MAGISTRATES
AND
PIONEERS

*Essays in the History
of American Law*

MAGISTRATES AND PIONEERS

Essays in the History of American Law

Warren M. Billings

THE LAWBOOK EXCHANGE, LTD.
CLARK, NJ

Copyright © Warren M. Billings 2011

ISBN 9781616191276 (hardcover)
ISBN 9781616191283 (paperback)

Lawbook Exchange edition 2011

THE LAWBOOK EXCHANGE, LTD.
33 Terminal Avenue
Clark, New Jersey 07066-1321

Please see our website for a selection of our other publications and fine facsimile reprints of classic works of legal history:
www.lawbookexchange.com

Library of Congress Cataloging-in-Publication Data

Billings, Warren M., 1940-
  Magistrates and pioneers : essays in the history of American law / by Warren M. Billings.
    p. cm.
  Includes bibliographical references and index.
  ISBN 978-1-61619-127-6 (hardcover : alk. paper) --
  ISBN 978-1-61619-128-3 (pbk. : alk. paper)
  1. Law--Virginia--History--17th century. 2. Virginia--Politics and government--To 1775. 3. Law--Louisiana--History. 4. Louisiana--Politics and government. I. Title.
  KF352.B55 2010
  349.73--dc22
                                      2010049177

Printed in the United States of America on acid-free paper

For Andrew Gregory Schafer
Beloved Grandson

Contents

Foreword	*xi*
Preface	*xvii*

ESSAY 1   1
Introduction
The Lure of the History of American Law

ESSAY 2   19
The Growth of Political Institutions in Virginia,
1634 to 1676

ESSAY 3   47
Law and Culture in the Colonial Chesapeake

ESSAY 4   71
English Legal Literature as a Source of Law and
Practice for Seventeenth-Century Virginia

ESSAY 5   93
Vignettes of Jamestown

ESSAY 6   117
Sir William Berkeley, A Cavalier Turned Virginian

ESSAY 7   153
Councils, Assemblies, and Courts of Judicature
*The Development of Representative Government in
Seventeenth-Century Virginia*

ESSAY 8   173
The Law of Servants and Slaves in
Seventeenth-Century Virginia

ESSAY 9 — 201
Pleading, Procedure, and Practice
The Meaning of Due Process of Law
in Seventeenth-Century Virginia

ESSAY 10 — 225
Louisiana Legal History and Its Sources
Needs, Opportunities and Approaches

ESSAY 11 — 245
A Judiciary Legacy
The Last Will and Testament of François-Xavier Martin

ESSAY 12 — 263
A Neglected Treatise
Lewis Kerr's Exposition *and the Making of Criminal Law in Louisiana*

ESSAY 13 — 295
The Supreme Court of Louisiana and the
Administration of Justice, 1813-1995

ESSAY 14 — 315
A Bar for Louisiana
Origins of the Louisiana State Bar Association

ESSAY 15 — 333
Mixed Jurisdictions and Convergence
The Louisiana Example

ESSAY 16 — 371
Politics Most Foul?
Winston Overton's Ghost and the Louisiana Judicial Election of 1934

CONTENTS   ix

ESSAY 17   399
Southern Caudillos
Harry F. Byrd, Sr., and Huey P. Long, Jr.

ESSAY 18   417
Needs and Opportunities in Virginia's Legal History
and Culture

Index   455

FOREWORD

Mark F. Fernandez

Nearly twenty years ago I had a wonderful conversation with the late John Hemphill about Warren Billings's work. Warren had just submitted the manuscript for what would become *Virginia's Viceroy: Their Majesties' Governor General Francis Howard, Baron Howard of Effingham* (Fairfax, Va., 1991). John, a ubiquitous force in the Chesapeake School of historians, was always available for a friendly chat about history to the graduate students at the College of William and Mary. These conversations often led us to unique discoveries about our own research and deep revelations about the works of other scholars. I had many talks like that with John in my five years at the College. Early on I learned to look polite, listen, and take notes in my head because one could gain a graduate seminar's worth of knowledge in the time it took to consume a cold beer or two. I was particularly fascinated with John's opinions of Billings's scholarship because Warren had introduced me to early American history and had become my good friend as well as a dear mentor. The direction of this particular talk also made me a bit nervous because John's criticisms were often biting, brutal, and always right on target. I didn't want him to shatter my estimation of one of my closest friends' life's work. Fortunately, he didn't. After praising many of Billings's early essays, Hemphill turned to the Effingham biography. He'd just read the manuscript as had I. John mentioned that he didn't much like the early chapter on Effingham's life in England, but then his eyes lit up and he said the rest of the book is "vintage Billings." I had to suppress my laughter knowing that John would want an explanation for my reaction, but I was delighted and somewhat proud to know that one of my friends had achieved so much that a critic as incisive as John Hemphill would recognize his work as "vintage."

And vintage it is. For four decades Warren Billings has been one of the most productive and prolific scholars of early American history. His books, all unanimously well received, and his "vintage" articles have stamped out impressive imprints in several different areas of American history. His work on the colonial Chesapeake ranks as nothing short of seminal. Leading his graduate students at the University of New Orleans and a handful of other interested scholars, Billings almost single-handedly laid the foundation for the vital field that he helped to christen the New Louisiana Legal History. Recently, he's been able to fuse these interests into deeper, thoughtful, and expansive synthetic essays on aspects of American history from 1607 to the present. This impressive array of interests is evident in the essays in this volume.

Billings's approach to history at first glance reveals the influence of twentieth-century legal and institutional historians such as James Willard Hurst, David H. Flaherty, Paul Murphy, Philip Alexander Bruce, and C. H. McIlwain. Closer investigation, however, suggests that Billings has transcended the methodologies of these early to mid-twentieth-century icons by adapting aspects of the *longue durée* and material world of the *Annales* School, the politico-social implications of scholars such as the New England and Chesapeake historians, and the New Social History. He also brings an appreciation of the ideological approach of Clifford Geertz that gained so much influence in the early American field in the 1960s and 1970s. His deep knowledge of antique law books and legal treatises also led him to an early interest in the history of the book. In his own unique way, Billings incorporates these influences and enhances them by creating a style that marries the tremendous antiquarian knowledge of the early institutional historians with more recent attention to culture and identity formation and the subtle relationships between the people and the state. Of course, Billings is not the only modern scholar to pull this off; many of his colleagues in the Chesapeake School followed similar paths. Yet Billings adds an artistic grace to his prose more reminiscent of other twentieth-century essayists such as C. Vann Woodward and Arthur M. Schlesinger, Jr. It is this artistic dimension, as it combines with meticulous, unimpeachable research, that made his work identifiable as "vintage" to a critic as discriminating as John Hemphill.

After completing graduate school and taking a job at the University of New Orleans, Billings focused his earliest published work on colonial Virginia. In the early 1970s he suggested to Thad Tate, then the director of the (Omohundro) Institute of Early American History and Culture that the Institute convene a meeting of early American scholars who had begun to undertake an aggressive research agenda on the colonial Chesapeake. Papers presented at that conference in November 1974 were later published in Thad W. Tate and David Ammerman, eds., *The Chesapeake in the Seventeenth Century: Essays on Anglo-American Society* (Chapel Hill, 1979). With the publication of that volume, Billings's insight helped forge a major realignment of early American history, which had been dominated by New England studies, as the burgeoning scholarship about the Chesapeake forced a re-imagining of colonial America.

Billings's important contributions to Chesapeake studies can be found in the essays published here as well as in his books and the two magnificent editions of the papers of Sir William Berkeley and Francis Howard, Baron Howard of Effingham. Three essays in this volume—"The Growth of Political Institutions in Virginia: 1634 to 1676," "Law and Culture in the Colonial Chesapeake," and "English Legal Literature as a Source of Law and Practice for Seventeenth-Century Virginia"—appeared in 1974, 1978, and 1979, respectively, and laid out an utterly new and original contribution to the scholarship on the early Chesapeake. Not only did Billings identify, explain, and interpret a tremendous amount of arcane legal and judicial material, but he also presented it in a manner that mimicked the very vitality of the political and legal culture of early Virginia and focused his analysis in such a way that it gave life to the elites who created and dominated that society. These three essays established Billings as a prominent scholar of early American history and the history of law. "The Law of Servants and Slaves in Seventeenth-Century Virginia," the eighth essay in this compilation, extends that scholarship by connecting Billings's elite world with subordinate ranks of the Chesapeake's social order.

"Vignettes of Jamestown" demonstrates another side to Billings's scholarship. Stemming from a talk that he gave to the Association for the Preservation of Virginia Antiquities (now Preservation Virginia) and published in *Virginia Cavalcade* in 1996, the essay represents a mature scholar at the top of his game making colonial history attractive to a popular audience. Although the essay builds on his book *Jamestown and the Founding of the Nation*, attentive readers will note that it not only sheds light on the history of the town, but it also serves as Billings's love song to the island where he lived as a boy.

"Sir William Berkeley, A Cavalier Turned Virginian" is another example of the public aspect of Billings's scholarship. Derived from the Mary F. Carroll Lectures he delivered at Mary Baldwin College, the essay, which appears for the first time in this collection, represents a brilliant distillation of the major ideas that Billings expanded on in his monumental biography of Berkeley. Although the essay cannot substitute for the biography, it offers an outstanding glimpse into the life of one of colonial America's most complicated men.

Seven of the essays illustrate Billings's influence over modern interpretations of Louisiana's history. In "Louisiana

Legal History and Its Sources: Needs and Opportunities" Billings adeptly plotted the outlines of the New Louisiana Legal History, a field in which he is the master architect. "A Neglected Treatise: Lewis Kerr's *Exposition* and the Making of Criminal Law in Louisiana" is a fine example of one of his most important contributions to American legal history, his love of the history of the book, and his determination to educate other historians about the role of legal treatises in creating culture—and what a culture! This analysis of Lewis Kerr's commentary on Louisiana's criminal laws in the territorial era, when joined with "Mixed Jurisprudence and Convergence: The Louisiana Example," adds new dimensions to the confusing, but essential understanding of the agencies of cultural fusion that make early Louisiana one of the most fascinating laboratories for the study of American identity. "Politics Most Foul?: Winston Overton's Ghost and the Louisiana Judicial Election of 1934" explores the dicey side of Louisiana's judicial and political culture as it matured in the twentieth century.

Essays 13 and 14 deliver masterful forays into the possibilities inherent in interpreting the contributions of a legal system to a society. "The Supreme Court and the Administration of Justice" provides a sturdy framework for understanding the inner-workings of Louisiana's judicial system in an essay that ranges from the beginnings of statehood to the end of the twentieth century. "A Bar for Louisiana" not only marks the first serious, scholarly investigation of the history of the state bar, but it also adds breadth and depth to the relationship between the association, its members, and their own community.

The final essays represent a new "vintage" dimension of Billings's work. His assessment in "Southern Caudillos: Harry F. Byrd, Sr., and Huey P. Long, Jr.," provides a remarkable glimpse at the possibilities inherent when a major scholar expands his focus into differing regions, eras, and milieus.

The concluding essay, "Needs and Opportunities in Virginia's Legal History and Culture," offers a virtuoso assessment of the history and present state of Virginia legal scholarship.

These essays, each in their own way, are "vintage Billings." Their variety of topical and technical approaches and their profound contributions to several different aspects of American history testify to the importance of his work. Perhaps more important, they are a joy to read.

When Warren and I spoke about the prospect of my writing the foreword to this volume several years ago the conversation stirred in me many mixed feelings. Of course, I was thrilled at the prospect of summing up his life's work for fellow scholars and new generations of students. At the same time, a collection such as this one seems more appropriate as a headstone on the grave of a great career—and Warren M. Billings is still very much alive. These essays attest to his vitality over the course of a long scholarly enterprise and give us tantalizing clues about what might come out of the productive retirement that he is just beginning.

PREFACE

Hurricane Katrina blew into New Orleans on 29 August 2005, and the city that I knew and loved for nearly forty years disappeared forever. Although my family and home survived intact, Katrina wrought destruction of another kind. Friends and colleagues who fled for safety ahead of her landfall never returned. The school I helped make into a significant urban university sustained massive damage to its physical plant and lost a third of its students, faculty, and staff, and its health is still tenuous. New Orleanians picked up the pieces, but there were the endless frustrations of living in a town where everything was broken and the simplest of life's most mundane routines required enormous and frequently unsuccessful expenditures of energy. No less vexing were the prevarications and the utter incompetence of government officials or the outsider's oft-heard thoughtless remark that taxpayer dollars ought not be squandered on rebuilding New Orleans. Those realities imposed something we residents acidly called "the new normal." Living this new normal exacted a steep psychological cost too, and its toll caused me to question my capacity ever to do history again. Assembling this book became the means of recovering that which I nearly lost.

What follows is an anthology of my shorter works. Five are published here for the first time, whereas the remaining essays appeared at intervals between 1974 and 2005. All speak to my engagement with the history of law in seventeenth-century Virginia and nineteenth-century Louisiana, and they are representative of lines of investigation that guide my research. A head note acquaints readers with the circumstances that led me to write the essay it precedes. Collectively the head notes also provide a measure of thematic continuity that gives this book coherence. I regularized the texts and the notes in the previously published articles to conform to a common copy style, and, where appropriate, I incorporated citations to newer scholarship. Aside from these emendations, those essays are unchanged.

References to manuscript Virginia county court records are to microfilm copies of the originals housed at the Library of Virginia, Richmond, whereas citations to Louisiana high court documents are to the manuscript archives of the Supreme Court of Louisiana held by the Earl K. Long Library at the University of New Orleans. Citations to all sixteenth-, seventeenth-, eighteenth-, and nineteenth-century legal treatises, manuals, dictionaries, abridgments, and case reports are always to witnesses of editions that are in my personal library.

The late Judge George A. Arceneaux, United States District Court for the Eastern District of Louisiana; Mary Sarah Bilder; Carol D. Billings; John B. Boles; Patricia Brady; Carl A. Brasseaux; Julie A. Campbell; Raphael Cassimere, Jr.; Georgia Chadwick; Ronald S. Chapman; the late Glenn R. Conrad; Judge James L. Dennis, United States Court of Appeals for the Fifth Judicial Circuit; the late Judge John A Dixon, Jr., Chief Justice of Louisiana; the late Mary Clark Roane Downing; Mark Engsberg; Marie Erickson; the late Emory G. Evans; Wayne M. Everard; Mark F. Fernandez; Betty Field; Linda K. Gill; Greg Granger; Christopher Grasso; Edward F. Haas; David D. Hall; Collin B. Hamer; James S. Heller; Wythe Holt; Florence M. Jumonville; Jon Kukla; Nelson D. Lankford; the late Michael L. Lanza; Michael S. Martin; Justice (ret.) Harry T. Lemmon, Supreme Court of Louisiana; Michael McGiffert; Ramona Meyers; Randal L. Miller; John T. O'Connor; John Ruston Pagan; John M. Price; Virginia Barrett Price; Martin H. Quitt; Sally K.E. Reeves; Kenneth Rudolph; Judith Kelleher Schafer; Philip J. Schwarz; Janice K. Shull; Janet Sinder; the late Judge Albert Tate, Supreme Court of Louisiana and United States Court of Appeals for the Fifth Judicial Circuit; Brent Tarter;

Thad W. Tate; Sandra Gioia Treadway; the late Joseph G. Tregle, Jr.; Marie E. Windell; and Jules Winterton took extraordinary interest in my work. Their counsel and support sustained me in more ways than mere words will ever convey. I always delighted in their friendship so it is pleasure to recognize them here.

Valerie L. Horowitz, my editor at The Lawbook Exchange, Ltd., deserves a special word of appreciation. She designed the book and shepherded it to print. Working with her was a pleasure, and I am deeply grateful for that opportunity.

Lastly, I avow my gratitude to the University of New Orleans. Being there took me in directions that I never could have imagined when I first arrived on campus. I had spacious latitude to progress as a teacher and an historian as well as to engage with the New Orleans community. It was my privilege to instruct wonderful students who contributed much to the life of the Crescent City or who became outstanding scholars in their own right. I profited from their questions, which prodded me to think my best thoughts and bound us in the excitement of shared intellectual inquiry. Those students are the principal reason I take enormous pride in having played a hand in making a university more or less from scratch. Such a gift comes rarely. It is one that I shall cherish always. My fondest hope is that UNO will thrive and become an even greater force for good and for the advancement of learning as New Orleanians struggle to recover from Hurricane Katrina.

Warren M. Billings
New Orleans
Spring 2011

ESSAY 1

INTRODUCTION

The Lure of the History of American Law

Growing up in Jamestown and Williamsburg meant that history and I were never strangers, though becoming an historian was no youthful aspiration of mine. Serendipity turned me toward history as a calling, and serendipity lured me to the history of American law as my particular preoccupation. To walk Duke of Gloucester Street or to tarry in Bruton Parish Church, however momentarily, was to feel the presence of Virginians who participated in the birthing of the nation or who are remembered no longer. Jamestown had no restored area, so it lacked the visual cues of Colonial Williamsburg, but enjoying free run of the place I could readily picture events that once transpired in that lost little metropolis. Friendship with Sam Robinson,[1] sexton at the memorial church and a marvelous yarn spinner, stoked my imagination with tales of the inhabitants of the church graveyard. An inspiring high school teacher, Spotswood Hunnicut Jones,[2] instilled in me her fondness for Jamestown

---

1. Employed by the Association for the Preservation of Virginia Antiquities, Robinson (1901–1965) supplemented his income with tips from the visitors he regaled with stories about the Virginians who lay buried about the churchyard. We spent countless hours together, we became fast friends, and in time I memorized all of his stories, which, if prodded, I can still repeat.
2. Jones (1925–2006) taught in the Williamsburg-James City County school system and private schools. She and Frances Butler Simkins co-authored a controversial history textbook for use in the public schools. See Adam Wesley Dean, "'Who Controls the Past Controls the Future':

too. At the College of William and Mary, I encountered Thad W. Tate who introduced me to the formal study of early American history. I took my degree with no thought of what happened next, but one thing became sharply clear after the president of the College handed my diploma to me. The tap from my father's dole closed abruptly, and I needed to find my own way.

Having apprenticed as a crane operator between terms at William and Mary, that work now seemed a promising occupation to try again. Directly I left Williamsburg, and I asked the business agent for the eastern Virginia affiliate of the International Union of Operating Engineers if he could find a full-time job for me. He did, and in short order I was bound to a feisty journeyman called Marion Payne whose skill with cranes and whose command of their mechanics was the marvel of the local and beyond. Payne was quick to pass his knowledge along to me as I acquired the rudiments of making lifts without causing a wreck or killing anyone whenever I spelled him. What especially fascinated me were his lessons in rigging and servicing our cranes. I learned how to disassemble those behemoths entirely and to put them back in running order, all of which satisfied an innate curiosity about how things worked.

Colleagues sought to convince me that my future lay in finishing my apprenticeship and earning my journeyman's ticket. Their blandishments enticed me. I was good at what I did, I liked the work, and I thrived on the rough and tumble camaraderie that bonds construction workers into a singular society. The money was plentiful too. Even so, I held back, not quite knowing why. Tugs of uncertainty would not go

---

The Virginia History Textbook Controversy," *Virginia Magazine of History and Biography*, 117 (2009): 318–355. A trustee and one-time president of APVA, Jones recruited me to chair the APVA's Jamestown Rediscovery Archaeological Advisory Board, a seat I held from 1995 to 2008.

INTRODUCTION 3

away, no matter my every effort to stifle them, and my qualms about the future grew more persistent. But what to do?

The more I pondered that question the more I felt the pull of doing history professionally. Having trifled at William and Mary, I doubted that I could realistically turn myself into an academician, and I verged on dismissing that unlikeliest of possibilities. Nevertheless, I took the precaution of sounding out Thad Tate before coming to a decision. Saying forthrightly that the odds in my favor were quite long, Tate urged me to try. He called in chits on my behalf, and in the fall of 1963 I matriculated the University of Pittsburgh as a provisional master's student.

Pitt's graduate regime was rigorous. M.A. candidates were on a fast track that ruthlessly drove them to earn their diploma and to enter the doctoral program within a single academic year or wash out. That was a daunting prospect, made all the more so after the chairman pulled me aside to say that he expected me to fail before the end of the fall trimester. His small regard for me stiffened my resolve and sharpened my sense of purpose. I exhilarated in the intellectual stimulation of bright colleagues, challenging classes, and tough mentors. Of the latter, the one who mattered most was the late Emory G. Evans, for he it was who interested me in Virginia's seventeenth-century court records and who became the dearest of friends. At his behest I began scouring the documents in hopes of gaining a fresh insight into that greatest assault on British authority in North American before 1776—Bacon's Rebellion. I still recall my chagrin upon putting a reel of microfilm up on the reader for the first time only to discover documents in hands that I could barely decipher. Thus began my mastery of antique handwriting and usage. I soon grew sufficiently adept at navigating though the records and used them in a seminar paper that pointed in the direction of my eventual dissertation on the causes of Bacon's Rebellion.[3]

Everything seemingly fell into place until a day in February 1964 when Evans called me into his office to say he was leaving Pitt to take up the chair at Northern Illinois University. My first question was could I go too. He demurred, noting that Northern's doctoral program was in its infancy and had yet to produce any graduates. That very newness, said he, could be an obstacle to my finding a job, but I was willing to venture the risk, and after I earned my M.A. that spring, off I went to DeKalb. The four following years at Northern were every bit as challenging as my time at Pitt, if not more so. I emerged soundly trained, and to this day I have never regretted my decision to follow Evans.

Jobs were more abundant than applicants when I sought one of my own. I had offers aplenty. The most appealing one came from Louisiana State University in New Orleans (now the University of New Orleans), which was a mere ten years old at the time. An opportunity to live in an exotic city until something better came along seemed too good to pass up. I arrived on campus in 1968 with no inkling that I would spend my entire career there. Such was my rare good fortune, however, that many unexpected opportunities fell my way over the ensuing decades. Not least of these was the chance to make UNO into one of America's consequential urban universities and a place that mattered in the lives of the people of the Crescent City, and I will always be unabashedly proud of having contributed to raising up such an institution. That environment enabled me freely to devote nearly equal portions of my time to serving the university and the community at large, to teaching, and to flourishing as a scholar.

---

3. Warren M. Billings, "'Virginias Deploured Condition': The Coming of Bacon's Rebellion, 1660–1676" (PhD diss., Northern Illinois University, 1968).

INTRODUCTION   5

From the outset, I routinely taught everything from survey classes to graduate seminars. Although I joyfully instructed great numbers of undergraduates, I probably made my greatest impact as a mentor of graduate students because I ran the graduate program throughout the 1980s, and again in 2004–2005. Eventually, I shepherded over sixty M.A. candidates to their degrees. Because the department does not offer doctoral work, I placed those of my students who were Ph.D. bound in top-flight programs elsewhere. They completed their work and went on to positions where they became valuable scholars in their own right. I delight in knowing that they turned into better historians than I ever hoped to be.

All of that was to come, and by ways and means that I could never have anticipated. My immediate concern in the fall of 1968 was settling into a new department and turning my dissertation into a book, which I likely would have done, were it not for James H. Hutson. Then editor of publications at the (Omohundro) Institute of Early American History and Culture at William and Mary, Hutson knew of my familiarity with Virginia's legal records, and he talked me into composing a documentary history of the colony as an Institute publication. Crafting that book—*The Old Dominion in the Seventeenth Century: A Documentary History of Virginia, 1606–1689* (Chapel Hill, N.C., 1975)—afforded lessons in documentary rendition and arrangement, as well as ways of introducing documents and themes to readers. I discovered how books became books and why genial relationships between authors, outside readers, and editors are vital to any publishing enterprise. By the time the book was printed, I had also gained something of even greater value.

Choosing the documents that went into *The Old Dominion in the Seventeenth Century* took me through the entire corpus of the court records anew. That laborious chore awakened a realization. I really did not want to write a book about

Bacon's Rebellion because I doubted my ability to add significantly to the literature on that much-debated upheaval beyond what I had already established in my dissertation, an article in the *Virginia Magazine of History and Biography*, and in a chapter in *The Old Dominion in the Seventeenth Century*. Charting the rise of the colony's legal order offered a fresher, more inviting way to proceed, so I redirected my emphasis in search of a deeper understanding of how legal institutions worked, the effects of personality upon early Virginia politics, and the ways law shaped, and was shaped by, an emerging colonial culture.[4]

My decision to go off in that direction was propitious, given its timing. By the early 1970s an energetic cadre of my contemporaries was well on its way towards becoming the Chesapeake school of early American studies. Multi-disciplinary in outlook, Chesapeake historians devised a new appreciation of the two tobacco colonies that relied greatly upon social science methodologies that supported rigorous quantitative analyses of local records. Their approach intrigued me, whereas their findings reoriented my thinking about the climate in which Virginians flourished from the collapse of the Virginia Company of London in 1624 to the end of the seventeenth century. Nevertheless, as much as I esteemed the originality of this new interpretation, and even envied its adherents, the angle of attack seemed better suited to Maryland than to the Old Dominion. Maryland records bore far fewer marks of destruction than those of Virginia, which made the chore of teasing out their data far easier than was so for Virginia. Then too, there was a critical mass of scholars—the so-called "St. Mary's City Mafia"—that was nonexistent among Virginia historians. That I had a plot of

---

4. Warren M. Billings, "The Causes of Bacon's Rebellion: Some Suggestions," *Virginia Magazine of History and Biography*, 67 (1970): 409–435 and Billings, ed., *The Old Dominion in the Seventeenth Century: A Documentary History of Virginia, 1606–1689* (Chapel Hill, N.C., 1975), pp. 236–251.

historical ground largely to myself encouraged me to head down a road not then taken by the Chesapeake scholars or traditional legal historians. But for the serendipity of befriending the late Albert Tate,[5] a justice of the Supreme Court of Louisiana, I would have happily continued along that path for time to come.[6]

Mutual friends introduced us at a dinner party in the mid-1970s. Shared interests in history, the business of courts, and the value of legal records as historical evidence incubated this first encounter into an abiding friendship that gave rise to an unexpected result. Judge Tate's concern for the security and preservation of his court's archives caused him to seek my advice on ways to safeguard the collection, which sat in a dank basement at the courthouse in New Orleans. The first time Tate took me down to the basement and showed me around, I beheld a sight little short of breathtaking. There sat a massive accumulation of records, a portion of which antedated the Court itself and bigger in size than anything I had ever beheld until that moment. Even though I knew absolutely nothing about the Court or Louisiana law, I immediately recognized the collection for what it then most

---

5. Tate (1920–1986) served on the Supreme Court of Louisiana from 1970 to 1979. He left that bench after President James Earl Carter appointed him to the United States Court of Appeals for the Fifth Judicial Circuit, where he remained until his death.

6. The records themselves are in the process of being digitized and mounted on the World Wide Web. Documents that are presently available in the digital environment may be accessed by pointing the reader's browser to http://library.uno.edu/help/subguide/louis/inventories/106.html, and navigating to the appropriate link. Warren M. Billings, "Confessions of a Court Historian," *Louisiana History: The Journal of the Louisiana Historical Association*, 35 (1994): 261–272. Warren M. Billings and Mark F. Fernandez, eds., *A Law Unto Itself?: Essays in the New Louisiana Legal History* (Baton Rouge, La., 2001), p. xii.

certainly was: the largest single untapped source of Louisiana history in existence.

The obvious way to protect the records would have been to transfer them to the Louisiana State Archives in Baton Rouge. That possibility was no option for Tate, because he and his brother justices rejected any suggestion that the records leave the Crescent City. Besides, State Archives was too understaffed to conserve the collection or to make it readily accessible. Of even greater concern, State Archives lacked a proper facility, and there was little likelihood of one rising in the foreseeable future. Thus, if the records went to Baton Rouge, they would be stored near the Mississippi River in a warehouse that lacked climate controls and risked water damage in flood season. I ventured the opinion that UNO might act as the Court's depository. The university sat a mere twenty-minute drive from the courthouse, it was a state institution, and its library satisfied environmental conditions that State Archives could not furnish. I offered to sound out the university librarian. After a bit of haggling with university officials, Tate and I drafted the order that the Court issued which deposited all its records from 1813 to 1921 in UNO's custody. That arrangement resulted in a unique cooperative venture between a high court and a public university.

Following the announcement of the deposit I thought my involvement was complete, but it was not. Every inquiry from genealogists, lawyers, judges, or scholars came to me, which compelled me to learn about the Court and its archives. The more I probed, the more the collection appealed to me, but I resisted mining the documents too deeply because that seemed to require a considerable retooling on my part. My attitude shifted gradually as the allure of this magnificent hitherto underutilized archive grew ever more irresistible. Here too was an opportunity to revivify a long dormant field. Retooling proved less of an impediment, once I discerned certain parallels between early Virginia and Louisiana legal

INTRODUCTION   9

developments. Those parallels were not entirely congruent, to be sure, but they were near enough to impart the worth of examining evolving legalities in both places, contrasting each not only with those of Great Britain and Continental Europe but also with those of other states in the Union. That recognition carried the further realization that the questions and methods that sustained my Virginia research could be tailored to a Louisiana setting. I discovered various descendants of seventeenth-century Virginia magistrates who pioneered the blending of American and Continental European precepts into a distinctive Louisiana system of law and practice. And, once my graduate students started using the collection for their documentary editing projects, seminar papers, and master's theses, they quite literally launched a reassessment of the state's distinctive legal order that became the New Louisiana Legal History. Being a part of that enterprise ranks among my most rewarding scholarly experiences because, as I once remarked, the students "challenged me to think my best thoughts, I learned much from their enquiries . . . [and best] of all we had, and continue to have much intellectual fun together."[7]

Comprehending what nineteenth-century Louisianians and seventeenth-century Virginians knew about their law required a mastery of the law books that informed them—a necessity that unexpectedly opened an allied branch of

---

7. Warren M. Billings, ed., *Historic Rules of the Supreme Court of Louisiana, 1813–1879* (Lafayette, La., 1985), pp. 9–11, 19, 29-30; Florence Jumonville, *Bibliography of New Orleans Imprint, 1764–1864* (New Orleans, La., 1989); Robert Feikema Karachuk, "A Lawyer's Tools: The Law Library of Henry Adams Bullard" (M.A. thesis, University of New Orleans, 1996); Rosemarie Davis Plasse, "Tools of the Profession: New Orleans Attorneys and Their Law Libraries from Statehood to Secession (1813–1861)" (M.A. thesis, University of New Orleans, 2000); Warren M. Billings, "A Course of Legal Studies: Books That Shaped Louisiana Law," in Billings and Fernandez, eds., *A Law Unto Itself?*, pp. 25–40.

inquiry for me. Starting with Virginia, I identified pertinent books by scouring studies of reading habits, legal bibliographies, and estate inventories before I wound up with a working list of some two hundred titles of dictionaries, clerk's manuals, statutory compilations, formularies, case reports, how-to guides, treatises, and parliamentary procedure manuals that circulated across the Old Dominion.[8] I composed a similar list of about fifty additional titles for Louisiana, which I derived from similar sources in addition to compilations of Supreme Court rules, which governed legal education throughout the state, and practitioners' libraries.[9]

Lists in hand, I set about locating witnesses to everything in them, whereupon I ran into an unexpected obstruction. Although items were available at law libraries in New Orleans, Baton Rouge, and elsewhere around the country, I could neither borrow nor photocopy any of them because of

---

8. Philip Alexander Bruce, *Institutional History of Virginia in the Seventeenth Century: An Inquiry into the Religious, Moral, Educational, Legal, Military, and Political Condition of the People Based on Original and Contemporaneous Records* (New York, 1910); Louis B. Wright, *The First Gentlemen of Virginia: Intellectual Qualities of the Early Ruling Class* (San Marino, Calif., 1940); Richard Beale Davis, *Intellectual Life in the Colonial South, 1585–1763* (Knoxville, Tenn., 1978); and W. Hamilton Bryson, *Census of Law Books in Colonial Virginia* (Charlottesville, Va., 1978); John Worrall, comp., *Bibliotheca Legum: Or, A Catalogue of the Common and Statute Law Books of this Realm* . . . (London, 1777); John William Wallace, *The Reporters, Chronologically Arranged: With Additional Remarks Upon their Respective Merits*, 3d ed. (Philadelphia, 1855); Morris L. Cohen, comp., *Bibliography of Early American Law* (Buffalo, N.Y., 1998). See also Essay 4 below.
9. The Early English Books in Microforms series is keyed to A.F. Pollard and G.R. Redgrave, comps., *A Short-Title Catalogue of Books Printed in England, Scotland and Ireland, and of English Books Abroad, 1475–1640* (London, 1926), and Donald G. Wing, comp., *A Short-Title Catalogue of Books Printed in England, Scotland, Ireland, Wales, ad British America, and of English Books Printed in Other Countries, 1640–1700* (New York, 1945–1951). Titles listed in the *STC* are still being filmed. Those that have been copied are also available via a subscription-based digital collection called the Early English Books Online.

their antiquity. UNO's library subscribed to the Early English Books in Microform series, which seemed to offer an alternative route of access to the Virginia-related books. Unfortunately, volumes I sought either awaited photo duplication or they were on reels that the library did not own. Not to be stymied, I chose to buy as many titles as I could locate on the antiquarian book market.

That was an easy decision to take because it stirred a penchant for book collecting that began in boyhood. Initially, I turned to Mary Clark Roane Downing, a Richmond book dealer friend, who acted as my informal tutor until her death. I poured over dealer and auction catalogues, partook of auctions, went to book fairs, visited shops, and gradually wove a web of booksellers that reached across the United States and Canada to Great Britain, Continental Europe, and even Australia. Searches became more efficient after the World Wide Web came into existence because internet queries instantaneously revealed the availability of a book at any given moment and whether the item on offer was one that I could afford.[10]

Louisiana titles, especially those imprinted at New Orleans, were rather more difficult to run to ground, though I succeeded eventually in acquiring almost everything I sought, just as I found nearly all of the Virginia items too. I kept costs down by purchasing serviceable copies irrespective of impression. The aim, after all, was creating a working library rather than larding my bookshelves with pretty, expensive first editions. Any contemporaneous printing in good repair sufficed, and in several instances I even bought reprints in facsimile. In time I became quite proficient at

---

10. Mary Clark, as friends knew her, found the first law book for my collection. It is second edition of William Waller Hening's *New Virginia Justice, Comprising the Office and Authority of the Justice of the Peace, in the Commonwealth of Virginia* (Richmond, Va., 1810).

finding desiderata for good prices in out-of-the way places. Truth be known, a singular tale lies behind the acquisition of each book in the law section of my library. How I stumbled across my witness to Michael Dalton's *The Countrey Justice: Containing the Practice of Justices of the Peace out of their Sessions* (London, 1618 and later) surely ranks among the more extraordinary of those stories.

The Countrey Justice was atop my Virginia list because it and Henry Swinburne's *Treatise of Testaments and Last Wills* (London, 1590 and later) were two volumes that enjoyed wide circulation on either side of the Atlantic, and the General Assembly required all county courts to own both. Catalogue searches and inquiries to dealers drew repeated blanks, which made me dubious of success. Then one day in 1972, while on a visit to London, I happened upon the stall of a Kensington bookseller who dealt in rare herbals. Stopping to admire his display of many handsome volumes, as I glanced over his stock, my eyes caught sight of a spine panel that read "The Countrey Justice/Dalton." Could it be? Eagerly but gingerly, I withdrew the book from the shelf and turned to its title page. *Voila!* Here was a twelfth edition, published in London in 1677, in excellent condition, and best of all, the asking price was a mere £27 (around $50 in 1972 dollars)! Hurriedly, I reached for my wallet, only to discover that I did not have that much cash in hand, so I tendered a credit card. The dealer hemmed and hawed before finally admitting that he did not know how to run the card through his billing device. Not about to be denied, I showed him what to do, we completed our transaction, and off I went, overjoyed by my good luck.[11]

After returning to New Orleans, I subjected the Dalton to an examination that I give to every book before it takes its

---

11. Seven years after that transaction, I finally located a copy of Swinburne, a fourth edition, which I purchased from a California bookseller.

place in the bookcase. I poured over it from cover to cover turning each page looking for traits that set it apart from known witnesses to its edition. The Dalton had a look, a smell and a feel all its own. Its binding was recent, albeit one that replicated those of seventeenth-century law books. The end papers were new as well. Apart from a bit of dampstaining, there were few signs of wear or damage to the text block itself.[12]

Others of my volumes retained their original leather coverings utterly intact and included additional notable attributes—fancy blind stamping, elegant gold tooling, even parchment hinge reinforcements cut from medieval illuminated manuscripts—though most, like the Dalton, had been rebound on one or more occasions in their lifetime. In contrast to the Dalton too, rounded page corners, missing pages, tears, wormholes, ink spills, dirt stains, and marginalia bore witness to heavy use, if not abuse, and such testimony suggested why other copies from the same press run or different impressions just wore out long before obsolescence overtook them. Whenever marginalia occurred they were the most eye-catching evidence of prior ownership. My predecessors doodled freely or endlessly practiced their penmanship on endpapers, flyleaves, or any other blank spaces that seemed handy for such exercises. Sometimes a previous owner helpfully recorded when and where she or he bought a book, as well as its purchase price. Other former owners inserted erudite commentary in the margins of the text or composed verse, cast accounts, recorded family lore, and made copious references to details of obscure lives. To this day, for instance, I wonder why of all places the eighteenth-century Englishwoman who had my copy of the 1592 printing of Fernando Pulton's *An Abstract of all the Penall*

---

12. I maintain a catalogue that records bookseller, date of purchase, price, author, title, printer and all physical characteristics of individual volumes.

Statutes which be gennerall, in force and use should have chosen to scrawl this sentence across one of the end leaves. "There was sene the 6th day of March a storme like two armies fighting in the aire at night in 1710."

Studying the books not only taught me greatly about old legal usages, but my growing familiarity with them also turned me in other unforeseen directions. For one, the crafts associated with the evolution of print culture caught my fancy, and I taught myself about papermaking, type founding, printing presses, binding, printers, booksellers, the book trade, and the history of the book. The foremost lesson I gained from those excursions was a wider awareness of the vital interplay between the creation of law as knowledge and the technology of information dissemination.

Before the coming of the modern digital information revolution, books were the principal means of categorizing and locating legal knowledge, which made them essential for anyone who attended to legal matters of whatever sort or for whatever reason. The perfection of moveable type and printing presses cheapened production costs and put law books within easier reach of users, causing markets to grow apace with a non-stop increase in the sheer quantity of legal information that went hand in hand with the rise of the early modern world. Consequently, printers continually experimented with technologies that realized economies of scale and enabled them to keep abreast of mounting demand. As a result, the number and variety of law books available to any literate individual grew exponentially between the fifteenth and nineteenth centuries, and that constant was reflected in the collecting tendencies of Virginians and Louisianians.[13]

---

13. A quick comparison of Worrall's *Bibliotheca Legum* with Cohen's *Bibliography of Early American Law* readily reveals the magnitude of the increase of law book titles that were available to colonial Americans and their nineteenth-century counterparts. The last edition of Worrall's

My library also provided clear indications of which books invested Virginians and Louisianians with their legal knowledge. That revelation became an important finding because it went a long distance to explaining how men, and women, who lacked formal training in English law, or had none at all, managed to adapt complex legal customs of the homeland to Virginia needs. Louisianans, by contrast, were trained practitioners who fashioned their state's mixed legal regime out of Anglo-American and Continental European customs, but they too relied upon particular books from which they drew the ingredients of that blended jurisdiction. Those insights prompted me to write a series of articles wherein I called attention to the importance of early law books as a window into the mindset of early American men of law.[14]

Then too, the books became attractive teaching tools. The students who filled my classes customarily were the first in their families to attend college. They held down jobs, they reared families, and they hungered for success, but they were neither well traveled nor widely read, and to them the history of American law was as alien as alien could be. As artifacts the books were tangible links to a remote time largely beyond their ken until their encounters with me.

My reading aloud of passages from Dalton's *Country Justice* on the meaning of "peace" or definitions from the first ever

---

bibliography is a small octavo volume of one hundred sixty-two pages in length, whereas Cohen's compilation embraces six massive quarto volumes, each of which is at least a thousand pages long.

14. Essays 3, 4, and 12 below; Billings, "Justices, Books, Laws and Courts in Seventeenth-Century Virginia," *Law Library Journal*, 85 (1993): 277-297; Billings, "Seventeenth-Century Virginia Law and Its Historians, With an Accompanying Guide to Sources" *Law Library Journal*, 87 (1995): 556-576; Billings, "An American Original: John Bouvier's Law Dictionary," *Legal History & Rare Books,* 6 (1996): 8-9; Billings, "A Course of Legal Studies: Books That Shaped Louisiana Law," 25-40.

American legal lexicon, John Bouvier's *A Law Dictionary, Adapted to the Constitution and Laws of the United States of America and of the Several States of the American Union, With References to The Civil and Other Systems of Foreign Law* (Philadelphia, 1839 and later), revealed how ordinary words and phrases took on different meanings in given legal contexts. Passing Dalton, Bouvier, the Louisiana *Civil Code*, or other volumes around quite literally gave the students a feeling for a past that they had not experienced heretofore. Invariably, whenever I put on such dog and pony shows, someone asked about the paper's rough texture, its mottled color, or why the book itself differed in look, smell, or heft from her textbooks, and why certain volumes bore signs of massive wear. Responding to such queries always were opportunities for me to note that to a trained observer such characteristics could impart degrees of insight quite beyond a book's content. Those questions became a conduit for my remarking on the likely impact of law books upon the Virginians and Louisianans who turned to them for inspiration or who relied upon them as authoritative sources. In that regard, I suggested, the books constituted a portal to worlds that are quite removed from the present but left marks of deep impression that are visible to this day.

Opening gateways took me down paths I never expected to walk. The itch to know the working of things drove decades-long visits to the past—that foreign country where people did legal things differently, to paraphrase the English novelist Leslie P. Hartley—and in making those journeys I gained a measure of appreciation of times long gone. Sharing my understanding via the spoken and the written word with students and colleagues has been an immensely satisfying experience. So also is the awareness that the study of the legal order in early Virginia and Louisiana is livelier now than it was forty years ago. The extent to which I bear any responsibility for enlivening that change is for others to gauge.[15]

---

15. L. P. Hartley, *The Go-Between* (London, 1953), p. 1.

Essay 2

The Growth of Political Institutions in Virginia, 1634 to 1676

Among my earliest published writings this essay provided a new explanation of Virginia politics, as they existed by 1676. Of equal importance for me, the piece signaled a shift of interest away from Bacon's Rebellion towards close investigations into the workings of Virginia's institutional arrangements. At the time, unraveling the social origins of colonial leaders, their ties to one another, and their routes to power intrigued me. I was equally taken by the idea that localism defined the courts in ways that decentralized power between county magistrates and provincial authorities as it bred institutional fragility and factionalism that characterized the Old Dominion from the 1630s to the 1670s. Consequently, I paid scant heed to the General Assembly, which I regarded merely as an amorphous nonentity with little value to my understanding of the nature of an embryonic political culture.

Placing the article in an issue of the premier journal of early American history was a heady accomplishment for a junior scholar not long removed from graduate school and anxious for recognition. More importantly, the essay joined an emerging body of new literature about the colonial Chesapeake, and it was widely cited following its appearance in 1974. Indeed, it remains something of a standard to this day.

Revisiting the essay decades after its publication, I see in it inklings of projects that were to come, which was the reason I chose to include it here. I also recognize its shortcomings, such as my failure to look more closely at the role of the General Assembly. No less apparent was my tendency to overplay the idea of Virginia as an inherently unstable society made more so by a chaotic brand of local politics. Those were the missteps of a novice.

Originally published as "The Growth of Political Institutions in Virginia, 1634–1676" in the *William and Mary Quarterly*, 3d ser., 31 (1974): 225-242, the article is reprinted here with the editor's kind permission.

Recent investigations into the texture of colonial America's political culture and the resurgence of scholarly interest in local records suggest the need for a fresh approach to the study of the growth of political institutions in seventeenth-century Virginia.[1] To provide a framework for reexamining those institutions between 1634 and 1676 is the purpose of this essay.

Central to this objective is the thesis that the General Assembly's creation of the county court system of local

---

1. Jack P. Greene, "Changing Interpretations of Early American Politics," in Ray Allen Billington, ed., *The Reinterpretation of Early American Politics: Essays in Honor of John Edwin Pomfret* (San Marino, Calif., 1966), pp. 159–176; J. R. Pole, *The Seventeenth Century: The Sources of Legislative Power* (Charlottesville, Va., 1969), pp. 1–73. Although they have no direct bearing on Virginia, the studies of Massachusetts's local institutions by John Demos, *A Little Commonwealth: Family Life in Plymouth Colony* (New York, 1971); Kenneth A. Lockridge, *A New England Town: The First Hundred Years, Dedham, Massachusetts, 1636–1736* (New York, 1970); and Philip J. Greven, Jr., *Four Generations: Family: Population Land, and Family in Andover, Massachusetts* (Ithaca, N.Y., 1970) revived interest in the use of local archives.

government in 1634 set in train changes which profoundly affected the character of Virginia's political institutions. Creation of the county courts divided the functions and powers of government between the newly erected local jurisdictions and those governmental organs already in existence at Jamestown. Over a thirty-year period after 1634 that division was greatly enlarged by statutory additions to the county courts' responsibilities, by customs, and by local conditions. As the courts' competence in local matters expanded, the General Assembly began to assume a more purely legislative function; the Assembly's development, however, did not keep abreast of the county courts. Furthermore, the governor's broad powers to direct the colony's political life were eroded by custom and the willing acquiescence of governors.

As the county courts became important centers of power, some Virginians began to view membership on the bench as a means to satisfy their rather large political, social, and economic ambitions. The court system therefore became the institutional mechanism whereby grasping men used the tools of kinship, patronage, deference, and money to lay the foundations of a ruling elite that possessed the attributes of the traditional English ruling classes. This process was played out in a political arena full of petty disputes, constant bickering, vicious infighting, and occasional violence. The tumultuous character of politics, which Bernard Bailyn has aptly designated "chaotic factionalism," combined with rapid changes in the structure of Virginia society to produce the chronic instability that marked the Old Dominion before 1676.

When it adopted the county court system of local government,[2] the Assembly was responding to a growing

---

2. There is no known extant text of the statute which established the county courts in 1634, but a précis of the act is printed in William Waller

colony's need for greater efficiency in the disposition of its affairs. Between 1607 and 1634 Virginia's colonized area had expanded from the original settlement at Jamestown. Plantations had sprung up along the James River from its falls to its mouth; colonists had seated much of the York-James Peninsula east of what is now Williamsburg, and some had already settled across the Chesapeake Bay on the Eastern Shore.[3] While Virginia's population remained small and the area of settlement lay close to Jamestown, the governor and his council could adequately perform the tasks of managing the infant colony. As early as the 1620s, however, necessity had caused some of these duties to devolve upon the proprietors of particular plantations and the judges of the several monthly courts that the Assembly had created in 1624.[4]

These changes pointed toward the statutory differentiation enacted in 1634 between the provincial and the local governments of Virginia. Reliance upon the proprietors and the monthly courts proved ineffective because it led to an irregular patchwork of jurisdictions that increased delays in obtaining justice while it added to the burdens of those men whose responsibility was local administration. In creating the county courts the Assembly not only devised a more efficacious method of governing Virginia but also anticipated extension of a uniform system of justice and government throughout the Old Dominion.

Hening, ed., *The Statutes at Large; Being a Collection of all the Laws of Virginia from the First Session of the Legislature, in the Year 1619*, facsimile edition (Charlottesville, Va., 1969), 1: 224.

3. Morgan P. Robinson, "Virginia Counties: Those Resulting from Virginia Legislation," *Bulletin of the Virginia State Library*, 9 (1916): plate 6.

4. Wesley Frank Craven, *The Southern Colonies in the Seventeenth Century, 1607–1689* (Baton Rouge, La., 1949), pp. 166–169; Hening, ed., *The Statutes at Large*, 1: 125.

In 1634 the Assembly divided Virginia into eight counties, each of which was governed by a court composed of justices of the peace,[5] a sheriff, a clerk, and several lesser officials. The functions of the justices of the peace were similar to those of their counterparts in England, but the scope of their authority was initially somewhat narrower.[6] Individually the justices served as magistrates who took depositions and settled minor disputes; collectively they disposed of civil causes below £10 and petty criminal offenses. Their more general obligation, as the title *justice of the peace* implies, was to maintain what a contemporary English jurist called "the Amity, Confidence and Quiet that is between men."[7] Although they were probably analogous to those of an English sheriff, the original duties of the colonial sheriff are obscure.[8] The office of clerk had no equivalent in English local government, although its prototype seems to have resulted from a mixture of the record-keeping functions of the *custos rotulorum* and his deputy, the clerk of the peace.[9]

---

5. The new judges were designated "commissioners of monthly courts" or "commissioners of the peace" until an act of Assembly adopted in Mar. 1662. See Hening, ed., *The Statutes at Large*, 2: 70. To avoid confusion, I have used the designation "justice of the peace" throughout this essay.
6. Cf. Hening, ed., *The Statues at Large*, 1: 224, with William Lambarde, *Eirenarcha: Or, the Office of Justices of Peace* . . . (London, 1581), Book 2, chap. iv, on the competence of a Virginia justice of the peace in 1634 and his English counterpart.
7. Michael Dalton, *The Countrey Justice: Containing the Practice of Justices of the Peace out of their Sessions*, 12th ed. (London, 1677), p. 9.
8. A not very useful comparison of the office in its respective settings is Cyrus Harreld Karraker, *The Seventeenth-Century Sheriff: A Comparative Study of the Sheriff in England and the Chesapeake Colonies, 1607–1689* (Chapel Hill, N. C., 1930).
9. In England the *custos rotulorum* was a senior justice of the peace who kept the court's rolls safe from destruction. The clerk of the peace was a scrivener who enrolled indictments, convictions, etc. From the beginning the clerk of court in Virginia never was a member of the commission of

Clerks discharged one of the court's primary responsibilities by providing a place of record for the business of court and colonist.[10]

The emergence of these courts coincided with a major increase of Virginia's population and expansion of its settled area. Beginning in 1634, if not earlier, the Old Dominion experienced its own "great migration," and in thirty years' time the number of inhabitants swelled from five thousand to forty thousand.[11] During those years the colonists rolled back the wilderness, settling all of present-day Virginia east of the fall line. Indicative of this growth was an increase in the number of counties. By 1648 two counties had been added to the original eight; within twenty more years the number had

---

the peace. See Lambarde, *Eirenarcha*, pp. 371–375; Dalton, *Countrey Justice*, p. 64; *The Compleat Justice. Being an Exact and Compendious Collection out of such as have treated of the Office of Justices of the Peace* . . ., 7th ed. (London, 1661), p. 69.

10. Early records indicate that the colonists first used the courts mainly as a place of registry for such things as land titles and business accounts. See Northampton County Order Book, 1632-1640, *passim*.

11. These population figures come from contemporary sources. The number 5,000 is drawn from a census taken sometime after the erection of the county court system; that of 40,000 is an estimate made by Sir William Berkeley in 1671. See "A List of the Nomber of men women and Children Inhabitinge in the severall Counties within the Colonie of Virginia, Anno Domini *1634*," C.O. 1/8, fol. 155, National Archives, Kew (formerly the Public Record Office), and "Enquiries to the Governor of Virginia" (1671), in Warren M. Billings, ed., *The Papers of Sir William Berkeley, 1605–1677* (Richmond, Va., 2007), pp. 393–397. In the 1970s the size and character of Virginia's 17th-century immigration had become a subject of renewed interest and debate among scholars. See, for example, Wesley Frank Craven, *White, Red, and Black: The Seventeenth-Century Virginian* (Charlottesville, Va., 1971), pp. 1–39, and Edmund S. Morgan, "Headrights and Head Counts: A Review Article," *Virginia Magazine of History and Biography*, 80 (1972): 361–372.

doubled. County building ceased for a time only when immigration slackened after 1668.[12]

As the Old Dominion grew, the Assembly turned over to the county courts increasing responsibility for local affairs. What began in 1634 as agencies of regional administration with narrowly prescribed powers emerged by 1662 as the units of government whose wide authority touched the colonists' lives far more immediately than did that of the Assembly or the governor. An explanation of this phenomenon is to be found in the problems of adjusting to an economic and social pattern marked by a progressively greater dispersal of settlement. An ever-broadening circle of colonization created communications difficulties with the capital, so that the settler who lived in remote parts of Virginia might have to wait days or weeks for a distant governor or assembly to take action that in some instances meant the difference between life and death. More immigrants increased the number of deeds, indentures, runaways, disputes, and other matters which required legal attention. Assigning such problems to local authority not only alleviated the burdens on the governor and council but put power into the hands of men who had the closest acquaintance with local affairs, the residents of the

---

12. New Norfolk was created in 1636. The following year the General Assembly divided it into Upper and Lower Norfolk counties. In 1642 the Assembly renamed four counties: Upper Norfolk became Nansemond, Accomack became Northampton, Warwick River became Warwick, and Charles River became York. From 1648 ten new counties were erected: Northumberland (1648), Gloucester (1651), Surry (1652), Lancaster (1653), Westmoreland (1653), New Kent (1654), Old Rappahannock (1656), Accomack (1663), Stafford (1664) and Middlesex (1668). The Assembly established no new counties until 1691. See Robinson, "Virginia Counties," *Bulletin of the Va. State Lib.*, 9 (1916): 90–93; Lancaster County Order Book, 1666–1675, fol. 128; Martha W. Hiden, *How Justice Grew. Virginia Counties: An Abstract of their Formation* (Williamsburg, Va., 1957), p. 15.

communities themselves. In short, the General Assembly, using statutes, fashioned the courts into an institutional instrument capable of serving the needs of a fast-growing colony.

Even a casual reading of Virginia's laws enacted between 1634 and 1676 reveals the Assembly's preoccupation with local government, as well as its inclination to give the county courts control of local affairs and many of the processes of justice. During the first eighteen years of their existence the county courts gained extensive additions to their jurisdictions. As early as 1640 they were empowered to punish such moral lapses as bastard-bearing and fornication—offenses which the English traditionally tried in church courts.[13] When it rewrote Virginia's legal code in 1643, the Assembly assigned to the courts the responsibility for maintaining bridges and ferries within a county's boundaries[14] and ordered the recording of mortgages in the courts' records.[15] Besides giving sheriffs power to distrain a man's goods for satisfaction of his debts,[16] the code of 1643 authorized the justices to hear civil cases below a value of sixteen hundred pounds of tobacco[17] and to oversee the estates of orphaned minors.[18] In 1644 the courts acquired limited control over tavernkeepers as well as the power to issue local orders which did not "enjoyne any obedience contrary to an act of Assembly."[19] At its February 1645 sitting the Assembly extended the courts' authority over the church by requiring the justices to punish churchwardens who were derelict in the performance of their office.[20] A

---

13. Hening, ed., *The Statutes at Large*, 1: 227.
14. Ibid., 269.
15. Ibid., 248–249.
16. Ibid., 266.
17. Ibid., 272–273.
18. Ibid., 260–261.
19. Ibid., 287, 264.
20. Ibid., 291.

significant addition to their authority came in November 1645 when the Assembly granted the justices of the peace power to hear all cases in common law and in equity. Before this change, the governor and his councillors, sitting in quarterly sessions, had tried all civil causes above £10, but "the great distance of many parts of the collony from James Citty" and an increased caseload had rendered that practice ineffectual. Necessity thus forced the provincial government to surrender much of its control over local government to county officials. After 1645 the General Court gradually took on the role of an appellate court. Although the 1645 act would be refined by later assemblies, the county courts had now gained original jurisdiction in most civil cases.[21]

The widening of the courts' judicial competence was paralleled by a broadening of their administrative duties. Typical was the Assembly's assignment of the power to probate wills.[22] Extending this authority to the courts was a radical departure from English practice, whereby that power belonged to ecclesiastical courts. Since the Anglican hierarchy had not been transferred to Virginia, the governor and the council inherited many of its responsibilities. Assigning the probation of wills to the county courts relieved the governor of a burdensome chore while it spared the remotely situated colonist an arduous trip to Jamestown. To the courts also fell responsibility for enforcing the colony's laws, which grew in complexity with each passing year.[23] Tax collection was another of the courts' duties.[24] In addition to serving as militia

---

21. Ibid., 303–304.
22. Ibid., 302–303.
23. Ibid., 244–246.
24. Ibid., 267, 280–283; Philip Alexander Bruce, *Institutional History of Virginia in the Seventeenth Century: An Inquiry into the Religious, Moral, Educational, Legal, Military, and Political Condition of the People, Based on Original and Contemporaneous Records* (New York, 1910) 2: 570–574; Martha

officers, the justices of the peace were required to secure sufficient arms and ammunition for defense.[25] Poor relief, the regulation of prices and wages, and the maintenance of roads were among the other concerns which came within the courts' administrative purview.

By 1652 the Assembly had thus transferred an appreciable degree of control over local affairs from the provincial government to the county courts. Although the surrender of the Old Dominion to Oliver Cromwell's rule in March 1652 raised the possibility of an alteration in Virginia's institutional arrangements, Cromwell proved to be more interested in bringing Virginia to heel than in social or political engineering.[26] Consequently, when the Assembly convened six weeks after the surrender to conform the colony's law to the changed situation in England, it did nothing to impair the county courts' powers.[27] In fact, it added to their powers by assigning them an admiralty jurisdiction together with the right to appoint surveyors of the highways and to judge capital offenses.[28]

Woodroof Hiden, "Virginia County Court Records: Their Background and Scope," *VMHB*, 54 (1946): 1–15.
25. Hening, ed., *The Statutes at Large*, 1: 277, 292–293, 315.
26. Craven, *Southern Colonies*, pp. 253–257, and Hening, ed., *The Statutes at Large*, 1: 363–365.
27. The revised code of Apr. 1652 does not appear in Hening's *The Statutes at Large*. The only known copy is in Surry County Deeds and Wills, Book I, 1652–1657, following p. 405. This manuscript also contains the acts of Assembly for Nov. 1652 and July 1653, which were unknown to Hening at the time he edited *The Statutes at Large*. I transcribed and edited the Surry manuscript and published it in *VMHB* 73 (1975): 22–72 under the title "Acts Not in Hening's *Statutes*, Acts of Assembly April 1652, July 1653, and November 1653."
28. Billings, ed., "Acts Not in Hening's *Statutes*, 51–52, 70, 71. In 1656 the Assembly repealed the courts' power to try capital crimes. Hening, ed., *The Statutes at Large*, 1: 397–398.

Over the next ten years, the Assembly continued to enlarge the courts' competence. At its November 1652 sitting, for example, it authorized the justices to enforce an act that imposed a ten-shilling duty on tobacco exported in Dutch vessels. It also charged them with laying out parish boundaries within newly formed counties.[29] Four years later, in another effort to reduce appeals to the General Court, the Assembly made the justices the final arbiters of civil suits below £16.[30] And when the entire legal code was revised again in 1658, the courts gained still wider powers.[31]

The restoration of royal authority in Virginia brought the county courts' statutory control over local government to its zenith. Restoration of old forms and practices required alterations in existing Virginia law. Hence in March 1661/62 the Assembly undertook what proved to be its last revision of the statutes during the seventeenth century.[32] As Wesley Frank Craven has observed, the primary concern of the revisal's architects was local government.[33] They left untouched the courts' expanded jurisdiction, for now the justices of the peace were empowered "to act, and doe all such things as by the laws of England are done by Justices of the peace there." In practical terms, this meant that the county courts combined various criminal, civil, ecclesiastical, admiralty, and administrative jurisdictions which in England belonged to separate courts or political subdivisions. Additionally, those revised laws which touched the church gave the county magistrates control over parish vestries. As if to seal their complete domination over local matters, the

---

29. Billings, ed., "Acts Not in Hening's *Statutes*," 73–74.
30. Hening, ed., *The Statutes at Large*, 1: 398.
31. Ibid., 1: 398, 429–493.
32. See ibid., 2: 41–148, for the revision.
33. Craven, *Southern Colonies*, p. 292.

Assembly gave the justices power to enact bylaws.[34] Save for incidentals or refinements, the division of responsibilities between provincial and local government, as legitimized by the 1662 revision, remained unchanged until 1676.

Since 1634 the Assembly had, in effect, transmuted the county court into the focal point of much of colonial life. Planters turned to the courts to record wills, deeds, or cattle brands. They depended upon local magistrates for settlement of most of their debts and other personal problems that required legal attention. Courts probated wills, collected taxes, fixed prices, and conducted elections. Collectively, they had become the linchpin of Virginia's entire legal and administrative structure. The result was decentralization of the political system, for the courts represented an intervening authority between governor and colonist. No longer was the power to govern the colony concentrated in one place; that power was now dispersed. Because most of government's concerns in seventeenth-century Virginia were private or local in nature, the justices of the peace were the agents of government with whom the planters dealt most directly and often. As the courts' powers grew, the settler turned more to the justices of the peace and less to the provincial authorities for solutions to his problems.

These developments had two gradual effects upon the growth of the colony's political institutions after 1634. The influence of the governor, the Council of State, and the General Assembly in local matters declined as the justices' statutory competence increased. In turn, the justices used their expanding power to translate themselves into Virginia's ruling elite. Over the years after 1634 the governor's control of local politics through his power to influence the justices

---

34. Hening, ed., *The Statutes at Large*, 2: 44–45, 70, 171.172; Bruce, *Institutional History*, 1: 540–550; Craven, *Southern Colonies,* p. 293.

diminished significantly. A single example illustrates the point. The power to appoint justices and other court officers had always belonged to the governor, but by 1662 usage and necessity had reduced that power to a mere formality.[35] For appointments to the benches of the eight original counties, Sir John Harvey had been able to draw from a reservoir of talent that included the councillors, the militia officers, and judges of the defunct monthly courts. Under the old system these men had gained some practical experience in local government. But the practice of naming councillors as senior justices did not continue much beyond the 1640s.[36] After 1648 the number of counties doubled, and there were not enough councillors to go around.[37] Moreover, a majority of the council had usually been selected from the three counties closest to Jamestown-Charles City, James City, and York.[38]

---

35. Instructions to Sir William Berkeley, 10 Aug. 1641, Billings, ed, *Berkeley Papers*, pp. 29–36.
36. The initial employment of councillors on the courts probably contributed to the later distinction between senior and junior justices, a distinction which became formalized when the governors began to designate justices-in-the-quorum in the commission of the peace. For an example of a commission of the peace, see Northumberland County Order Book, 1650–1652, fol. 76.
37. Down to 1676 councillors occasionally sat in on the deliberations of county courts, as was their prerogative. Indeed, for a time in the early 1660s they were required to act as circuit judges, but as the requirement proved unworkable it was discontinued. Hening, ed., *The Statutes at Large*, 2: 64–65, 179.
38. Between 1634 and 1676, 73 men sat on the Council of State. Sixteen resided in York County, 15 in James City County, and 10 in Charles City County. The remaining 32 councillors' residences were as follows: 5 men lived in Warwick County; 4 in Gloucester County; 3 each in the counties of Lancaster, Lower Norfolk, and Northampton; 2 each in the counties of Elizabeth City, Isle of Wight, and Nansemond; 1 each in Henrico, New Kent, Northumberland, Old Rappahannock, Surry, and Westmoreland counties. Accomack, Middlesex, and Stafford counties were

For the new county courts the governors had to turn to men who had little or no judicial experience. An insight into how the problem of staffing a new court was solved during the 1650s is afforded by the circumstances leading to the formation of Rappahannock County.[39] In 1656, at the request of the inhabitants, the Assembly partitioned the then Lancaster County into two smaller counties, Lancaster and Rappahannock. The bench of the parent county was similarly divided, with half of the justices going to each of the new courts. To bring the two counties' benches up to their statutory limits Governor Edward Digges then appointed men who had had no previous service on the parent court.[40]

Then, too, as the number of counties grew the distances from court to capital rendered it impractical to seek advice from the governor, and as the Assembly reduced the chief executive's direction of local affairs his familiarity with local government diminished. The net effect of all these developments was to give the justices of the peace effective control over appointments to their courts. Increasingly after 1648 the judges recommended to the governor new members of the bench, sheriffs, and clerks, and he complied with their

---

unrepresented on the Council before 1676, and residence for four Council members could not be established. This group of councillors was compiled from county records; Hening's *The Statutes at Large*; Annie Lash Jester, *Adventurers of Purse and Person: Virginia 1607–1625*, 2d ed. (n.p., 1964); Lyon G. Tyler, *Encyclopedia of Virginia Biography* (New York, 1915). Subsequently, I folded them into an electronic database for the years between 1619 and 1700 that consists office-holder names, vital statistics, places of origin, kin connections, occupations, offices, and size of land ownership.

39. The Rappahannock County of the 17th century ceased to exist in 1692 when it was divided into Essex and Richmond counties. But use of the name was revived in 1833 when the General Assembly created the county that presently bears the name. So to avoid any confusion, the use of the word *old* has been employed here to distinguish between the two counties.

40. Lancaster County Order Book, 1657–1666, fol. 319.

recommendations. Evidence of the practice can be found as early as the 1630s; by the 1650s it was a customary procedure; and during the 1660s it became virtually inviolable.[41]

After 1634 the duties of the Council of State became more specialized. Its role as a court of original and appellate jurisdiction evolved into that of a high court of appeals. The Council retained original jurisdiction in all cases of felony and civil suits above £16.[42] Since the number of such cases was comparatively small, much of the Council's time was taken up in hearing appeals from the county courts. The growing competence of the local courts reduced the Council's concern for routine local affairs and administrative detail. Released from the task of solving local problems, the councillors could devote more time to their roles as advisors to the governor and legislators.[43]

Owing to the destruction of most of the Council journals, it is difficult to trace the evolution of the Council's advisory and legislative roles after 1634. In their capacity as advisors, the councillors assisted the governor in arriving at decisions affecting his administration of public affairs. Apparently some councillors also worked with the burgesses as floor managers and assisted in the drafting of legislation. The Council's assent was of course necessary for a bill to pass into law.

---

41. Northampton County Order Book. 1632–1640, 77; 1651–1664, fol. 108; 1664–1674, fols. 65–66, 229; 1674–1679, fol. 50; Lower Norfolk County Order Book, 1656–1666, fols., 124, 312–313, 435; 1666–1675, fols., 116, 132, 162; Lower Norfolk County Deed Book No. 4, fol. 16; Accomack County Order Book, 1673–1676, fol.19; Old Rappahannock County Deeds and Wills No. 3, 1663–1668, fol. 307; York County Records No. 5, 1672–1694, fol. 89. During the 1650s the Assembly wrote the practice into law, but its statutory basis was eliminated in later revisals of the colony's legal code. See Hening, ed., *The Statutes at Large*, 1: 392, 402.
42. Bruce, *Institutional History*, 1: 665–690.
43. Ibid., 2: 374–376.

Generally, the councillors' close relationship with the governors, together with their wide experience and superior knowledge of the law, made the Council the dominant component of the General Assembly before 1676.

Throughout the period of the county courts' expansion the House of Burgesses underwent no comparable transformation. Indeed, not until after Bacon's Rebellion did the House begin to emerge as a counterpoise to the powers exercised by the courts or the Council. The Assembly met annually before 1676,[44] but the House probably did not sit as a body separate from the Council until the 1680s.[45] Although the prerogatives of the House were ill defined, it is evident that by 1676 the House had won some control over legislation and taxation. Together with the governor and the councillors the burgesses performed the important task of enacting statute law. Still, for much of the period the impetus for such legislation came from the governor. Gradually, as the Assembly's concerns became more local in nature, some of the initiative shifted to the burgesses. One of the earliest clear examples of this shift occurred in 1663 when Edmund Scarburgh, burgess for Northampton County, moved adoption of some legislation desired by his constituents. The Assembly's passage of Scarburgh's motion indicates that by the 1660s the burgesses had already acquired a degree of freedom in drafting and enacting laws not initiated by the colony's chief executive.[46] The power of the purse had first been claimed by the burgesses in 1624, when the Assembly prevented the governor from imposing taxes. Thereafter

---

44. Cynthia Miller Leonard, comp., *The General Assembly of Virginia, July 30, 1619–January 11, 1978: A Bicentennial Register of Members* (Richmond, Va., 1978), pp. 4–40.
45. Wesley Frank Craven, "'. . . And So the Form of Government Became Perfect,'" *VMHB*, 77 (1969): 131–145.
46. Hening, ed., *The Statutes at Large*, 2: 201–203, 185.

House members gained some control over drafting budgets, fixing salaries, and requiring county courts to collect the taxes that were levied at each Assembly session. By 1666 the right to raise public revenues was recognized as an exclusive prerogative of the House of Burgesses.[47]

Despite the slow growth of clearly defined powers, a significant alteration in the basis of House membership had occurred by 1662. At the time the Assembly had established the county court system, church parishes constituted the legislative districts from which burgesses were elected, and a parish could elect as many burgesses as its parishioners chose to pay. The introduction of the county form of local government induced a new basis of representation, and for a while both parochial and county burgesses sat in the House. In time, however, the justices succeeded in supplanting the parochial burgesses by tying membership in the House to court membership. During the 1640s and 1650s, for example, members of local courts usually managed to insure the election of one of their number.[48] By 1660 it had become customary to regard the county as the sole unit of representation in most parts of the colony,[49] and an act of Assembly of March 1661/62 finally eliminated the parish as an electoral district.[50] Thereafter until June 1676 no man sat

---

47. Ibid., 1: 124, and H. R. McIlwaine, ed., *Journals of the House of Burgesses of Virginia, 1659/60–1693* (Richmond, Va., 1914), 43; Warren M. Billings, *A Little Parliament: The Virginia General Assembly in the Seventeenth Century* (Richmond, Va., 2004).

48. Hening, ed., *The Statutes at Large*, 1: 267, 299, 520–521.

49. Craven, *Southern Colonies*, 266n-268n. Cf. the burgesses for Lower Norfolk in the 1650s given by Leonard in *Bicentennial Register of Members*, with the justices of the peace who attended the Lower Norfolk County Court. Lower Norfolk County Order Book, 1646–1651, *passim*, 1651–1656, *passim*, 1656–1666, *passim*.

50. Hening, ed., *The Statutes at Large*, 2: 106.

in the House of Burgesses who was not simultaneously a justice of the peace.[51]

This monopoly on House membership points to the emergence of the county courts as the base for Virginia's ruling elite. Greater reliance upon these courts had enhanced the office of justice of the peace. Not only was it a badge of success and a source of power, but it was the instrument with which successful colonists fashioned political domains for themselves and their progeny. The enhancement of the office led also to the formation of a variety of competing interests. In turn, the competition for county offices invested politics with its distinctively chaotic quality.

Trebling the number of counties in the decades after 1634 generated an unanticipated need for men to fill county offices. The demand soon outstripped the supply of qualified residents and opened the way to advancement for talented immigrants. For the ambitious immigrant membership on a county court offered certain advantages. It was useful in obtaining land. It also gave a man the opportunity to use whatever business connections he had to acquire economic influence in his county. A strategic marriage could connect him with established colonial families, assuring a rise in status. Moreover, a court system whose power grew with each ensuing year afforded the chance to shape and direct the entire colony's political affairs. A place on the court opened the door to membership in the House of Burgesses and possibly even in the Council of State. These reasons for seeking office were of vital importance to colonists whose desire for social betterment was a compelling motive for moving to Virginia.

---

51. Warren M. Billings, "'Virginia's Deploured Condition,' 1660–1676: The Coming of Bacon's Rebellion" (Ph.D. diss., Northern Illinois University, 1968), pp. 103–106.

Having acquired the power and social prestige of political office, the successful immigrant sought to consolidate his gain and to transfer it to succeeding generations of his family. While he may not have sprung from the English ruling classes, he was in his "social origins just close enough to establishment in gentility to feel the pangs of deprivation most acutely."[52] He recognized an intimate nexus between social position and political authority, for he knew that the English squire who enjoyed high social standing was the same man who enforced the law and the king's decrees.[53] That knowledge led him to use the office of justice of the peace to duplicate the familiar relationship in the Old Dominion. In short, by 1662 the office had been transformed into the cement between the layers of society and government in Virginia.

How this transformation occurred may be illustrated by examining two sets of men who held political office between 1634 and 1676—the justices of the peace, 215 in all,[54] in

---

52. Bernard Bailyn, "Politics and Social Structure in Virginia," in James Morton Smith, ed., *Seventeenth-Century America: Essays in Colonial History* (Chapel Hill, N. C., 1959), p. 100.
53. Ibid., p. 91.
54. These four counties were chosen because they satisfied three conditions: first, they had to be counties whose records spanned all or a major part of the period under investigation in unbroken or nearly unbroken runs. The Lancaster records are virtually complete from the county's inception in 1652. Likewise the records of Lower Norfolk are all but intact from 1637 on. Only the first two years of the Northumberland order books are missing. The York records are broken between 1648 and 1657 and between 1662 and 1665. Second, since relationships between service on the courts and House membership were sought, the counties chosen had to have surviving tax records from which House membership could be determined. All four of these counties met this requirement. Third, in order to view the growth of the county courts over as much of the period from 1634 to 1676 as the sources allowed, the records of the oldest counties had to be examined. York is the only one of the original

Lancaster, Lower Norfolk, Northumberland, and York counties, and the members of the Council of State. The justices shared certain traits. Most were substantial landowners whose holdings ranged from five hundred to fifteen thousand acres.[55] Some were the major economic forces in their communities.[56] Frequently these men monopolized the important county offices, served in the House of Burgesses, and acquired seats on the Council. Their families were closely interrelated by kinship and personal affiliation. Yet the justices lacked an important attribute-a sense of social and political responsibility—probably because of their lack of previous experience in government.

In their backgrounds and origins the justices had much in common. For example, of the eighty-nine men whose English occupations can be determined, over 60 percent were merchants. Twelve were gentlemen, two were yeomen, and the remainder practiced a variety of professions or skilled crafts ranging from baker to surgeon. Many of the justices had migrated from England's urban areas. Original residences

---

eight with abundant surviving records. Lower Norfolk was established in 1637, Northumberland in 1648, and Lancaster in 1652.

55. Since the 17th-century deed books for the four counties have not survived intact, I have used Nell M. Nugent, comp., *Cavaliers and Pioneers: Abstracts of Virginia Land Patents and Grants, 1623–1666*, vols. 1 and 2 (Richmond, Va., 1934, 1977), in computing the landholdings for both justices and councillors. There is an inherent error in this method since it reveals only the land which a man patented, and not the ultimate disposition of a tract. It is also useless for determining land which an immigrant purchased. By this method of computing landholdings, land ownership for 153 justices could be established. The size of the average tract was nearly 1,100 acres. Unfortunately it is not possible to say how that holding compares with landholdings for Virginians in general, because no one has yet made a systematic analysis of Virginia's land records.

56. The point is based upon data which were compiled from local records on each justice of the peace.

for seventy-five men can be established; excluding six who are known to have been born in Virginia, nearly half came from London and Bristol, while the remainder lived in smaller cities and towns or in the country.[57]

Often those justices who had followed commercial pursuits had come to Virginia seeking trade outlets for themselves, their families, or their friends. In the Old Dominion they became tobacco planters and used their business acumen to establish themselves as intermediaries between their neighbors and English-based merchants. Their links to England's commercial centers drew their fellow planters to them for credit and easier access to the tobacco markets. Gradually, as their acquaintance with the other colonists grew, these men enlarged the range of their activity and influence. Often they extended their business dealings over several counties and numbered among their customers other justices of the peace, burgesses, councillors, and even governors. Using this newly acquired economic role, as well as any other connections they might have gained through

---

57. Note 38, above. As noted in the text, the most frequent occupation was "merchant." That designation carried a double meaning in the 17th century. It was applied loosely to anyone who engaged in trade, but it also carried a specific meaning, as in the case of a man who belonged to the London Company of Merchant-Venturers. Unfortunately, the surviving evidence is not precise enough to allow one always to distinguish between the two uses of the word. The breakdown of the 89 according to occupation is as follows: 55 were merchants, 12 were gentlemen, 3 each were grocers and ship captains, and 2 each were coopers, doctors, innkeepers, merchant-tailors, and yeomen. A baker, a book-binder, a carpenter, a mariner, a salter, and a surgeon rounded out the total number. Of the 75 men whose residences may be fixed, 25 came from London, 8 from Bristol, 5 from Yorkshire, 3 from Kent, 3 from Rotterdam, 2 from Kilkenny, Ireland, 2 from Norfolk, 1 each from 21 other cities, towns, or counties in England, and 6 were probably born in Virginia.

marriage or political alliances, they pushed their way onto the county courts.

The immigrant justices of the peace attained their positions fairly rapidly, and having won office they retained it until they died, retired, or were elevated to higher office. It is possible to fix the dates of appointment, length of service, time of arrival, and time of death for 133 of the 215 justices who served in the four counties.[58] Of that number, 72 (54 percent) were appointed to office within a decade of their arrival in Virginia. Another 34 (26 percent) had lived in the colony no more than fifteen years before securing their appointments. None of the remaining 27 (20 percent) had been a resident for more than twenty-five years before his nomination to the bench.[59] Some of these men held office for

---

58. Note 38, above. It should be noted that arrival and appointment dates are often approximations of reality. Seldom does one find documentary evidence that precisely establishes when an individual came to Virginia. In the absence of such documentation the individual's first appearance in local records or the date when he sued out his first land patent has to suffice. There is, of course, an inherent error in such a method of fixing arrival dates. As anyone who works with 17th-century Virginia land records quickly learns, a lag of several years often obtained between the time someone took up a tract of land and when he had his patent recorded in the Secretary of the Colony's office. Dates of appointment may be fixed with considerably more precision, however. Usually copies of individual justices' commissions are preserved in the records of the four counties. In those cases where such commissions exist, the date of issue has been taken for the date of appointment. Where the commissions do not exist two other methods of fixing the time of appointment were used. Often a clerk recorded that at a regular meeting of the court a particular individual appeared and was by order of the governor sworn a justice of the peace. Lacking even that kind of documentation, the date of first appearance on a court has been used as time of appointment.

59. A number of explanations may account for the longer lapse of time between the coming of these 27 men to Virginia and their appointments to office. Nine emigrated to the colony between 1610 and 1634, and they

as little as a year, while others served for more than forty; the median length of service was approximately twelve years, the average length approximately seventeen.

Of these 133 justices a bare majority, 67 individuals, emigrated to the Old Dominion between 1645 and 1660. Another 60 settled in the colony before 1645, and the 6 remaining men went there during the interval from 1660 to 1676. As significant as the time of their establishment in Virginia was the longevity of the justices. Of the 133 for whom such information is available, 44 died between 1634 and 1660, only four of these before 1645. Another 42 were deceased by 1676, but 47 survived after that date.[60] In effect, there does not appear to have been a sharp break between an old and a new elite caused by the deaths of the pre-1645 immigrants. Rather, the gradual passing of these men indicates a slow transfer of power from their hands to those of later arrivals. Furthermore, the justices who had settled prior to 1645 gave to their successors an entrée into the power structure by providing the familial and political connections that were necessary for advancement.[61]

These data suggest a high degree of continuity of political control by the men who became justices of the peace. That

---

came to their respective benches shortly after the courts were erected. At least two were small children at the time of their arrival. Conceivably some of the others were likewise quite young at the time of their arrival. Two men had lived in counties other than the four studied in this essay. The absence of records for those particular counties prevents a determination of whether or not these individuals had previously been justices. Another man had been brought to Virginia as an indentured servant and had served out his indenture before entering into the colony's political life. For the remaining 13 no other explanation is possible than they lacked the ability, luck, or connections needed for advancement.
60. Note 38, above.
61. Bailyn, "Politics and Social Structure," in Smith, ed., *Seventeenth-Century America*, pp. 94–98.

suggestion is reinforced by three other pieces of evidence. First, 22 of the immigrants' sons succeeded to seats on the county courts. Second, there is in the careers of all 215 justices a discernible pattern of multiple officeholding and succession to higher political positions. At least 64 justices held the shrievalty one or more years. Another 50 were burgesses, and 16 others held seats in the Council of State. Third, there is a nexus between membership on the Council and prior service on the county courts. Thus the seventy-three councillors who held office between 1634 and 1676 had similar backgrounds.[62] Most Council members had been long-term residents of Virginia, living there from ten to twenty-five years before their appointments. During that interval they had served on the county courts, been sheriffs, and sat in the House of Burgesses. Their wide experience in local government was invaluable preparation for discharging the duties of the office of councillor. Indeed, following the creation of the county courts, governors soon came to realize the importance of prior service at the local level in making their appointments to the Council. After 1650 virtually all of the men named councillors had had some previous experience in Virginia's politics. Just as there was a gradual turnover of officeholders at the county level, there was no sudden introduction of outsiders to membership on the Council. While fifty-five councillors died or retired before 1676, membership on the Council did not open up to later immigrants.[63] Replacements came instead from the county courts.

Another link between county and provincial officeholders is revealed in the second generation of conciliar families.

---

62. Note 41, above.
63. The precise breakdown of deaths from 1634 to 1676 is as follows: 1634–1645, 8; 1645–1660, 17; 1660–1676, 30, post 1676, 16.

Nearly one-third of the seventy-three councillors had sons who followed in their fathers' footsteps to seats on the county benches and in the House. Five sons eventually reached the Council itself. One of these sons even became governor of the colony.[64]

Continuity in leadership did not insure political stability. Indeed, the reverse may have been true, for the power of the established justices limited the opportunities for advancement in older counties like Lower Norfolk and York. In these counties the ambitious newcomer had to compete for minor offices, family connections, and influence with men already in political control. He could move to counties like Lancaster and Northumberland and try to parlay his talents into a position of power, but even in these newer counties he still faced competition from established settlers.[65] This intense rivalry for place and preferment provided one basis for the chaotic factionalism which characterized Virginia politics before 1676.[66] County building, however, tended to relieve some of the pressure by providing an outlet through the multiplication of local offices.

---

64. Samuel Mathews, Jr., was governor between 1656 and 1660.
65. At least a dozen of the justices in Lancaster and Northumberland Counties lived elsewhere in the colony prior to their settlement in those counties. Some of these men had been burgesses, and probably justices of the peace, but the records of their previous service are difficult to obtain because the men emigrated from counties whose records are now destroyed.
66. J. Mills Thornton III, "The Thrusting Out of Governor Harvey: A Seventeenth-Century Rebellion" *VMHB*, 76 (1968): 11–26; Accomack County Order Book, 1663–1666, fol. 120; 1660–1670, fols. 176-181; Susie M. Ames, "The Reunion of Two Virginia Counties," *Journal of Southern History*, 8 (1942): 536–548; Hening, ed., *The Statutes at Large*, 2: 364–365; Charles City County Order Book, 1655–1666, fols., 555–561; "Charles City Grievances 1676," *VMHB*, 3 (1895–1896): 132–147; "Defense of Col. Edward Hill," ibid., 249–252.

During the years of rapid county expansion there were opportunities to fill new offices, but after 1660 a significant alteration occurred in the pattern of acquiring political office. The earlier easy access to office was now cut off. Between 1660 and 1676 the General Assembly erected only three new counties, and men who had been on the parent courts or men who had migrated to Virginia before 1660 filled the positions on the new courts. The effect of the slowdown in the availability of offices for well-to-do immigrants was dramatic. Between March 1660 and June 1676, Sir William Berkeley appointed eighty-two justices of the peace and thirty-two councillors. Only six of the appointments went to men who had arrived after 1660.[67]

County building was an artificial stimulus to advancement. As long as it continued at the rate of the 1650s, the well-placed newcomer who demonstrated an ability to wring material gain from the wilderness could expect to obtain a justice's commission. The office served to distinguish him as a person of exceptional ability and skill, but not necessarily as a person of the best family. Once the artificial stimulus had all but disappeared, opportunity declined. The key to political success became less a matter of outdoing one's peers and more of gaining the sponsorship of someone already in a county ruling elite. Such sponsorship had always existed—the quickest way for a man to gain acceptance into a local elite before 1660 was to be ushered into it by a strategic connection—but as more offices tended to be passed down to sons, and as the county courts became the exclusive domains of a few families, sponsorship assumed increased importance.[68]

---

67. Billings, "'Virginia's Deploured Condition,'" 14n.
68. Ibid., 134–136.

This change in the means of attaining office was unsettling. Competition for social position continued as in the past, but economic success no longer assured a person of office. As a result, the struggle for offices probably intensified after 1660. Thus the narrowing, or closing off entirely, of the avenues to political office induced tension in Virginia's social system. As long as there was a limited number of available offices, few men's aspirations for these positions would be realized. This situation laid a second foundation for political factionalism. Factions could form around those men who controlled the offices and those who desired to control them.[69]

Factionalism was also inherent in a system of government where a small group of men exercised as much unrestrained power as the county courts had acquired before 1676. Moreover, Virginia society lacked the means of controlling a tendency toward fragmentation, because no institutions existed that could give it coherence. Widely scattered settlements prevented any discernible interaction between counties, except in extreme emergencies. Since it was still in a transitional phase of development, local government could not provide much stability. The House of Burgesses reflected disparate county interests, while the Council displayed no particular concern for local affairs. Failure to comprehend the evolving nature of the colony's institutions prevented the governors from moving resolutely to check rampant political factionalism. Continually proroguing the General Assembly, distributing patronage to the councillors, or trying to tie stability to economic diversification were not effective solutions because these devices depended for success upon the very men who were the sources of turbulence.[70]

---

69. Ibid., 68–79, 9–92.
70. Ibid., 181–230; Bailyn, "Politics and Social Structure," in Smith, ed., *Seventeenth-Century America*, 101–102; John C. Rainbolt, "The Alteration in

In effect, Virginia society was extremely fragile. There was little in its institutions to give the colonists a sense that change was occurring within an orderly and gradually evolving framework. The uncertainties bred by competition and the novelty of institutional arrangements carried the potential for violent upheavals. Prior to 1676 there was no effective mechanism to dissipate social tensions. Bacon's Rebellion was the result.

In the end the hope for understanding the unstable quality of seventeenth-century Virginia politics lies in the investigation of local institutions and the men who ran them. What happened in 1676 becomes much clearer in light of the train of events set in motion by the establishment of the original county courts in 1634. That single step, taken in response to the necessities imposed by Virginia's novel environment, fragmented political power in the Old Dominion and determined the character of the colony's political life for the next forty years.

---

the Relationship between Leadership and Constituents in Virginia, 1660–1720," *WMQ*, 3d Ser., 27 (1970): 414–415.

ESSAY 3

LAW AND CULTURE IN THE COLONIAL CHESAPEAKE AREA

I developed this essay out of a presentation at a conference on colonial law, which the (Omohundro) Institute of Early American History and Culture put on at Cornell University in March 1978. That paper represented an initial step towards my linking law with culture as a means of explaining early Virginia in ways that other Chesapeake scholars did not. The argument I set forth would underpin my subsequent work on the Old Dominion and I would later bend it into a mechanism to explain legal developments in Louisiana. Shortly after the Cornell conference, John M. Price, then the managing editor of *Southern Studies: An Interdisciplinary Journal of the South*, inquired if I might submit the paper for his consideration. I acceded to his request, figuring that a bird in hand was better than two in a bush. Price accepted the essay with the stipulation that I enlarge it into the version that follows.

Originally published as "Law and Culture in the Colonial South" in *Southern Studies: An Interdisciplinary Journal of the South*, 17 (1978): 333-349, the article is reprinted here with the editor's kind permission.

No one would dispute the eminence that seventeenth-century Marylanders and Virginians attached to things legal, just as no one would deny that the emergence of a body of vernacular law was a key ingredient in the nascent colonial culture. Yet, the growth of law in the colonial Chesapeake area has gone largely unnoticed. Several reasons explain why that is so. In the current rush to reassess the history of early Maryland and Virginia, scholars who are votaries of social history dominate most of the research. As such—while they use the stuff from which colonial law was fashioned—their aim is not to describe how the Chesapeake colonists nurtured their respective legal institutions. Instead, their concern lies with elucidating the demographic patterns they have so painstakingly wrung from legal records.[1] Once they have done that, they are content to leave the law to others, thereby continuing the practice in American historiography of assigning the interpretation of the law's development to specialists in legal history. Specialists have made significant contributions to our appreciation of law in the colonial period, though their energies have not often been spent in examining the colonial south, let alone Maryland and Virginia.[2] But their emphasis on what is deemed autonomous about the legal order—rules, procedures, jurisdictions, courts, precedents—plainly heightens the notion that only those students who speak the special language of the law are competent to interpret its history to others. This species of scholarship, which may be termed "internal legal history," tends to divorce the law from its cultural anchors in the past and very often renders its study didactic, mechanical, and

---

1. Two convenient collections of the social historians' work are Aubrey C. Land, et al., eds., *Law, Society and Politics in Early Maryland* (Baltimore, Md., 1977) and Thad W. Tate and David L. Ammerman, eds., *The Chesapeake in the Seventeenth Century: Essays on Anglo-American Society* (Chapel Hill, N.C., 1979).
2. David H. Flaherty, ed., *Essays in the History of Early American Law* (Chapel Hill, N.C., 1969), pp. 12–14.

sometimes just a trifle dull.³ Historians who lack formal legal training therefore usually fear to venture into what appears as a field of historical inquiry that lies beyond their ken.

We lay historians should not be so easily frightened. Indeed, a smattering of legal erudition may be more of an advantage than an impediment. Our training does not bind us to ask the same questions as our colleagues who have prepared primarily as lawyers and secondarily as historians. While we may attend to what specialists regard as the central theme of early American legal history—the transfer of common law to the colonies—our concern need not be wholly with distinctively legal-appearing things.⁴ We can look beyond colonial law as an independent entity to ponder its broader implications for the transplantation of English culture to the New World. There is, after all, more to the transfer of common law to the Chesapeake than statutes, precedents, and customs, or courts, procedures, and decisions. Colonial law was an integral part of a developing culture, and its emergence reveals what aspects of the colonists' Old World heritage could be appropriated unchanged, what could be bent to new settings and what was useless. Additionally, this larger perspective affords a less restrictive view of the sources of colonial legal history. Besides, the obvious legal sources such as statutes or court records, it is possible to draw from those sources used by social or institutional historians. We may also link legal developments to the social and economic growth of the Chesapeake, thereby giving the region's early history a unity that has hitherto been lacking. So, instead of allowing legal

---

3. Robert W. Gordon, "J. Willard Hurst and the Common Law Tradition in American Legal Historiography," *Law and Society Review* 10 (1975): 10–11; Warren M. Billings, "Law in the Colonial South," *Journal of Southern History*, 73 (2007): 603–616.

4. Flaherty, ed., *Essays in the History of Early American Law*, p. 5.

formalities to intimidate us into passing lightly over colonial law or ignoring it altogether, we ought to see in it an opportunity to enrich our own understanding of the Chesapeake colonies. As we grow in that appreciation, we may eventually surpass the limitations of social history and begin to reach towards a synthesis of the two colonies' cultural development.[5] One way of approaching such a synthesis is outlined in the following sketch of the growth of law in Virginia between 1606 and 1700.

Throughout the seventeenth century the founders of Virginia exhibited marked penchant for establishing serviceable laws and legal institutions in their corner of America. Their proclivity was natural, for they had gone to a place that, by their reckoning, was bereft of civilization. If

---

5. While the current revision has produced several attempts at synthesizing the individual histories of Virginia and Maryland, as yet there is no general synthesis of the region's cultural development. The need for such a synthesis was suggested as early as 1974, when Rhys Isaacs challenged Chesapeake historians attending the (Omohundro) Institute of Early American History and Culture's 34th Conference on Early American History to raise their work to a higher level of generalization. In a paper, "The Social and Economic History of the Colonial Chesapeake: Toward a Synthesis," which Alan Kulikoff delivered at the 43rd annual meeting of the Southern Historical Association, he tried to articulate a broad scheme for interpreting Chesapeake history. His argument rested largely upon a demographic and economic analysis of court records. While it was an alluring interpretation, it lacked persuasiveness because it paid so little attention to other ingredients in the process of cultural change. That shortcoming points up a limitation of the techniques of social history as they are presently understood and utilized. The focus on family and economic relationships all but ignores other aspects that were very much a part of the movement of English culture to the Chesapeake. Since the date of the aforementioned convention *Southern Studies: An Interdisciplinary Journal of the South* devoted the winter 1977 issue to this subject. See especially articles by Russell Menard, Allan Kulikoff, and Michael Greenberg. A somewhat different approach to the problem of culture transfer is James Axtell's "The Ethnohistory of Early America: A Review Essay," *William and Mary Quarterly*, 3d. ser., 35 (1978): 110–145.

they hoped to achieve an orderly society in this new land, settlement required the adoption of rules to govern their developing economic, political, and social relations. And so they moved haltingly, gradually, sometimes even painfully and cruelly towards adapting a richly complex legal heritage to its new setting. By 1700, they had succeeded in devising serviceable legal institutions and laying some of the foundations of American law.

Their cultural background intensified their feelings of immediacy. Seventeenth-century Englishmen sprang from a culture that emphasized the primacy of law as the sinew that drew men together in civilized society.[6] Like other western legal systems, English law comprehended man's precious possessions, life, family, property, and beliefs. But its form was what gave it distinctiveness. Distinguished then as now from continental systems by the phrase "common law," English law was uncodified, pluralistic, and without a central focus.[7] Evolving as statute, case law, custom, and precedent for centuries before 1600, common law represented an accumulation of wisdom about the constitution of a proper social order. It afforded the realm protection by maintaining peace among its members, and it, fixed standards of taste, manners, and morals. Its forms and its rituals served to remind all men that it was the arbiter of their conduct. But it was more than these things. Taken in its broadest sense, common law was the ultimate statement of English culture because it defined the identity that set Englishmen apart from their fellow Europeans.

---

6. Edward Bulstrode, *Reports* (London, 1657), 1: "The Epistle Dedicatory."
7. In his commentary on the composition of English law, Sir Edward Coke noted some fifteen species that fell under the general rubric of common law. See Coke, *Institutes of the Laws of England* (London, 1660), 1: fol. 114b.

An Englishman need not have been professionally versed in law to appreciate its cultural significance, for it pervaded his daily existence. Everywhere he looked about him, he found his life enmeshed in some piece of common law's wide fabric. From birth he absorbed the precepts that regulated the household as he observed the relations between his parents and himself. As he grew older, he came across rules affecting a larger society outside his home. When he took up a calling, got married, had children, acquired property, or changed residences, he again discovered himself bound by a time-honored code of behavior. No matter where he turned, he learned that law was an inescapable part of life. The perceptions thus gained through observation and experience became the basis for much of the knowledge that the colonists who became lawmakers tried to incorporate into their own legal system in the Old Dominion.

Virginia lawmakers were part of that socio-political elite whose collective markings are so well known as to require no recapitulation here. The noteworthy thing about these social characteristics, however, is the impression that they left upon the colony's law. Virginia attracted the sort of middling Englishmen who were lured by the hope of exchanging the intricate legal webbing that bound them to medieval order for the nearly perfect freedom to quest for private gain. Their favored position gave them a competitive advantage, thereby allowing them to exploit the opportunity with shameless abandon. Indeed, indentured servitude and chattel slavery are two testaments to their search for wealth and power that remind us of some of the more cruel aspects of English culture's transit to Virginia.[8]

---

8. Bernard Bailyn, "Politics and Social Structure in Virginia," in James Morton Smith, ed., *Seventeenth-Century America: Essays in Colonial History* (Chapel Hill, N.C., 1959), pp. 90–105; Warren M. Billings, *A Little Parliament: The Virginia General Assembly in the Seventeenth Century*

Once in the Old Dominion these colonists soon discovered that there was more to living in their new world than the exclusive pursuit of private ends. To seek those goals, they first had to survive, and, as many an acquisitive settler discovered to his dismay, ambition alone guaranteed neither survival nor success. At first, merely staying alive in a strange place was chancy. Even as the colonists grew in proficiency at coping with the wilderness, the routine rhythms of life still demanded regulation. Without it, debts could not be settled, estates could not descend, and property, human or real, could not be acquired. Because these and dozens of other social needs would remain matters of intense concern, these settlers could not escape all the restraints of their background. Complete freedom would bring not only chaos but also the loss of cultural identity. The latter was a terrible prospect, made the more frightful by the separation from England and the chronic social instability that typified Virginia for so much of its first century. Confronted by such grim possibilities, leading colonists soon looked to their legal roots in order to pluck from them the means of giving their society definition and direction. These men therefore became the instruments by which English law was fashioned to its Virginia setting, and it is instructive to examine their creative impulses.

In their quest to create a viable legal tradition, Virginia lawmakers drew inspiration from several sources. The governors, representing first the Virginia Company of London and then the crown, provided one such impetus, which was usually directed towards the implementation of some specific policy. Another was the cultural impulse, whose transformation into usable laws demanded only an awareness and a willingness to act on the part of the lawmakers. Their

---

(Richmond, Va., 2004), pp. 87–115; Edmund S. Morgan, *American Slavery, American Freedom: The Ordeal of Colonial Virginia* (New York, 1975), *passim*.

grounding in commerce and skilled trades had led to frequent brushes with certain parts of English law. In the ordinary conduct of their business they had learned the intricacies of bills of exchange, charter-parties, deeds, letters of attorney, and even wills. Settling debts or other disputes put them in touch with courts and courtroom procedures. These and similar contacts provided instruction in how to bring suit, how to give and take evidence and how to discharge the obligations of attorneyship. Collectively, such encounters invested prospective lawmakers with a working understanding of the English judicial system. It was the acquisition of such skills that accounts for so many of them finding Virginia an attractive place in which to pursue their ambitions. Their talents enabled them to promote new opportunities for gain, as well as to tend the established interests of family and friends. Upon settling in Virginia, they quickly discovered that even the barest rudiments of legal expertise qualified them for entrance into the colony's political life.[9] Once insinuated into politics, it was but a short, logical leap to using one's knowledge to participate in erecting the Old Dominion's legal system.

Finally, there was the impact of books about English law. From the introduction of printing presses into England late in the fifteenth century until the settlement of Jamestown, dozens of legal titles circulated throughout Britain. In the next hundred years their number grew as the seventeenth-century's political and constitutional crises enlivened Englishmen's enthusiasms about their law. Books that

---

9. Although he was by no means a legal illiterate, William Fitzhugh is a good illustration of an immigrant who parlayed his limited learning in law into great personal advantage as he played as influential role in shaping some parts of Virginia law. For an assessment of Fitzhugh, see Richard Beale Davis, ed., *William Fitzhugh and his Chesapeake World, 1676–1701: The Fitzhugh Letters and Other Documents* (Chapel Hill, N.C., 1963), pp. 1–57, especially, pp. 9, 24–27.

reported cases, abridged statutes, provided learned commentary, or gave practical instruction to local magistrates—all were eagerly devoured by lawyer and layman alike. Here, then was an expansive treasure trove of inspiration that opened the law's mysteries to any colonial lawmaker who turned to it for guidance.

When we moderns contemplate this antique literature, we too frequently think only of the names of the few most famous authors. For in assessing the old writings' effects in America, it is most tempting to look to the likes of Sir Thomas Littleton, Sir John Fortescue, or, of course, Sir Edward Coke, to assign preponderant weight to their work and go no further. It is demonstrable, however, that Coke's *Institutes* or his *Reports* had scant influence in Virginia, if anywhere else in America before 1700.[10] Instead of depending upon Coke, Fortescue, or Littleton for enlightenment, early lawmakers relied upon more prosaic writers whose names and works are by now so obscure as to be unknown to most of us. But a bit of digging soon yields those books whose contents can give the enterprising scholar a further insight into the colonists' own grasp of law.

Here it must suffice merely to enumerate the types of law books that circulated and to suggest their probable effect. Philosophical commentaries, procedural studies, case reports, abridgments of statutes, and dictionaries all found their way to Virginia, but their impact is difficult to assess because seldom is there a direct link between any of them and specific laws or institutions. Furthermore, these sorts of writing

---

10. One of the earliest examples of Coke's authority being invoked in the Virginia courts occurred in 1685 (Westmoreland County Order Book, 1675–1689, pp. 374–377); David Allan Grayson, "In English Ways: The Movement of Societies and the Transfer of English Local Law and Custom to Massachusetts Bay, 1600–1690" (Ph.D. diss., University of Wisconsin, 1975), p. 6.

tended to be overshadowed by a more mundane species that might be termed "how-to-do-it books." "How-to-do-it-books" were sources of practical knowledge that were usually written by men widely experienced in their respective fields. There were guides for justices of the peace and directories for attorneys, clerks, constables, and sheriffs, as well as manuals on how to plead cases, write will, convey property, and draft other legal instruments.[11]

All how-to-do-it books were of a similar format. When an author described the responsibilities of a justice or a sheriff, for example, he first examined the office for its origins and its evolution to his own time. Next, he discussed the duties and powers of the office, and these discussions were almost always arranged alphabetically by topics. The manuals gave detailed instruction in what constituted violations of law and how those offenses should be treated. Books that instructed one in preparing and maintaining records were also basically alike. Their authors commented upon the importance of record keeping, the origins of documents, their functions, and the circumstances under which they should be employed. Most important of all, such manuals provided the reader with sample copies of each instrument in Latin and English. For men who were not always conversant with Latin, which was the language of legal instruments, the English translations stripped away some of the law's mystery.

The appeal of this class of law books to Virginians is self-evident. To men lacking in formal training, a scrivener's guide was a useful model upon which to pattern a county court's records, while the advice in a manual for justices afforded direction in how a magistrate should discharge his duties. The statutes, precedents, and customs, which the authors of how-to-do-it books invoked, could be cited to provide one foundation of tradition upon which to ground law and

---

11. Essay 4, below.

procedure in Virginia. Colonial lawmakers had only to borrow appropriate sections out of the books and apply them to a given problem.

These books made two other impressions on the Old Dominion's early lawmakers. Not only did they provide models, but also they were authoritative sources that sanctioned the colonists' handiwork. To men who possessed only practical learning in a complex, difficult, and sometimes-arcane branch of English culture, the written word carried a validity that their own recollections could not. In this regard, the how-to-do-it books solaced uncertain men by being a direct, tangible link with home. Because they drew attention to how local magistrates discharged their duties, they also augmented the importance of those officeholders. In turn, they accented the primacy of local law and custom. That emphasis served to strengthen the colonists' past contacts with English law by reminding the lawmakers of their previous experiences, and it reinforced the idea that English local traditions were the most suitable for their requirements in Virginia.

How the Virginians perfected their impulses into law is revealed in their creatures, the General Assembly, the courts, the statutes, and the court records. The institutional development of the General Assembly and the courts requires no additional comment since these are the most intensely studied parts of the colony's legal apparatus.[12] What merits further consideration, though, is

---

12. Philip Alexander Bruce, *Institutional History of Virginia in the Seventeenth Century: An Inquiry into the Religious, Moral, Educational, Legal, Military, and Political Condition of the People Based on Original and Contemporaneous Records* (New York, 1910), I: 463–696; 2: 229–637; Wesley Frank Craven, *The Southern Colonies in the Seventeenth Century, 1607–1689* (Baton Rouge, La., 1949), pp. 169–172; Billings, *A Little Parliament*; Morgan *American Slavery, American Freedom*, pp. 133–147; Martin H. Quitt, "Virginia House of Burgesses, 1660–1706: Social, Educational & Economic Bases of Political

the role of these bodies in the transmission of English culture to the Chesapeake. The Assembly wrote the laws that the courts implemented and interpreted. Thereby both became the institutional mechanisms with which the colonists fashioned their knowledge of their background to their own needs. To examine the statutes and the court records, however briefly, is to learn what colonial lawmakers esteemed about the past, what they sought to improve, and where they struck off in new directions.

From its beginnings in 1619, the Assembly arrogated to itself an authority to write law for Virginia, a power that its members gradually and haphazardly enlarged over the length of the century. By 1700, there were few areas touching the Old Dominion's internal polity where they felt incompetent to legislate. While the acquisition of this legislative power is obscured by the destruction or loss of most of the assembly journals, its results exist in abundance. The most accessible collection of seventeenth-century written laws is, of course, William Waller Hening's *The Statutes at Large*.[13] Historians owe a continuing debt to Hening; his compilation is the largest collection of Virginia's colonial statutes, and although there are important gaps in the edition, *The Statutes at Large* remains the basic source of knowledge about the colony's written laws. Despite its obvious value as historical evidence, Hening's work is seldom employed as a research tool. The reason for that lies in the compilation's form. As the title implies, Hening arranged the statutes in chronological order consistent with their enactment by the Assembly. There is no

---

Power" (Ph.D. diss., Washington University in St. Louis, 1970). A complement to the Quitt study is Jon Kukla, *Political Institutions in Virginia, 1619–1660* (New York, 1989).

13. Published between 1809 and 1823 in thirteen volumes at Richmond, New York, and Philadelphia, and re-issued in a facsimile edition by the University of Virginia Press in 1969. The latter is the source of references to Hening throughout this essay.

logical categorization of the laws according to their subjects or types, and, as it stands, the work's usefulness is not immediately apparent. That difficulty may be overcome, however, if one first examines the content of the Assembly's periodic complete revisions of the entire corpus of written law and then abridges their subsequent amendments.

In 1632, the General Assembly finished the first of five overhaulings of the colony's laws that occurred in the seventeenth century. Two more were done in 1642 and 1652, while the fourth came in 1658, and the final one was undertaken in 1662.[14] As the preamble to the 1632 "revisal," to use the contemporary idiom, indicates, the legislators found existing laws "in some cases defective and inconvenient," and they therefore wished to make "a clearer explanation of some of them, as likewise some additions and alterations."[15] Practical considerations were not the only motives underlying this and later reforms, however. The revisals of 1642, 1652, and 1662 followed on the heels of significant political changes in Virginia, such as the crown's appointment of Sir William Berkeley as governor, the reduction of Virginia to Oliver Cromwell's government, and the restoration of royal authority. Each of these events signalled the need to adjust to new realities. Beyond these consequences lies the fact that periodic revisions are also evidence of the assemblymen's desire to reduce colonial law

---

14. The revisals of 1632, 1642, 1658, and 1662 are in Hening, ed., *The Statutes at Large*, 1: 178–202, 429–505; 2: 41–148. That of 1652 was unknown to Hening. The only extant copy is in Surry County Deeds and Wills, 1652–1672. A printed version of the Surry manuscript is Warren M. Billings, ed., "Some Acts not in Hening's *Statutes*, The Acts of Assembly, April 1652, November, 1652, and July, 1653," in *Virginia Magazine of History and Biography*, 83 (1975): 22–72. A sixth revision was undertaken in 1699 but not completed until 1704 (Billings, *A Little Parliament*, pp. 194–198).

15. Hening, ed., *The Statutes at Large*, 1: 179.

to an orderly system. They were not "codes" within the civilian or modern meanings of codification. Instead, they were rough groupings of statutes according to area of activity requiring regulation. It is this characteristic which makes the revisals helpful in abridging the other laws.

Abridgments are compilations that summarize statutes and arrange them according to subject matter.[16] Laying them side by side topically rather than chronologically shows what leading colonists regarded as their social imperatives, what were recurring matters of interest, which laws worked, which did not, and what new species of law grew out of unique conditions. A single example, the Assembly's treatment of the institutional church, illustrates the point.

While the colonists drew spiritual solace from the church, they also recognized that its precepts and its organization could be employed to support traditional cultural values. That awareness led them to try to encourage the movement of the Anglican establishment to Virginia by laying some of its foundations. To that end, the assembly, almost from its inception, devoted considerable attention to church affairs. In fact, putting church law at the head of all the revisals signifies the importance that the lawmakers attached to the need for a well-ordered religious establishment.[17]

---

16. Abridgements of statutes were among the first law books printed in England, and a useful guide to them is John D. Cowley, comp., *A Bibliography of Abridgements, Digests, Dictionaries and Indexes of English Law to the Year 1800* (London, 1932). On both sides of the Atlantic, it was not uncommon for individuals to compile manuscript abridgments for their personal use. Only one such survives from 17th-century Virginia, that of Philip Ludwell. The original manuscript now rests in the collection of the Virginia Historical Society, Richmond, while an imperfect edition of it was published in *VMHB* 9 (1901): 274–288.

17. Hening, ed., *The Statutes at Large*, 1: 122–124, 180–185, 240–243, 433–435; Billings, ed., "Acts Not in Hening's *Statutes*," *VMHB*, 83: 31–32.

By 1662, these expectations proved illusory. Virginia lacked a bishop, a sufficient number of clergymen, and, until 1693, even the means of training prospective candidates for the priesthood. There were no church courts to manage family relations, probate wills, or guard the public morals. In the absence of churchmen to lead or institutions to support, many ecclesiastical functions fell to others. When ministers could be induced to trade their English livings for sojourn in the Virginia wilds, the governors inducted them into service. The Assembly set parochial boundaries, created new parishes and vested county courts with the authority that traditionally lay with church courts. It also transformed parish vestries from relief agencies into the instruments of control in local churches. The laity who filled the vestries assumed the burdens of recruiting rectors, voting taxes maintaining church buildings, presenting offenders to the county courts, and attending to other routine affairs of the parish. Consequently, canon law or its Roman antecedents did not compete with common law, as was the case in England. Furthermore, the institutional church's failure to strike root in Virginia led to a more secular life there and pointed in the direction of an eventual separation of church from state.

To be sure, many of the laws governing the church, labor, land, or the county courts were primitive examples of the legislator's art. All too often they lacked specific meaning and intent, which rendered them difficult to interpret or enforce. Sometimes they devolved too much unchecked power into the hands of local magistrates, who were themselves only partly skilled in governing others. They were also weighted heavily in favor of the more privileged members of colonial society. These imperfections should not, however, obscure the importance of fixing institutions and social relations in written law. Statute, not the accretion of judicial opinion, was the means of adapting English law and culture to their uses in Virginia.

At first blush, this reliance upon statute seems curious because of the lawmakers' obvious lack of professional education. That dependence is explained by several considerations. New law, such as that governing labor or Indian relations, which arose from the peculiarities of the American situation, needed to be written. Because judges from the General Court to the local benches were well versed neither in English law nor their own, colonial law had to be set down in writing. That is why the Assembly compelled magistrates to purchase law books and clerks of court to keep on record copies of all Virginia statutes.[18] Without that guidance there would have been little uniformity in the administration of justice across the colony. Above all else, any variance from English law required statutory definition to prevent mistaking what was and what was not law in the Old Dominion. This continuing need for written laws gradually gave formal definition to those parts of the English cultural tradition that were transformed into colonial culture, just as it slowly taught the members of the assembly the skills of their craft. That very process of adaptation and schooling also embraced local justices and their courts.

Responding to the pressures of rapid expansion, the General Assembly moved as early as the 1630s to establish a uniform system of local government for Virginia and to develop it into a focal point of colonial life.[19] Within a matter of three decades, the county courts resembled their English counterparts. As at home, they enforced the law and ministered to their communities' needs. The men who sat on the benches soon fashioned their offices into the bridge between the colony's political and social strata, and themselves into its ruling elite. In the process, they recreated

---

18. Hening, ed., *The Statutes at Large*, 2: 246; Lancaster County Order Book, 1661–1680, fol. 132; York County Order Book, 1665–1672, p. 361.
19. Hening, ed., *The Statutes at Large*, 1: 224.

the familiar tie between high station and great power that was so much a part of traditional English society. The courts in these respects linked the colonists to higher legal and social authority.

Despite such similarities, singular differences distinguished Virginia courts from their English models. Unlike the situation in England, colonial courts owed their existence to a legislature rather than the custom of immemorial usage. Moreover, their power was largely fixed as described in the statute. That very power was broader than that which English county courts enjoyed, for it encompassed the jurisdictions of the mother country's admiralty, civil, criminal, ecclesiastical, and equity courts. Because judicial processes had to be intelligible to men of limited understanding, a casual informality governed colonial courtrooms. Few written rules existed, and when they did, they were stripped to bare essentials.[20] English supplanted Latin as the language of court. Pleadings, summonses, and writs all found their way into court proceedings, but like procedural rules, they were simplified and divested of technical language. In fact, pleadings were often no more than the merest summary of an argument, while petitions frequently replaced writs as the means of initiating trials. Even the record of court business was different. Apart from being kept in the vernacular tongue, colonial court records contain matters, such as land transfer: inventories of estates, and wills, that were never kept by English local courts.

The scheme of these and other notable departures from the past followed no preconceived design. Instead, they happened naturally, as the Virginians sought to satisfy the needs of a growing colony. Momentary problems became the excuse to borrow some piece of tradition, enact it into statute, test it at the local level, and then cast it aside for

---

20. Lancaster County Order Book, 1660–1680, p. 208.

something else if it failed. Once a desired legal solution had been found, it became a precedent for a future appropriation of English law. Slowly, this gradual testing gave the colonials experience in the mysteries and arts of lawmaking, as it eventually gave formal definition to an indigenous culture.

Although this process of adjustment was haphazard, there is a discernible pattern to the growth of Virginia law over the length of the seventeenth century. Colonial lawmakers made their adaptations in five stages that spanned irregular intervals between 1606 and 1700. The first commenced with the initial settlement and continued until 1619; the second existed between 1619 and 1652; the third lasted from 1652 to 1660, and the remaining two ran from 1660 and 1677 to 1700 respectively. Each of the stages coincided with major events in the colony's growth, and legal developments generally mirrored significant changes in the emergence of colonial society.

Because the original founders of Virginia intended something other than the full-scale transplantation of their native culture, they gave little thought to creating a legal establishment for their colony. Beyond the vague references to common law that appear in the Charter of 1606 and the instructions to the resident leaders, the question of law got short shrift.[21] The first specific attempt to resolve the matter came with the revision of the Virginia Company of London's charter in 1609 and the subsequent promulgation of the *Lawes Divine, Morall and Martiall*.[22] Sir Thomas Dale's vigorous enforcement of that draconian code of military law saved the colony, but the colonists' hostility to the alien species of law,

---

21. Philip L Barbour, ed., *The Jamestown Voyages under the First Charter, 1606–1609*, Hakluyt Society Publications, 2d Ser; 136–137 (Cambridge, 1969), 1: 31, 35–36.

22. First published in 1612, a modern edition of the *Lawes Divine, Morall and Martiall* was prepared by David H. Flaherty and published in 1969 by the University of Virginia Press.

plus their eagerness to pursue their own interests and the company's desperate need to find a way of salvaging an unprofitable venture led eventually to the first turning point in Virginia's legal history. The decision to introduce familiar forms of law and legal institutions was perhaps the Virginia Company's most enduring attainment. It was not without unfortunate consequences, however. In trying to save the colony by capitalizing on its one obvious resource, the land, the company enhanced the possibility that Virginia would be shaped by callous, greedy men who were ruthless in their exploitation of others.

That possibility became reality in the three decades following 1619. Events on both sides of the Atlantic combined to loosen Virginia's ties with the mother country. Following the crown's dissolution of the Virginia Company and its takeover of Virginia, Charles I's domestic difficulties prevented the government's active involvement in colonial affairs. Free of constraints from abroad, the colony experienced rapid population growth, geographic expansion, and economic development. That the Virginians could act in relative freedom is demonstrated most dramatically by their expulsion of Governor Sir John Harvey in 1635. This state of near independence peculiarly suited the buccaneering style of the successful settlers who emigrated to Virginia in the 1630s, 1640s and 1650s. Seizing the precedent established by the convening of the first General Assembly, they used it to institutionalize their conception of a proper legal order. They created a fundamental decentralization and dispersal of power by dividing the authority of government among the county courts, the governor, and the assembly. Using the time-honored tools of family ties and social influence, they turned local government into a device for assuring their continued dominance. By mid-century they had succeeded in fixing the legal order's outlines as they fastened their grip on the access to power, prestige, and wealth.

A challenge to these arrangements came in 1652 when Sir William Berkeley surrendered the Old Dominion to Oliver Cromwell's government. After the disputes between Charles I and the parliament men had given way to civil war a decade earlier, the Virginians remained aloof from the conflict. Once the issue had been settled in the Puritans' favor, the situation changed as Cromwell moved to gain Virginia's submission. It soon developed that the new masters had no inclination to upset things unduly. Moreover, a series of inept governors served to strengthen lawmakers' hands, and the colonists stayed on the course they had charted years earlier. Growth continued as the uncertainties at home drove more immigrants to the Chesapeake. The problems caused by expansion still required appropriations of English law: so there was a steady enlargement of the legal system throughout the Interregnum. In the end, the eight years of Commonwealth rule served mainly to quicken the pace of legal adaptation. Otherwise, parliamentary rule had little lasting impact in Virginia.

The 1660s and 1670s were years of adjustment to realities different from those of the Interregnum. Sir William Berkeley's return to power in 1660 heralded the reversion of Virginia to its old allegiance. Many colonists expected that the restoration of royal authority meant that the crown would resume its former benign indifference to its loyal dominion, but that was a vain hope. Parliament's passage of the first navigation statutes signalled the home government's intent, and thereafter followed more rather than less interference. The trade laws also intensified the problems inherent in a single-crop economy, worsened already by chronic overproduction of tobacco. Concern for the future of the colony's economy was reflected in the various schemes for crop diversification that Governor Berkeley pushed into law.[23] Lack of stability plagued the political sphere just as it did the economy. Although colonial leaders finally managed to monopolize all of the colony's lucrative political and legal offices, they had yet to acquire the qualities of leadership that would translate them from a gang of buccaneers into a ruling class.

The pace of institutional development slowed as the county courts matured. Recognition of that maturity came in 1662, when the assembly raised the court's statutory control over local government to its zenith.[24] The colony's social structure also acquired a more permanent shape. One evidence of that is to be found in the efforts by the assembly and the courts to give legal definition to chattel slavery.[25] With these changes came a gradual hardening of the lines of authority and a growing restiveness among those colonists who enjoyed neither success nor influence. Their discontent surfaced as Bacon's Rebellion, which drove an embittered old Governor Berkeley back to England to die in disgrace and closed a political age.

As the seventeenth century's eighth decade closed, Virginia entered a new era. Bacon's Rebellion forced the crown to pay closer heed to the Old Dominion than at any time since the 1620s. One result of that attention was closer scrutiny of the colony's law and legal institutions and an effort to bring both more nearly in line with English practices. County courts, for example, lost some of their

---

23. John C. Rainbolt, *From Prescription to Persuasion Manipulation of Seventeenth Century Virginia Economy* (Port Washington, N.Y., 1974); Warren M. Billings, *Sir William Berkeley and the Forging of Colonial Virginia* (Baton Rouge, La., 2004), pp. 136–163, 174–210.
24. Hening, ed., *The Statutes at Large*, 2: 44–45, 70, 171–172.
25. Lower Norfolk County Order Book, 1665.1675, fol. 73; Charles City County Order Book, 1677–1679, p. 216; Hening, ed., *The Statutes at Large*, 2: 170, 260, 288.

control of local affairs and officeholding.[26] Another consequence was the crown's attempt at a more centralized colonial administration. These and similar changes went to the heart of the political contests that engaged Berkeley's successors and the General Assembly down to 1700, and their occurrence signals a shift of focus away from local issues to ones of provincial and imperial concern. The rebellion also affected the men who had stood at the head of colonial society in 1676. While they retained their hold on society's top rung, the upheaval shocked them into a greater appreciation of those beneath them. This heightened sensitivity altered the relationship between leaders and constituents, and as that modification happened, a ruling class that resembled England's finally emerged.[27] By the 1680s and 1690s sufficient time had also passed to turn frontier outposts into settled communities. There was stability to life that had not existed fifty years earlier, and second and third generation Virginians were more at ease with their surroundings than their parents had been. They accepted Virginia for what it was and were less concerned about what it ought to have been. It was their country and their home. They did things their way, and that way was inscribed in their law. Colonial law, like its English antecedents, now defined what was distinctive about Virginia culture.

Like that culture, colonial law was passing from adolescence to maturity. It resembled its English parent, although some of its parts approached uniqueness. Still fluid, it remained receptive to influences other than the English local traditions that had prevailed down to 1700. Its supporting institutions were set, but they too were open to

---

26. Accomack County Order Book, 1683–1692, p. 4.
27. John C. Rainbolt, "The Alteration in the Relationship between Leadership and Constituents in Virginia, 1660–1720," *WMQ* 3d Ser., 27 (1970): 411–413; Billings, *A Little Parliament*, pp. 49–63.

further refinement. These changes would come with the rising professionalism of eighteenth-century men of law.

Viewed from this side of 1700, the growth of law in seventeenth-century Virginia is at once a dismaying and impressive phenomenon. Colonial law bespoke a culture that exhibited the grosser attributes of a society founded on the pursuit of private gain. Yet, the slow working-out of legal forms to realize those ends invested the first English colonists and their descendants with a priceless legacy of self-government and liberty. That paradox reaches across the centuries to our own time.

ESSAY 4

English Legal Literature as a Source of Law and Practice in Seventeenth-Century Virginia

I did the research for this and the previous essay more or less simultaneously. They were published within months of one another, and I intended them as companion pieces, although they appeared in different magazines. In this one I contemplated which colonists tailored English law to its Virginia setting, what they knew about English law, and the sources of their inspiration. The article identified colonial lawgivers in terms of their backgrounds and political stature. These men, I suggested, were laymen, not lawyers. Their knowledge was at once cultural and practical, but it also proceeded from a treasure trove of law texts that circulated freely in Great Britain and Virginia and lay within reach of any literate colonial. Much of the essay turns on a description of titles and their contents.

Originally published as "English Legal Literature as a Source of Law and Practice for Seventeenth-Century Virginia," in the *Virginia Magazine of History and Biography*, 87 (1979): 403–417, the article is reprinted here with the editor's kind permission.

The broad dimensions of Virginia's legal history in the seventeenth century are well known. For colonial Virginians the interval between 1607 and 1700 was a period of experimentation during which they ransacked their heritage to discover laws and legal institutions suitable for a novel environment. Gradually, they devised acceptable legal practices grounded alike in an ancient tradition and a new environment, thereby setting the stage for the maturing of Virginia society in the next century. Although there is a familiar ring to this summary, the details of how the colonists proceeded to mold their legal inheritance to their use remains obscure. For, as David H. Flaherty has aptly observed, the Old Dominion's legal history has languished from serious neglect.[1] Consequently, inadequate answers have been provided to some fundamental questions: Who was responsible for adapting English law to colonial needs? What was the extent of the colonists' legal training? And, how did they acquire their knowledge of English law and its practice?

Throughout the nearly two decades that the Virginia Company managed the colony, company officials recruited the colony's leaders from England's ruling classes. Therefore, the men who the company selected as its governors and councillors had more than a passing acquaintance with the realm's customs. They had, after all, enjoyed the educational and professional advantages of their privileged station. At all times before 1624 offices in the colony were filled by experienced men who had attended the universities or the Inns of Court and who possessed close ties with the king's court or Parliament.[2]

---

1. David H. Flaherty, ed., *Essays in the History of Early American Law* (Chapel Hill, N.C., 1969), p. 12.
2. Bernard Bailyn, "Politics and Social Structure in Colonial Virginia," in James Morton Smith, ed., *Seventeenth-Century America: Essays in Colonial History* (Chapel Hill, N.C., 1957), pp. 92–94; William Strachey, comp., *For the Colony in Virginea Britannia, Lawes Divine, Morall and Martial, etc.*, ed. by David H. Flaherty (Charlottesville, Va., 1969), p. xv.

Despite the qualifications that they brought to their places, these men left a negligible impression upon Virginia's legal system. More than a few succumbed to the rigors of settlement. Others found Virginia too great a hell to endure and fled home at the first opportunity. Still others had no intention of remaining in Virginia any longer than it took to slake their thirst for adventure. The inability of early leaders to adapt to Virginia plus the uncertainty about the direction in which the colony should proceed postponed necessary decisions and reserved to those colonists who assumed positions of leadership after 1624 the greatest influence in shaping English law to fit the colonial setting.

Those men who assumed leadership upon the demise of the Virginia Company fall into two groups. The smaller but more conspicuous of the two consists of the royal governors whom the crown selected throughout the remainder of the seventeenth century. In background and in training these individuals were similar to their company counterparts, and in virtue of their position they were situated so as to be able to shape colonial law. In London's view theirs was the most powerful and prestigious office in Virginia, and their royal masters often counseled them to rule "as near as may be to the laws of England."[3] Moreover, as the king's surrogates and the colony's chief magistrates they could propose laws to implement their instructions and to facilitate their government of colonial affairs. One might therefore conclude that Virginia's royal governors played a preeminent role in transferring English law to the colony, but such a conclusion is unwarranted.

From 1619 onward, governors shared with the General Assembly the responsibility for making laws for Virginia, and

---

3. Instructions to Sir William Berkeley, 10 Aug. 1641, in Warren M. Billings, ed., *The Papers of Sir William Berkeley, 1605–1677* (Richmond, 2007), p. 29.

as the century wore on the assembly came to enjoy a greater measure of legislative authority. Furthermore, the accretions of local custom lessened the governors' influence, particularly in cases of their acquiescence, which were often made necessary by a lack of royal guidance and support. In the end, default as much as design guaranteed that other hands than those of the governor would assume the task of reforming English law to suit Virginia's needs.

The other hands belonged to men who were part of that migration of "vexed and troubled Englishmen,"[4] who following the company's downfall left a disturbed homeland committed to finding a stable and prosperous life in America. By the mid-1630s what had begun as a trickle of settlers became a flood that did not run its course for more than forty years.[5] Arriving in such numbers, these new immigrants soon burdened Virginia's existing legal and institutional structures beyond their capacity to meet the requirements of an expanding frontier community. Responding to the need for a fundamental change in the colony's government, the General Assembly as early as the 1630s established the county court system, thereby creating a need to adapt more English law to new conditions.[6] Beyond that, the new system proliferated the

---

4. The phrase is Carl Bridenbaugh's.
5. Wesley Frank Craven, *White, Red, and Black: The Seventeenth-Century Virginian* (Charlottesville, Va., 1971), pp. 1–39.
6. William Waller Hening, ed., *The Statutes at Large; Being a Collection of all the Laws of Virginia from the First Session of the Legislature in the Year 1619* (Richmond, New York, and Philadelphia, 1809–1823), 1: 224. The rise of Virginia's legal institutions is too well known to be rehearsed here. See, for example, Philip Alexander Bruce's monumental *Institutional History of Virginia in the Seventeenth Century, An Inquiry into the Religious, Moral, Educational, Legal, Military, and Political Condition of the People Based on Original and Contemporaneous Records* (New York, 1910); Wesley Frank Craven, *The Southern Colonies in the Seventeenth Century, 1607–1689* (Baton Rouge, La., 1949); Essay 2, above; Edmund S. Morgan, *American Slavery, American Freedom: The Ordeal of Colonial Virginia* (New York, 1975).

number of offices in the colony, and the prospect of acquiring one of these posts lured ambitious colonists. Thus it was the post-1630s immigrants who became clerks of court, justices of the peace, sheriffs, burgesses, and councillors, who were most responsible for effecting the transfer of England's legal patrimony to Virginia.

Unlike their predecessors, the post-1630s colonial leaders did not spring from the traditional ruling stock. They arose instead out of that variegated social class of seventeenth-century England called "the middling sort." Their background was quite different from that of the men they succeeded. To be sure, some were gentlefolk, but for the most part they were merchants, bakers, salters, vintners, or practitioners of some other skilled calling. As such, they were not, however, part of the mercantile establishment that had promoted colonial undertakings at the beginning of the century. Rather, they belonged to that group of commercial men who assumed a controlling interest in the colonial trade after 1624.[7] While a majority of these men resided in London or Bristol at the time they left England for Virginia, they were often of country origin and had gone to the metropolis in search of opportunities. Frequently in their formative years they had benefited from the improved educational opportunities that were an English hallmark in the years between 1560 and 1640. But no more than a handful were university graduates or matriculants at the Inns of Court.[8] Such formal training as the majority of them received likely

---

7. Robert Paul Brenner, "Commercial Change and Political Conflict: The Merchant Community in Civil War London" (Ph.D. dissertation, Princeton University, 1970), pp. 1–145.

8. Louis B. Wright, *Middle Class Culture in Elizabethan England* (Chapel Hill, N.C., 1935), Chapter II; Martin H. Quitt, "From Elite to Aristocracy: The Transformation of the Virginia Ruling Class," unpublished paper read at the annual meeting of the Southern Historical Association, Houston, Texas, 1971, pp. 6–8.

went no further than grammar school or an apprenticeship. The remainder of their education came in the school of hard knocks.[9] These men differed from their earlier company counterparts in one other important respect. They lacked close connections with the home government, and until they settled in Virginia[10] they had little experience in drafting laws or administering justice.

Given these circumstances, how did men with seemingly so little expertise in so complex an institution as the law succeed in transporting it to Virginia? There are several possible answers to the question. In the first place, the men who effected the transfer were not completely ignorant of the law and its customs. No Englishman was, nor could be, because the law was very much a part of his culture. A belief that a set of rules governed society and its members had long been a guiding cultural assumption in England, and for centuries successive generations of Englishmen learned to respect the law as the sinew that bound society together.

---

9. The experience of Obedience Robins is typical of these immigrants. Born in Northamptonshire in 1600, at age twenty Robins was bound as an apothecary's apprentice in London. He moved to Virginia in 1621, settling on the Eastern Shore, where he became involved in the area's political life, serving as a monthly court judge, justice of the peace, burgess, and councillor. At his death in 1662 he had amassed large landholdings and was a power in colonial politics at both the provincial and county levels. These data were compiled from the court minute books of the Worshipful Company of Apothecaries at the Guildhall in London and the records of Northampton County, Virginia.

10. The conclusions drawn in this paragraph rest largely upon information compiled for Virginia's local and provincial officeholders in the period from 1619 to 1700. That information was taken from the Virginia county court records, guild records at the Guildhall Library, London, the archives at the Bristol Archives Office, Bristol, microfilm copies of English records that comprise part of the Virginia Colonial Records Project, the family papers that are housed at the Virginia Historical Society, and such genealogical sources as the *Virginia Magazine of History and Biography* and the first and second series of the *William and Mary Quarterly*.

Almost from birth the colonists slowly absorbed this conception of law. By mere observation, they discovered the rules that governed their family's household. As they grew older, they came upon the more formal regulations that touched the relationships between their own and other families, and individuals, the church, the guilds, and the state. Little by little, they came to understand that a well-ordered society was a regulated community that kept its members at peace with one another and out of harm's way. Hence, by the time they became adults, they had learned to appreciate a fundamental maxim of English law: "*salus populi suprema lex est*," that is, "the safety of the people is the chief law."[11]

This view of the law's purpose was an important item in the post-1634 immigrant's intellectual baggage. In order to transform his perceptions into usable laws for Virginia, a colonist did not need to be a lawyer. He needed only an awareness of this general function of law, a concern for the well being of his fellow settlers, and a willingness to act.

Then too, colonial lawmakers had received more than a cultural exposure to English law. Their backgrounds in commerce and the skilled trades frequently led to participation in legal proceedings. In the normal course of doing business they gained practical experience in drafting documents such as powers of attorney, charter parties, deeds, bills of exchange, indentures, and even wills. Settling debts or other business disputes brought them into contact with the judicial process. These contacts were valuable lessons in how to bring suit, how to take and give evidence, and how to discharge the duties of attorneyship. Together, these and similar encounters gave the lawmakers a layman's working understanding of how the English system of justice operated.

---

11. The seventeenth-century legal writer William Fulbeck expounded these views at length in his *A Direction or Preparative to the Study of the Lawe* (London, 1600), Chapter 1.

These acquired talents explain why some of the men had gone to Virginia in the first place. Their skills qualified them to promote new outlets for business as well as to protect the established interests of family and close friends. Once in the colony they soon discovered that a proficiency in legal matters facilitated their entrance into the local political life. And it required little effort for them to employ their practical knowledge in helping to create Virginia's legal system.

Besides cultural inspiration and practical acquaintance, the colonists drew their legal knowledge from the large corpus of printed works about English law which had come into use in the one hundred fifty years before Jamestown's settlement. Since the invention of printing made books far cheaper to produce, the middle of the fifteenth century witnessed a revolution in learning. By the 1480s the first printed law books were available in England.[12] Throughout the next century the number of legal titles multiplied as their popularity increased and as more learned lawyers sought to pass their knowledge on to others through the medium of print. By 1600 more than fifty volumes of a variety of legal works were already in circulation.[13] The great constitutional struggles of the seventeenth century insured that the law would remain a lively topic, and authors and printers struggled to keep pace with demand. Numerous editions of Sir Edward Coke's monumental *Reports* and the *Institutes*,[14] for

---

12. Except where otherwise noted, the bibliographic data mentioned in this paragraph were compiled from A. W. Pollard and C. R. Redgrave, eds., *Short-Title Catalogue of Books Printed in England, Scotland and Ireland, and of English Books Printed Abroad, 1475–1640* (London, 1926), and D. G. Wing, ed., *Short-Title Catalogue of Books Printed in England, Scotland, Ireland, Wales, and British North America and of English Books Printed in Other Countries, 1640–1700* (New York, 1945–1951).
13. Bertram Osborne, *Justice of the Peace, 1361–1848: A History of the Justices of the Peace for the Counties of England* (Shaftsbury, Dorset, 1960), p. 12.
14. Pollard and Redgrave, *STC*, pp. 121–122; Wing, *STC*, pp. 350–351.

example, were printed between 1606 and 1697. Sir Francis Bacon's *Elements of the Common Lawes of England*[15] went through three editions, while John Kitchin's *Jurisdictions*[16] and Sir William Noye's *Compleat Lawyer*[17] went through five and eight printings respectively. Here, then, was a vast treasure-trove of legal information to which Virginia lawmakers could turn for guidance.

Documenting the colonists' use of the literature that was available is easy enough. In addition to estate inventories in manuscript and in print, there are numerous studies written about the colonial Virginian's reading habits.[18] These sources provide a reasonably accurate indication of the titles that circulated in Virginia. They show a wide variety of subjects—abridgments of statute and case law, legal dictionaries, case reports, and books that dealt with the law's philosophical and procedural underpinnings.[19] Another group consisted of books of a more practical nature, which might be termed "how-to-do-it" books. Examining the contents of some of these books reveals the wide range of legal information which a Virginia lawmaker could command.

---

15. Pollard and Redgrave, *STC*, p. 27.
16. Wing, *STC*, p. 301.
17. Ibid., p. 496.
18. A useful guide to printed inventories of estates that included their owners' libraries, as well as studies of reader habits is David Gillespie and Michael H. Harris, compilers, "A Bibliography of Virginia Library History," *Journal of Library History*, 6 (1970): 72–90. I derived my list of law titles read by seventeenth-century Virginians from these sources and others that are mentioned below. Mr. Harris kindly provided me with a copy of the bibliography. See also William Hamilton Bryson, *Census of Law Books in Colonial Virginia* (Charlottesville, Va., 1978).
19. For an example of what a colonist's law library might contain see "An Inventory of the Goods Chattels Wares and Merchandizes belonging to the Estate of Arthur Spicer 8 Feb. 1701/02," Richmond County Wills and Inventories, 1699–1701, fols. 36–41.

Abridgments of statutes and case law were among the first legal books printed in England.[20] The compilers arranged their summaries in roughly alphabetical order, according to subject matter.[21] A reason for their existence seems to have been a desire to furnish law students with convenient finding aids to the statutes and the yearbooks, the predecessors of the law reports.[22] Since the abridgments facilitated access to both statute and case law, they became popular with lawyers, and their popularity caused them to be reprinted in many editions prior to 1700.

Of the many abridgments compiled down to the end of the seventeenth century, those of Sir Anthony Fitzherbert,[23] Sir Robert Brooke,[24] William Rastell,[25] and Edmund Wingate[26] enjoyed wide use in England, and copies of all four authors' works found their way to Virginia. Their influence, as well as

---

20. A useful bibliographic guide to the abridgments is John D. Cowley, comp., *A Bibliography of Abridgments, Digests, Dictionaries and Indexes of English Law to the Year 1800* (London, 1932). Cowley's introduction acquaints the reader with some of the mechanics of publishing legal literature from the fifteenth to the nineteenth centuries.

21. For example, see the entry "action sur le case" in Sir Robert Brooke, *La Graunde Abridgement, Collecte a escrie per le judge tres reverend Syr Robert Brooke Chivalier, nagdairs chief Justice del Common banke* (London, 1576), fols. 4–8.

22. Theodore F. T. Pluncknett, *Concise History of the Common Law*, 5th edition (London, 1956).

23. Sir Anthony Fitzherbert, *La Graunde Abridgement, Collecte par le Judge tres-reverend monsieur Anthony Fitzherbert . . .*, 2d ed., (London, 1565). The first edition, published in 1516, had no attribution of Fitzherbert's authorship (Cowley, comp., *Bibliography of Abridgments*, pp. xliii–xlvi).

24. Brooke's abridgment was first published in January 1573/74 (Cowley, compiler, *Bibliography of Abridgments*, p. 30).

25. William Rastell, *A Collection of all Statutes (from the beginning of Magna Carta unto the yere of our Lords, 1557) which were before that yere imprinted* (London, 1557). Between 1557 and 1625 Rastell was reprinted, with additions, twenty times.

26. Edmund Wingate, *An Exact Abridgment of All Statutes in Force and Use* (London, 1641).

that of lesser-known abridgments, upon Virginians is questionable, however. Abridgments of case law were printed in Latin or law French, which most colonial legislators probably could not read. The appearance of Fitzherbert and Brooke in some inventories does, of course, suggest that certain individuals had the facility to read those works and draw inspiration from them. But no direct evidence which links either Brooke or Fitzherbert to colonial statutes or court decisions has been forthcoming. Because they abridged statute law, Rastell's and Wingate's compilations may have been helpful to the colonists; they could be used both as guides to English statutes and as models for colonial laws.

Although their contribution is difficult to document precisely, the utility of law dictionaries for colonists without formal legal training is readily apparent. At least six compilers of legal dictionaries flourished between the 1520s and 1700, but John Rastell's *Termes de la ley* and John Cowell's *Interpreter* probably had the most extensive circulation in Virginia.[27] Composed by the printer John Rastell, the first edition of *Termes de la ley* appeared in 1527.[28] The first dictionary of any sort ever printed in England, its popularity was such that it went through twenty-eight editions before going out of print in 1819. Early editions of *Termes de la ley* were more limited in scope than later dictionaries; they contained only the most commonly used legal terms and a bit of antiquarian lore about the origin of words and phrases. Later editions included an

---

27. Among the other dictionaries available to the colonists were Henry Spelman's *Archaeologus* (1626), Edward Leigh's *Philogicall Commentary, or, an Illustration of the Most Obvious and Useful Words in the Law* (1652), and Thomas Blount's *NOMO-ΛΙΞΞΙΚΟΝ: A Law Dictionary* (London, 1670). See also Cowley, comp., *Bibliography of Abridgments*, pp. lxxxi–xc.

28. The original title was *Expositones terminorum in legum anglorum*. Because the dictionary was first printed in law French, it soon became popularly known as *Termes de la lay*.

expanded number of definitions as well as a parallel English translation of the entire dictionary.

Cowell's *Interpreter*[29] is of a wholly different character. Its coverage is more extensive, its author was more erudite than Rastell, and its publication entirely in English was an improvement over Rastell's dictionary. Published by a professor of civil law at Cambridge, the *Interpreter* initially appeared in 1607. Unlike Rastell, from whom he borrowed heavily upon occasion, Cowell cited precedents, statutes, and authorities for his definitions. That the prose is lucid and direct in its explanation of sometimes-complicated terminology is the *Interpreter's* great strength. Despite its value, the *Interpreter* was suppressed in 1610 because of a parliamentary controversy over certain passages which Cowell had written about the monarch's absolute sovereignty.[30] It reappeared in 1637 and was republished with additions six times in the next ninety years.

To read through *Termes de la ley* and the *Interpreter* is to gain some feeling for their probable effect upon the colonists. Certainly both dictionaries are quite helpful in rendering seventeenth-century English law and practice more intelligible to modern scholars.

Case reports came into vogue shortly after the compilation of the last of the yearbooks was completed around the year 1535.[31] At first the reports resembled the yearbooks in that they were little more than notes or rough summaries of selected cases. In time their reportage became more formal and complete, thereby making them a more

---

29. John Cowell, *The Interpreter: or Book Containing the Signification of Words . . .* (Cambridge, 1607).
30. The story of this controversy, plus a brief biography of Cowell, may be found in the 1727 edition of the *Interpreter*.
31. For a listing of the various reports published before 1776 see John William Wallace, *The Reporters, Arranged with Incidental Remarks . . .*, 4th edition (Boston, 1882).

valuable reference tool than their predecessors. By the seventeenth century, a number of compilations of reports were already in print, and those attributed to James Dyer[32] and Edmund Plowden[33] were especially esteemed until they were superseded by the reports of Sir Edward Coke. Coke, of course, soon dominated this branch of legal literature just as he did every other matter of law that attracted his interest. Such was his reportorial prowess that the work of other compilers, like Edward Bulstrode[34] and Sir George Croke,[35] seems pale by comparison.

Dyer, Plowden, Coke, Bulstrode, Croke, and other reporters all appear in colonial inventories, but the degree of their influence in Virginia is difficult to determine. The fact that the early reports were in law French probably precluded their widespread use in the colony. Coke's *Reports* were not published in English until 1658, about the same time that Bulstrode's and Croke's English reports appeared. It may be, then, that reports of any kind did not have much of an effect until after mid-century. That they were used in Virginia after that time is substantiated by the presence of the reports among the law books belonging to men who migrated to Virginia or who came to intellectual maturity after 1650. William Fitzhugh, Ralph Wormeley II, Richard Lee II, and Arthur Spicer, for instance, all owned some parts of Coke's *Reports*, and Fitzhugh's surviving correspondence shows that

---

32. Sir James Dyer, *Cy ensuont ascuns nouel cases* (London, 1585). Dyer's reports went through nine printings in law French down to year 1622. Five abridgments in English appeared after 1648.
33. Edmund Plowden, *Les Commentaries, ou les reports de deyvers Cases* . . . (London, 1571). It went through a succession of printings before an English abridgment was done in 1650.
34. Edward Bulstrode, *The Reports* (London, 1657–1659).
35. Sir George Croke, *The Reports, Collected and Written in French by Himself; Revised and Published in English by Sir Harbottle Grimston* (London, 1661).

he at least consulted Coke frequently.[36] Moreover, in a case heard before the Westmoreland County Court in 1685, Coke's authority was invoked by the defendant in a dispute arising from an alleged violation of the Navigation Acts.[37] Other examples of the reporters' influence must await further study of the relationship between the reports and an evolving Virginia legal system.

There were many books that dealt with the philosophical and procedural aspects of law published in England before 1700. Such titles as Coke's *Institutes of the Laws of England*,[38] Henry Finch's *Law, Or a Discourse Thereof*,[39] Sir John Fortescue's *A Learned Commendation on the Politique Lawes of England*,[40] William Fulbeck's *A Direction or Preparative to the Study of the Lawe* and his *A Parallele or Conference of the Civill Law, the Canon Law and the Common Law of this Realme of England*,[41] and Sir Thomas Littleton's *Tenures*[42] enjoyed a wide circulation throughout the English-speaking world. Coke's *Institutes* are too renowned to require any comment here, other than to lament the lack of a modern edition and to

---

36. Richard Beale Davis, ed., *William Fitzhugh and his Chesapeake World, 1676-1701: The Fitzhugh Letters and Other Documents* (Chapel Hill, N.C., 1963), pp. 49–50, 65–66, 66n, 68–69n; Louis B. Wright, *The First Gentlemen of Virginia, Intellectual Qualities of the Early Colonial Ruling Class* (San Marino, Calif., 1940), pp. 202–203, 225; "A Inventory . . . of the Estate of Arthur Spicer."
37. Westmoreland County Order Book, 1675–1689, pp. 374–377.
38. The *Institutes* were published in London in four parts between 1628 and 1644.
39. Finch's work first appeared in 1627.
40. Fortescue's book was first printed in Latin. The parallel Latin and English edition cited here was published in London in 1567. A modem translation is S. B. Chrimes, *Sir John Fortescue De Laudibus Legum Anglie* (Cambridge, 1942).
41. Fulbeck's books appeared in 1600 and 1601 respectively.
42. First printed in 1481, Littleton's *Tenures* went through many editions. An English translation appeared in 1604.

suggest the need for someone to undertake a careful assessment of their use by seventeenth-century Virginians. By the seventeenth century, Fortescue's and Littleton's works had already been recognized as classic commentaries on English law. A charming little book, *A Learned Commendation of the Politique Lawes of England* was written around 1471 to instruct the young Prince Edward in the mysteries of England's legal customs. Fortescue constructed the book in the form of a dialogue between himself and the prince. In it he stressed two main themes, the rule of law and the limited character of the English monarchy—two ideas whose time had come by the 1600s. Whereas Fortescue was concerned with general legal principles, Littleton's *Tenures* is a technical treatment of English property law. In the book Littleton discussed estates, types of tenures, joint ownerships, and the special doctrines of real property that were known when it was published in the 1480s. Littleton's intelligent style, his reduction of complex law to a logical system, and his abstraction of sound legal principles made the book a required text for all who would become proficient in the laws of real property. The more obscure writings of Finch and Fulbeck are noteworthy not so much for their authors' erudition as for what their use reveals about the readers. Neither author is now remembered for having any lasting effect upon the course of English legal history; their works are rather pedestrian. But use of both books by the colonists suggests a certain eclecticism on the Virginia lawmakers' part. It was as though the Virginians turned to any and every theoretical study that might aid them in finding serviceable legal traditions. Furthermore, their use of these books should alert scholars to the necessity of going beyond the obviously seminal treatises like Littleton and Coke to examine the work of numerous lesser lights.

To this point, the discussion of colonial tastes in legal literature has centered on those books whose influence was more general than specific. For that reason, it is particularly difficult to measure a book's effect. The impact of the "how-to-do-it books" can be calculated with much greater certainty.

How-to-do-it books were an important element in the legal literature to which any sixteenth- and seventeenth-century Englishmen could turn for instruction. A source of practical knowledge, they covered a broad range of subjects, and they were usually authored by men who were highly competent in their fields. A case in point is William Lambarde. The author of a very popular guide for justices of the peace,[43] Lambarde was himself a member of the bench in Kent.[44] As he noted in his preface, he was moved to write the book because upon coming to his office he had known so little about it. Accordingly, he hoped his work would be an inspiration to others. Lambarde's was but one of a large number of similar manuals for justices of the peace.[45] There were in addition to the manuals for justices, directories for clerks, sheriffs, constables, and lawyers, as well as guidebooks

---

43. William Lambarde, *Eirenarcha: Or the Office of Justices of Peace* . . . (London, 1581). Between 1581 and 1620 the *Eirenarcha* went through 13 editions.

44. On Lambarde's judicial career see Wilbur Dunkel, *William Lambarde, Elizabethan Jurist* (London, 1965).

45. Among these were Sir Anthony Fitzherbert, *The New Boke of Justices of Peace* (London, 1554); Michael Dalton, *The Countrey Justice: Contayning the Practice of the Justices of the Peace Out of their Sessions* (London, 1618); *The Compleat Justice, Being an Exact and Compendious Collection Out of Such as Have Treated of the Office of Justices of the Peace* . . ., 7th edition, (London, 1661); Wa. Young, *A Vade Mecum, or Tale Containing the Substance of Such Statutes; Wherein Any One or More Justices of the Peace are Inabled to Act* . . ., 7th edition, (London, 1663); William Sheppard, *The Whole Office of the Countrey Justice of the Peace* (London, 1650); Joseph Keble, *An Assistance to the Justices of the Peace, for the Easier Performance of their Duty* (London, 1683). There was a marked tendency for the writers of such manuals to borrow most liberally from each other's work.

on how to plead cases, write wills, convey property, or draft a variety of legal documents.[46]

In form, all how-to-do-it books were pretty much alike. If the author discussed the duties of a justice or a sheriff, he began with an examination of the office and traced its development down to his own time. Then he described the duties of the officeholder and what powers were vested in him. Generally these descriptions were arranged alphabetically in a fashion similar to the abridgments of statute and case law. In those situations where the officeholder was likely to confront breaches of law, the manuals gave instruction in what constituted criminal offenses, and told how to make arrests, collect evidence, and hold trials. Books that dealt with the preparation and keeping of legal records were basically alike. They explained the importance of records, the derivations of particular documents, their functions, and the conditions under which they should be employed. Most important of all, such guidebooks furnished the reader with sample copies in English and Latin of each instrument.

Of all the how-to-do-it books which the colonists owned, Michael Dalton's *Countrey Justice* and Henry Swinburne's *Briefe Treatise of Testaments and Last Willes* deserve special attention. Apart from their being superior examples of the genre, each made a demonstrable impression upon Virginia law. In a word, they provided many of the models for both law and procedure in the colony.

---

46. See for example George Billinghurst, *Arcana clericala: or The Mysteries of Clerkship* (London, 1673); Michael Dalton, *Officium Vice comitum, The Office and Authoritie of Sherifs* (London, 1623); William Lambarde, *The Duties of Constables, Borsholders, Tithingrnen, etc.* (London, 1583); Sir William Noye, *The Compleat Lawyer* (London, 1651); Henry Swinburne, *A briefe Treatise of Testaments and Last Willes* (London, 1590); John Godolphin, *The Orphans Legacy: Or a Testamentary Abridgment* (London, 1674); William West, *Symboleographia, Which May Be Termed the Art, Description, or Image of Instruments, Covenants, Contracts, etc.* . . . (London, 1590).

"For the better conformity of the proceedings of the courts of this country to the lawes of England," an act of the General Assembly in 1666 required both volumes to be purchased by the county courts, the General Assembly, and the General Court.[47] Even before the legislature ordered their use in the colonial courts, however, there are indications that some magistrates had long depended upon Dalton and Swinburne for advice on legal matters.[48] Copies of both volumes are recorded in some inventories that date from the 1640s and 1650s. In Lower Norfolk County the justices bought the *Countrey Justice* as early as the 1650s. And Swinburne's comments on the heritability of status seem to have been influential in persuading the Assembly in 1662 to entail slavery upon mulatto children whose mothers were held in life service.[49]

The appeal of such books to Virginians is clear. For men with no formal training, a scrivener's guide like William West's *Symboleographia* was an invaluable pattern upon which to model a county's records. Dalton's or Swinburne's opinions on the magistrate's duties or on the making of wills gave the necessary advice on how these responsibilities should be discharged. The statutes, precedents, and other authorities that these writers cited could be invoked to provide a foundation of tradition upon which to rest law and procedure in the Old Dominion. One had merely to lift

---

47. Hening, ed., *The Statutes at Large*, 2: 246; Lancaster County Order Book, 1661–1680, fol. 132; York County Order Book, 1665–1672, p. 361.
48. *Cf.* the oath administered to Virginia magistrates in Hening, ed., *Statutes at Large*, 1: 169, with the justice's oath in Dalton, *Countrey Justice*, 12th edition, p. 13; Accomack County Order Book, 1666–1670, fols. 150 ff, 179 ff.
49. *Cf.* Swinburne, *A Briefe Treatise of Testaments and Last Willes*, pp. 75-76 and the act defining the status of mulatto bastards in Hening, ed., *Statutes at Large*, 2: 170. The citation to Swinburne used here is taken from the third edition, which was published in London in 1635.

appropriate sections out of these volumes and apply them to a given problem. That Dalton, Swinburne, West, and other authors of how-to-do-it books were more popular with colonial lawmakers than Coke, Bacon, or Littleton is evidence of their collective work's considerable effect in Virginia.

Their writing had another significant consequence for Virginia's early legal history. Since it drew attention to how local officials discharged their public obligations, it tended to magnify the eminence of these officeholders. It also emphasized the importance of local law and custom. That emphasis served mainly to reinforce the colonists' previous exposure to English law by calling to mind their past experience and by sanctioning the idea that local traditions were the most suitable to their own needs in the New World. Colonial dependence upon the how-to-do-it books is therefore one proof of the preeminent role English local law played in seventeenth-century Virginia.

In the end, the combination of culture, experience, and book learning produced surprising results. Some, like the emergence of a body of law governing slavery and Indian relations, were tragic and had the most unhappy consequences in the long run. The amalgamation of various civil, criminal, admiralty, equity, and administrative jurisdictions into a single system of local courts, which was under one appellate court,[50] simplified the judicial process. That change probably made the dispensation of justice somewhat more efficient in Virginia than it was at home. Using the vernacular in all laws, court proceedings, and documents was an improvement over the situation in England, as was the employment of the county courts for the

---

50. Until the 1680s the General Assembly could hear appeals from the General Court. See Warren M. Billings, *A Little Parliament: The Virginia General Assembly in the Seventeenth Century* (Richmond, Va., 2004), pp. 149–173.

safekeeping of all kinds of legal records.[51] The county courts' gradual assumption of the powers of ecclesiastical courts and control over church-related affairs led to a secularization of colonial society and the eventual decline of the church's hold over the worldly activities of colonial Virginians.

These and other breaks with the past may be explained as the offspring of necessity or as the inevitable consequence of crude attempts to imitate things badly remembered. The compulsion of necessity cannot, of course, be overlooked. In the absence of firm direction from home, the demands of a harsh environment often forced the colonists to depart from tradition. No one can deny the fact that the men who brought English law and institutions to Virginia were often woefully ignorant of the system's basic customs. Over time, ignorance produced differences between how things were done in England and in Virginia.

The variances may also be explained another way. That explanation is revealed in a paradoxical attribute peculiar to so many of the Englishmen who transformed their legal heritage in its Virginia setting after the 1630s. Being English, they strove mightily to render a faithful replication of that birthright. But being laymen in the law as well, they did not have the same sort of dedication and reverence for the law and its forms as did judges and lawyers. Theory and general principles often gave way to practical considerations; substance was more important than form. What worked, in short, was frequently more significant than either precedent or the wisdom of the ancients.

Nowhere perhaps are the implications of this behavior more clearly illustrated than in a 1662 statute that defined the status of bastard mulatto children born to black bondswomen. An increase in the number of such children

---

51. Land records and wills, for instance, were not recorded in English county archives.

had heightened concern about the children's condition. In part, the worry was due to an inflation in the incidence of court actions brought by mulattos claiming that their English paternity prevented their enslavement.[52] English hostility to blacks, mulattos, and bastards also played a part in the legislators' quest for a statutory means to prevent the increase of such children. Searching the past for help provided few guidelines. English local law, the statutes, and case law were of little help because none of these had contemplated the mulatto's existence or the situation that brought him into the world. Lacking the sanction of common law, the Assembly borrowed the civilian doctrine *partus sequitur ventrum*, which some burgess probably had found while rummaging through his copy of Swinburne: It made a mulatto's freedom or bondage dependent upon his mother's condition of servitude. In English common law such a manoeuvre would have been most irregular, but because it worked, it satisfied the Virginians. Moreover, because their solution had come from an authoritative source, it satisfied their urge to remain faithful to the past while solving the immediate legal problem of what to do with a peculiar species of person.

At the end of the seventeenth century Virginia boasted a legal system that was already verging on maturity. The handiwork of men lacking in formal legal education, it resembled its English parent, but was different enough in certain aspects to claim a nearly unique distinctiveness. Still in a fluid state, it was receptive to infusions from English legal traditions other than the local ones that had dominated developments since 1618. Such changes would be brought about in the next century by more professional men of law who had a much better acquaintance with English procedure

---

52. For an example of such a suit see Northumberland County Record Books, 1652–1658, fols. 66–67, 85; 1658–1660, fol. 28; Northumberland County Order Book, 1652–1665, fols. 40, 46, 49.

and case and statute law than did their predecessors. Their task would be made easier because they had inherited a common characteristic from their colonial forebears—a temperamental willingness to accept change and variance with the past as the price for doing business in the New World.

ESSAY 5

VIGNETTES OF JAMESTOWN

This piece appeared in *Virginia Cavalcade*, a lovely historical magazine that the Library of Virginia issued until budgetary cutbacks forced its discontinuance. I based it upon a talk that launched the annual Jamestown Lecture Series, which the Association for the Preservation of Virginia Antiquities (now Preservation Virginia) inaugurated in 1993. The prospect of speaking to a Williamsburg audience greatly appealed to me because of the special hold Jamestown has upon me. Then too, Spotswood Hunnicutt Jones, APVA president in 1993, introduced me, and that was a delight because she was a friend and a one-time high school history teacher of mine.

Preparing the talk was easy enough. I had recently published a small book, *Jamestown and the Founding of the Nation* (Gettysburg, Pa., 1991) that grappled with the problem of recreating the little metropolis where the General Assembly convened between 1619 and 1698 to do the business of legislatures—making the statutes that magistrates enforced throughout the Old Dominion. Unlike colonial capital cities elsewhere in British North America, there were few above ground traces of Jamestown, aside from the church tower ruin, and its documentary outlines were equally sketchy. Consequently, archaeologists and historians could not always agree on the import of artifacts recovered from the ground or bits gleaned from fragmentary records. Efforts in the 1930s and the 1950s to pinpoint the location of the first fort proved frustratingly futile, and in 1993, the opinion that the fort had long ago washed into the James River remained firm, although that prevailing wisdom was about to change in a most dramatic fashion.

Plans were afoot to observe the quadricentennial of Jamestown's founding in various ways. The APVA started the Jamestown Lecture Series as a precursor to the commemoration, but it also mounted a much more ambitious project. Months before I gave my talk, the board of trustees committed the organization to finding the site of the first fort. To that end, the trustees sanctioned the appointment of Dr. William M. Kelso, a renowned archaeologist of wide experience with digging early Virginia sites, as director of archaeology. Based upon a reconsideration of a map of the fort drawn in 1608 by a Spanish spy, Kelso drew the conclusion that the fort sat nearer the church tower ruin than previously thought. If he had interpreted the map correctly, then traces of the fort probably survived and awaited rediscovery. To validate his theory, he drew up an initial five-year plan for a systematic investigation of the spot where he thought the footprint lay. And by the time I handed the text of the article over to the editor of *Virginia Cavalcade*, Kelso had uncovered encouraging evidence that he had found the fort, though he forbore publicly announcing his discovery until September 1996.

Originally published as "Vignettes of Jamestown" in *Virginia Cavalcade*. 45 (1996): 164–180, the article is reprinted here with the kind permission of the director of publications and educational services at the Library of Virginia.

---

13 May 2007 will mark the four-hundredth anniversary of the founding of Jamestown. The approach of the quadricentennial bids a reconsideration of Jamestown as both an artifact of Virginia's colonial past and a symbol of national identity. However, anyone seeking to apprehend its

significance sooner or later confronts an incontestable reality. Jamestown disappeared following its abandonment in 1699, and it is now mainly an imaginary place.

To be sure, it may be envisioned more sharply than was possible a hundred years ago, when the Association for the Preservation of Virginia Antiquities acquired the land that encompasses the church tower ruin, the statehouse foundations, and the site of the original fort. Present-day depictions derive from conceptual assumptions, investigatory techniques, archaeological evidence, and records that were unknown in 1893.[1] Nevertheless, questions regarding the plan of Jamestown, its buildings, its population, or its development vex us still. Such puzzles linger because the tangible remnants of the little metropolis, while far from scarce, are too few to re-create the town in the manner of, say, Colonial Williamsburg. Even so, the reminders are sufficient to glimpse Jamestown at intervals across the span of the seventeenth century. Together, such sightings form a series of vignettes that document its existence during the nine decades it was the capital of the Old Dominion.

John Smith, with characteristic hyperbole, proclaimed the vicinity of Jamestown "a verie fit place for the erecting of a great cittie."[2] In truth, as he and later residents learned, the natural features of the site made it rather an unfit place on which to plant a "cittie," great or small. The town the colonists came to know variously as "James Fort," "James Cittie," or "Jamestown" arose on a pear-shaped patch of ground that was situated along the north bank of the James

---

1. James M. Lindgren, *Preserving the Old Dominion: Historic Preservation and Virginia Traditionalism* (Charlottesville, Va., 1993), pp. 66, 91–94.
2. John Smith, *A True Relation of such occurrences and accidents of note, as hath hapned in Virginia, since the first planting of that Colony, which is now resident of the South part thereof, till the last returne.*, in Philip L. Barbour, ed., *The Complete Works of Captain John Smith (1580–1631) in Three Volumes* (Chapel Hill, N.C., 1986), 1: 29.

River, some sixty miles west of the entrance to Chesapeake Bay. About three miles long and a mile broad, "James City Island" was joined to the mainland by a narrow isthmus that has since eroded away. Much of the land was marsh, punctuated by stretches of high ground that either rimmed the perimeter or ran out, finger-like, into the mire. Wet terrain bred, as it still does, great hordes of mosquitoes, blood-sucking flies, and other insect pests that ferociously preyed upon human or animal flesh. There were no fresh water springs, whereas the water in the marsh and river was brackish—partly salt, partly fresh—and quite undrinkable. Then too, the island was hunting ground for a nearby nation of Indians, the Paspaheghs, who took less than a conciliatory view of the foreigners' intrusion.

The first colonists chose their site without regard to native sensibilities or the potential for urban amenities; considerations of defense governed the selection. Lying deep in the interior, Jamestown Island was safe from surprise assaults from the Spanish, which was not a fanciful assumption in 1607, given that Spaniards claimed the region for their own, and barely three years had passed since a peace treaty ended the Anglo-Spanish War of 1588–1604. Being surrounded almost entirely by water also rendered the island reasonably secure from the natives. Moreover, the main river channel ran close by the south shore, and that made the task of off-loading supplies from shipboard less difficult during the first stages of settlement.

Despite Smith's pronouncement, neither the backers of the Virginia Company nor the colony's resident leaders expected to erect a city in any modern sense of the word. Their original intention was to found a permanent stronghold from which to exploit Virginia's undoubted potential for profit. Time and circumstances altered that expectation, but throughout two decades of company management (1607–

1624), fort and town were virtually synonymous. Thus the first vignettes of Jamestown are of it as a military outpost.

Edward Maria Wingfield, the titular leader of the first complement of colonists, carried instructions not "to offend the naturals," and he initially permitted no "fortification but the boughs of trees cast together in the forme of a halfe moone."[3] An attack by the Indians soon changed Wingfield's mind, whereupon he ordered the construction of defenses more substantial than a ring of brush. The work moved with some dispatch. By mid-June 1607, "we had built and finished our Fort which was triangle wise, having three Bulwarkes at every corner like a halfe Moone, and foure or five pieces of Artillerie mounted in them," as George Percy later told it.[4] That fort, together with the buildings it protected, burned in January 1608, and it was promptly rebuilt, presumably along lines similar to those Percy described.

The look and placement of these forts are matters of conjecture, in large part because contemporary descriptions such as Percy's lack precision and also because they cannot easily be corroborated by extant evidence. Conventional wisdom has long held that the site lay within the property of the APVA and that it slowly eroded into the James River after 1607. Lyon G. Tyler, the historian, and president of the College of William and Mary, first articulated that opinion

---

3. "Instructions given by way of Advice," ca. Nov.-Dec. 1606, in Philip L. Barbour, ed., *The Jamestown Voyages Under the First Charter, 1606–1609, Works issued by the Hakluyt Society*, 2d ser., 136, 137 (Cambridge, 1969), p. 51; William Simmonds, *The Proceedings of the English Colonie in Virginia since their first beginning from England in the yeare of our Lord 1606, till this present 1612, with all their accidents that befell them in their Journies and Discoveries* (Oxford, 1612), p. 4.
4. "Observations gathered out of a Discourse of the Plantation of the Southerne Colonie in Virginia by the English, 1606. Written by that Honorable Gentleman Master George Percy," in Barbour, ed., *Jamestown Voyages*, p. 142.

more than ninety years ago. It gained additional credence a short while later, when a United States army engineer, Colonel Samuel H. Yonge, studied the available hydrographic data and reached similar conclusions. In the 1930s, George C. Gregory, a Richmond banker whose interests ran to early Virginia history, revisited the question and rejected the Tyler-Yonge view. Using various land records and other information, he contended for an alternate location—the so-called Elay-Swann site—which lay about half a mile down river from the APVA holdings. Gregory's interpretation drew support at the time from the architectural historian Henry Chandlee Forman.

Archaeological excavations conducted by the National Park Service in the 1930s and the 1950s failed to confirm either location, so the debate continues. Recently, however, William M. Kelso, Director of Archaeology at APVA, has undertaken a new search for the fort. He premised his investigation on the assumption that the fort sat farther back from the riverside than has been supposed and that it encompassed the land in the vicinity of the church tower ruin.[5]

Whatever the outcome of Kelso's digs, which are in progress, this much is indisputable. As the purpose of the colony changed so did the colonists' conceptions of Jamestown. The winter of 1609–1610, which Jamestonians

---

5. Tyler, *The Cradle of the Republic: Jamestown and James River*, 2d ed. (Richmond, 1900), p. 112; Yonge, "The Site of Old 'James Towne,'" 1607–1698," *Virginia Magazine of History and Biography*, 11 (1903–1904): 257–276, 393–414; 12 (1904–1905): 33–54, 113–133; George C. Gregory, "Jamestown, Site of First Fort,"(n.d.), Colonial National Historical Park, Virginia; Henry Chandlee Forman, *Jamestown and St. Mary's: Buried Cities of Romance* (Baltimore, 1938), pp. 331–337; Virginia Harrington, "Theories and Evidence for the Location of James Fort," *VMHB*, 93 (1985): 36–54; Allan Mardis, "Visions of James Fort," ibid., 97 (1989): 463–499; Kelso, *Jamestown: The Buried Truth* (Charlottesville, Va., 2006), pp. 9–44.

long remembered as the "Starving Time" that brought the settlement to near ruination, marked the turning point. When Thomas West, third baron De La Warre, and Sir Thomas Gates relieved the colony in May 1610, they found "pallisadoes [that were] tourne downe, the portes open, the gates from the hinges, the church ruined and unfrequented, empty howses ... rent up and burnt."[6] Thereafter Gates, who succeeded de la Warre as governor, together with the determined assistance of the colony's marshal Sir Thomas Dale, labored to put things right. The sole representation of their eventual achievements comes from the colonist Ralph Hamor, author of *A True Discourse of the Present Estate of Virginia*. By Hamor's account, which was published in London in 1615, Gates and Dale rebuilt the town into a "hansome forme," which consisted of

> two faire rowes of howses, all of framed Timber, two stories, and an vpper Garrett, or Corne loft high, besides three large, and substantiall Storehowses, joyned togeather in length some hundred and twenty foot, and in breadth forty, and this town hath been lately newly, and strongly impaled, and a faire platforme for Ordenance in the west Bulwarke raised: there are also without this towne in the Island, some very pleasant and beutifull howses, two Blockhouses, to observe and watch least the Indians should at any time should swim over the back river, and come into the Island, and certaine other farme howses.[7]

---

6. Thomas West, third baron De La Warre, Sir Thomas Gates, and the Council of Virginia to Sir Thomas Smythe, 7 July 1610, as quoted in Alexander Brown, comp., *The Genesis of the United States* (Boston, Mass., 1890), 1: 405.

7. Ralph Hamor, *A True Discourse of the Present Estate of Virginia* (London, 1615), p. 33.

Hamor skimped on particulars, but his sketch is still instructive. In general, it documented how the two Sir Thomases turned Jamestown into a village patterned after a well-known model that English soldiers employed in Ireland, the fortified garrison town.[8] That they should have seen in such a plan a solution to their problem is hardly startling, considering that both men were well-schooled army officers. Beyond that, Hamor's observation about Jamestown having been "lately newly, and strongly impaled" reveals that Gates and Dale either razed the triangular fort or altered it significantly, as does his comment about the erection of a "faire platforme for Ordenance" in the "west Bulwarke."

Hamor also called attention to a tendency that remained commonplace for the rest of the seventeenth century, the scattering of houses and small farms on high ground beyond the town limits. Finally, his remark about the "two Blockhouses," while imprecise, suggests that those fortifications sat on strategic points of high ground and faced northward toward the mainland. The likeliest locations for these bastions may have been an area beneath or near the still-visible rifle pits Confederate military engineers threw up in 1861, though the exact positioning awaits archaeological confirmation.

Gates and Dale likewise broadened the areas of settlement up and down the James River basin, they encouraged agricultural trials, and they changed the nature of the colonial enterprise by introducing a measure of private landholding. Such inducements led John Rolfe to try his hand at cultivating desirable West Indian strains of tobacco. Rolfe's success started a fever that seized the entire colony when his fellow settlers sought to imitate him.

---

8. John W. Reps, *Tidewater Towns: City Planning in Colonial Virginia and Maryland* (Charlottesville, Va., 1972), pp. 8–20.

The changes siphoned off Jamestown's inhabitants and slowed its growth. As of 1616, for example, the population dwindled to a mere fifty men, plus a smaller number of women and children. Physical deterioration set in as well, so much so that when Deputy Governor Samuel Argall landed in town the following year, he saw "but five or six houses, the Church downe, the Palizado's broken, . . . the Well of fresh water spoiled; the Store-house they used for the Church, the market-place, and streets, and all other spare places planted with Tobacco."[9] Argall forced the residents to make necessary repairs, including the construction of a new frame church that stood until the 1630s. However, his efforts at renovation "did exceedingly trouble" the settlers, whose disgruntlement was one consideration among many that led officials of the Virginia Company in London to mount yet another scheme to make the colony prosper. Out of that determination came decisions that moved Virginia from a quasi-military settlement toward something akin to a more traditional agriculture-based society. Company leaders promulgated new forms of land tenure, introduced rules similar to English local law, and improved resident administration. They also provided a more representative governing authority, the General Assembly.[10]

Need for a place to hold sessions of the General Assembly and somewhere for the governor and his council to meet soon turned Jamestown into the de facto administrative center of the colony. That requirement abetted an effort by

---

9. John Smith, *The Generall History of Virginia, New-England, and the Summer Isles: with the names of the Adventurers, Planters, and Governours from their first beginnings Ano: 1584 to this present 1624* (London, 1624), in Barbour, ed., *Works of Captain John Smith*, 2: 262.

10. Wesley Frank Craven, *The Dissolution of the Virginia Company, The Failure of a Colonial Experiment* (New York, 1932), pp. 47–81; Sigmund Diamond, "From Organization to Society: Virginia in the Seventeenth Century," *American Journal of Sociology*, 63 (1958): 457–475.

the Company to polish the settlement into a more attractive place. In 1621, company treasurer Sir Edwin Sandys recruited a surveyor named William Claiborne and sent him to America with a new governor, Sir Francis Wyatt. Claiborne's main charge was to fix accurate boundaries for the many tracts of land that Sandys used as bait to draw colonists, but the surveyor also laid out an expansion of Jamestown. "New Towne," as they styled the development, lay about half a mile down river of the existing village and was bounded on the east by Orchard Run. No plan of Claiborne's scheme exists, but it can be approximated from details in extant property descriptions of the town lots. Claiborne projected two parallel main streets that ran on an east-west axis. One was a "high way close to the bank of the Maine River" that linked up with a "Great Roade" that passed the fort on its way over the isthmus to the mainland and beyond. Two or three cross streets joined the other thoroughfare, called the "Backe Street," to create a rough gridiron. Uncertainties bred by the Anglo-Indian War of 1622–1629, the downfall of the Virginia Company, and the transfer of the colony to the crown all impeded the development of New Town, though it attracted some of the more prominent colonists. John Harvey, a future governor, took up a large parcel that sat between Back Street and the river road in the eastern extremity of New Town. On it he erected an orchard, gardens, and various dwellings, including a two-unit abode. His neighbors numbered George Menifie, a merchant-planter and councillor of state; John Chew, also a merchant; Ralph Hamor, sometime secretary of the colony; and Richard Stephens, who often quarreled with Harvey. The physician John Pott, once acting governor, who used his medical knowledge to poison the natives, was among the others who lived along Back Street, or just north of it. So were Governor Wyatt and Edward Blaney, William Pierce, or Roger Smith, all of whom sat at various times as burgesses in the General Assembly.[11]

Unfortunately, the establishment of New Town failed to bring about the desired goal of building a vital community. Once the danger from the Indians receded, the distinction between New Town and the older section diminished, especially after the fort fell into disuse, as seems to have been the case at the close of the 1620s. Jamestown was barely more than a collection of private residences, a church, and a storehouse. No taverns accommodated colonists who came to town to press suits at court or to transact other affairs. There was no statehouse from which to conduct the colony's business. Instead, the "quire" of the church doubled as a meeting hall for the General Assembly, the governor's front parlor provided the venue for sessions of the Council of State, or the General Court, and the secretary of the colony used his residence as a public record office. Nonetheless, the settlers regarded "James Cittie" as the center of their colony, and they remained imperviously resistant to locating it some place else.[12]

The character and look of Jamestown changed considerably during the administration of Sir John Harvey. Charles I named Sir John governor and captain-general in 1628 and commanded him to develop the town out of the belief that urbanization was key to controlling the colony and its future growth. Harvey, a prickly man, is best known to

---

11. Virginia Land Patent Book 1, pt. I, 1624–1637, *passim.*, Library of Virginia, Richmond, Va.; Sarah S. Hughes, *Surveyors and Statesmen: Land Measuring in Colonial Virginia* (Richmond, Va., 1979), pp. 8–10; Warren M. Billings, *Jamestown and the Founding of the Nation* (Gettysburg, Pa., 1991), pp. 72–73.
12. Sir John Harvey and the Council of State to the Privy Council, Jan. 1638/39, Colonial Office Papers, Class 1, vol. 10, National Archives, Kew.

history for falling foul of leading Virginians, who drove him from office in 1635, but he did launch the alteration of Jamestown. His incentive to build up the place went quite beyond the king's commandments. As governor, he constantly used his spacious house as a "rendezvous for all sorts of strangers" and "a general harbour for all comers." For that reason, despite his troubles with members of his Council of State, he convinced the General Assembly to enact legislation that altered Jamestown significantly. A law of February 1632, for example, declared Jamestown Virginia's sole port of entry, thereby confining the tobacco trade to the capital. Another statute compelled craftsmen to perform their trades and to refrain from planting "tobacco or corne or doe any other worke in the grounde," whereas a 1633 act gave the town storekeeper oversight of the colony's official weights and measures. Yet another statute promised a house lot and garden plot to anyone who took up residence and raised a dwelling within six months of his settling.[13]

Writing to the Privy Council in January 1639, Harvey reported on the success of his endeavours. There were, he noted,

> twelve houses and stores built in the Towne, one of brick by the Secretary [Richard Kemp], the fairest that ever was known in this countrye for substance and uniformity, by whose example others have undertaken to build frame howses to beautifye the place, consonant to his majesties Instruction that wee should not suffer men to build slight cottages as heretofore.
>
> Such hath bene our Indeavour herein that our of our owne purses wee have Largely contributed to the building of a brick church and both masters of shipps and others of

---

13. William Waller Hening, comp., *The Statutes at Large; Being a Collection of all the Laws of Virginia from the First Session of the Legislature in the Year 1619*, facsimile edition (Charlottesville, Va., 1969), 1: 206, 208, 221.

the ablest Planters have liberally by our persuasion underwritten this work. A Levye likewise by his majesties commands is raised for the building of a State howse at James Cittie, and shall with all diligence be performed.

"There was not," he concluded, "one foote of ground for half a mile together by the Rivers syde in Jamestown but was taken up and undertaken to be built."[14]

Harvey revealed several characteristics about the extent of the growth that his urgings had prompted. There was a considerable addition to the existing stock of buildings and an increase in the inhabited area, both of which indicate a degree of integration between New Town and the old quarter. Moreover, his pointed reference to Secretary Kemp's brick house argues that that dwelling was the first of its kind in town, especially in light of his observation that other residents had built "frame howses" in emulation of Kemp's example. Then there is his comment about the erection of a brick church, which is the earliest extant documentation that such a house of worship was abuilding, though not necessarily completed as yet. For certain, though, the statehouse was never built because Harvey left office before he could find an undertaker for that project. With him out of the way, the General Assembly used the levy to buy his residence for that purpose.

Sir Francis Wyatt became governor in 1639, and during his short tenure he merely followed up on Harvey's lead. He did, however, push through an act of assembly in 1640 that actually denominated Jamestown as the colony's "chief town." The law was also unusual in that it was the first to compel the governor and his successors to reside at Jamestown. Consequently, Kemp sold his house to Wyatt and

---

14. Sir John Harvey and the Council of State to the Privy Council, 18 Jan. 1638/39, *VMBH* 3 (1895): 30.

moved to new quarters on the mainland near Middle Plantation. Another of Wyatt's laws began the regulation of retail liquor sales, which is the first testimony to the presence of innkeepers and public houses at Jamestown. Wyatt likewise persuaded the Assembly to renew its earlier commitment to "the making of a Towne," when he secured passage of a statute that required "aunciant proprietors" to build on their town lots or forfeit them.[15]

That same law authorized Wyatt and the Council of State to plan the construction of a "platt forme," to defend the town. Whether Wyatt actually oversaw the project is unclear; perhaps he did not, given that the law was passed just months before he and Sir William Berkeley entered into negotiations for the sale of his office. For certain the colonists subsequently built an earthen rectangular bastion several hundred yards to the east of the old fort site. It stood guard over the town until the 1660s, when it was replaced by a larger fortification on an upriver site overlooking Sandy Bay. Recent archaeological excavations have confirmed its location.[16]

In early 1642, when Sir William Berkeley alighted on the dock at Jamestown, he stepped into another world. The one he left behind had been the pivot of public life; the new one lay at the margins of British civilization. Little about the colony's sole metropolis conjured images of London, the court, or Berkeley's cultured circles of princes and courtiers. It amounted to scarcely more than a tiny English village with an indifferent collection of houses, taverns, breweries, and commercial properties. Few trappings bespoke Jamestown as

---

15. Hening, ed., *The Statutes at Large*, 1: 226, 229; "Nine Acts of the Grand Assembly of Virginia, 1641," p. 7, typescript of a transcription by Jon Kukla from a manuscript text in the Library of Virginia, a copy of which is in my possession.
16. Ibid.

capital of Virginia or Berkeley's dignity as the king's vicegerent. The inhabitants themselves were a rough-hewn lot too, consisting as they did of small planters who farmed the land beyond the town limits, indentured servants, slaves, renters, a few craftsmen, and even fewer families.

Berkeley soon settled into the Kemp-Wyatt House, which came to him in the deal that made him governor, and went about the business of performing his duties. He brought orders for every planter who held more than five hundred acres of land each to build a brick house in the capital. Moreover, Charles authorized Berkeley "to choose such other Seate for the Chiefe Town," if he wished, and the new city would retain "the Ancient name of James Town."[17] Because Berkeley sought to draw the leading planters to him, he made no effort to move the seat of government elsewhere. He elected instead to build up Jamestown and to lead by his example. And so he began construction on a three-unit brick row house sometime around the year 1643, but he also started work on his country estate, Green Spring House. Berkeley's schemes of urban development did not progress very far before the outbreak of the English Civil Wars and the Anglo-Powhatan War of 1644–1646 disrupted them.

Strife in England drove thousands of immigrants to Virginia. Few of them saw opportunities in town living, so they generally avoided Jamestown as their place of new beginnings, settling instead north and west of the York River watershed. Renewed warfare with the natives not only forced Berkeley into a hurried trip to England in search of weaponry, but it distracted leading politicians who were less than eager to spend time or money on perfecting James Cittie.

---

17. Instructions to Sir William Berkeley, 10 Aug. 1641, in Warren M. Billings, ed., *The Papers of Sir William Berkeley, 1605–1677* (Richmond, Va. 2007), p. 33.

Even so, Berkeley persisted. He succeeded in attracting and keeping various craftsmen and artisans. Brewmasters, for example, found Jamestown an especially congenial place to practice their calling, for as a contemporary observer noted "Six publike Brewhouses" flourished there. Bakers, boatwrights, brickmakers, carpenters, coopers, limeburners, masons, potters, sawyers, and assorted others also followed their traditional occupations. Some plied their trades at various locations, but there was a tendency to concentrate in particular areas, such as the commercial zone along the riverside, near the docks just east of the church, or at the rim of the Pitch and Tar Swamp, toward the mainland.[18]

Berkeley gave Jamestown a commercial boost and the semblance of an English market town at the General Assembly of 1649. He introduced legislation that provided for a "weekly markett, to be holden upon every Wednesday and Saturday." The act designated a tract of land "bounded (vizt.) from the Sandy Gutt, comonly called and knowne by the name of Peter Knight's store westward and soe to the gutt next beyond the house of Lancelott Elay eastward, and bounded on the north side with the back river" as the market place, which would open between eight in the morning and six in the evening on market days. A clerk of the market, who presided over transactions, kept the official weights and measures, recorded all sales, and judged disputes that arose from disagreements over pricing and such matters.[19]

As of mid-century, the town reached the pinnacle of its development. All the improvements since Harvey's administration resulted in noticeable changes that gave Jamestown the look and feel of a stable community. The turf fort commanded the approach to the town. Vessels, stuffed

---

18. [John Ferrar], *A Perfect Description of Virginia* (London, 1649), p. 3; Billings, *Jamestown and the Founding of the Nation*, pp. 75–79.
19. Hening, ed., *Statutes at Large*, 1: 362.

with tobacco bound for European markets and with cargoes from Dutch, English, New England, or West Indian ports, lay at the docks. Berkeley's row house and the statehouse epitomized the town's political significance as well as the links that tied the colony to England. The brick church was a now-familiar landmark, and it served both to solace the godly spiritually and to provide a regular outlet for parishioners to trade gossip or talk of weather and politics. New Town still retained its residential quality, though the distinctiveness of the area disappeared once construction filled in the space between the old and new quarters. Dwellings of different materials and design reflected the variations of wealth and standing of the occupants. Thatched cottages of wattle and daub lodged poorer residents or new arrivals, whereas a number of brick homes also dotted the townscape, but sturdy frame structures were the most prevalent house types. The houses of craftsmen did double duty as places of business, meaning that their plans were more functional than aesthetic.

In March 1652, blueprints for additional modernization came to an abrupt halt. Governor Berkeley surrendered to the parliamentary regime that overthrew and beheaded Charles I. The new rulers in London provided little encouragement for town building, whereas Richard Bennett, Edward Digges, and Samuel Mathews, Jr., who governed during the Interregnum, lacked Berkeley's commitment to urban planning or redevelopment, and with Sir William out of the picture the effort languished. Furthermore, the onset of the First Anglo-Dutch War (1652–1654) raised the possibility of invasion, and those fears pushed concerns for the future of Jamestown even deeper into the background. As a consequence, much of the progress was undone within a decade of Berkeley's capitulation.

Fire, always a danger, played its part too. It consumed the statehouse (the old Harvey place). Homeless, the General Assembly and the General Court contracted with a resident named Thomas Woodhouse, who leased them space in his house, which they occupied until 1657, when the provincial government acquired a brick structure for a capitol building. It sat a little north and west of the Harvey residence, but its use as the seat of government was short lived because fire destroyed it about the time Berkeley became governor pro tem in February 1660. That sequence of occurrences is established by four orders of the General Assembly of October 1660, two of which ordered disbursements "out of the levye the next year" to Woodhouse and one Thomas Hunt as rents "for the use of [their] house[s]." The others requested "that the right Hon. Sir William Berkeley would take into his care the building of a state-house" at public expense and empowered the governor to "presse tenn men of the ordinarie sort of people" for workers.[20]

Berkeley chose not to act on this authorization immediately. The restoration of royal authority in Virginia and the crown's emerging colonial policies dictated his return to England in the spring of 1661 to protect the colony's interests as well as to advance his plan for the diversification of the Virginia economy. His scheme had important consequences for the future of Jamestown. Landing in London in July 1661, Sir William remained at court for over a year before he received Charles II's limited blessing for his economic ideas and a new set of instructions. One of those latter enjoined "that care be taken to dispose the Planters to be willing to build Towns upon every River which must tend very much to their security, & in time their profit ... and that you begin at James River, which being first seated wee desire to give all Countenance, and to settle the Government

---

20. Ibid., 1: 425; H.R. McIlwaine, ed., *Minutes of the Council and General Court of Colonial Virginia*, 2d ed. (Richmond, Va., 1979), pp. 514–515; patent to John Baldwin, Oct. 1656, Virginia Land Patent Book 4, 1655–62, 88, Library of Virginia; Hening, ed., *Statutes at Large*, 2: 12, 13.

there." That royal commandment led to a flurry of urban renewal at Jamestown.[21]

As soon as Berkeley landed in Virginia he summoned the General Assembly to a meeting that convened just days before Christmas 1662. Reporting on the results of his London excursion, he called upon the legislators to implement the king's order, and they complied by adopting an act for rebuilding Jamestown, which he drafted. That law surpassed all others both in its detailed stipulations for financing and managing new construction as well as for its comprehensive specifications of the layout of the new city and its buildings. The town would consist of "thirty two houses, each house to be built with brick, forty foot long, twenty foot wide within the walls, to be eighteen foote high above the ground, the walls to be two brick thick to the water table, and a brick and a halfe thick above the water table to the roofe, the roofe to be fifteen foote pitch and to be covered with slate or tile." These new buildings would be "regularly placed on by another in a square or such other forme as the honorable Sir William Berkeley shall appoint most convenient." Ratepayers in each of the counties bore the costs of seventeen houses, while members of the Council of State and private undertakers accounted for the remaining fifteen. The act also banned wooden construction of any sort, just as it forbade repair of existing frame structures, which were supposed to be replaced by brick buildings once they fell into dilapidation.[22]

Complementing the statute was a request from the Assembly in September 1663 for the governor to proceed with the erection of a new statehouse. In their memorial the members urged the project on the grounds of sparing

---

21. Instructions to Sir William Berkeley, 12 Sept. 1662, Billings, ed., *Berkeley Papers*, 177–180.
22. Hening, ed., *Statutes at Large*, 2: 171–176.

taxpayers the continual expense of renting space and the "dishonour of our Lawes and Judgments given in Alehouses." They likewise voted to expend thirty-thousand pounds of tobacco, plus "what ever more it shall amount to next yeare" to cover building costs.[23]

This third capitol building, according to Secretary Thomas Ludwell, was finished by 1665, and it sat at the western end of the island. If the renewal of Jamestown went as projected, Ludwell's siting of the statehouse suggests the probability that all the new construction took place on land northwest of the church. Documentary records are too few to provide definitive answers, so until archaeological explorations are undertaken, the matter remains speculative.[24]

Whatever its precise location, the whole project never proceeded exactly as Berkeley intended it should. At most, less than a third of the planned houses were ever raised. Worse still, the goal of urban renewal died by the 1670s. Berkeley met with resistance from members of the Council, who were slow to buy into the scheme from the outset, and their reluctance discouraged lesser planters. His own enthusiasm could not sustain the initial rush of expectation, especially after concerns over other issues raised doubts as to the desirability of the redevelopment. Two more wars between England and Holland (1664–1667 and 1672–1674) brought the costly matter of defending against Dutch invasions to the forefront of politics; so did the taxes that undergirded the effort at economic diversification. Berkeley's

---

23. H.R. McIlwaine, ed., *Journals of the House of Burgesses of Virginia, 1659/60–1693* (Richmond, Va., 1914), p. 27.
24. Thomas Ludwell to Henry Bennett, 1st earl of Arlington, 10 April 1665, CO 1/19, fol. 75, National Archives, Kew. Based upon subsequent archaeological investigations, and my discovery of some overlooked documentary records, I would conclude that the statehouse Berkeley projected was at this site. See Warren M. Billings, *Sir William Berkeley and the Forging of Colonial Virginia* (Baton Rouge, La., 2004), pp. 178–182.

overconfidence and physical decline led to a concomitant deterioration in his ability to lead. The combination of these and other problems that plagued Berkeley throughout his last years as governor not only stopped the revitalization project, but they contributed to Bacon's Rebellion and the burning of the capital.

In September 1676 Jamestown sustained extensive damage from the fire that Nathaniel Bacon and his rebels. The church, the statehouse, and every other brick structure lost its roof or worse, whereas all of the frame buildings went up in flames. With the public buildings in ruins, the provincial government and the James City County Court were hard put for meeting space. Shelter was an immediate concern for the permanent residents; even as the embers still smoldered some took the first steps toward rebuilding. For a time there was talk of relocating the capital to a more central location inland. The idea appealed to the colonists who lived at considerable distance from Jamestown, and it progressed to a point in February 1677 where the General Assembly actually debated moving to Tindal's Point (across the York River from modern-day Yorktown). In the end, though, resistance on the part of the inhabitants of Jamestown scotched the possibility.[25]

Reconstruction of the taverns and other private buildings went forward, and by the early 1680s most of that work was done, as were the necessary repairs to the dock and the fort. Parishioners refurbished the church and added the tower as a refinement, but Berkeley's town house never was repaired, which meant that none of his successors had an official home until the erection of the Governor's Palace at Williamsburg. Until the restoration of the capitol complex, neither was there a place for the legislature or the James City County Court to

---

[25] McIlwaine, ed., *Journals of the House of Burgesses, 1659/60–1693*, pp. 110, 106, 78.

meet. The General Assembly sat at Green Spring House, whereas the county court held sessions in the home of Otho Thorpe near Middle Plantation and Secretary Ludwell's house at Rich Neck served as the public record office. Enough public houses were in operation to provide meeting space after 1680, and either Ann Macon, Henry Gawler, or William Armiger rented out rooms for the conduct of public business.[26]

The arrangements sufficed until Governor Francis Howard, fifth baron Howard of Effingham, cajoled the General Assembly into letting a contract for repair of the statehouse ruin. After much pulling and hauling, all parties agreed in May 1684 to engage Philip Ludwell as the contractor. Within a year, the feisty colonel moved the work to a point where the partially reconditioned building could accommodate the Council of State and the House of Burgesses, but another decade passed before another contractor, Henry Hartwell finished the job.[27]

Why did the work on the state house proceed so slowly? The short answer is politics. Colonel Herbert Jeffreys, Thomas Culpeper, second baron Culpeper of Thoresway, and Effingham were under strict orders to curb the powers of the General Assembly, and they kept it from meeting in annual sessions, as had been the practice before 1677. All three feuded with colonial politicians, who held hostage any plans to restore the capitol. Then too, rebuilding was costly, and the prospect of taxing colonists during the bad economic times of the post-Bacon's Rebellion years was none too inviting to

---

[26] Ibid., p. 70, 174, 226, 257; George Carrington Mason, *Colonial Churches of Tidewater Virginia* (Richmond, Va., 1945), pp. 13–14.

[27] McIlwaine, ed., *Journals of the House of Burgesses, 1659/60–1693*, p. 245; Warren M. billings, *A Little Parliament: The Virginia General Assembly in the Seventeenth Century* (Richmond, Va., 2004), pp. 147–148.

leaders who feared increasing the public levies might inspire yet another revolt.

Impeded by political squabbles, the renewal crept along, and as of 1698, the town consisted of about thirty residences and taverns, a stout jail, the church, and the nearly complete state house block. To all appearances Jamestown seemed to have recovered to a semblance of its former self, but looks were deceiving. No longer was James Cittie the colony's only town. Hobbes his Hole (now Tappahannock), Norfolk, Urbanna, and Yorktown all had sprung up after the General Assembly adopted the town act of 1680, and their presence presaged the decline of the ancient metropolis as a commercial center.

Its demise came quicker than anyone could have imagined. On Halloween, 1698, yet another fire swept the town, and within a matter of hours it was a smoking ruin once more. This time there was no effort to rebuild because Governor Francis Nicholson inveigled the General Assembly to move the capital to a new site at Middle Plantation, which became Williamsburg.

As the years passed, the remnants of the community disappeared from view. Earth, roots, and water covered brick foundations, shards of pottery and a discarded helmet.[28] Jamestown slipped into the realm of the imagination.

---

[28] The essay as it appeared in *Virginia Cavalcade* was profusely illustrated, and one of those illustrations was of a pot helmet that was among the early artifacts that Bill Kelso's team recovered from the fort site. Between 1995 and 2004, the Kelso produced eight booklets, each entitled *Jamestown Rediscovery*, that reported on the progress of the excavations. The University of Virginia Press released his *Jamestown: The Buried Truth* in 2006.

ESSAY 6

SIR WILLIAM BERKELEY, A CAVALIER TURNED VIRGINIAN

In the mid-1980s, I yielded to a long-felt temptation to write the first ever book-length biography of Sir William Berkeley (1605–1677). An inescapable presence in seventeenth-century Virginia, the governor-general and I had often bumped into each other as I explored his world. I recognized in the Berkeley of my encounters someone who marked his adopted homeland like no other figure of his era. He ranked with the premier statesmen of the first British Empire, he encouraged the General Assembly to become a bicameral representative legislature, and in so doing he propelled an important precedent for American self-government. An inveterate exponent of agricultural experimentation, he nearly weaned the planters from their dependence upon a tobacco economy. Virginia represented a place of new beginnings for him, and he became the foremost of the planter aristocrats who pushed their way to the head of an emerging social hierarchy. His beloved Green Spring plantation operated as a model for the great planters. Ultimately, his schemes for Virginia's betterment foundered, and his failures led to Bacon's Rebellion, his disgrace, and to tighter control of the colony from London. In these and other ways, as my acquaintance deepened, I discovered a Berkeley quite at odds with the stereotypical villain who oppressed small planters and savagely crushed Bacon's uprising.

This Berkeley's was a worthy story, but a conspicuous obstacle stood in the way of telling it in full—the lack of a Berkeley archive. After he died in 1677, his estate papers passed to his second wife, the redoubtable Dame Frances Culpeper Stephens Berkeley (1634–1695?). She later married Philip Ludwell, and afterwards the estate collection commingled with family documents of the Ludwells and their Lee relations. Virtually all of those Berkeley papers went missing throughout the eighteenth and nineteenth centuries. A second group, his public papers, lasted until fire consumed them in 1865 when in the waning days of the Civil War retreating Confederate officials set fire to warehouses in Richmond that stored Virginia's seventeenth-century provincial archives. The remainder constituted a third portion, but until someone gathered them no one knew to a certainty if their number and scope were sufficient to sustain a book. Thus, reassembling those survivors became a necessary first step for me. Clues in readily identifiable Berkeley documents, plus goodly doses of serendipity, pointed me towards repositories widely scattered across the United States, Great Britain, Ireland, the Netherlands, Virginia, and even Sweden. The hunt soon produced a steady increase of finds, and whenever a new paper came to light, I transcribed it and entered it chronologically into a searchable digital database. Eventually, I recovered over 900 items—a mere fraction of what once existed, to be sure, but one of sufficient proportion to provide a sound evidentiary foundation for my projected book.

As the papers accumulated there were repeated opportunities for me to comment upon never-before-noticed features of Berkeley's life or to refine my assessment of his place in Anglo-Virginia history.[1] None of those occasions

---

1. "Berkeley and Effingham: Who Cares?" *Virginia Magazine of History and Biography*, 97 (1989): 33–47; "The Search for Sir William Berkeley,"

proved more important to how I ultimately designed my book than the result of an invitation from Mary Baldwin College to become the 1992 Mary F. Carroll Lecturer. As a Carroll Lecturer, I was expected to deliver two public presentations on a subject of my choosing. That prospect suited me because I could use those lectures to profile Berkeley at greater length than I had ever done up to that point. I entitled them "Sir William Berkeley, A Cavalier Turned Virginian." The ensuing essay, a condensation of my Carroll Lecture notes, appears here for the first time.

Sir William Berkeley dominated Virginia as few of its governors, colonial or modern. He possessed a temperament at once winning and wrathful, and much about him repelled rather than captivated. Yet he was a gifted, clever man with an inventive turn of mind. He presided over the Old Dominion for a third of the seventeenth century, during

delivered at the Staff Break Series, North Carolina Department of Archives and History, Raleigh, Sept. 1990; "Sir William Berkeley: Portrait by Fischer, A Critique," *William and Mary Quarterly*, 3d Ser. (1991): 598–607; "Sir William Berkeley: From Cavalier to Virginian," delivered at the annual meeting of the Southern Historical Association, Ft. Worth, November 1991; "Sir William and the Invention of Self," delivered at the annual conference of the British Association of American Studies, Sunderland, Eng., April 1993; "Imagining Green Spring House," *Virginia Cavalcade*, 44 (1994): 84–95; "Sir William Berkeley: Carolina Proprietor," *North Carolina Historical Review*, 72 (1995): 329–343; "Sir William Berkeley and the Diversification of the Virginia Economy," *VMHB*, 104 (1996): 433–455; "The Return of Sir William Berkeley," *Virginia Cavalcade*, 47 (1998): 100–110. "Sir William Berkeley: Governor of Virginia," presentation at a scholars' round table convened by the National Park Service at Jamestown, June 1998; "Sir William Berkeley, Virginia Planter and Politician;" Delivered at the 1999 Heritage Lecture Series sponsored by the Jamestown-Yorktown Foundation, Jamestown, April 1999; "Sir William Berkeley's *A Discourse and View of Virginia*: A Note on Its Authorship," *Documentary Editing*. 24 (2002): 33–36.

which he stamped deep marks upon its people, its institutions, its politics, and its relationship to England, just as he had much to do with the settlement of the Carolinas, westward exploration, and economic development. His own passage from cavalier to Virginian epitomized a personal transformation that happened to women and men who traded the uncertainties of an Old World in turmoil for a confrontation with the American wilderness.

Like his nemesis Nathaniel Bacon, though, no one quite knows how to interpret Berkeley. Contemporaries disagreed mightily about his character and motives. Those disputes still find voice in the words of scholars, who have characterized him, sometimes bitterly, as either a staunch Stuart loyalist, a merciless despot, a friend of Indians, or the architect of creole culture. A practical reason accounts for this contrariety of opinion in large measure. Berkeley's papers scattered following his death, and significant portions were destroyed after 1677—conditions that made him a less than inviting subject of close inquiry. Now that the surviving documents have been reassembled, and are in preparation for publication, it is appropriate to reconsider this most controversial of seventeenth-century figures.[2]

William Berkeley descended from a many-branched family, whose members prospered from an ancient tradition of service to the Crown. He was born in 1605 at Hanworth Manor, Middlesex, home of his maternal grandparents. His mother Dame Elizabeth Killigrew Berkeley came from well-off gentry stock. Like other highborn women of that time, she fulfilled the purpose in life that English society demanded of her, making an advantageous marriage and bearing children. Thus, there is little to learn about her beyond the bare record of her existence, and so her influence upon

---

2. Warren M. Billings, ed., *The Papers of Sir William Berkeley, 1605–1677* (Richmond, Va., 2007).

William and his siblings can only be guessed. Her husband, Sir Maurice, sprang from the Somerset Berkeleys, who resided at the Abbey, in the town of Bruton. He won a knighthood while soldiering with Robert Devereaux, second earl of Essex, and served as a justice of the peace for Somerset as well as a member of the House of Commons for several West Country constituencies. The owner of substantial properties in Somerset, Gloucestershire, and London, he also invested in the Virginia Company of London.

Besides William, Maurice and Elizabeth brought six other children into the world. Charles (b. 1600), their first-born, was followed in turn by Henry (b. 1601), Maurice (b. 1603), John (b. 1607), Margaret (b. 1611), and Jane (b. 1613). All seven lived to adulthood and beyond, though only Charles, William, and John had public careers. As such, they are the only ones about whom there is much to know.

Sir Maurice died in 1617. The terms of his will made adequate provisions for his wife and minor children. William therefore grew toward manhood secure in the knowledge that he would share in every benefit to which his status entitled him. Details of his early education are few, but he likely enrolled in grammar school either in Middlesex or Somerset, where he received his first formal learning. Just before he turned eighteen, he followed his forebears and matriculated at Queen's College, Oxford, thereby honoring a longstanding family custom, but for reasons unknown, transferred to St. Edmund Hall, which awarded him an A.B. in 1624. His mother and his brother Charles evidently intended that he should prepare for life as a barrister or a local magistrate. That supposition is borne out by his two-year stint at the Middle Temple, where he encountered a fellow student, Edward Hyde, the future earl of Clarendon, who would figure prominently in his later career.

Berkeley perhaps balked at satisfying his family's expectations of him because he was not called to the bar or to county office. Instead, he returned to Oxford and entered Merton College, where he became Master of Arts. The latter accomplishment won his election as a college fellow, though he had other ideas than continuing in academe. Young Stuart gentlemen sometimes traveled continental Europe in search of adventure. Such a possibility took the fancy of Master Berkeley, and in February 1630, he petitioned the Merton faculty to grant him a leave of absence. They did. Armed with a passport from the Privy Council, he and two companions set out to spend up to three years abroad, though they promised not to go to that center of Roman Catholicism, Rome. Although no details of the trip have come to light, some indications hint at a probable itinerary. For a time Berkeley may have joined brother John, who soldiered with English troops in Holland, which gave William a taste of military life and an acquaintance of the Dutch. Next, he visited France and Italy. Then he ignored the restrictions of his passport and went to Rome, because, like others of his countrymen, he would have regarded a visit there as an essential element in his travels and education.

Berkeley returned to England in 1632. Dwindling resources entailed upon him the necessity of finding a settled existence. One possibility was to return to Merton; another was to follow in his father's footsteps, but neither of those options appealed to him. Instead, he took the course of many another younger, impoverished gentry son: he sought preferment at court. His family credentials afforded him an edge that sufficed to win him a place as gentleman of the king's privy chamber. Though seemingly a minor post, the office gave its holder proximity to the monarch as well as manifold opportunities with which to fashion an honorable, profitable career.

Charles I was at the pinnacle of his power when Berkeley joined the court. An outwardly peaceable and prosperous kingdom, which Charles was determined to rule without resort to Parliament, allowed him to indulge his tastes for the arts and learning. Together with Queen Henrietta Maria he patronized scores of artists, architects, gardeners, poets, playwrights, scholars, wits, and adventurers. Just being among such an entourage opened Berkeley to a spacious world of intellectual stimuli that fixed his personal relationships and outlook for years to come. He encountered Sir Francis Wyatt and George Sandys who shared their experiences of Virginia, just as he observed the policy debates over the future of that faraway colony. The two John Tradescants, the royal gardeners, sharpened his interests in landscaping, horticulture, silk making, and agricultural experimentation. His acquaintance with the architect Inigo Jones exposed him to the Italianate idiom that Jones introduced in his set designs for masques at court and his plans for buildings such as the royal silk works at Oatlands or the Banqueting Hall at Whitehall Palace.

A more immediate influence resulted from Berkeley's inclusion in overlapping circles of courtiers. One, known as "The Wits," and named by the poet Sir John Suckling, grouped around the queen. A second centered on Lucius Carey, second viscount Falkland, and it gathered at Great Tew, his estate in Oxfordshire. The affinity between Berkeley and these luminaries was natural enough. Some were relatives, others were friends, and he had literary ability too.

Berkeley dabbled, as did they, at verse making and play writing. His poems disappeared centuries ago, as have all but one of his plays, *The Lost Lady: A Tragi-Comedy*, which he penned in 1637. It was performed first at court during that Christmas season and again in February and March 1638 at Blackfriars and the Cockpit. *The Lost Lady* is a nearly forgotten bit of Caroline literature owing chiefly to the scarcity of witnesses to its texts. Cast in ancient Greece, the play is not easily summarized in a few words because Berkeley wove numerous characters into a convoluted tale of love and deception. The intricacies of the plot seem overwrought to a modern reader, but they resonated with Berkeley's audiences, who expected to be amused by incredible story lines, ghosts, portents, heroes, villains, word plays, classical allusions, romantic scheming, and political chicanery. Likewise, chattiness and slow moving pace were standard fare of Caroline court dramas.

Playwrights often employed those very conventions for more than mere entertainment. They used them as subtle devices to express their displeasure with the excesses of court life or the current political scene. Such was certainly true of Berkeley. Setting *The Lost Lady* in a context of war and intrigue spoke to his anger at the loss of his brother Maurice in the abortive English raid on the French coast in 1627, his dismay at the crown's aloofness to the Thirty Years' War, and his despair at the king's growing troubles with the Scots over the church. Characters who resorted to artifice for the sake of their love suggest his rising frustration with the twists and turns of court politics, just as their criticism of absolutism hint at misgivings about Charles I.

Two sources fed Berkeley's views, his associates and his own lack of fulfillment. Among his acquaintances and friends, Sir Thomas Roe, the viscount Falkland, and Edward Hyde stood foremost as his political mentors. Each was dubious of Charles, and each chafed at a sovereign whom they considered weak and untrustworthy, but all three held monarchy to be the rock layer of English polity, and they saw no choice except to use their prodigious talents to mediate between Charles and his censors. Their example inculcated in Berkeley an abiding devotion to the crown and an equally abiding wariness of Stuart kings. Those were lessons he never forgot. From Roe, Falkland, and Hyde, as from other colleagues, he partook of the skills and mannerisms of an accomplished courtier and honed them to a fine edge, though he did not follow the example of some and indulge in scandalous behavior. Instead, he maintained a high reputation throughout London and at court.

Keen abilities and a good name alone failed to assure Berkeley's aggrandizement, which, after all, was the point of his going to court in the first place. A decade of service to Charles I garnered Berkeley neither riches nor power nor did it forecast promises of brighter days. To be sure, he received some royal gifts, but all of them amounted to little when compared to the successes of his brothers Charles and John or to other members of his circle, who ranked higher in the inner group of royal confidants than he or whose literary achievements surpassed his. He remained a privy chamber man, and there was little to mark him apart from run-of-the mill courtiers who approached middle age.

If there was a single episode that at last soured Berkeley on the courtier's life, though, it was his participation in the First and Second Bishops' Wars against the Scots. In the first war, he joined his fellow privy chamber men who formed a guard for Charles I. Marching off to Scotland in March 1639, the guardsmen saw limited action because the fighting amounted to little, although Berkeley gained knighthood for his services. Sir William held a staff position during the second war, acting as a messenger between the army and Secretary of State Sir Francis Windebanke. Sometimes he also arranged exchanges of prisoners or spied on the Scots. The latter occupation embarrassed him exceedingly after he accused his superior officers of giving intelligence to the enemy. Unable to prove his assertions, he was sharply rebuked, and he left the army a much-embittered man.

Bitterness mingled with rising worry about how he might be affected by the troubles that inched the British Isles toward civil war. Taking stock in the spring of 1641, Berkeley saw little that encouraged him. His income suddenly diminished after the Long Parliament abolished the Court of Star Chamber and overturned his rights to the treasury of the Court of Common Pleas. The impeachment of Thomas Wentworth, first earl of Strafford, vexed him too. He had small regard for that luckless minister, but his brother John, his cousin Henry Jermyn, and members of his circle conspired to rescue Strafford from the Tower of London. Discovery of the Army Plot not only endangered them but it cast suspicion on him and doomed the hapless earl. Once Charles fecklessly signed the warrant for Strafford's head, Berkeley saw confirmation of his worst opinions of the king.

These things pointedly reminded Berkeley of the precariousness of his situation. A pinched pocketbook and his political moderation put him on ground that eroded increasingly. Therefore, about the time of Strafford's execution (12 May 1641), he concluded that his days at court were done and that he would go abroad. Seeking a graceful exit and a means of livelihood, he sought the counsel of Sir Thomas Roe. Roe urged consideration of Constantinople and even found a suitable place there for his protégé. Anxious to leave England, Berkeley seized on Roe's advice and began packing, but amidst his preparations, he unexpectedly changed his mind, and lobbied to become governor-general of Virginia.

An obstacle in the form of Sir Francis Wyatt, the incumbent governor-general, stood in the way. An unknown person prevailed upon Wyatt to sell out even as Berkeley pressed Charles for the appointment and dickered with Sir Francis. The wheels of the royal bureaucracy ran faster than the negotiations with Wyatt. Charles commissioned Berkeley governor and captain-general of Virginia on 31 July 1641, and sealed the appointing documents ten days later. The Wyatt negotiations lasted into September before Sir Francis came to terms. Berkeley agreed to give Wyatt £300, to buy Wyatt's house at Jamestown, and not to assume office before 14 January 1641/42, which allowed Wyatt to collect a full year's salary.[3]

Berkeley's preparations for his passage to Virginia lasted into mid-November. Because there is no account of his voyage, it is impossible to pinpoint the date of his landing at Jamestown. A routine crossing would have put him at his destination anywhere between mid-January and early February 1641/42, but true to his agreement with Wyatt, he did not swear his oaths of office until 8 March.

When Governor-General Berkeley alighted on the Jamestown docks, he stepped into another universe. His old one had been at the pivot of public life. The new one lay at the margins of British civilization. Little in the colony's sole town conjured images of London, the court, or the cultured circles of princes and courtiers. Jamestown was scarcely more than a tiny English country village and a mean one at that. Its buildings amounted to an indifferent collection of houses, taverns, breweries, and commercial properties that numbered only a few dozen at most. All were of wood save for the house Berkeley bought from Wyatt and the partially constructed town church, which were of brick. A residence that once belonged to a predecessor of Berkeley's, Sir John Harvey, sufficed as the meeting place of the General Assembly and the General Court, as well as an office for the secretary of the colony. Aside from this so-called "statehouse," there were few, if any, trappings that bespoke "James Cittie" as the capital of the colony or Berkeley's new dignity as the king's vicegerent. The inhabitants were a rough-hewn lot too, consisting of small planters, who farmed the land beyond the town limits, indentured servants, renters, a few craftsmen, and even fewer families.

What Berkeley observed at Jamestown reflected the colony as a whole. The main features of an economy based

---

3. Billings, *Sir William Berkeley and the Forging of Colonial Virginia*, pp. 1–39.

on tobacco, bondsmen, and foreign commerce were set already by the time of his landing. Plantations scattered along the James-York peninsula, south across the James River, north toward the Potomac, and over the Chesapeake Bay to the Eastern Shore. The mostly male population grew ten times in the years after Virginia became a crown colony, and that increase led to the beginnings of the county court system of local governance as well as an alteration of the purposes of the General Assembly. An emerging elite, composed of fractious, vaulting colonists, was bent on controlling the future of Virginia as it plotted the basic outlines for self-government, a legal order, and a structured society.

His remaining papers supply none of the initial impressions this place and its people made on the polished Berkeley, but he had little time to brood over his situation. There was work to be done. Getting settled and his servants to their tasks were his first concerns. Unlike other colonists, though, finding a place to live and land to farm took little time and outlay beyond his initial investment of £1000 on the laborers and supplies that accompanied him to America. Wyatt's house afforded him a comfortable, if cramped shelter, while a three-thousand acre plot of ground known as "the Governors Land" enabled him to take up planting almost at once.

Land was the most precious and durable thing Stuart Englishmen might possess, and the prospect of ownership drew them to Virginia by the thousands. Berkeley was no exception to that rule. Like anyone else, he could claim head rights on himself and the servants he brought at his expense, and by that means, he became in time one of the colony's largest landholders. He gained his first property in the spring of 1643, when he patented a thousand-acre tract about three miles west of Jamestown. There he began construction of Green Spring House, which he enlarged over the years into one of the first stately mansions in English North America.

The fields about the plantation became proving grounds for experiments with staples that Berkeley hoped to substitute for tobacco. Within a decade, he was producing vendible quantities of silk, rice, small grains, wines, and other crops that he marketed around the Atlantic rim. These successes, plus his partnerships with Indian traders made him wealthy beyond anything he had known in England, and they deepened his attachments for Virginia. His roots sank deeper still following his marriage to his first wife, whose identity defies discovery.

Accomplishments in farming and commerce explain Berkeley's strengthening conviction that the way of the future for Virginia laid in diversified agriculture, compact communities, and a deferential social order. Such a colony would immensely benefit England as it lessened the planters' reliance upon tobacco. That vision, it is true, found impetus in the instructions that Charles I gave every royal governor, but Sir William had imbibed deeply of diversification theory long before he set foot in Virginia. His faith in diversification made him the first of the colony's chief executives who believed in its possibilities and who worked tirelessly towards its implementation. As a first step, he recognized that he must make it succeed at Green Spring, and if it did, then he might persuade other planters to emulate him. Initially, however, the duties of office diverted his grand design.

Berkeley assumed office in trying political circumstances. His charge—governing in the interests of king and colonist—presented an exquisite trial of his governing skills: to hold Virginia loyal, to carry out Charles's instructions, to steer between competing factions of leading Virginians, and to keep the good will of the Puritans in Parliament. Practical concerns, not sentiment, cemented Virginians' loyalty to Charles. The king guaranteed their land titles and their political arrangements, while his dithering kept at bay those English mercantile interests who saw in a revived Virginia

Company the means to manage the colony in a profitable manner. Civil war, which broke out in August 1642, put colonial allegiances to the test. War compelled the settlers to take sides, and it threatened commercial relationships that were vital to their prosperity. Then too, a mere seven years had passed since the Council of State toppled Berkeley's predecessor Sir John Harvey after a dispute over a governor-general's power to act independent of the councillors' wishes. Most of the very men who ousted Harvey off still held places on the Council, and they were quick to dare Berkeley.

Sir William responded adroitly for one who had no first-hand experience of governing. His approach to the task and his courtly style certainly benefited him. Concluding that his royal master's interests would be served best if he led by example, he made common cause with the great planters. That was an easy step for his personal aspirations and theirs were one. He tempted members of the Council, showering them with lands and offices, and he was especially solicitous to his potential rivals. His treatment of William Claiborne, for one, typified his method. Claiborne had wide mercantile affiliations that connected him to parliamentary interests. Long resident in the colony, he sat on the Council of State and commanded a consequential political following, which the governor could ill afford to offend. A possibility of winning him presented itself soon after Sir William assumed office. Death had vacated the lucrative office of treasurer of Virginia, and he chose Claiborne to fill the vacancy.

Berkeley also reached out to members of the General Assembly and the county courts. He landed at Jamestown during an assembly session, which had been called mainly to deal with Parliament's attempt at reconstituting the Virginia Company. That possibility was anathema to many of the burgesses. Seeing an opportunity to enhance his popularity with another constituency, he associated with the opponents and assisted them in drafting a protest to King Charles. He followed that move with another, when he not only encouraged the General Assembly of March 1642/43 to proceed with the revision of the colony's statute law and reforms of local administration, but he also urged the burgesses to become a House of Burgesses that sat apart from the Council of State. As such, the House, newly created, became a counterpoise to the council and a place where Berkeley could to win over colonial politicians who were not part of any conciliar faction. He requited local magisterial interests by strengthening the county courts in ways that enhanced the reach and prestige of the justices.

Doing these things yielded results that altered the political landscape for years to come. Dividing the General Assembly launched it on the way toward becoming a little Parliament with prerogatives that exceeded its model in certain respects: adding to the power of the county courts incrementally decentralized authority and invested county elites with nearly unchecked control of local affairs. And Berkeley gained relative freedom to keep Virginia clear of the English troubles and to promote the Dutch trade.

Commerce with the Dutch appealed to those colonists who were not allied to the London merchants as it dovetailed with Berkeley's dream of economic diversification. A free trader in the sense that the governor opposed restricting the privilege of marketing to a favored few vendors, whether Londoners or Virginians, Berkeley favored selling Virginia goods wherever there was call for them. He himself developed extensive connections with Dutch, English, Maryland, New England, and West Indian merchants.

An unexpected boost to Berkeley's leadership came in the wake of renewed war with the Indians. Threatened sorely by the influx of colonists and the spread of their plantations, the Powhatans tried to stem the tide. Their great werowance, Opechancanough, as he had done in 1622, laid plans for a swift, surprise stroke to drive out the English. He attacked them on Holy Thursday, 1644. The blow was costly to individual colonists. Five hundred died that April day, but Virginia itself was in no danger of destruction, whereas the assault gave Berkeley the chance to prove his mettle as a warrior. Hurriedly, he called the General Assembly into session, and it sent him back to England to find arms and ammunition. He commissioned Secretary of the Colony Richard Kemp acting governor and gave temporary command of the militia to William Claiborne before booking passage eastward late in June.

Once in England, he soon grasped the folly of his mission. Virginia could expect no help from Charles, who had his own need of weaponry to carry his fight to the parliamentarians. Seeing no advantage in lingering, Berkeley planned a speedy return to the colony, but a campaign with the king detained him. In the field, he might have emulated his brother John and pressed for a command, but he rejected that choice and went home as quickly as he could find a Virginia-bound vessel.

Landing at Jamestown in June 1645, he discovered that the fight with Opechancanough had gone badly in his absence. Claiborne proved an indifferent general who was more interested in using the militia to settle a personal vendetta with the Maryland government than in defeating the Indians. Berkeley put him aside and took the field himself. He sprang a trap on the natives, which resulted in capture or death of a number of lesser werowances, though Opechancanough eluded him. Next, Berkeley pillaged the Indians' cornfields and torched their villages until the coming of cold weather quieted the campaign. The following spring Berkeley met with the General Assembly, and together they perfected a plan that ended the war. They drafted a special force of militia for the express purpose of taking Opechancanough. Those troops tracked their quarry and found him at length. A messenger brought the news to Sir

William who, with a troop of cavalry caught him by surprise. Berkeley brought his captive to Jamestown, intending to ship him to England, but a militiaman killed the old man while he laid a prisoner in the town jail. Necotowance, who replaced Opechancanough, sued for peace. The treaty, which Berkeley drafted, was ratified in October 1646, and it kept the eastern tribes peaceful for the next thirty years.

In those instances when he underestimated his constituents, his popularity and sure-handedness sustained Berkeley. The most serious of these missteps happened when he launched a policy of strict conformity to the Church of England. Such a measure complied with his instructions, which he was honor bound to implement to the fullest of his abilities; doing so jeopardized his hold on office. For one thing, he opened himself to a too-close identification with the king's religious views, thereby giving his detractors in England a cudgel with which to club him. For another, Virginia Anglicans showed little taste for punishing the nonconformists in their midst, especially as they were themselves rather lax in their own religious habits. Finally, there were few colonists who wished for Virginia a replication of the strife that set Anglican against Puritan back home. Especially not Berkeley. He was a devout son of the Church who had little patience with dissent from its teachings, but he rejected the theological rigidities of Archbishop William Laud and the king. His experiences in the Bishops' Wars taught him the disastrous consequences of trying to drive people of faith too hard in directions they balked at taking. Accordingly, once he recognized the political liabilities of his religious policy, he downplayed it and avoided lasting damage to his credibility.[4]

The ascendancy of the parliamentarians and the beheading of Charles I put Berkeley in a precarious spot.

---

4. Ibid., pp. 39–113.

News of the king's overthrow reached Virginia a few months after his execution, and the governor acted swiftly to hold the colony loyal. Proclaiming Charles II Virginia's rightful ruler, he dispatched a defiant remonstrance off to Whitehall wherein he damned Parliament for overturning the monarchy. He used his royalist contacts to communicate with the young monarch and to urge cavaliers with military training to come to him and use the colony as a base from which to war on Oliver Cromwell. At his insistence the General Assembly enacted legislation making treasonable any words that questioned the succession of Charles II or justified regicide.

On their side, the parliamentarians moved slowly but designedly. Upon reading Berkeley's remonstrance, the Council of State referred it to the Committee of the Admiralty for recommendations about bringing Virginia to heel. The committee's advice led to an order-in-council of 14 August 1650 that interdicted English commerce with the colony. Parliament followed up with a statute that prevented foreigners from trading there too.

Now it was the governor's turn to retaliate. Scarcely had he scanned a text of the statute when Berkeley summoned the General Assembly for a daylong meeting. He delivered the opening speech, which was vintage Sir William. "By the grace of God," cried he, "we will not tamely part with our King, and by all these blessings we enjoy under him." Should defiance meet with force, "do but follow me," he cajoled his listeners, and "I will either lead you to victory, or loose a life which I cannot more gloriously sacrifice then for my loyalty, and your security." When he finished, a clerk read out the act, and the members of both houses unanimously condemned it with a joint declaration of their own. Then, with characteristically dramatic flair, Berkeley sent copies of both papers to friends at The Hague who published them for distribution throughout the Netherlands and England.

For Parliament, combating Charles II's campaigns to recover his throne took higher priority than reining in Berkeley. Cromwell dispelled the threat from the would-be king on 3 September 1650, when he routed a royalist army at the battle of Worcester, and soon thereafter Parliament sought to end its Virginia difficulties. Advice on how to do that came from Benjamin Worsley, a functionary close to key members of the commons. He asserted that Virginia would never submit to Parliament so long as Berkeley remained governor, nor would it profit the new regime while its colonists traded with the Dutch. Enlarging on these premises, he went on to outline his plan for conquering Virginia. The Council of State should appoint a commission to lead troops to America. These individuals, in his opinion, must be Virginians whose loyalties were with Parliament, and they should resort to force only if they failed to negotiate Berkeley's surrender. Worsley's final suggestion called for legislation banning the Dutch from Virginia waters.

Parliament translated Worsley's advice into policy almost to the letter. On 26 September 1651, the Council of State picked Richard Bennett, William Claiborne, Edmund Curtis, Robert Dennis, and Thomas Stegge as a commission to reduce Virginia, gave them forces for that purpose, and sent them on their way. Two weeks later, the Navigation Act of 1651 passed into law.

Dennis and Stegge perished at sea, but the convoy reached its landfall in January and took up station at an anchorage in the lower James River. Bennett, Claiborne, and Curtis dispatched messengers upriver to Berkeley seeking his surrender. When he refused them an answer, they sailed to Jamestown. Ever the dramatist, he prepared a spirited show for them. He called out a thousand militiamen and placed them strategically about the little capital as if he would contest the invaders. A tense standoff lasted several days before he signed articles of capitulation on 12 March 1651/52.

In reality, Berkeley intended two results from his show of arms. One was to maintain credibility with Charles II. The second was to gain concessions that preserved the colony's political and social establishment and left Virginians free of meddlesome outsiders. His ploy succeeded because the commissioners' main goal was gaining Virginia for Parliament. Thus they accepted terms that left the status quo mainly intact, and they were generous to him as well. Although they turned Berkeley out, he was not required to swear loyalty to Parliament. They allowed him to write an explanation of the surrender for Charles II and to send it unopened via his own personal courier. He was also given a year in which to liquidate his assets and join the royalists in Holland.

After handing Virginia over to Richard Bennett, William Claiborne, and Edmund Curtis, Berkeley returned to Green Spring and prepared an explanation of the surrender for Charles II. He entrusted its delivery to his friend and military confidant, Colonel Francis Lovelace, whom he dispatched to Europe on 11 May 1652. Barely two pages in length, the letter was an apologia cast in the muted, deferential language of the courtier who had failed in his duty but sought his master's forgiveness. With it safely gone to Holland, Berkeley turned to the question of honoring those articles of surrender that compelled him to sell his estates and to leave Virginia.

Apparently no one expected him to keep those promises. Governor Bennett and Secretary Claiborne signaled as much in October 1652, when both signed a patent reconfirming the title to all Berkeley's properties. The following summer the General Assembly used the outbreak of the First Anglo-Dutch War as an excuse to lengthen his stay for an additional eight months. That extension came and went without anyone's notice. Thereafter, the subject of his departure never arose again, and he stayed at Green Spring, where he lived quietly for the remainder of the Interregnum.

His activities during those years are mostly hidden because so few papers remain to document his retirement. There is the rare, revealing glimpse, however. At first, Berkeley seems to have scrambled to make ends meet. His return to private life and the disruptions of the Dutch war significantly cut into his income. Gone were the salaries and the considerable profits from the numerous other perquisites that went with being governor, whereas conflict with the Netherlands disrupted his commercial ties to New Amsterdam and hampered the sale of his crops. Strapped for capital, he sold portions of his Chipokes plantation in Surry County to William Claiborne, one of his Jamestown row houses to Governor Bennett, and the leaseholds for several of his town lots. Then too, he pressed the General Assembly for the arrears it still owed him, while he sued his debtors to collect from them. Those remedies slowed the losses, although he probably did not regain his financial equilibrium before the mid-1650s.

Diminished fortunes did not stop improvements at Green Spring. At some point Berkeley began an enlargement of the house and a further refinement of the grounds. Agricultural trials continued as before, although he perhaps concentrated on silk. Promoting sericulture was once again in vogue, especially with intellectuals of the Samuel Hartlib circle who advised Parliament on colonial matters, and Berkeley seems to have warmed to them. His continuing efforts to diversify even won him notice from like-minded Puritans in England, who praised him for his experiments.

Ever the astute politician, the former governor-general cocked a weather eye on politics at home and abroad. He kept his distance from Governors Bennett, Edward Digges, and Samuel Mathews, Jr., although he remained on cordial terms with them and observed their difficulties with the burgesses. Friends and former colleagues in the General Assembly discretely talked politics with him too. He noted the increasing independence of the House of Burgesses and the growing power of the county courts. Similarly, he saw how little influence Cromwell wielded in the colony, especially in matters of trade. His sources in England told a different story. There Cromwell's grip was firm and showed no indication of relaxing in the immediate future. Secret communications with the royalist exiles revealed the ineptitude of the king's supporters, which probably weakened Berkeley's faith in the likelihood of Charles's restoration in the near future. Even so Berkeley hoped for the best.

Starting in 1658, he had reason to hope. Cromwell died that September, leaving his son Richard to follow him. The new lord protector enjoyed a momentary popularity, but he was no Oliver, and he abdicated within a year of his succession. Word of his abdication and an aborted royalist uprising found its way to the colony. Months rolled by before tales reached Green Spring of the expulsion of the Rump Parliament and rumors that Charles would soon return to his throne. Berkeley also heard accounts of an increasingly unstable situation in England.

Reports such as these at once encouraged and alarmed him. The snail's crawl at which news crossed the Atlantic quickened his anxieties because it compounded his difficulty of sifting fact from rumor. Distance only magnified his uncertainty, about which side, if any, controlled Whitehall.

Who ruled England took on an unexpected significance for him in January 1660. A mortal illness felled Samuel Mathews, Jr., and suddenly Virginia had no governor. Just as suddenly, Berkeley emerged as the obvious candidate to replace him. Put plainly, there was no other choice. Richard Bennett, the senior councillor and nominal acting governor-general, was tainted by his Puritan leanings, and he was unacceptable to the House of Burgesses, who held the power of election. Secretary Claiborne bore similar liabilities. Former Governor-General Edward Digges was abroad on colony business. The remaining councillors, while able, lacked stature. That left Berkeley. The times required a vigorous chief executive, and his capacity to govern was unmatched. He still retained the loyalties of the planters, and they would follow him in uncertain times. He could reconcile the disputes between the Council and the House of Burgesses that had riven provincial politics in recent times. And his connections to the Stuarts were an asset in holding Virginia safe from royal interference in its affairs in the event Charles resumed the throne.

Considerations such as these led to negotiations with the Council of State that began within days, if not hours, of Mathews's death. Who first approached whom is not known because the record of the talks, if any, was lost long ago. Conceivably, William Claiborne made the overture. He and Berkeley were opposites, but they had occasionally dealt with one another on friendly terms in the past. Whoever it was, he, or they, dealt with a reluctant Berkeley. Perhaps the former governor-general, who neared his fifty-fifth birthday, wished to live out his remaining days unburdened by affairs of state. Publicly, he hesitated from fear of what the government in England, Puritan or royalist, might do to him. He was too proud to assume his former place only to be removed from it a second time as soon as the situation clarified in London. Perhaps his reluctance was just a bargaining stance. In the end, he put his fears aside out of his sense of duty, and around mid-February he informally became governor-general.

His recall remained incomplete until it won the approval of the House of Burgesses. The General Assembly convened at Jamestown on 13 March to consider it. Declaring that no duly constituted authority existed in England, the burgesses proclaimed that the ultimate power of government lay with them, and so it would continue until orders to the contrary came from London. That was one in a series of conditions the House intended to extract from Berkeley. Additionally, they expected him to govern according to the ancient laws of the realm and those of the colony. They required him to summon the General Assembly every other year, but they forbade him to dissolve it without their consent. Finally, subject to their approval, they permitted him to pick the secretary of the colony and the Council of State.

Berkeley was not entirely comfortable with these demands. The monarchist in him balked at the burgesses' assertion of their sovereignty. He reiterated his concerns about how the outcome of the events in England could affect him, as well as the colony. The burgesses held firm, he relented, and on 19 March, he agreed to the House's stipulations in writing.[5]

Berkeley's restoration preceded that of his sovereign by two months—too short an interval for news of it to reach the king before he returned to London in May 1660. Rather quickly thereafter, Charles II set about reasserting his authority in the colony. Reclaiming it required no more than paperwork because he regarded the commission he had given Berkeley a decade earlier as still in force. Thus, in June he commanded a warrant for his signature that formally returned Sir William to his place. Secretary of State Sir Edward Nicholas sent the commission and an official notification of the Restoration on its way to the Chesapeake in July, and the two documents reached their destination by mid-September.

Now the task of constitutionally returning the colony to its former loyalty fell to Berkeley. Toward that end, he hurriedly drew up two proclamations on 20 September 1660, which he ordered read throughout the colony. One declared Charles the rightful ruler of Virginia and ordered all colonists

---

5. Ibid., pp. 113–123.

to submit to the king. The other continued all public officeholders in their places until further notice.

Berkeley reconvened the General Assembly a month later to complete the transition to royal government. By then, he had also formulated schemes to convert Virginia to a diversified economy, and he presented them to the legislators. The support of the Assembly was a necessary precondition. Free trade was vital. Curbs on tobacco were also essential, but any limitation in Virginia would not succeed unless there was a corresponding reduction in Maryland. Inducing Virginians to give up tobacco demanded a level of financial incentives that was quite beyond the means of the provincial government. Capital, huge sums of it, was also needed to recruit skilled workers who could instruct planters and their servants in the techniques of raising the substitutes for tobacco. Those inducements could come only out of England, and Berkeley argued he must win the backing of Charles II if he hoped to make diversification prosper colony-wide as it had at Green Spring.

The General Assembly readily bought his ideas, and in the spring of 1661, Berkeley returned to England in search of royal approval for them. Back in London, he set about the pleasant task of renewing old acquaintances. His brothers and his friends assured Berkeley a ready hearing at court, and so, he discovered, did his seat on the newly formed Council for Foreign Plantations. Those connections benefited him personally as well in that they led to his becoming a proprietor of Carolina. Mainly, though, he lobbied energetically for his reforms of the Virginia economy.

The set piece of that lobby was a printed memorial entitled *A Discourse and View of Virginia*, which Berkeley directed to Charles II and the Privy Council. Drawing on his experiences as someone who had lived and prospered in Virginia for twenty years, he put forth his prescriptions for its improvement in rhetorical tones reminiscent of his playwriting days. The colony was a glorious place; blessed with advantages that surpassed the king's other American dominions. Virginians were substantial, energetic subjects who deserved the king's grace because of their loyalty and industry. Conceding that tobacco brought more revenue to the Crown than all the other colonies combined, he nonetheless argued that a variety of staples would be of greater "publick advantage" to England than a single cash crop that was chronically overproduced. Developing these commodities required free trade, royal encouragement, and the Crown's financial backing. With such help, Berkeley concluded, he could persuade the planters to follow his example, and Virginia would soon blossom into the jewel of the empire.

His politicking yielded mixed results, which were embodied in new instructions the crown handed him when it ordered him back to America in September 1662. The instructions affirmed his goal of diversification, although Charles refused to buttress his affirmation with support from the royal coffers. Instead, he commanded Berkeley to use any taxes that the General Assembly might pass to encourage crop experimentation. He warmed to the possibility of limiting tobacco as well. To that end, he empowered Berkeley to seek an agreement with the government of Maryland. He also reconfirmed his father's instruction for raising towns throughout Virginia. He emphatically turned aside Berkeley's plea for free trade, however.

The reason for his denial was this. Berkeley's argument favoring freedom of trade for Virginia stood at odds with a key element in the Crown's unfolding colonial policy. Charles and his advisors envisioned Virginia as part of an empire grounded upon the subordination of colonial interests to those of England, and Whitehall's regulation of foreign commerce. Achieving those goals required the imposition of military security, political obedience, social discipline, and the exclusion of the Dutch from colonial markets. Of course, those purposes were the core of the navigation system, which the later Stuarts and Parliament settled on the colonies over the last forty years of the seventeenth century.[6]

Chastened, but not undaunted, Berkeley left London, firmly resolved to bend the king's instructions as he saw fit. That was one in a series of misjudgments and misadventures that at last destroyed him. At first, his plans for the economy appeared to work. He easily mesmerized the General Assembly, which enacted all the requisite legislation and raised the necessary taxes. Statutory inducements persuaded a number of colonists, who willingly tried their hands at starting such enterprises as saw mills, tanneries, and salt works. Others emulated Berkeley's example and actually cultivated exportable quantities of silk, hemp, or potash. There was a flurry of urban renewal at Jamestown and an attempt to spawn more towns. As for limiting tobacco, envoys from Maryland, Virginia, and North Carolina successfully negotiated a so-called "stint," which Cecilius Calvert, second baron Baltimore, vetoed, and the Crown eventually withdrew its tentative endorsement of the proposal. Despite that setback, Berkeley kept the faith and pressed forward. In the end, however, he abandoned diversification in the early 1670s.

As a matter of public policy, diversification was doomed aborning because Berkeley predicated it upon premises that were inconsistent with the Crown's conceptions of empire. He neither fathomed nor accepted the Stuarts' meddlesome brand of imperialism. That misapprehension derived as much from ignorance as from hubris. He grasped little of the rationale that underlay colonial policy after the Restoration. His experiences were not those of the architects of the navigation system, so he ignored what he could not comprehend.

---

6. Ibid., pp. 123–163.

His own successes at Green Spring beguiled him into an overconfidence that blinded him to a hard reality. Few colonists approached his fortune, his technical competence, or his access to skilled labor, let alone his steadfast faith in improving Virginia through diversification. Lacking his depth of commitment, or his resources, this dubious majority declined to follow his lead. Better, they thought, to stick with tobacco than to chase pipe dreams. Their doubts only intensified as they bore the expense of the increased taxes that underwrote costly experiments. For ordinary planters, diversification became a nightmare that yielded them little tangible relief from the scourges of a single-crop economy.

Then too, their governor overlooked less expensive and difficult ways to advance diversification. For example, he ignored the inherent possibilities of the grain trade. The sugar revolution in the West Indies raised a demand for foodstuffs, a need Virginians could have easily filled merely by switching from tobacco to grain. Berkeley acknowledged as much in the *Discourse and View of Virginia*, when he remarked how Barbadian planters were forced to spend a fifth of their income to purchase foodstuff from abroad. Ironically, even he himself exported grain to the Caribbean, but the commerce was no more than one in an eclectic range of his enterprises.

Perhaps that early chronicler of Virginia, the historian Robert Beverley, provided the ultimate reason for the failure of diversification. "Sir William Berkeley," he wrote in 1704, "was full of projects, so that he was always very fickle, and set them on foot only to shew us what might be done, and so never minded to bring them to Perfection."

Bad luck dogged Berkeley throughout his second term as governor. He never bargained for the loss of the Dutch trade, war with the Hollanders, the revival of the Northern Neck proprietary, the breakdown of peace with the Indians, natural disasters, or his own declining health. Closure of foreign markets further devalued tobacco and increased dependency on London merchants, whom Berkeley despised as being "avaricious persons, whose sickle hath bin ere long in our harvest already." The Second and Third Anglo-Dutch Wars jeopardized the safety of Virginia in ways he was helpless to prevent. Over his strenuous objections, and at great expenditure to rate payers, the Crown compelled the governor to build a worthless fort at Old Point Comfort. In 1667, and again in 1673, Dutch raiders sailed into the James River out of range of the fort's guns and easily destroyed convoys of tobacco ships. Charles's renewal of a long dormant land grant to the Arlington-Culpeper interests threw Northern Neck real estate titles into question and necessitated a protracted, expensive, though not wholly successful effort to buy out the proprietors. Berkeley might slow, but he could not stop intermittent cultural clashes and frontier skirmishes with the natives that at length broke into the warfare that sparked off Bacon's Rebellion. Neither could he control the elements. Rains and a devastating hurricane destroyed much of the year's tobacco harvest in 1667, whereas disease killed an estimated fifty thousand head of livestock during the bitter winter of 1672–1673.

Mishaps such as these magnified other misfortunes that beset the aging governor and his beloved Virginia. For one thing, Berkeley's influence at court waned noticeably. Shifting court politics destroyed a principal patron, Edward Hyde, first earl of Clarendon, the lord chancellor. Death claimed Charles Berkeley, first viscount Fitzhardinge of Berehaven, treasurer of the royal household, while the other brother, John Berkeley, first baron Berkeley of Stratton, took up residence in Dublin as lord lieutenant of Ireland. Retirement removed other protectors, and the sum of these departures left Berkeley few defenders in Whitehall by the mid-1670s. Charles II and the younger imperialists owned no great investment in him, and they came to regard him as something of a nuisance, though they lacked the will to remove him until Nathaniel Bacon gave them an excuse.

Poor health dulled Berkeley's political instincts and significantly altered his personality. Secretary Thomas Ludwell noted a physical deterioration in Berkeley as early as 1667, and thereafter he often expressed to correspondents his fear that the burdens of office might kill the governor. Other observers also noticed a similar decline, though, except for deafness, no one specified the exact nature of his impairments. Deafness caused people to shout at Berkeley, which probably contributed to an intensifying irascibility, to which all testified. Even Berkeley seemed to realize the toll his advancing years demanded of him. He made several requests to be replaced in the late 1660s that I know of. Each time, though, the Crown, ignored him, and at length he gave up trying.

When close friends on the Council of State or the county courts died, Berkeley appointed younger politicians or newer immigrants to succeed them, but few of the replacements earned his trust. He depended instead upon a diminishing circle of intimates, none of whom wielded greater sway than his second wife, the redoubtable Frances Culpeper Stephens Berkeley, who he married in 1670. She was a formidable political presence whose patronage resulted in favors for those who earned it, just as her ill will closed the door to preferment. In a word, she was for her husband what First Lady Edith Bolling Wilson was for President Woodrow Wilson. And like Mrs. Wilson, Dame Frances's proximity to Sir William gave rise to rumblings that this quick witted, lively woman wielded undue influence over a sickly old man. Whatever the reality, there was sufficient leeway for much bickering and jockeying as everyone around him elbowed for the best place against the day when he either fell into the king's disfavor or dropped dead.[7]

Virginians who stood beyond the circle of favor, or felt the sting of his opprobrium, or dared cross Berkeley were slow to question his ability to lead. Their unwillingness to make the frustrations of the disgruntled their own spared him until the summer of 1675, when a party of Indians raided a plantation in frontier Stafford County. On its face, the raid was similar to incidents that were commonplace along the margins of English settlement. This one, however, precipitated the disagreements over Indian policy between Berkeley and Dame Frances's cousin Nathaniel Bacon that by the spring of 1676, ripened into rebellion.

Of course, Bacon's Rebellion defined Berkeley as no other event in his entire career. His part in fostering and curbing the revolt forms the crux of the controversy that has surrounded him from that day to this. I am not quite prepared to join that debate because I have not yet fully digested the relevant Berkeley papers in the context of other evidence. But I will offer this tentative conclusion. Berkeley's handling of the uprising was more visceral than tyrannical.

His failure to counterattack the Indians as speedily as he had in 1644 made him appear cowardly and coldhearted, whereas his insistence upon an antiquated plan of defense aroused the fears of frontier planters, who turned to Nathaniel Bacon as their savior. Declaring Bacon a rebel while calling for new elections to the General Assembly unwisely pitted angry voters and their newfound hero against Berkeley and eroded his leadership. Forgiving Bacon and then permitting him to slip away to his plantation at Curles Neck encouraged the upstart "darling of the people" and swelled his following. Daring Bacon, who was Berkeley's junior by forty years, to settle their accounts with rapiers was more

---

7. Ibid., pp. 163–232.

theatrical than brave, and Bacon's refusal to take the bait made the challenge seem grotesque. After the revolt degenerated into a fight for control of Virginia, the governor stumbled repeatedly as he struggled to defeat Bacon. At length, however, Bacon's own missteps, his sudden death from dysentery, the skill of Berkeley's lieutenants, and the well-timed aid of half a dozen armed merchant ships ended the rebellion.

By the first weeks of 1677 the worst was over, and the remaining rebels surrendered as Berkeley restored order. Except for Bacon, and Richard Lawrence, who reportedly escaped to New England, the ringleaders were the governor's prisoners. Their treasons were capital offences, and they could hope for no clemency from their adversary. He showed them none. They were court martialled one by one, then sentenced and hanged, usually within a matter of a few hours' time. Lesser participants, who might have expected mercy, were executed with equal alacrity. Those who managed to elude the gibbet paid in other ways as Berkeley seized their estates to compensate for their offenses. The seizures quickly surpassed the pillaging the rebels had done, and for a time there seemed to be no end to the governor's vengeance.

No one who knew Berkeley expected him to be gentle with the ex-rebels. In truth, few thought he should, but the fury his visited upon his enemies astonished even the most hardhearted of his followers. Rather than using confiscations and hangings as dreadful examples of the consequences of rebellion, a vengeful Berkeley seemed hell-bent on slaking a fierce taste for blood. He was.

Berkeley despised rebels to the core of his soul. Vile men, they threatened the established order like no other for their wicked deeds struck at society's very vitals. Rebels had murdered his royal master, and they had driven him from office. Bacon's revolt was a bitter cup for Berkeley to taste, especially because he had given so much of himself to

Virginia and its interests. He never saw the flaws in his method of governing nor did he quite comprehend why, after so many years of what he considered mild administration, his people turned on him so suddenly and so completely.

Begging to be replaced was a humiliating admission of his incapacity to govern in the midst of trouble. It galled that the parvenu Bacon should dare to extort by force of arms a general's commission from him, the king's governor and captain-general. He was angered to see the smoldering ashes of Jamestown, the capital he had worked so diligently to build up. The sight of his beloved Green Spring, which looters had laid waste to the tune of some £10,000, was an exquisitely painful sight to him. And, he was greatly embarrassed at being called to London to answer for his conduct. Such injuries to a proud old man could not heal without revenge. His desire for vengeance conflicted with the crown's plans for pacifying Virginia.

News of the rebellion reached England in the summer of 1676, and by fall a thousand redcoats and a three-member commission of inquiry were dispatched to America. Sir John Berry, Herbert Jeffreys, and Francis Moryson, the commissioners, brought orders recalling Berkeley to England, a commission naming Colonel Jeffreys lieutenant governor, and a pardon for all the rebels, save Bacon and his chief subordinates. They arrived in late January 1677, well after there was any need for the soldiers. The commissioners conducted their inquiry, the result of which damned the way Berkeley ruled and blamed him for the upheaval. Sharply critical in tone, their report castigated his suppression of the rebels, and it concluded that Virginia was too independent of the crown's direction.

Understandably, Berkeley clashed with the commissioners almost as soon as their convoy dropped anchor in the James. He resented their presence and their tendency to second-guess him. They faulted him for his lack of compassion.

There were angry words over Berkeley's treatment of the ex-rebels and the extent of the commissioners' right to interfere in the Virginia government. Berkeley refused immediate publication of the royal pardon, which infuriated Berry, Jeffreys, and Moryson too. For months, he declined to accede to Jeffreys, who insisted on displacing him as governor-general. He yielded only when he realized that the highly exasperated colonel might grab him and ship him off to London in chains. Nevertheless, the temptation to have the last word proved irresistible. Berkeley shot off a tart letter to Jeffreys in which he taxed his adversary with an "irresistible desire to rule this country" and forecast that "the inhabitants of this Colony will quickly find a difference between your management and mine." As if to dig the needle deeper, he signed himself "Governor of Virginia til his most Sacred Majestie shall please to determine otherwise of me." Finally, he bade Dame Frances goodbye, boarded his ship, and on 5 May 1677, sailed away.

The crossing went swiftly because he reached England within six weeks of his departure. How different London seemed from his visit in 1661. He was at the peak of his abilities then, and he had ties to the highest court circles. People in government, the king among them, valued his opinions on Virginia. Things were different now. Broken in body and reputation, no one sought him. His allies were all gone. Only one thing mattered, and that was the compulsion to clear himself with Charles II. He petitioned for a royal audience. A response came through Secretary of State Henry Coventry, who sent a note that said the king would speak with him. He never did. On 9 July 1677, Berkeley died in London. Embalmers prepared the corpse. Funeral arrangements were made. The body, wrapped securely in lead foil, was laid to rest in Twickenham on the 13th, not three miles distant from the place of his birth.[8]

I'd like to conclude by musing momentarily on Berkeley's importance. Mine was a fuller, more telling sketch than any of the conventional portraits of Virginia's most controversial governor. I might therefore recommend contemplating Berkeley's character as an end in itself. I won't because I believe his significance lies elsewhere. It is to be found, I think, in the juxtaposition of colonists with colonization, a linkage that invites plain but profound questions about the meaning of the act of settlement. Why did colonists colonize? How did the experience of colonization change their lives and alter their views of themselves? In what ways did the presence of individual immigrants give shape or purpose or quality to the colonies they settled? These queries are pertinent to Berkeley because his career, the events that formed it, and his literary remains are useful for fashioning answers.

Born into a prominent West Country family, Berkeley rose to manhood in Caroline England, expecting to prosper in service to the crown. As a courtier, he won notice for his literary and diplomatic abilities, but he abruptly quit the court for a fresh start Virginia. Thereafter, he stood prominently in the middle of Anglo-American politics, and for more than thirty years tirelessly promoted the colony's interests above all others. Allying with leading planters, he became like them, a Virginian; that is, his colonial experiences defined his identity more than his English roots. He participated in the transformation of Virginia into a land where a privileged minority slipped the restraints of their origins and magnified themselves at the cost of the majority of settlers who were lesser planters, indentured servants, and slaves. Empowering his great planter allies enhanced habits of self-rule that grew into the fundamentals of American politics. Sadly, though,

---

8. Ibid., pp. 232–267.

liberty for the few translated into deprivation for the many. After 1660, Virginia moved to Berkeley's beat, which put it off step with English imperial policy and frustrated Stuart dreams of empire. Bacon's Rebellion not only destroyed the old governor, but it also compelled royal officials to interfere in Virginia affairs as never before. Seizing the moment, they recast the imperial connection on terms more favorable to the crown, and Berkeley's like was never seen again.

This then was the mark of a cavalier who turned himself into a Virginian.

ESSAY 7

COUNCILS, ASSEMBLIES, AND COURTS OF JUDICATURE

The Development of Representative Government in Seventeenth-Century Virginia

My phone rang late one afternoon in the fall of 1993, just as I was about to quit my office for the day. At the other end of the line was Joseph A. Gutierrez, Director of Education at the Jamestown-Yorktown Foundation. He asked if I might be the first presenter in a series of talks he was organizing to mark the three hundred seventy-fifth anniversaries of the arrival of the first Africans in Virginia and the founding of the General Assembly. Without hesitating, I agreed to speak on how the General Assembly matured after 1619, little imagining where that reply would eventually lead me. The lecture, which I gave in January 1994, got a favorable reception from an enthusiastic audience who had gathered at the Yorktown Victory Center. At one point in the question and answer session that followed, someone asked for the title of the book upon which I had based my talk. I replied that no such volume existed, though I quickly added that someone should have written it a long time ago.

I thought no more about that exchange after I returned home. Months later, however, I mentioned it in passing to Mark F. Fernandez who encouraged me to write such a book. His suggestion caught my fancy because I needed a break from my ongoing Berkeley and Louisiana projects.

I was also intrigued by the challenge of pulling disparate bits and pieces of the General Assembly's early history into a coherent, extended treatment of how the oldest representative legislature in the Western Hemisphere worked throughout the seventeenth century. My lecture could readily be fashioned into the basis for just such a study, and I set about turning it into a book.

From an intellectual standpoint, that lecture is important because it represented a marked change in my thinking about seventeenth-century Virginia politics. My earlier writings stressed the importance of a chaotic localism to the near exclusion of any consideration of the General Assembly. That interpretive stance reflected an unquestioning acceptance of traditional explanations as well as a shallow familiarity with sources and means that could illumine relationships between Crown, province, and county in ways that surpassed conventional wisdom. In other words, the talk anticipated something that I was better equipped to write in the 1990s than, say, when I wrote "The Growth of Political Institutions in Seventeenth-Century Virginia" decades earlier, and it became the blueprint for *A Little Parliament: The Virginia General Assembly in the Seventeenth Century*, which the Library of Virginia, in partnership with Jamestown 2007/Jamestown-Yorktown Foundation, published in 2004. Printed here for the first time is a lengthier, more refined iteration of the lecture, which I delivered from notes.

Once I accepted Joe Gutierrez's invitation to speak about how the General Assembly began and how it matured after 1619, I considered how I might frame my remarks, and the more I thought, the more the assignment gave me pause. I say that because the rise of representative government in English North America is a well-known tale from our early history. The Virginia part of that story, especially as it played out during the seventeenth century, is one whose telling is impeded by great losses of the documentary record. Just to make that point, let me cite three examples. Of all the men who sat in the governor-general's chair between 1619 and 1700, papers of a mere four—Sir William Berkeley, Thomas Culpeper, second baron Culpeper of Thoresway, Francis Howard, fifth baron Howard of Effingham, and Francis Nicholson—exist in appreciable quantities, and only those of Berkeley and Effingham are, or will be, available in modern letter press editions.[1] Most of the assembly's journals before 1680 survive no longer, and, aside from one or two pieces, all of its working papers are gone too.[2] Consequently, the test for me was two-fold: to work around yawning gaps in the evidence and to find new variations on a familiar theme.

A number of possibilities ran through my mind before I recalled an item that I had recently transcribed for inclusion in my future edition of Sir William Berkeley's papers. That document, a set of interrogatories that the governor-general received in 1670 from the Council for Foreign Plantations in London, solicited information about conditions in Virginia so that the councillors might advise King Charles II on "the care and management of things relating to his Plantations." I pulled up the text on my computer screen and reread it. One of the queries, and Berkeley's response, immediately caught my eye. "What Councells Assemblies and Courts of Judicature," it asked, "are within your government and of what nature and kinde?" To which Sir William responded,

---

1. Warren M. Billings, ed., *The Papers of Sir William Berkeley, 1605–1677* (Richmond, Va., 2007); Billings, ed., *The Papers of Francis Howard, Baron Howard of Effingham, 1643–1695* (Richmond, Va., 1989).
2. For a discussion of the extant legislative sources, see Billings, *A Little Parliament*, pp. 215–219.

"There is a Governor and Sixteene Councellors who have from his Sacred Majesty a Commission of oyer and Terminer who judge and determine all Causes that are above £15 Sterling. For what is under there are particular Courts in every County which are Twenty in Number. Every yeare at least the Assembly is Called before whome lyes Appeales And this Assembly is Composed of Two burgesses out of Every County. These lay the necessary Taxes as the necessity of the Warr with the Indians or other exigencies require."[3]

Berkeley accurately depicted his government as it existed in 1670. Indeed, few of his contemporaries knew it better than he, and fewer still were those who had done as much as he to give it the form he now described to the king's advisers. Nevertheless, he forbore giving his superiors an explanation of how or why it had attained that shape. Filling in what Berkeley left unfilled therefore afforded me a means of illuminating the subject of my remarks tonight.

Throughout the seventeenth century, contests between monarch and subject over who should rule England led the contestants to inquire deeply into the nature of English polity. Such questioning informed the emergence of representative government in Virginia, though it was not the colonists' sole source of inspiration. An ocean between Jamestown and London, the desire to find private gain in a place free of European restraints, the necessity of raising taxes, settling litigation, and defending Virginia—these perceived imperatives provided an ample environment for learning adequate forms of governance and the uses of power.

The actual beginning of representative government was an unintended consequence of colonizing Virginia. None of the investors in the Virginia Company of London ever imagined that a representative legislature, and all that it might

---

3. Billings, ed., *Berkeley Papers*, pp. 381, 392–397, esp. 393.

imply, would flower on the banks of the James River. In a sense, it is not too much of a stretch to say that self-government merely happened. Hewing to no grand design, a succession of governors-general, councillors of state, and burgesses modified the purposes of the General Assembly and augmented its prerogatives as the need arose, and their solutions of the moment translated into fixed customs. Bit by bit, novice assemblymen grew schooled in the arts and mysteries of governing those they presumed to represent. That quality of happenstance invested the evolution of the General Assembly with a distinctive pattern of growth over the eight decades between its first session and the end of the seventeenth century.

First came a formative period that began in 1619 and lasted until 1639. Provisions for an assembly were among the steps the managers of the Virginia Company employed to salvage their colonial venture. They envisaged this assembly as a resident corporate appendage to dispose of routine administrative, legislative, and judicial matters. The apt analogy would be between that entity and an English town council rather than Parliament, as is commonly thought. Thus, the General Assembly convened for its first session in July 1619.[4]

Before I proceed farther, allow me to clear up a widely held misconception. From its inception the General Assembly never was synonymous with the House of Burgesses, and the two should never be conflated. It always consisted of the governor-general, councillors of state, and burgesses. Actually, in 1619, there was not yet a House of Burgesses. Everyone sat together as a single body in the Jamestown church, and they would remain a unicameral assembly until the 1640s.

---

4. Billings, *A Little Parliament*, pp. 5–13.

Events after 1619 dictated an outcome that differed from investor expectations. The rescue scheme proved overly ambitious, which led to the company's dissolution in 1624. A year later, Charles I proclaimed Virginia a royal dominion. The failure of the company jeopardized the General Assembly because the Crown was in no way obliged legally to retain it. In fact, when Charles commissioned Sir Francis Wyatt as the colony's first royal governor-general, he neglected to instruct Wyatt to call the Assembly on a regular basis. Charles's oversight had more to do with his own ignorance of Virginia and his impending wedding to his queen, the French princess Henrietta Maria, than with his supposed animus towards representative government. No matter his reasons, his mistake threw the Assembly into constitutional limbo. Even so, Wyatt and his successors set precedents for its continuance by regularly summoning it to legislate on such issues as defense, tobacco pricing, or statutory revisions. Then too, leading colonists quickly regarded the Assembly as a congenial means of governance. Others even held it as a bulwark against a revived company that the Crown was thought to have preferred as the way to manage Virginia. Both groups aggressively campaigned, as a memorial to the Privy Council put it, to "retaine the libertie of our generall Assemblie, the which nothing can more conduce to our satisfaction or the publique utilitie."[5]

Such persistence bore fruit at length. In 1639, when Wyatt again returned to Virginia as governor-general, he brought the king's instructions commanding him to convene the General Assembly annually. That mandate finally bestowed Charles's sanction on the body. It also contained an implicit right of the Crown to interfere in the Assembly's

---

5. H.R. McIlwaine, ed., *Journals of the House of Burgesses of Virginia, 1619–1658/59* (Richmond, Va., 1915), p. 27.

business, though that was a seldom-exercised prerogative before 1676.

The General Assembly that Wyatt met upon his return in 1639 differed considerably from the ones over which he had presided a decade earlier. And though it remained unicameral, its continued existence provided ample fodder for claims that certain colonials were of right entitled to share largely in governing Virginia and that the General Assembly was an appropriate mechanism by which they should exercise their dominion over their fellow settlers. As an institution, the Assembly also had become the primary lawgiver for Virginia, and as that responsibility widened, the body had assumed a number of important attributes of representative legislatures as well as the duties of a high court of appeals.[6]

Such modifications opened the way to a second stage of growth that started in the early 1640s and ran for a third of a century thereafter, which also coincided with the Berkeley years. Arguably no other politician did more in those years to fashion the General Assembly into a miniature parliament than did Sir William. Charles I commissioned Berkeley to succeed Wyatt in the summer of 1641. When Sir William landed at Jamestown in February 1642, he had no friends or allies among leading colonials. Quite the contrary, the great men regarded him with suspicion because he had shunted the ever-popular Wyatt aside and because of their uncertainty of his willingness to share power with them. He understood enough about his new constituents to appreciate the necessity of winning a following among them. That realization led him to encourage the burgesses to sit apart from him and the Council of State as a House of Burgesses. And so the General Assembly divided in 1643.[7]

---

6. Billings, *A Little Parliament*, pp. 14–23.
7. Warren M. Billings, *Sir William Berkeley and the Forging of Colonial Virginia* (Baton Rouge, La., 2004), pp. 32–38, 90–93.

The maneuver was one among many Berkeley initiated throughout his long tenure that decentralized political power and led in the direction of bicameralism and greater degrees of self-rule. By the 1660s, therefore, the Assembly had grown into a little parliament that was quite independent of direction from the Crown. It enjoyed most of the customary procedural courtesies, but it also possessed prerogatives that often surpassed those of the Parliament at Westminster. For example, the Assembly met annually, whereas Parliament convened irregularly at the whim of the sovereign. It held considerable sway over the raising and disbursing of public revenues, just as it could create towns, counties, church parishes, and local offices. The Council of State acted as a high court of appeals, and in certain instances the whole General Assembly served as the tribunal of final resort. Whereas the burgesses arrogated a generous measure of the legislative initiative to their house, they also claimed a virtually unrestrained liberty to appoint their clerks and speakers or to discipline unruly members.[8]

To be sure, these and similar changes were not entirely of Berkeley's making. Some resulted from Stuart indifference or to the consequences of the English Civil War and the era of parliamentary rule that came with the overthrow of the British monarchy in 1649. Others can be traced to the assemblymen's particular desires to manage their own affairs with as little interference as possible from governor-general, king, or Parliament, while others still reflected an evolving sophistication of Virginia's polity. Even so, in the 1660s, when the General Assembly achieved its greatest degree of autonomy at any point before the American Revolution, it was far from omnipotent. Its very existence depended upon royal sufferance, which always carried the possibility of the Crown's diminishing its legislative powers. The foundations of

---

8. Billings, *A Little Parliament*, pp. 25–47.

its prerogatives rested on local usages and Berkeley's willing acquiescence instead of ages' old settled habits, written warrantees, or practices akin to those that sustained Parliament. The Crown's response to Bacon's Rebellion revealed the frailty of those supports.

Nathaniel Bacon's uprising threatened English authority in North America as no other event before 1776, and it compelled the Crown to intervene in Virginia affairs in ways it had not since the 1620s. Consequently the General Assembly passed through its third stage of development, which I shall characterize as a time of adjustment to new realities, the upshot of which was a significant diminution of its autonomy.

A different breed of governors-general followed Berkeley after 1676. Sir William always believed that what was best for Virginia was best for Crown and country. His style of governing was to become a Virginian and to make common cause with the great planters with whom he shared his power as he deferred to their sensibilities. His successors would have none of that. King's men all, they were royal clients who shared the later Stuarts' visions of a disciplined, ordered empire, and they were determined to bend the Old Dominion according to the wishes of their masters. Their commitment dovetailed neatly with the calculus of other royal bureaucrats who regarded the General Assembly as far too independent and therefore dangerous to a proper relationship between king and colony. They aimed to diminish the Assembly by pruning all of its privileges that lacked the sanction of English constitutional precedent. First to go was the practice of annual legislative sessions, a change that the Londoners effected merely by strictly instructing Berkeley's successors not to hold "too frequent assemblies." The Assembly conceded its place as the colony's court of last resort, it gave up a large share of its control of the public fisc, and the burgesses lost their right to choose their clerk without gubernatorial intrusion.

These changes provoked an adversarial relationship between governors-general, councillors, and burgesses that continued for the remainder of the colonial period. They ushered in an era of dominance by the Council of State because it was the only branch of the General Assembly that routinely met in its advisory and judicial capacities. The focus of colonial politics also shifted away from localism toward a more provincial and imperial outlook as the assemblymen attempted to check the Crown. And, by century's end, the legislature was increasingly filled by a younger, native-born generation of members. They regarded Virginia as part of an Atlantic imperial community that centered on London, just as they accepted a diminished General Assembly as a reality that distinguished them from their father's political world.[9]

The governors-general, councillors, and burgesses who comprised the General Assembly varied greatly in the talents and skills that they brought to their tasks. That said, they shared some common characteristics, and this is the appropriate point for me to discuss them individually and severally, starting with the chief executives.

Twenty-two men sat in the governor's chair between 1619 and 1700. Ten were councillors who warmed the seat for periods running from a few months to several years as acting governors. The Crown named two—Herbert Jeffreys and Francis Nicholson—as lieutenant governors. Richard Bennett, Edward Digges, Samuel Mathews, Jr., and Berkeley were all elected governors during the Interregnum. Sir George Yeardley, Sir Francis Wyatt, Sir John Harvey, Berkeley, Thomas Culpeper, second baron Culpeper, Francis Howard, fifth baron Howard of Effingham, Sir Edward Andros, and Nicholson each received a commission from the king as "Governor Generall of our Colony of Virginia."[10]

---

9. Ibid., pp. 49–63, 213–215.
10. Billings, ed., *Effingham Papers*, p. 9.

Save for Berkeley, Culpeper, Effingham, and Nicholson, most of the twelve governors-general under the Virginia Company, the parliamentary regime, or the Crown remain elusive figures who are difficult, if not impossible, to know in any depth beyond certain outward characteristics shared by all. They sprang from the upper echelons of British society, which is an unsurprising discovery, given the prevailing view of leadership. As a widely-read sixteenth-century social commentator, Sir Thomas Elyot put the point "Where vertue is in a gentyll man it is commenly mixte with more sufferance, more affibilitie, and myldnesse, then for the more parte it is in a persone rural or of a very base lineage, and when it hapneth otherwise, it is to be accompted loathesome and monstruous." Furthermore, Elyot cautioned, when a leader was "worshypfull, his governance, though it be sharpe, is to the people more tolerable, & they therwith be the less grutch [i.e., complaining] or be less disobedient." Consequently, the twelve were well connected to the court or to Parliament. They all confronted the same task of governing in the interests of Crown and subject. Those interests often deviated as much as they converged, and that divergence compelled them to decide where their greater duty lay, in Jamestown or in London. In Berkeley's case, the Old Dominion commanded the greater measure of his loyalties, whereas it was just the opposite choice for his successors.[11]

A similar full roster of councillors and burgesses is impossibility because of incomplete records. At a minimum, however, I can identify one hundred and forty-eight men who became councillors, and another six hundred twenty-three individuals who were burgesses. I do not propose to mention them all by name because that would soon exhaust your patience.

---

11. Sir Thomas Elyot, *the boke named the Governour, devised by Sr. Thomas Elyot, knight* (London, 1531), fols. 83–98, 106–106; Billings, *A Little Parliament*, pp. 65–87.

The men who got to be councillors or burgesses were of a different sort than the governors-general. They sprang from that much-storied lot of immigrants who streamed into the colony in ever increasing numbers after 1619 and who belonged to a variegated social class that Stuart Britons laconically styled "the middling sort." Standing above poverty, but below greatness, some were of genteel origins, although the predominant background was mercantile. A majority had little more formal education beyond grammar schooling or an apprenticeship, but others could barely read let alone write the vernacular tongue, and few, if any, sat in Parliament or held office in England. Ties of blood and affinities of interest related them one to another. Some—the Wests, Mathewses, Yeardleys, Willoughbys, for example—established themselves in Company period and sustained their families through succeeding generations into the eighteenth century and beyond. Others—the Carters, Lees, Ludwells, Corbins, Custises, Byrds, to mention an obvious few—settled during the time of the great migration from the 1620s to the 1660s and amassed considerable wealth in land, tobacco, overseas trade, and laborers as they pushed their way to the head of Virginia society, where they remained well after the Revolution.[12]

For the most part, all started out as political neophytes. That quality of being novices raises the intriguing question of how they assumed places of leadership. Let me suggest an explanation.

Lack of formal education and political experience did not equal profound ignorance of British polity. The idea of governance—that is, who ruled and by what warrant—was well understood by any Briton. Everyone knew that

---

12. Billings, *A Little Parliament*, pp. 87–115, 247–253. See also Emory G. Evans, *A "Topping People": The Rise and Decline of Virginia's Old Elite, 1680–1790* (Charlottesville, Va., 2009).

government differentiated the powerless from the powerful; it cherished good subjects and chastised bad ones; its rulers ordered the goings and comings of civilized society; and its magistrates enjoyed the deference of the ruled. This knowledge formed, if you will, part of a cultural genetic coding that all English settlers carried with them across the Atlantic.

Virginia represented a place of new beginnings where the privileged few could pursue their dreams of aggrandizement by exploiting others. Even freedom had its limits. Without the restraints of law, there could be neither order, nor control, nor the possibility of fulfillment. If Virginia were to be rendered civil, then it must be bound by rules. Hence, the Virginia Company of London introduced the General Assembly as a means of governing its colony. Trouble was nothing worked as planned. The company bankrupted, the Crown took over, but left the settlers to fend for themselves and after 1624 the General Assembly became the principal source of law for the better part of fifty years.

Situated thus, assemblymen of necessity set about imposing order where they thought none existed. Their quest for authority led them to experiment, and they fell back upon their cultural traditions, drawing from them what they knew, or thought they knew, about English law and politics. Much of what they took they gleaned from that vast body of legal literature that circulated on both sides of the Atlantic and manuals such as Henry Elsynge's *Ancient Method and Manner of Holding Parliaments in England* or William Hakewill's *Modus tenendi Paraliamentum, Or the Old Manner of Holding Parliaments in England*, which entered circulation around the time of the Civil War. Ultimately, they gauged their handiwork by the measure of utility. What worked counted for more than strict adherence to ancient tradition. Trial and error afforded invaluable instruction in the arts and mysteries of self-governance. Sadly, though, such testing resulted in perversely clever adaptations, such as chattel slavery, whose malign consequences are with us still.[13]

How did the respective members of the General Assembly gain their places? Until its dissolution, the Virginia Company designated the governor-general, and after 1624, he was a Crown appointee, except during the Interregnum when the House of Burgesses elected him. Each new governor-general received written warrant, signed and sealed by the monarch, which was known as a commission. A commission set forth the governor-general's authority in broad terms, whereas he received more specific mandates for how he should exercise those powers in another document, his instructions, which the Crown might supplement from time to time. There was no set term of office. Instead, an incumbent remained at the royal pleasure or until death or retirement carried him off.[14]

A council seat was the highest office a colonial politician could gain, which made it the uttermost political achievement for those Virginians who gained one of the chairs Generally, councillors were large land holders with long-time political experience in local government and service in the House of Burgesses. Typically, they tended to live in the counties nearest to Jamestown because that proximity readily assured the presence of a quorum at council meetings. Rather than receiving individual commissions, councillors were listed by name and order of seniority in the governor's commission, and they held office for life, though after Bacon's Rebellion, the Crown dismissed several recalcitrant ones for their unrelenting opposition to its policies. Whenever vacancies occurred, the governor-general nominated replacements, and the Crown usually confirmed his appointments.

---

13. Billings, *A Little Parliament*, pp. 131–139, 256–258.
14. Ibid., passim.

Between 1619 and 1776, a place among the burgesses was the only elective political office in Virginia, and so I ought to comment on electoral practices in the seventeenth century before I say anything about the members themselves. First off, a word about members who came to be styled "burgesses" is in order. Burgesses sat for boroughs, cities and towns, in the House of Commons, and in 1618 the Virginia Company rearranged the colony into a series of boroughs and styled representatives from those jurisdictions "burgesses." The name stuck, and it remained in use until 1776.

Early on, however, burgesses spoke for a hodge-podge of constituencies—boroughs, private plantations, church parishes, and any other precinct where electors agreed to compensate a representative. After the General Assembly instituted the county court system of local government in the 1630s, the counties emerged as units of representation and the political base of Virginia's great planter elite. That transformation was completed in the1670s, by which time the Assembly restricted representation to the counties and to Jamestown, reduced the number of burgesses to two per county, and exacted stiff fines from any county where voters failed to elect the requisite two members.[15]

The notable characteristic about these arrangements was the tying of representation to a particular group of voters who lived in a specific geographic location. Unwittingly born of distinctive colonial conditions, the practice gave rise to a later American conception of a representative as someone who serves first and foremost the interests of the voters who elected her or him. That understanding contrasted with the British view, which held that the constituencies of members

---

15. William Waller Hening, comp., *The Statutes at Large; Being a Collection of All the Laws of Virginia, from the First Session of the Legislature, in the Year 1619* (Richmond, 1809–1823), 2: 20, 272–273, 282–283.

in the House of Commons comprised the whole body politic, not merely those voters who sent them to Westminster.

I should caution you to banish from your mind everything you know about the conduct of modern elections because most of what we take for granted was non-existent back then. The idea of elections contested by organized political parties was completely foreign, as were party platforms, campaign rallies, stump speeches, or media advertisements. Women cast no votes. Conversely, Governor-General Sir George Yeardley extended the franchise to all adult free white males in 1619, which made the franchise in Virginia more generous than in Great Britain, and so it remained for six decades. Declaring that the "lawes of England grant a voice . . . only to such as by their estates real or personall have interest enough to tye them to the endeavour of the publique good" the General Assembly undercut the privilege in 1670 by restricting the vote to landowners and householder. Six years later, Sir William Berkeley suspended the statute as a ploy to erode the popularity of Nathaniel Bacon, but it was revived on the direct order of Charles II after Bacon's Rebellion, and the right to vote remained tied to property until the Virginia constitution of 1851 adopted universal white male suffrage.[16]

A right to vote did not confer a concomitant liberty to run for the House of Burgesses. Burgesses to a man were all substantial landowners, they were related to one another, and they were invariably justices of the peace, at least until the 1680s when generational changes and a shifting away from localism began to alter the political landscape. What determined which members of the county courts actually sat in the House is not readily apparent. Senior justices rarely, if ever, stood for election, and neither did sheriffs. Being a burgess was not an especially attractive occupation. Members

---

16. Ibid., 280; Billings, ed., *The Berkeley Papers*, pp. 520–521.

received no compensation beyond expenses, and their access to lucrative provincial offices was far fewer than for councillors. Travel to Jamestown and sitting through sessions was unappealing too. Moreover, no burgess looked upon politics in the same way as modern politicians, who regard public life as their profession and source of livelihood. And so incumbents came and went frequently, though some tarried for years on end. Perhaps Lemuel Mason who represented Lower Norfolk County was the most notable example of a long-timer. First elected in 1654, he sat continuously for the next forty years.

Burgesses did not serve fixed terms, and elections did not always precede Assembly sessions. The concepts of rotation in office and regular elections were still in their infancy on both sides of the Atlantic. Thus, if a governor-general happened to have an especially congenial group of burgesses, he could extend the life of an Assembly by proroguing it— that is recessing it to a date certain. The notable example of this practice was the General Assembly that lasted from March 1661 to May 1676. Even in that instance, though, there were elections whenever retirements or death created vacancies.[17]

An election could not occur until the governor-general sent an authorizing writ to every sheriff across Virginia. A writ usually went forth as much as forty days ahead of a session and was read out at court, in church, or any other place of public gathering. It announced when the General Assembly would convene and commanded the sheriff to round up the electors to cast their votes. In turn, the sheriff set the day of the poll and conducted the voting, which was done orally. Then he recorded the winner's name on the back

---

17. Billings, *A Little Parliament*, pp. 104–114.

of the writ, which he signed and sent to Jamestown as proof that he had done his duty.[18]

Burgesses, councillors, and the governor-general gathered on the appointed day, so let me show a snapshot of how the General Assembly did its business. Sessions customarily lasted no more than three weeks. As soon as everyone got to town, the burgesses organized their house. They took an oath that averred their allegiance to the Crown and another that affirmed their acceptance of the king as head of the Church of England. Then the members nominated their Speaker before they joined with their council colleagues to listen to the rector of James City Parish, or some other priest, invoke divine guidance in their debate. Afterwards, everyone gathered in the council chamber to hear the governor-general give an address that denoted the formal opening of the session. His remarks, which were akin to a modern State of the Commonwealth or State of the Union speech, were fundamental to the legislative process in that they set forth his expectations or orders from London. Crafted by a clever politician such as Berkeley, or an insistent one like Effingham, the opening address usually ensured the desired result.

Burgesses and councillors retired to their respective chambers, where resolutions were introduced, debated, amended, or rejected, and adopted into statute law. Certain house structures and procedures were in place well before the burgesses existed as a separate body. Secretary John Pory, a sometime member of the House of Commons, can be credited for instructing his colleagues in the General Assembly of 1619 about legislative customs. Their successors built on Pory's lessons, and by mid-century procedural rules in the Assembly bore close similarity to those that governed

---

18. Warren M. Billings, ed., *The Papers of Francis Howard, Baron Howard of Effingham, 1643–1695* (Richmond, Va., 1989), p. 66.

Parliament. House committees originated in 1619 too. They were employed on an ad hoc basis at first, but after the Assembly divided several became permanent fixtures for vetting bills.

A bill passed through the House after it received three readings. The first was a formality in the sense that the clerk introduced it for consideration by reciting it aloud for the members' benefit. Then the Speaker invited discussion or assigned it to a committee, as he deemed appropriate. Following modification on the floor or in committee, the clerk read the bill a second time. Then the clerk reduced the approved version to a fair text and it received its third reading. If at that point the Speaker saw fit, he might allow additional debate, but because a third reading was equivalent to passage, he rarely permitted further deliberation.

Once the House adopted the bill it went up to the councillors, who disposed of it in one of three ways: they rejected it, they modified it, or they accepted it as received. Because its records have not survived in great quantities, we know little about how the Council worked in its legislative capacity so its procedures lie in the realm of speculation. Given its small size, it probably did not resort to a committee structure akin to that of the House of Burgesses. Absent an equivalent great officer of state no one played the part of the Lord Chancellor who was Speaker of the House of Lords in England. Instead, the governor-general presided. The only certainty is that councillors had to concur before approving a measure and sending it to the burgesses for their agreement.

No bill became law unless the governor-general agreed to it. Unlike a modern governor of Virginia, he enjoyed what amounted to a double veto. Being president of the Council gave him a vote in legislative deliberations. His opposition usually stopped passage of a measure, but if his colleagues outvoted him, he could withhold his signature, thereby preventing a bill from becoming law. So far as I am aware, Sir

William Berkeley never exercised these prerogatives, though his successors did, which contributed to the adversarial relationship between chief executives that marked the post-Berkeley era. In any event, once all of the bills were passed, scribes engrossed a fair text of the acts, which the governor-general and the Speaker signed. That done, councillors and burgesses returned home to await a call to assemble on another day.[19]

Councils, Assemblies, and Courts of Judicature had not come to the Old Dominion all at once. Each was an unintended consequence of settlement. They had all grown by fits and starts, and as they did, the habits of self-rule took on peculiarly Virginia twists by 1700. Ultimately, they made a distinctive cord in the fabric of America's political culture.

---

19. Billings, *A Little Parliament*, pp. 8–10, 173–191.

ESSAY 8

THE LAW OF SERVANTS AND SLAVES IN SEVENTEENTH-CENTURY VIRGINIA

Servitude and slavery were hardly unknown to Stuart Britons. Countless numbers of them traced their fortunes to royal service or to apprenticeships. Their Bible was replete with stories of good slaves and bad. Wanderers among them sometimes experienced actual enslavement as an accident of piracy or war. Bound labor in early Virginia resembled those precursors, but it was governed by a decidedly different set of regulations that diverged meaningfully from its antecedents. Those differences emerged slowly over the seventeenth century as a distinctive body of statutory and case law.

I sketched several features of the colony's labor law in a small piece—"The Cases of Fernando and Elizabeth Key: A Note on the Status of Blacks in Seventeenth-Century Virginia"—that appeared in the July 1973 number of the *William and Mary Quarterly*, where I also stated an intention to look more deeply into the subject. That project remained wishful thinking for more than a decade until an invitation to contribute to a conference on early American law at the New-York Historical Society occasioned the spoken version of this essay. Members of the audience urged me to revise that text for publication, but I set it aside owing to other commitments. It grew dusty on the shelf for a number of years before I took it down, dusted it off, and made extensive changes that were based upon additional research and the helpful comments from a number of readers. That reworked rendition appeared as "The Law of Servants and Slaves in Colonial Virginia in the *Virginia Magazine of History and Biography*, 99 (1991): 45–63 and is reprinted here with the kind permission of the editor.

Servants and slaves were a peculiar species of property that figured prominently in the settlement of Virginia. They have long been the subjects of intense inquiry, but there are only a few sustained analyses of how the law pertaining to bondsmen came to be woven into the legal fabric of colonial Virginia.[1] That shortcoming has prevented recognition of the

---

1. The literature on servants and slaves in seventeenth-century Virginia is a body of voluminous proportions. For a representative sample, see Philip Alexander Bruce, *Economic History of Virginia in the Seventeenth Century, An Inquiry into the Material Condition of the People, Based upon Original and Contemporaneous Records* (New York and London, 1896), 1: chap. 9; 2: chaps. 10–11; James Curtis Ballagh, *White Servitude in the Colony of Virginia: A Study of the System of Indentured Labor in the American Colonies*, The Johns Hopkins University Studies in Historical and Political Science, ser. 13, nos. 6, 7 (Baltimore, Md., 1895); James Curtis Ballagh, *A History of Slavery in Virginia* (Baltimore, New York, and London, 1902); Richard Brandon Morris, *Government and Labor in Early America* (New York, 1946); Abbot Emerson Smith, *Colonists in Bondage: White Servitude and Convict Labor in America, 1607–1776* (Chapel Hill, N.C., 1947); Wesley Frank Craven, *White, Red, and Black: The Seventeenth-Century Virginian* (Charlottesville, Va., 1971); Edmund S. Morgan, *American Slavery, American Freedom: The Ordeal of Colonial Virginia* (New York, 1975); T. H. Breen and Stephen Innes, *"Myne Owne Ground": Race and Freedom on Virginia's Eastern Shore, 1640–1676* (New York and Oxford, 1980); Carl N. Degler, "Slavery and the Genesis of American Race Prejudice," *Comparative Studies in Society and History*, 2 (1960): 49–66; Oscar Handlin and Mary F. Handlin, "Origins of the Southern Labor System," *William and Mary Quarterly*, 3d ser., 7 (1950): 199–222; Winthrop D. Jordan, 'Modern Tensions and the Origins of

development of laws that departed significantly from English common law. It has also clouded the perception of how the legalization of servitude in Virginia influenced the definition of slavery. Preoccupation with the roots of modern racism obscures attitudes other than prejudice that allowed Englishmen to find in chattel slavery solutions to their problems with labor and social control. Although it is true that servitude and slavery both sprang up piecemeal, the mechanics of their legitimation reveal more calculation than is implicit in the characterization of the enslavement of black Virginians as an "unthinking decision."[2]

Mystery cloaks the precise origins of indentured servitude; nevertheless, certain details regarding its beginning are clear enough. Seventeenth-century Englishmen were no strangers to the idea of service, which was anchored deeply in

---

American Slavery," *Journal of Southern History*, 28 (1962): 18–30; David Galenson, *White Servitude in Colonial America: An Economic Analysis* (Cambridge, London, and New York, 1981); James Horn, "Servant Emigration to the Chesapeake in the Seventeenth Century," in Thad W. Tate and David L. Ammerman, eds., *The Chesapeake in the Seventeenth Century: Essays on Anglo-American Society* (Chapel Hill, N.C., 1979), pp. 51–96; Russell R. Menard, "British Migration to the Chesapeake Colonies in the Seventeenth Century," in Lois Green Carr, Philip D. Morgan, and Jean B. Russo, eds., *Colonial Chesapeake Society* (Chapel Hill, N.C., and London, 1988), pp. 99–132. Paul C Palmer, "Servant into Slave: The Evolution of the Legal Status of the Negro Laborer in Colonial Virginia," *The South Atlantic Quarterly*, 65 (1966): 355–70, and chapter 1 of A. Leon Higginbotham, *In the Matter of Color: Race and the American Legal Process, The Colonial Period* (New York and Oxford, 1978) are recent efforts to study the legalization of slavery. Palmer's article is suggestive, but Higginbotham's treatment is marred by so many factual errors and misconceptions that its worth is greatly diminished.

2. Winthrop D. Jordan, *White Over Black: American Attitudes Toward the Negro, 1550–1812* (Chapel Hill, N.C., 1968), chap. 2.

their feudal past.³ Untold numbers of Englishmen served in the households of the mighty, while others were bound to labor in recompense for their misdeeds. By 1607, a more common type of servitude was apprenticeship—an arrangement whereby a young man contracted with a craftsman to learn a skilled trade. Apprenticeship also had its roots in the Middle Ages, having been first devised by members of the craft guilds to control competition as well as to assure the proper training of craftsmen. All of that changed after 1563, when Parliament enacted the Statute of Artificers, the purpose of which was to impose a national system of apprenticeship upon all who would enter industrial occupations.[4]

Under the law, apprentices and household servants were bound to their masters by an instrument that Stuart Englishmen rather loosely styled an "indenture." More exactly, an indenture was a form of deed known as a "covenant merely personal," a written "consent of two, or more, to one thing, to give somewhat . . . or to serve."[5] The apprentice or the servant thus contracted with a master for a specific period of service, during which he would be maintained while he was being trained. Upon the completion of his service, he was given a written release, which

---

3. Sir Edward Coke, *The First Part of the Institutes of the Laws of England* . . . (6th ed.; London, 1664), fols. 74, 116; Sir John Fortescue, *A Learned Commendation of the Politique Lawes of England* . . . (London, 1567), fol. 101.

4. Sir Thomas Smith, *De Republica Anglorum. The Maner of Governement or policie of the Realme of England* . . . (London, 1583), pp. 107–115; 5 Eliz. I, 4, in Ferdinando Pulton, *An Abstract of all the Penall Statutes Which be Generall, In Force and in Use* . . . (London, 1592), fols. 178–183. The statute was subsequently amplified in 1 Jas. I, c. 6, in Edmund Wingate, *An Exact Abridgement of all the Statutes in Force and Use* . . . (London, 1670), p. 328.

5. John Cowell, *A Law Dictionary: or the Interpreter of Words and Terms Used Either in the Common or Statute Laws of Great Britain* . . . (London, 1727) (originally published at Cambridge in 1607 as The Interpreter), under "covenant" and "apprentice."

constituted legal proof of his having satisfied the conditions of his indenture. Indenturing meant the loss of personal freedom in that apprentices were obliged to do their masters bidding and not to marry and that their contracts might be sold or willed to others. The latter possibility temporarily translated would-be craftsmen into chattels that might be disposed like any other sort of personal belonging. If either party broke the specific provisions of the covenant, the other had recourse in the courts. Well before the passage of the Statute of Artificers, there was a considerable body of legislation and case law that enforced these contractual arrangements. Among other things, a master could punish an unruly servant and seek restitution from a bondsman who pilfered or ran off. An apprentice could turn to judicial authorities for protection from an abusive master and might be released from the service of one who could not furnish proper support, maintenance, or training.[6]

These customs had ready application to the settlement and subsequent development of Virginia. The first settlers covenanted with the Virginia Company of London to trade their labor for shares in the venture's anticipated profits. Within a decade of settlement, company officials modified the terms of their offer. In order to attract settlers, they began promising land in return for labor, and that change, coupled with the success of John Rolfe's experiments with raising West Indian tobacco, revolutionized the Virginia venture.[7]

Conversion from a colony built along military lines to one modeled on a more traditional social pattern quickly attracted grasping settlers who saw in land and labor the way to power,

---

6. Michael Dalton, *The Countrey Justice: Containing the Practice of Justices of the Peace out of their Sessions* . . . (London, 1677), chap. 58, "Laborers."

7. Susan Myra Kingsbury, ed., *The Records of the Virginia Company of London* (4 vols.; Washington, D.C., 1906–1935), 3: 314; Ralph Hamor, *A Trve Discovrse of the Present Estate of Virginia* . . . (London, 1615), p. 24.

position, and wealth. Success in realizing those objectives depended upon recruiting laborers in England, providing them the means of getting to the colony, and finding a way of legally holding them to a period of service. With a little modification, apprenticeship could be tailored to suit each of those needs.

Such alterations occurred in practice well before 1619, when the customs of indentured servitude began to be fixed in written law. The first General Assembly required the recording of indentures as a way to enforce labor contracts, to prevent double dealing, and to stop servants from marrying in secret.[8] Thereafter, a principal concern of subsequent Assemblies was the regulation of servitude, and to that end the legislators crafted numerous statutes. Such legislation fell into four broad categories: one defined terms of the labor contract, another aimed at restraining what the legislators perceived as the servants' vicious habits, a third established the masters' property rights, and the last afforded minimal protections to the servants. Collectively those acts provide an insight into the process of legalization and certain of the lawmakers' cultural assumptions about labor and laborers.

The Assembly's concern in defining contractual obligations was to prevent bondsmen from serving shorter terms than was considered just compensation for the expenses of their passage and their keep. In the early days some prospective servants landed in the colony before becoming indentured. They then negotiated a contract with a planter, who in turn compensated the shipper for his expenses in transporting the servants. Starting in the 1620s the number of such laborers increased, and their presence raised the issue of what length of service could be legally

---

8. H. R. McIlwaine, ed., *Journals of the House of Burgesses of Virginia, 1619–1658/59* (Richmond, Va., 1915), pp. 13–14.

required of them. As more servants arrived without indentures the question became more contentious, causing legislators to search for a solution to a touchy problem. Assemblymen who were aware of the English law found the precedents not to their liking. They knew the accepted rule of common law held, in Sir Edward Coke's words, that "if a man shall retain a servant, without expressing any time, the law shall construe it to be for a year."[9] Plainly, if that rule were left to stand in Virginia, it would undermine labor relations because it would eliminate any incentive for servants to contract for long-term service. Therefore, because "divers controversies [had] risen between masters and servants being brought into the colony without indentures or covenants," the General Assembly moved to clarify the status of unindentured servants in March 1642/43. It specified terms that varied according to the servants' ages: adults (those twenty and older) served four years, while adolescents (those between the ages of twelve and twenty) and children could be held five and seven years, respectively.[10] The statute proved unworkable, and it was altered in March 1657/58. One evident difficulty, determining servants' ages, was resolved by allowing the justices of the peace to decide how old individual servants were. Once age was determined, the new law provided that anyone over sixteen would be bound for four years but that children would serve until they reached the age of twenty-one.[11] Four years later, the Assembly further modified the law. It obligated adult laborers for five years, but children under fifteen would remain in service "untill they be

---

9. Coke, *First Part of the Institutes*, fol. 42b; Dalton, *The Countrey Justice*, pp. 129–130.
10. William Waller Hening, ed., *The Statutes at Large; Being a Collection of all the Laws of Virginia* . . . (13 vols.; Richmond, Philadelphia, and New York, 1809–1823), 1: 257.
11. Ibid., pp. 441–442.

fower and twenty yeares old, that being the time lymitted by the laws of England."[12]

The General Assembly tried to solve this matter legislatively, but it never drafted a model indenture to spell out the precise requirements of the master-servant relationship. One of the earliest indentures on record—the agreement struck in 1619 between Robert Coopy and the proprietors of Berkeley Hundred—demonstrates why it did not. Such a model was unnecessary. Coopy's indenture was a variation on the traditional wording of a covenant merely personal.[13] Suitable examples were readily accessible in one of the numerous clerks' manuals known to Englishmen on both sides of the Atlantic, any of which could easily be tailored to the specific needs of individual contractors.[14] Printed copies of indentures akin to Coopy's were generally available by 1636, and these were also derivative. Furthermore, the numerous forms of the covenant merely personal were flexible enough to encompass whatever conditions someone might negotiate, which explains why extant indentures vary so widely in their wording and in their substance.[15]

Another reason colonial lawmakers showed little disposition to draft a statutory model indenture related to how laborers were procured. Planters often took servants with them when they went out to Virginia to settle, but once there few returned to England to recruit additional workers. Prospective bondsmen bargained with an English merchant, a planter's agent, or a ship captain, and upon arrival in the

---

12. Ibid., 2: 113–114.
13. Kingsbury, ed., *Records of the Virginia Company*, 3: 210–211.
14. For example, *The Compleat Clerk, Containing the Best Forms of all sorts of Presidents, for Conveyances & Assurances; And other Instruments now in Use and Practice* . . . (5th ed.; London, 1683), pp. 466–608; Smith, *Colonists in Bondage*, p. 17.
15. Northampton County Order Book, 1640–1645, ff. 94, 150; Middlesex County Order Book, 1680–1694, p. 343.

colony their indentures were sold at dockside. That was a satisfactory arrangement, and there was little necessity for the legislators to amend it. This unwillingness to tinker for tinkering's sake or from any tender regard for the servants reveals the pragmatism and self-interest that marked the way in which English law was refashioned in Virginia. Those characteristics are abundantly evident in the laws designed to curb what planters perceived as the servants' dangerous tendencies.

Indentured servitude taxed laborer, master, and legislator alike. Planters could be brutal, and, given Virginia's shortage of women, they sometimes subjected their maidservants to sexual abuse. Even under the best of conditions, tobacco farming was an arduous routine. The work was unceasing, seldom relieved by amusement or relaxation, and shelter or provisions were frequently lacking. Loneliness broke the spirit, work weakened the body, disease contributed to ill health, and many servants died before they fulfilled their indentures.

Servants responded to their lot in different ways. Some ran off at the first opportunity; others stole from their owners or attacked them; still others found momentary solace in drink or casual sexual liaisons. Planters viewed such behavior as a clear and constant danger to an orderly society and to their own economic well-being. And why not? As a group, the servile population accounted for half of Virginia's settlers. It was young, mostly male, resentful of authority, and difficult to manage in a colony where the ruling elite possessed few means to make any of the inhabitants answer for their conduct. Collectively, those laborers constituted a class to which the planters were tightly bound. Runaways, pilferers, bastard bearers, and the unruly diminished their masters' investments, just as such miscreants caused losses of time that, in the planters' minds, might be put to profitable uses. Masters therefore looked to the General Assembly for relief. Assemblymen required little prodding to action, because they were themselves among the colony's largest employers of servant laborers.

The response of the Assembly took several forms. To address the perennial trouble with runaways, they enacted a series of statutes requiring such punishments as added service, whippings, hair croppings, or, in the instance of habitual offenders, brandings, which were all variations on English vagrancy laws.[16] They adapted traditional laws in their effort to curb sexual appetites. Fornicators were liable to public penance, whipping, and an extra six months of service. Women servants who bore bastards were to be lashed and were to have their terms extended by two years. If known, the fathers were treated more kindly: regardless of their status, such men were fined and forced to bear the expense of their children's rearing. For men servants, these penalties usually translated into an additional period of servitude.[17] Several laws attempted to prevent secret marriages that were supposedly the cause of servants "neglecting their works and often perloyning their masters goods and provisions," while others were intended to check "Ill disposed persons [who] did secretlye and covertlye trade, and truck" with and hire laborers. Bondsmen who stole or committed violent acts were also subject to the colony's criminal laws.[18]

Although the deterrent value of these statutes is debatable, such legislation reinforced the customary property rights of the masters by throwing the weight of colonial legal authority behind them. Servants constituted an important

---

16. Hening, ed., *The Statutes at Large*, 1: 253–255, 401, 483, 517–518, 539–450; 2: 21, 26, 116–117, 187–188, 239, 266, 273–274, 277–279, 283–284, 299–300; 3: 12, 28–29.
17. Ibid., 1: 240, 253, 310, 433, 438–439, 551–552; 2: 114–115, 167, 168, 170; 3: 74, 139.
18. Ibid., 2: 114; 1:252-253, 438; Warren M. Billings, ed., "Some Acts Not in Hening's *Statutes*: The Acts of Assembly, April 1652, November 1652, and July 1653," *Virginia Magazine of History and Biography*, 83 (1975): 47.

element of their owners' property. Consequently, they were exchanged as commodities, were used as security in debt proceedings, and frequently formed portions of marriage settlements or inheritances. As was true of apprentices in England, servants were deemed "chattels personal," meaning there was no legal distinction between them and clothing or furnishings or livestock. That being so, traditional English regulations governing the uses of personal possessions sufficed in the colony with little or no modification by the General Assembly.[19]

Thus did the planters acquire the lawful means to control a valuable, albeit unruly, class of colonists. Brute force became a principal element in the definition of the law of servants. Nevertheless, the legislators were at some pains to minimize some of the law's harder features. Compelling shippers to furnish prospective laborers with adequate food and clothing eased the rigors of passage to Virginia and helped assure the landing of healthy servants.[20] Requiring the recordation of indentures and servants' ages guarded against the unscrupulous owner who might try to extend the time of bondage. Regulating the conditions under which masters and servants might negotiate additional contracts lessened the owners' "averitious, temper and unreasonable desire."[21] Outlawing "barbarous usage" and insisting upon the provision of "competent dyett, clothing and lodging" assured some measure of fair treatment.[22] Giving servants access to the courts, which was sanctioned by statute in the early 1640s, allowed them a means to air complaints of misuse.[23] Furnishing the custom of the country—that is, freedom dues

---

19. Northampton County Order Book, 1640–1645, ff. 26, 176, 225.
20. Hening, ed., *The Statutes at Large*, 2: 129.
21. Ibid., p. 388.
22. Ibid., pp. 117, 118.
23. Ibid., 1: 255, 440, 2: 118.

in the form of corn, clothing, and occasionally land—seemed to augur the promise of a start to those who served out their indentures.[24]

These adaptations of traditional servants' rights softened the harshness of indentured servitude, it is true, but such modifications were not born of the assemblymen's kinder instincts. Instead, they demonstrated a hardheaded reaction to practical realities. The colony had acquired a justly deserved reputation as a deathtrap during the years of the Virginia Company. Promoters, try as they might, never entirely shook that image with their portrayals of Virginia as a fabulous new Eden.[25] Planters understood that one way of diminishing the unfavorable reputation still further lay in making servitude seem, on paper at least, much like apprenticeship. In the end, though, whatever the safeguards, the protection would be only as good as the men who enforced the laws guaranteeing it.

The quality of that enforcement becomes easier to assess once the county court system and its records came into

---

24. These freedom dues were not specifically set in the statutes until the Assembly adopted the revision of 1705 (ibid., 3: 451), though they were often implied in earlier statutes; for example, ibid., 2: 388. Whether a servant was entitled to a tract of land as the custom of the country was also not a matter of settled law. His receiving any land usually depended upon his ability to negotiate a provision for acreage into his indenture. Eventually the crown took some notice of the matter. Governor Effingham's instructions required that every servant who completed his time receive fifty acres of land ("Instructions for Our Right Trusty and well-beloved Francis Lord Howard of Effingham . . . ," in Warren M. Billings, ed., *The Papers of Francis Howard, Baron Howard of Effingham, 1643–1695* [Richmond, 1989], p. 27).

25. Samuel Purchas, *Purchas His Pilgrims; or, Relations of the World and the Religions Observed in All Ages . . . in Foure Parts . . .* (London, 1613), pp. 631–32 (quoted in Warren M. Billings, ed., *The Old Dominion in the Seventeenth Century: A Documentary History of Virginia, 1606–1700* [rev. ed., Chapel Hill, N.C., 2007], pp. 371–372); Sir William Berkeley, *A Discourse and View of Virginia* (London, 1662), pp. 1–5.

existence after 1634. Those records bear vivid witness to a dreary litany of privation, overwork, beatings, harassment, and other abuses, in addition to indications of dockets clogged by cases of runaways, bastard bearings, petty thievery, and other infractions.[26] Such evidence shows the justices' disposition to hear a myriad of servants' complaints.[27] Within limits, the willingness to entertain such suits is noteworthy, but the justices were not in the habit of searching for abuses wherever they existed. Lodging the complaint and the burden of proof lay with the servant, and if he failed to make his case, he bore the brunt of his failure. For this reason, the number of instances in which such suits are recorded is only a partial measure of how the local magistrates worked to protect bondsmen because there is no way to calculate the abuses that went unreported.

The general impression that emerges from examining the county records, however casually, is one of a pitiless labor system, designed to favor the masters, and by them punitively enforced. Such a search also reveals the desire by the planters to profit handsomely upon the backs of others, and it indicates a callous neglect of the least fortunate of settlers. Could it have been otherwise? Sadly, the answer to that question is no. Indentured servitude was a creature of the masters. Moreover, the masters' eagerness to extract the last ounce of work from their laborers reflected the inequities in English society, which colonists accepted unquestioningly as the normal course of things. Few, poor or rich, bound or free, would have rejected the injunctions of the anonymous

---

26. Lower Norfolk County Order Book, 1646–1651, fol. 120; Accomack County Order Book, 1663–1666, fol. 67; Charles City County Order Book, 1655–1665, p. 53; Accomack County Deeds, Wills, and Inventories, 1678–1690, ff. 389–390; Middlesex County Order Book, 1680–1694, pp. 309–310.

27. Northampton County Order Book, 1632–1640, p. 2; Accomack County Order Book, 1678–1682/83, p. 260.

English author of *The Whole Duty of Man* who counseled servants to serve obediently, faithfully, diligently, and submissively, while he cautioned masters to be just and moderate and to set good examples.[28] Furthermore, indentured servitude differed from its model. It was not intended to teach skilled crafts; rather, its purpose was to get footloose young Englishmen to Virginia and then to turn them into submissive agricultural laborers. That done, once the servants had finished their time, they were at liberty to shift for themselves—providing they had lived through the perils of their indentures.

The steps toward transforming apprenticeship into indentured servitude were often without precedent. Accordingly, the legislators set the law of servants into the statutes, and that action provided one way in which indentured servitude influenced the legalization of slavery. To the extent that statutes rendered bondsmen into chattels, to that degree the law of servants also prefigured the definition of slaves as things. Another of servitude's effects was less direct. By its very nature, servitude caused a continual turnover in workers, and planters were constantly concerned with replenishing their labor force. Procurement was a lengthy and risky undertaking. It required time, money, and contacts, things that planters did not always have. Shippers regularly lost cargoes to the hazards of the sea, servants did not always withstand the effects of the crossing, and the supply was occasionally disrupted by political changes at home or by foreign wars. In time, planters came to see in slavery a solution to these difficulties as well as a means of lessening their vexations with a troublesome class of their own countrymen.

---

28. [Richard Allestree?], *The Whole Duty of Man, Laid Down in a Plain and Familiar way for the Use of All, but especially the Meanest Reader* (1658; London, 1727), pp. 311–317.

The enigma of the enslavement of black Virginians is more bedeviling than the origins of indentured servitude because of the lack of evidence. Surviving details are not easily interpreted, assuring that the question of the beginnings of slavery will remain the lively and tendentious subject that it has always been. Despite the difficulties created by the dearth of information, and the disagreements of the past, some parts of the riddle are to be doubted no longer. There may have been Africans in Virginia well before that renowned but anonymous Dutch skipper unloaded, in John Rolfe's words, his "20. and odd Negroes" at Jamestown in 1619.[29] The Dutchman's cargo did not commence a massive black migration to the colony. Virginia's African population as late as 1700 numbered, according to one estimate, somewhat

---

29. Wesley Frank Craven, "Twenty Negroes to Jamestown in 1619?" *Virginia Quarterly Review* 47 (1971): 416–420; John Rolfe to Sir Edwin Sandys, January 1619/20, Ferrar Papers, Box 9, no. 960, Magdalene College, Cambridge; "A relation from Master John Rolfe, June 15, 1618," in Philip L. Barbour, ed., *The Complete Works of Captain John Smith (1580–1631)* (Chapel Hill, N.C. and London, 1986), 2: 267–668. That blacks settled in Virginia before 1619 can neither be proved nor disproved conclusively. One piece of evidence suggests that at least one landed in the colony before that date. A census of all colonists taken in 1625 listed "Angelo, a Negro woman, in the *Treasurer*," meaning that she had come to Virginia aboard the ship *Treasurer*. The only known vessel bearing that name called at Jamestown in 1613, 1614, and 1618. In the absence of contrary evidence, to assume that Angelo arrived as early as 1613 but no later than 1618 seems plausible. Her arrival thus gives credence to the possibility that blacks preceded those about whom John Rolfe wrote. The census was printed from a manuscript (CO 1/3) in John Camden Hotten, *The Original Lists of Persons of Quality . . . and Others who went from Great Britain to the American Plantations, 1600–1700* (London, 1874), pp. 201–265; the reference to Angelo is on p. 224. The landing dates of other colonists aboard the *Treasurer* are scattered throughout the census. None is later than 1618, which suggests that the *Treasurer* stopped calling after that date.

more than six thousand, most of whom had arrived after 1660. Not every black Virginian was cast into slavery.[30]

At first, whether or not an African fell into slavery depended upon circumstances that are not now grasped easily, although religion and previous condition seemed to determine one's fate at the hands of the English.[31] Wary of all foreigners, the English were singularly hostile toward blacks, whose color and alien ways stirred intense feelings of suspicion, but Virginia Englishmen were slow to define a specific legal relationship between themselves and these strangers.[32] Slavery existed in fact long before it received statutory definition, a process that accelerated after 1662 and culminated in 1705, when the General Assembly wrote a slave code into the revised statutes.[33]

Still, why the English finally decided to adapt their law to accommodate slavery remains debatable. In truth, there was no single, fateful decision; there were many, each of which resulted from an interplay of emotion and self-interest. Slavery gained wider acceptance as the number of enslaved Africans grew, and with the increase came the troubles associated with the employment of any bondsmen. Slaves, like servants, rebelled, ran away, stole, and indulged in illicit sex. White Virginians wished to curb miscegenation and to keep existing slaves and their progeny from becoming free.

Wherever blacks and whites lived and worked together, it was not easy to separate the two or to prevent

---

30. Craven, *White, Red, and Black*, pp. 73–111; Alden T. Vaughan, "The Origins Debate: Slavery and Racism in Seventeenth-Century Virginia," *VMHB* 97 (1989): 311–354.
31. Alden T. Vaughan, "Blacks in Virginia: A Note on the First Decade," *WMQ*, 3d ser., 29 (1972): 469–478.
32. Jordan, *White Over Black*, chap. 1.
33. Hening, ed., *The Statutes at Large*, 3: 233–234, 269–275, 277, 333–335, 447–462.

miscegenation.[34] Englishmen's attitudes toward the commingling of the races were conditioned by their antipathies toward Africans, their prejudices against sexual intercourse outside of marriage, and the not impractical matter of what should become of the mulatto offspring of unions between blacks and whites. In English eyes, casual sexual relations offended against the laws of God and the sanctity of marriage, but as such relations were deemed largely an offense against morality rather than law, they were a matter for regulation by church courts. Brothel keeping, "open and notorious lewdness," and bastardy were among several sexual misdeeds of which common law took cognizance, at least until 1650, when the Puritan Parliament declared adultery and fornication capital crimes. That law had no real influence in Virginia. Besides, it was repealed at the Restoration, when, as Sir William Blackstone pithily remarked a century later, "men, from an abhorrence of the hypocrisy of the late times fell into a contrary extreme, of licentiousness, it was not thought proper to revive a law of such unfashionable rigour." Such laws might be bent to apply to indentured servants, but what of their relevance to mulattoes?[35]

In England a bastard, although child to no one and child to everyone, differed from an illegitimate colonial mulatto in important ways. The former was both Christian and English, meaning that while he might be bound, he could not be enslaved. In Virginia such children were routinely baptized and put into service. They could not be held past their thirty-first birthdays. Colonial statutes were quite specific on these matters, and there was no lawful way for those unfortunate

---

34. Ibid., 1:146; Lower Norfolk County Order Book, 1646–1651, fol. 113; ibid., 1681–1686, fol. 139; Henrico County Deed Book, 1677–1692, fols. 192–195; Charles City County Order Book, 1689–1695, fol. 225.
35. Sir William Blackstone, *Commentaries on the Laws of England in Four Books* (5th ed.; Dublin, 1773), 4: 63, 64.

children to escape the penalties of their parents' indiscretions. Not so the mulatto bastard. One of the parents was an African, who could be a slave or a heathen or both. What then? Was he or she a slave?

Might he or she escape slavery through baptism or through the claim of English parentage? Here was a puzzle for which English law could not provide a ready answer because it did not contemplate the existence of mulattoes or the circumstances of their conception. Colonial lawmakers had to construct their solutions out of whole cloth, and, lacking many useful precedents, they were inclined to move with cautious, purposeful deliberation. They stood in sharp relief to their countrymen who settled the West Indies, where, according to Richard S. Dunn, the English "plunged into the slaveholding business."[36]

Mulatto slaves, like full-blooded African slaves and servants, had access to the courts for much of the seventeenth century, a right that kept questions concerning their status alive even as it moved the General Assembly toward incorporating slavery into colonial statutes. The number of known case records in which such slaves sued for their freedom is small, but several suits are suggestive because of their influence upon the statutes. Of these cases, the most complete is the suit of Elizabeth Key. Key was the bastard daughter of an unnamed slave woman and one Thomas Key, a sometime member of the House of Burgesses who died about 1636. About the time of her father's death, Elizabeth Key was sold into servitude by her godfather, Humphrey Higginson, a member of the Council of State, to whom she had been indentured. Thereafter, in circumstances that are now obscure, she became the property of John Mottrom, a justice of the peace for Northumberland County, who kept

---

36. Richard S. Dunn, *Sugar and Slaves: The Rise of the Planter Class in the English West Indies, 1624–1713* (Chapel Hill, N.C., 1972), p. 226.

her for a slave. When Mottrom died in 1655, Key sued the executors of the Mottrom estate for her freedom. Her attorney argued her case before the Northumberland county court, basing his claims upon three grounds: Key's father was English, and so she should be free; she had been baptized, and as a Christian she could not be enslaved; she had been sold by Higginson to Mottrom for a term of years, and that had long since passed. A jury found for Key, but Mottrom's executors appealed to the General Court, which set aside the county court's judgment. Key had one last appeal to the General Assembly, which heard the matter and remanded it to the Northumberland justices, who finally freed her.[37]

Key's case is significant for what it reveals. Evidently some mulattoes were able to bring litigation grounded in the gray areas of existing law and, if their suits succeeded, to escape a life of slavery. So long as there were doubts about the condition of children born to slave women and free men, anyone who owned such offspring was a target for lengthy and costly lawsuits. Even if a planter prevailed he was out of pocket, because a slave could make no restitution for the master's loss of time and money. The obvious remedy lay in closing this loophole by statute, a step that the General Assembly finally took in a perversely clever way.

In December 1662 the Assembly moved decisively to quell any doubts "whether children gott by any Englishman upon a negro woman should be slave or free" by making a

---

37. The records of the case are in the Northumberland County Record Books, 1652–58, ff. 66–67, 85; 1658–60, fol. 28, and Northumberland County Order Book, 1652–65, ff. 40, 46, 49. They are also printed in Billings, ed., *The Old Dominion in the Seventeenth Century*, rev. ed., pp. 195–199. It is also one of the few surviving examples of cases appealed from the General Court to the General Assembly, and apart from its significance for the statutory definition of slavery, it thus provides evidence of appellate procedures in Virginia before the 1680s, when the Assembly lost its power to sit as a high court of appeals.

mulatto child's freedom dependent upon the mother's condition. The law further stipulated that "if any Christian shall committ ffornication with a negro man or woman, hee or she soe offending shall pay double the ffines imposed by the former act"; this was the first statutory indication of who might be a slave. In addition, the assembly sought to keep whites and blacks apart, it undercut the mulatto's chances to win freedom through the courts, and it made a seldom-used doctrine of civil law into a precedent for future slave codes.[38]

The burgesses and the councillors took that doctrine from Henry Swinburne's *Treatise of Testaments and Last Wills*, which, after Michael Dalton's *Countrey Justice*, was the most widely circulated English law book in Virginia. At one point in the *Treatise*, Swinburne, an Elizabethan judge of the Prerogative Court of York, commented upon who might legally make wills. Slaves could not, he wrote, because they were "in servitude or bondage to another, even against nature." He then went on to describe what conditions of birth determined a child's status. Although he was a canon lawyer, he incorporated common law precedents as well as civil law doctrines in his commentary, and thus he drew attention to the civilian precept *Quia partus sequitur ventrem*; that is, "the child inherits the condition of the mother." Significantly, he emphatically reminded his readers that

> it is otherwise by the laws of this realm, for the child doth follow the state and condition of the father: and therefore in England the father being a bond-man, the child shall be in bondage, without distinction whether the mother be bond or free: so that the child be begotten or born in lawfull matrimony. But a bastard shall not be bound, because the law doth not acknowledge a father in this case:

---

38. Hening, ed., *The Statutes at Large*, 2: 170.

for by the law a bastard is sometimes called *filius nullius* ... sometimes *filius vulgi*.[39]

Colonial lawmakers found in Swinburne's comments an authoritative source that enabled them seemingly to adhere to English law while solving matters for which it had no remedies.

Another assault on the mulatto's access to liberty through litigation came in September 1667, when the Assembly declared that "baptisme doth not alter the condition of the person as to his bondage or ffreedome."[40] The adoption of this act may well have resulted from a suit argued in the Lower Norfolk county court one month before the legislative session. During their August meeting the Lower Norfolk justices heard a slave named Fernando argue that he ought to be freed from his master's service because "hee was a Christian and had been severall yeares in England." He presented some documents as proof of his claims, but the clerk noted these were in "Portugell or some other language which the court could not understand." Unmoved by his pleas, the justices found against him, but Fernando took an appeal to the General Court. The resolution of the appeal is unknown because the high court's records no longer exist, but the proximity of Fernando's suit and the assembly's passage of the statute on baptism seems more than coincidental.[41]

---

39. In the London edition of 1677 the relevant passages are found on pages 52 and 53. Although copies of the *Treatise* circulated in Virginia as early as the 1630s, its widespread usage may be attributed in part to a statutory requirement that each county court own a copy (Hening, ed., *The Statutes at Large*, 2: 246). Thomas D. Morris, "'Villeinage ... as it existed in England, reflects but little light on our subject': The Problem of the 'Sources' of Southern Slave Law," *American Journal of Legal History*, 32 (1988): 95–137, minimizes the influence of Swinburne.
40. Hening, ed., *The Statutes at Large*, 2: 260.
41. Lower Norfolk County Order Book, 1666–1675, fol. 17; Billings, ed., *The Old Dominion in the Seventeenth Century*, rev. ed., p. 200.

The fate of all mulattoes was eventually sealed in 1691. In "An act for suppressing outlying Slaves," the Assembly banished "whatsoever English or other white man or woman being free shall intermarry with a negroe, mulatto, or Indian man or woman bond or free." It also levied fines of £15 or five years' service on English women who bore bastards by black, Indian, or mulatto fathers. A portion of the fines went to support the upkeep of the children, who were bound to serve until their thirtieth birthdays. As a further discouragement, the law required banishment of any mulatto whose master was disposed to free him.[42]

A desire to separate the races was clearly present in the movement toward the statutory definition of slavery, but fear and avarice were also no strangers to the minds of colonial legislators. Lawmakers recognized a potential threat to their safety as early as January 1639/40, when they excepted blacks from a provision requiring masters to furnish firearms to all members of their households capable of using them.[43] The wisdom of that prohibition seemed plain enough the following July, when a rising in Lower Norfolk County by some servants and an African named Emanuel was suppressed.[44] Thereafter concern abated, and minor infractions were dealt with according to existing statutes or customs.

The growth of the black population brought new legislative restrictions. In 1680, for example, Secretary of the Colony Nicholas Spencer brought the Council of State "Intelligence of the Discovery of a Negro Plott, formed in

---

42. Hening, ed., *The Statutes at Large*, 3: 86–88. Under Maryland law, such children were held until they were thirty-one (Raphael Cassimere, Jr., "The Origins and Early Development of Slavery in Maryland, 1633 to 1715" [Ph.D. diss., Lehigh University, 1971], chap. 2).
43. "Acts of General Assembly, 6 Jan. 1639–40 (concluded)"; *WMQ*, 2d ser., 4 (1924): 147. The Marylanders adopted a similar law. See Cassimere, "Origins and Early Development of Slavery in Maryland," chap. 4.
44. "Decisions of the General Court" (1640)," *VMHB*, 5 (1898): 236–237.

the Northern Neck for the Distroying and killing his Majties Subjects . . . with a designe of Carrying it through the whole Collony of Virga."[45] The Council moved swiftly to quell the rebellious slaves. It ordered trials of the principal actors and commanded local authorities to restrict the slaves' freedom of movement. Then the councillors joined Governor Thomas Culpeper, second baron Culpeper of Thoresway, and the House of Burgesses to pass "An act for preventing Negroes Insurrections." Beyond making it illegal for slaves to carry anything that might be employed as a weapon, the new statute instituted a pass system and provided whippings for slaves who went abroad without passes or who presumed "to lift up [their] hand[s] in opposition against any Christian."[46] In time, the act was augmented by the law to suppress outlying slaves and a statute of 1692 entitled "An act for the more speedy prosecution of slaves committing Capitall Crimes," which established a special system of tribunals for handling slave offenses with dispatch.

The latter legislation empowered the governor to commission justices of the peace as courts of oyer and terminer to try "every negro or other slave which shall . . . commit or perpetrate any cappitall offence which the law of England requires to be satisfied with . . . death . . . or loss of member." Upon being commissioned, the justices arraigned the accused, saw to his indictment, and collected witnesses in preparation for the trial. So long as the circumstances were "pregnant," the act allowed the testimony of a single witness, instead of the customary two, as compelling proof of wrongdoing. It even permitted the justices to try the cases

---

45. H. R. McIlwaine, Benjamin J. Hillman, and Wilmer L. Hall, eds., *Executive Journals of the Council of Colonial Virginia* (Richmond, Va., 1925–1966), 1: 86–87.

46. Hening, ed., *The Statutes at Large*, 2: 481–482; Cassimere, "Origins and Early Development of Slavery in Maryland," chap. 4.

"without the sollemnitie of a jury," and there was no appeal from their judgments. Obviously, the authors of this law, as well as the justices of the peace who enforced it, were more intent on assuring the safety of their fellow planters than they were on protecting the procedural rights of accused slaves.[47]

In the conduct of such trials, matters were left entirely to the discretion of local magistrates. The case of Tom Cary provides an insight into how the justices tried accused slaves. In June 1693 Cary, a slave of Northampton County planter John Swan, broke into the house of Thomas Richards, stole some items, and fired the building. He was apprehended shortly thereafter, whereupon the Northampton county court reported the incident to Governor Sir Edmund Andros, requesting that he authorize it to try Cary. Andros complied, issuing his commission on 5 July; a week later Cary came to trial before the Northampton justices of the peace sitting as a court of oyer and terminer. It was a short trial, lasting no more than a few hours, and the outcome was a foregone conclusion.

The first order of business was to call Cary to the bar. Next, the clerk intoned Andros's commission and the enabling statute. Then he read the indictment, to which Cary pleaded "not guilty." Several witnesses were called, and each testified against him. Cary's defenses were meager because he, like everyone else in seventeenth-century Virginia, had none of the safeguards that pertain to modern felony trials. He had

---

47. Hening, ed., *The Statutes at Large*, 3: 102–103. Virginia lawmakers were not the only colonials who departed from the two-witness tradition in English criminal law. Courts in Massachusetts Bay sometimes accepted the testimony of a single witness as sufficient proof of capital offenses. See William H. McBratney, "The One Witness Rule in Massachusetts," *American Journal of Legal History* 2 (1958): 155–60; Philip J. Schwarz, *Twice Condemned: Slaves and the Criminal Laws of Virginia, 1705–1865* (Baton Rouge, La. and London, 1988), chaps. 1, 3.

no counsel, he had no prior notice of the evidence against him, he subpoenaed no witnesses in his behalf, and he presented no exculpatory testimony. The most he could do was hope to gain some measure of mercy. Hearing Cary out, the justices retired to consider a verdict. They soon found him guilty, and they sentenced him to die. Cary then tried to escape death by claiming benefit of clergy, but the court overruled him. In doing so, it cited as its authority a statute from Henry VIII's time that denied benefit of clergy to those who, like the prisoner, stood convicted of forcible entry, robbery, and arson. Their ruling doomed Cary. Two days after the trial, William Kendall, the sheriff of Northampton, hanged him in view of the fire-gutted hulk of Richard's house.[48]

---

48. The record of Cary's case is in the Northampton County Order Book, 1689-1696, fols. 236–239 and is printed in Billings, ed., *The Old Dominion in the Seventeenth Century*, rev. ed., pp. 186–189. The case is among the earliest surviving examples of litigation under the slave trial statute. It contains Andros's commission of oyer and terminer, though it lacks the witnesses' depositions. If a convicted felon could read or recite Psalm 51, verse 1, he might claim benefit of clergy and so escape the punishment of secular law. That doctrine was rooted in a practice that began in the Middle Ages (see Cowell, *Law Dictionary*, under "clergy"). By the seventeenth century, a convict's ability to escape punishment by claiming the benefit was circumscribed by English statutes such as the one the Northampton justices employed to deny Cary. The law, 23 Henry VIII, c. 1, specifically forbade the claim in instances where felons stood convicted of the same crimes committed by Cary (see Pulton, *Abstract of all the Penall Statutes*, fol. 50, sect. 13). Following Cary's execution, Kendall attempted to collect nearly six thousand pounds of tobacco from the General Assembly as his "expence and fees" for his part in Cary's prosecution. The House of Burgesses turned Kendall's petition aside and noted that "the charge of obtaining the commission of Oyer & Terminer ought to be defrayed by the Country and that ye lawfull charge of prosecuteing the said Criminall is a County charge" (H. R. McIlwaine, ed., *Journals of the House of Burgesses of Virginia, 1659/60–1693* [Richmond, Va., 1914], p. 458).

Despite the fears that were inspired by deeds such as Cary's, masters continued to be eager to ensure their property rights to their slaves. Statutes aimed at keeping blacks and mulattoes in slavery afforded one guarantee. Those that turned black persons into black things provided yet another warrant.

The black Virginian's descent in law from humanity to property happened gradually but not haphazardly. At first, the English considered black bondsmen as chattels personal, although colonial lawmakers were slow to put even that understanding into writing. An act of March 1642/43, the earliest of such laws, implied as much when it required owners to regard African women, as well as black males, as tithable for tax purposes. (English servant women were not so taxed.) Subsequent laws defining tithables invariably included similar provisions, but none explicitly comprehended slaves as chattels before 1671, when the Assembly passed an act for the disposition of blacks in the estates of "orphans" whose parents died intestate.[49] In 1705 the assembly abandoned its tendency toward characterizing slaves as chattels in favor of declaring:

> all negro, mulatto, and Indian slaves, in all courts of judicature, and other places within this dominion, shall be held, taken, and adjudged, to be real estate (and not chattels;) and shall descend unto the heirs and widows of persons departing this life, according to the manner and custom of land of inheritance, held in fee simple.

According to the preamble of the statute, its purpose was "for the better settling and preservation of estates."[50]

---

49. Hening, ed., *The Statutes at Large*, 1: 242; 2: 19, 84, 288.
50. Ibid., 3: 333–335 (emphasis added). The act was modified in 1727 to construe slaves as chattels "whenever any person shall, by bargain and sale, or gift, either with or without deed, or by last his will and testament,

This act was one in a new series that dealt wholly or partially with slavery, a collection the assembly drafted in conjunction with its latest revision of the entire body of the colony's statute law. Accordingly, several acts were merely reworkings of earlier ones that the revisers of 1705 deemed suitable to the needs of their constituents. Others tidied messy situations, such as new regulations for office holding that for the first time unequivocally forbade blacks and mulattoes from serving in "any office . . . or any place of publick trust" or testifying "in any cases whatsoever." All of the revised statutes represented the culmination of decades of legislative searching for the definition of a legal relationship between masters and slaves. They also constituted the first "black code" in Virginia and provided the basis of all slave law down to the destruction of the peculiar institution.[51]

Taken together, the black code of 1705 and its predecessor statutes reveal how the General Assembly legalized slavery. Chattel slavery evolved gradually, and that evolution was influenced by the regulation of servants. The code also demonstrated that there were large holes to close in the institutional edifice before the law of slaves completely bound blacks. Although mulatto slaves lost the courts as routes of escape, other slaves did not. They continued to sue for their liberty as late as 1705 and beyond. Freedom by manumission or purchase remained unrestricted openings

---

in writing or by any nuncupative will, bargain, sell, [or] give" his bondsmen away (ibid., 4: 223). By the early nineteenth century, slaves were defined as "personal estate" (William Waller Hening, *The New Virginia Justice, Comprising the Office and Authority of a Justice of the Peace* . . . [2d ed.; Richmond, Va., 1810], p. 545).

51. Hening, ed., *The Statutes at Large*, 3: 251.The revisal of 1705 was the sixth undertaken by the assembly. Of these, the first occurred in 1632/33, to be followed in turn by the revisions of 1642/43, 1652, 1657/58, and 1661/62. After the revisal of 1705, the assembly did not attempt another until 1748.

through which a few slaves might still slip.[52] Some scholars have seen in all of this an aimlessness that proves the English made an unthinking decision to enslave black Virginians. Yet reviewing the early law of bondage suggests otherwise.[53] True, the legislation that governed slavery emerged intermittently, but so did all of the colonial modifications of English legal traditions—as, for that matter, did the common law of England itself. The authors of the law of servants and slaves demonstrated a streak of inventiveness not ordinarily associated with men who give no thought to the consequences of their actions.

---

52. Elizabeth City County Order Book, 1684–1699, fol. 107; Charles City County Order Book, 1655–1565, pp. 604–605; Accomack County Order Book, 1682/83–1692, fols. 92, 98; Surry County Deeds and Wills, 1657–1672, p. 349; H. R. McIlwaine, ed., *Minutes of the Council and General Court of Colonial Virginia, 1622–1632, 1670–1676* (2nd ed.; Richmond, Va., 1924), p. 354.

53. Winthrop D. Jordan developed the "unthinking decision" thesis at length in chapter 2 of *White Over Black*. That interpretation has worked its way into other scholars' work, including my own. It was one to which I subscribed when I compiled the documents and wrote the introduction for chapter 4 of the 1975 edition *The Old Dominion in the Seventeenth Century*. My thinking changed, however, as I read the evidence more closely and considered the effect of the influences I discussed in this essay.

Essay 9

Pleading, Procedure and Practice

The Meaning of Due Process of Law in Seventeenth-Century Virginia

I no longer recall the inspiration for this essay, which attempted to unwind the mechanisms that moved litigation to and through the courts. Then, as now, those devices resided under the rubric "due process of law." I obviously realized that ancient phrase conveyed quite different meanings to seventeenth-century Virginians than it did for twentieth-century Americans. And so the essay offered an explanation of the differences. Interpretatively, it was at variance with Felix Frankfurter's view of due process as an intentionally vague legal concept that was left to gather meaning through experience or the argument that colonial lawmakers concerned themselves with defining procedural rules as guarantors of individual liberties. I delivered an abbreviated rough cut of the essay at the annual meeting of the Southern Historical Association in St. Louis in 1978.

Originally published as "Pleading, Procedure, and Practice: The Meaning of Due Process of Law in Seventeenth-Century Virginia" in the *Journal of Southern History*, 46 (1981): 569–584, the article is reprinted here with the editor's kind permission.

Due Process of law is a venerable Anglo-American tenet. Modern Americans cherish it as a sturdy bulwark against the state's whimsical intrusion into their lives or belongings. The Supreme Court of the United States regularly employs it as a flexible instrument of judicial review and constitutional interpretation.[1] Legal historians describe its evolution as central to the growth of liberty in England and America.[2] In the estimation of scholar, justice, and layman alike, the utility of due process as freedom's guarantor springs from its ability to acquire new content with the passage of time. Felix Frankfurter, for example, once declared that great legal concepts like due process "were purposely left to gather meaning from experience."[3] Similarly, Wallace Mendelson has written that it doubtless was "designed to have, the chameleon's capacity to change . . . [its] color with changing moods and circumstances."[4]

These conceptions have fostered a distinctive theory about the adaptation of English legal customs to American circumstances. This theory supposes that seventeenth-century American lawmakers were acutely sensitive to defining and protecting individual rights when they turned their knowledge of common law into a system suitable to

---

1. Norman J. Small, ed., *The Constitution of the United States of America: Analysis and Interpretation* (Washington, D. C., 1964), pp. 959–986.
2. See for example Rodney L. Mott, *Due Process of Law: A Historical and Analytical Treatise of the Principles and Methods Followed by the Courts in the Application of the Concept of the "Law of the Land"* (Indianapolis, Ind., 1926). While it is dated in many ways, Mott's work remains the only book-length study of due process in its American manifestation.
3. *National Mutual Insurance Co. v. Tidewater Transfer Co., Inc.*, 337 U.S. 582 (1948), at 646.
4. Mendelson, *Justices Black and Frankfurter: Conflict in the Court* (Chicago, 1961), viii.

a new environment. That being so, as the legatees of a presumed tradition which emphasized due process as the primary guardian of their English birthrights, they claimed it as their own and easily fashioned it to similar uses in the colonies. In effect their adaptation exemplifies Frankfurter's "meaning [gathered] from experience," and it therefore follows that the development of due process is a paramount theme in the movement of English law to America in the seventeenth century.

On its face, this theory of the origin of American law seems plausible enough. Measuring it against the colonists' own understanding and use of due process, however, yields a result quite different from the one envisioned by Mr. Justice Frankfurter or Professor Mendelson. Far from being a term of "convenient vagueness,"[5] due process of law conveyed to colonial Englishmen a narrow meaning that had little to do with restraining the powers of government. They did not venerate the phrase as the cornerstone of the freedom that America provided them. Indeed, it rarely appeared in seventeenth-century statutes or other colonial legal documents.

As England's oldest American colony Virginia provides the earliest examples of how due process fared in the New World down to 1700. Inquiring into its evolution there also affords an opportunity to acquire greater appreciation of those mechanisms by which common law was placed in American surroundings. But there is more to be gleaned by such an inquiry than the New World origin of narrowly legal things. Law is, after all, more than the tool of its practitioners, colonial or modern. In the broadest sense law gives any society cultural distinction by formally defining what sets it

---

5. The phrase is Judge Charles M. Hough's. See Felix Frankfurter, *Mr. Justice Holmes and the Supreme Court* (Cambridge, Mass., 1961), p. 19.

apart from other societies.[6] Examining ideas peculiar to English law therefore shows something of how this part of English culture was transplanted to the southern Chesapeake, how the settlers there molded it to the region's requirements, and how their adaptations eventually contributed to the generation of an indigenous culture. Achieving these ends depends upon apprehending what the concept of due process of law signified to seventeenth-century Englishmen and seeing how they applied that meaning to a Virginia setting.

The phrase "due Process of the Law" was coined in a statute enacted by Parliament in 1354.[7] At that time it referred only to the manner of summoning accused persons to the Privy Council.[8] Over the next three hundred years the phrase never appeared in the statutes, and it attracted little notice until the seventeenth century. Interest in due process revived in the late 1620s when opponents of Charles I tried to use it as a contrivance to combat the king's imposition of forced loans by linking it to Chapter 29 of Magna Carta, which guaranteed that no one should be deprived of life, liberty, or property except by judgment of his peers or by the law of the land. Even as Charles's policy sharpened English tastes for defending liberty against Stuart tyranny, Sir Edward Coke was in the midst of revising his *Institutes of the Laws of England*. Esteemed by his countrymen for possessing the sharpest legal mind in the realm, Coke had steadfastly opposed the king. As he worked on his revision, he could not forbear the chance to confound Charles further by cloaking the opponents' linkage of due process and Magna Carta with the mantle of his erudition. Vintage Coke, the treatment in the second *Institute*

---

6. E. Adamson Hoebel, "Fundamental Legal Concepts as Applied in the Study of Primitive Law," *Yale Law Journal*, 51 (April 1942): 951–966.
7. 28 Ed. III, ch. 3, *The Statutes of the Realm* (London, 1810–1822), 1: 345.
8. Keith Jurow, "Untimely Thoughts: A Reconsideration of the Origins of Due Process of Law," *American Journal of Legal History*, 19 (1975): 265–271.

is an exhaustive, if not exhausting, commentary on the great charter. When he explicated Chapter 29, which had figured so prominently in the recent controversies, Coke equated the phrase "by law of the land" with "due process of law." In his mind the two carried identical meanings, as his citations to past statutes and precedents were meant to prove. His commentary is an example of how Coke sometimes constructed interpretations of English law from whole cloth. In this instance, he sought to prove that Charles's antagonists, not the king, had right, tradition, the law, *and* Sir Edward Coke on their side.[9] Whatever may have been the grip of Coke's scholarship upon the minds of Englishmen in the 1620s and Americans in later years, his interpretation of a relationship between due process and Magna Carta was not universally shared by his contemporaries. Nor was it confirmed by past usage. Legal lexicographers, case reporters, and compilers of statutory abridgments did not associate the two. In fact, these authorities devoted little space in their books to the phrase "due process of law." It passed unnoticed in the widely circulated writings of such respected authors as John Cowell, Michael Dalton, William Lambarde, and Edmund Wingate, men whose work had an important influence in Virginia.[10] These and other writers were somewhat more attentive to the word "process," to which they attached distinct and precise meanings not related to Magna Carta. In his dictionary Cowell noted: "Sometimes that only is called The Process, by which a Man is called into the Court, because it is the Beginning or the principal Part thereof, by which the Rest of the Business is directed . . . ." But he also defined process as "the Manner of proceeding in

---

9. Coke, *The Second Part of the Institutes of the Laws of England* . . . (London, 1797), pp. 50–55.
10. Essay 4, above.

every Cause."[11] In short, the word referred to what is now called "procedural due process," that is, the means of getting criminal and civil issues to court and moving them in orderly fashion through successive stages to a conclusion. Cowell's understanding fit the meaning of due process of law in 1354; it had not changed much by the seventeenth century, and it was the one the Virginia colonists took to America.

Before the Virginia colonists could put their idea of due process into practice, they had first to construct a workable system of courts. Following a period of groping toward a satisfactory method of settling litigation, the General Assembly in 1634 divided judicial power between county and province.[12] The ultimate consequence of that step was the appearance of a simplified system of inferior and appellate courts that combined the jurisdictions of such English courts as the leet, quarter sessions, the assizes, king's bench, common pleas, chancery, and the admiralty, as well as that of the church courts. In this respect Virginia courts differed sharply from their English parentage, just as they contrasted noticeably with those of other colonies. In Massachusetts and New York, for example, the number and variety of courts more nearly approximated the situation in England.[13]

---

11. Cowell, *A Law Dictionary: or the Interpreter of Words and Terms Used Either in the Common or Statute Laws of Great Britain* . . . (London, 1727: originally published at Cambridge in 1607 as *The Interpreter*), under "process."

12. William Waller Hening, ed., *The Statutes at Large; Being a Collection of All the Laws of Virginia* . . . (13 vols.; Richmond, Va., New York, and Philadelphia, Pa., 1819–1823), 1: 224; Philip Alexander Bruce, *Institutional History of Virginia in the Seventeenth Century: An Inquiry unto the Religious, Moral, Educational, Legal, Military and Political Conditions of the People Based on Original and Contemporary Records* (New York and London, 1910), 1: 485–486; Wesley F. Craven, *The Southern Colonies in the Seventeenth Century, 1607–1689* (Baton Rouge, La., 1949), pp. 169–172, 270–289; Essay 2, above.

13. Joseph H. Smith, ed., *Colonial Justice in Western Massachusetts (1639–1702): The Pynchon Court Record* (Cambridge, Mass., 1961), pp. 65–88; Julius

The General Assembly devoted much energy in the six decades after 1634 toward fixing and describing the courts' jurisdictions in statutes, but it did not simultaneously prescribe how that authority was to be exercised. Unlike its counterpart in Massachusetts, it wrote nothing comparable to the Puritans' book of "Presidents and Formes"[14] to pattern what John Cowell called "*The Process,* by which a Man is called into the Court. . . ." Nor did it draft rules to guide judges in conducting trials in a regular, orderly manner. Lacking any such guidance, courts were at liberty to improvise their own forms of due process. This was a freedom not necessarily sought or much enjoyed by colonial justices, for most were innocent of formal training in English law. To such men experimentation was unsettling. It added one more touch of impermanence to an already tenuous existence in Virginia. Still, if the courts were to work, the magistrates must resolve the question of what forms of procedure suited their emerging legal system. For their answers, they called upon knowledge acquired by personal experience or the gleanings from such texts as those of Cowell, Dalton, or Lambarde. Gradually they shaped the mechanisms for suppressing crime and settling civil suits.

While the year 1634 is an appropriate point from which to start a discussion of how criminal procedure developed in seventeenth-century Virginia, it is apparent that some colonists had begun to adapt English practice at an earlier date. Throughout the 1620s the governor's council was the only institution vested with criminal jurisdiction, and its members were thus the first Virginians to wrestle with the problem of finding suitable judicial procedures. The few criminal cases that survive from that decade are indicative of their solutions. First

---

Goebel, Jr., and T. Raymond Naughton, *Law Enforcement in Colonial New York: A Study in Criminal Procedure (1644–1776)* (Montclair, N. J., 1970), pp. 59–121.

14. Smith, ed., *Colonial Justice in Western Massachusetts,* p. 140.

of all, the governors-general and councillors may be credited with introducing the idea that criminal due process must comprehend such steps as indictment or presentment, arrest, bail, examination, trial, judgment, and execution of sentence. When they borrowed verbatim the wording of indictments, judgments, or other forms, they demonstrated that much of English criminal practice was wholly suitable to the Old Dominion. Furthermore, trying all cases in one place instead of several demonstrated the efficiency of consolidating jurisdictions into a less-complicated scheme than that offered by the mother country's example, just as it opened the way to continued experimentation after 1634.[15]

As the new court system was settled upon the colony, the county courts were given general jurisdiction in three areas of criminal prosecution. First, they tried all petty criminal and ecclesiastical offenses. Next, they were sometimes authorized by commissions of oyer and terminer to judge certain types of felonies,[16] even though felony jurisdiction generally remained the exclusive province of the Council of State, known in its judicial capacity as the General Court.[17] Finally, they assisted the General Court by conducting the preliminary procedures in felony trials. The discharge of each of these responsibilities

---

15. Henry R. McIlwaine, ed., *Minutes of the Council and General Court of Colonial Virginia, 1622–1632, 1670–1676* (2nd ed., Richmond, Va., 1979) (2nd Ed., Richmond, Va., 1979), pp. 4–5; Sir James Fitzjames Stephen, *A History of the Criminal Law of England* (London, 1883), 1: 346–351.

16. Felonies were crimes that were punished by loss of life or member. Theodore F. T. Plucknett, *A Concise History of the Common Law*, 5th ed. (Boston, Mass., 1956), pp. 442–54.

17. Before the Assembly's revision of all colonial statutes in March 1661/62 the General Court was called the Quarter Court. That designation stemmed from the fact that in the years just after 1634 it held quarterly sessions. By the 1650s, however, the terms had been reduced to three; so the revisers sought a name more appropriate to the court's actual function. I have everywhere here used the designation "General Court" because of its wider familiarity to modern colonial historians.

required particular steps, which, when taken together, constituted criminal due process in the local courts.

Before a court could try an offender, someone had to accuse him of wrongdoing, a responsibility that was first left to the settlers, the churchwardens, or the magistrates themselves. That arrangement proved unsatisfactory, and the General Assembly moved in 1645 to correct the defect when it passed an act appropriating the grand jury for use in Virginia. The new law required local justices to convene grand juries "to enquire of the breach of all penal laws and other crimes and misdemeanors not touching life or member" and to make their presentments to the courts. Although modified by later additions, this statute embedded the grand jury system into Virginia law, just as it provided a more efficient means of detecting and prosecuting criminal misconduct, and within a few years of its passage, the grand jury became the chief means of initiating trials.[18]

Following grand jury presentment, the next step was to compel the alleged malefactor to answer the charge against him. Traditionally, an arrest warrant, directed by the court to the sheriff or his deputies, served this purpose, but the Virginians followed a slightly different course. Virginia magistrates usually ordered the sheriff to summon the accused orally rather than by warrant. Moreover, in those instances where a warrant did issue from the bench its substance bore slight resemblance to anything used in England. It was little more than a few sentences commanding the arresting officer to detain the suspect and have him present at the next session of court. Here, then, is an illustration of how the Virginians borrowed English forms but altered their substance.[19]

---

18. Hening, ed., *The Statutes at Large*, 1: 304, 463; 2: 74; Henrico County Deed Book, 1677–1692, p. 336.
19. Compare the arrest warrants in Charles City County Order Book, 1655–1665, p. 556, and Northampton County Order Book, 1657–1664,

However defendants were brought to the bar, they were tried in one of two ways, summarily by the justices or by a jury. The procedure in a summary trial was quite uncomplicated. There were no prosecutors or defense lawyers, and the trial began with the clerk's reading of the charges and the defendant's response. If the defendant responded with an admission of guilt, the case proceeded no further. The justices pronounced sentence, ordered it executed by the sheriff, and directed the clerk to record the case's disposition. If the defendant contested the allegation the court called those persons who had witnessed the offense. By act of assembly all witnesses were required to appear in open court and to give their testimony under oath in the defendant's presence. After giving their testimony they could be questioned further by the justices, who might also put questions to the accused. Anything and everything that the defendant or witnesses said was deemed cogent evidence. When the court had heard all that it considered pertinent to the matter, it passed judgment and pronounced sentence.[20]

A limited guarantee of trial by jury was enacted by the General Assembly in 1642. A further act of 1658 provided that anyone who wished a jury trial might have it, provided he bore the expense of calling a jury. Although the wording of the law did not make plain whether or not the act extended to petty criminal causes, its modifications in later statutes left open that possibility. Indeed, as a result of the Assembly's revision of the whole corpus of statute law in March 1661/62, county courts

---

fol. 206, with Chap. 174 in Michael Dalton, comp., *The Countrey Justice: Containing the Practice of the Justices of the Peace Out of Their Sessions . . .* (London, 1677), pp. 478–494.

20. Hening, ed., *The Statutes at Large*, 1: 305; 2: 23–24, 64, 74, 79, 315; Northumberland County Order Book, 1650–1652, fol. 43; Charles City County Order Book, 1655–1665, p.45; Lower Norfolk County Order Book, 1637–1646 (transcript), 100-101, 120; Surry County Deed Book, 1671–1684, fols. 41-43; and Surry County Order Book, 1671–1692, pp. 41–42.

were required to call petty juries at the start of each of their sessions. To comply with that requirement local courts merely impaneled twelve men from the bystanders around the courthouse and brought cases before them as needed.[21]

The procedure in jury trials carried no assurance of better protection for a defendant since he did not enjoy many more rights under that mode of trial. Perhaps the single advantage of a jury trial lay in the possibility that jurors might be more sympathetic than the justices. What constituted due process of law in a jury trial is revealed in the case of Robert Hayes. In January 1664/65 Hayes and a confederate were indicted for petty larceny by the Northampton County grand jury. On trial day the sheriff brought Hayes into court, whereupon the clerk read the indictment. Hayes pleaded not guilty, and the justices asked, "How wilt thou be tryed?" to which he responded, "By God and the County." At that juncture, the court summoned the grand jury, who, after having been sworn, returned a true bill upon the indictment. Jury selection followed, during which Hayes had the chance to challenge prospective jurors, but he did not exercise his right. As soon as the jury was seated the clerk called the witnesses and again read the indictment. With the swearing in of the witnesses the testimony began, and in short order the case went to the jury. A little while later the jury convicted Hayes, and he was sentenced to receive a public whipping.[22]

Hayes presented no defense because, guilty or not, people in his situation had little opportunity to prepare one. As in summary proceedings, defendants in jury trials were not entitled to legal counsel. They did not have the power to subpoena witnesses in their own behalf, and until they went to trial they did not know what evidence the prosecution would present against them. So the outcome of Hayes's trial was never in doubt.

---

21. Hening, ed., *The Statutes at Large*, 1: 273–274, 474; 2: 73–74.
22. Northampton County Order Book, 1657–1664, fol. 205.

Despite the modern affection for trial by jury, it was not the preferred mode of handling petty crimes in colonial Virginia. Again and again, court records demonstrate that the preponderance of these cases was dispatched summarily. Several reasons explained this phenomenon. The employment of summary trials was a direct borrowing of English practice. In fact, there was little procedural difference between the Virginia variation and its English counterpart. To seventeenth-century Virginians presentment or indictment by a grand jury carried the automatic presumption of guilt. That presupposition probably explains why so large a number of defendants chose to confess to their crimes in open court rather than contest them before the judges or a jury. Servants charged as runaways or pilferers could not afford to pay jurors' expenses, and their masters certainly would not be put out of pocket either. Many freemen also chose not to incur this expense as part of the cost of their misdemeanors. Summary justice was also swift—so much so that we moderns might find its speed not deliberate enough for our tastes. Finally, Virginians seem also to have satisfied themselves that trial by jury should be reserved for crimes more serious than Sabbath-breaking, swearing, or petty theft. This attitude was consistent with that of colonists elsewhere in English North America, for they also relied heavily upon summary procedures to try minor offenses.[23]

---

23. Felix Frankfurter and Thomas G. Corcoran, "Petty Federal Offenses and the Constitutional Guaranty of Trial by Jury," *Harvard Law Review*, 39 (1926): 917–1019. It is possible that the existence of a crude system of plea bargaining might also explain why so many offenders pleaded guilty, for, as J. S. Cockburn has shown, plea bargaining was a familiar practice in England. See Cockburn, "Tried by the Book? Fact and Theory in the Criminal Process, 1558–1625," in S.H. Baker, ed., *Legal Records and the Historian* (London, 1978), p. 73. There exists no evidence that such a system existed in seventeenth-century Virginia as it did in England.

No matter the mode of trial, the judgment of the local court in criminal cases was final. Unlike the English procedure the possibility of review by the General Court through a writ of error did not exist. The only relief a convict might expect was a pardon from the governor-general, which in misdemeanor offenses was so rare as to be nonexistent.

In addition to their exclusive jurisdiction over petty crime, local magistrates were sometimes empowered to try felonies. As the king's vicegerent any governor-general could issue commissions of oyer and terminer to the justices of the peace. Such an authorization translated the justices into an *ad hoc* court to hear and determine a case against an indicted felon. Once that defendant had been judged, the commission immediately lapsed.

Until late in the century the governor-general authorized courts of oyer and terminer by letter, which he sent to a county's senior justice of the peace. In it he directed that such a court be convened to try the case that he was committing to it. At the appointed time the presiding justice read the governor's missive, whereupon he and the others declared themselves a court of oyer and terminer, and the case went to trial. Unless the defendant confessed his guilt he was tried by a jury. No appeal could be made to the General Court, and the sentence was carried out immediately.[24]

Down to the 1690s courts of oyer and terminer were not widely used. Their potential for dispatching and reducing the General Court's case load seemed to make them a serviceable mechanism for disposing of a growing number of felonies committed by the colony's enlarging slave population, and in 1692 the Assembly enacted a statute that institutionalized these courts for that purpose. The act permitted the governor to grant a *dedimus potestatem*—literally we give you power—to local magistrates ordering them to sit as courts of oyer and

---

24. Northumberland County Order Book, 1652–1665, pp. 110–111.

terminer. As such the justices were to cause the defendant's arraignment and to collect evidence. In what the act called "pregnant circumstances" the testimony of a single witness, instead of the two that Virginia law usually specified, was sufficient proof of a crime. Even though the charges were always capital, the trial could be heard "without the sollemnitie of a jury." There was no appeal of the court's verdict.[25]

While county courts usually lacked competence to adjudicate felonies, they aided in their prosecution by conducting the preliminaries that preceded the trial itself. How the justices proceeded in instances of murder, for example, provides the easiest illustration of how such assistance was rendered. In a county where a death occurred as a result of suspicious or mysterious circumstances the court ordered an inquest to ascertain if murder had been committed. Frequently, this inquiry was conducted by a coroner and coroner's jury, a practice taken directly from England. At the inquest the coroner, acting as interrogator, put written questions to witnesses, who answered under oath, and the jury based its decision on what it heard. The jury's verdict and the sworn statements became part of the record, for they were passed on to the grand jury. Following the grand jury's action the justices ordered the sheriff to arrest and detain the suspect. He also collected the witnesses, who, together with the defendant, were bound over for trial in the General Court.[26]

Occasionally, these preliminaries were not so elaborate. Although Virginians employed coroner's inquests as early as

---

25. Hening, ed., *The Statutes at Large,* 3: 102–103. For examples of such trials see Accomack County Order Book, 1690–1697, fol. 35; and Accomack County Deeds, Wills, and Depositions, 1692–1715, fols. 58-59; Northampton County Order Book, 1689–1696, pp. 236-39.
26. Accomack County Order Book, 1678–1683, pp. 159–168.

1624, that practice had no statutory sanction before 1677.[27] Some counties simply did without coroners, and in those instances the justices themselves convened and conducted the inquest. Then too, when courts were notified of a killing, sometimes they merely ordered everyone connected with the incident held for transportation to Jamestown. Evidently, where serious crimes like murder, arson, or rape were suspected procedural regularity was less desirable than prompt action. What seemed to matter most was the swift restraint of people who endangered the colony's safety, the more so if the suspect was a servant accused of a violent crime.[28]

By a tradition established in the 1620s and set in law in March 1661/62 the fourth day of each General Court session was reserved for clearing the criminal docket. Since that docket's cases involved the taking of life or member they were put to a jury, except of course in those instances of a defendant's admission of guilt. Once the clerk called the case and the defendant entered his plea a jury was chosen. The method of jury selection differed from that of the county courts, however. Like other Englishmen, the Virginians professed belief that a jury should be composed of the peers of one's neighborhood. But in a colony where widely dispersed settlements were the rule it was difficult to get twelve supposedly impartial men to go off to Jamestown for an extended stay. Consequently, the colonists turned to a procedure that English judges used when a jury lacked its full complement of jurors. The device, known as *tales de circumstantibus*, allowed a sheriff to complete a deficient jury by pressing into service the needed number from the bystanders present in the courtroom. As the practice developed in Virginia sheriffs compelled six

---

27. McIlwaine, ed., *Minutes of the Council and General Court*, p. 38; "An Act Ascertaining Coroners Fees," Acts of Assembly, October 1677, Colonial Office Papers, Class 5, Vol. 1379, p. 100, National Archives, Kew, Surrey.
28. Charles City County Order Book, 1655–1665, pp. 158, 242, 243.

disinterested local men to go along with the defendants and the witnesses to the capital. Then on trial day, when a sheriff received the General Court's writ of venire facias, he served it on those six and any six spectators who stood by in the council chambers. In this way the colonists came "as neere . . . as we possibly may" to English law while solving a procedural problem which that law did not comprehend.[29] As to the trial itself, it followed the fashion of the local courts. Similarly, in criminal cases there was no appealing of a judgment of the General Court, colonial judges tended to weight their proceedings against defendants, and in so doing they failed to mitigate noticeably the harshness of English criminal law. There is irony in that failure, considering that the seventeenth century was a time when Englishmen stoutly defended their liberties against the Stuart kings' pretensions to rule by divine right. At the same time, neither the Virginians nor their contemporaries in other colonies or at home paid heed to improving the protections afforded to those individuals charged with criminal misconduct.[30]

The reasons for such a failure lie in the colonists' attitudes towards crime. Despite profound concern for defending personal, political, and property rights from the crown's interference, in criminal matters the English still placed the whole of society's interest above that of the individual. That

---

29. Cowell, *Law Dictionary*, under "Tales"; Hening, ed., *The Statutes at Large*, 2: 63-64; Robert Beverley, *The History and Present State of Virginia*, ed. by Louis B. Wright (Chapel Hill, N.C., 1947), p. 258; Surry County Deed Book, 1671–1684, fol. 69; "Further Representation of [Thomas] Lord Culpeper [to the Committee for Foreign Plantations]," 30 Sept. 1683, CO 5/1356, 155–160.

30. Julius Goebel, Jr., "King's Law and Local Custom in Seventeenth Century New England," in David H. Flaherty, ed., *Essays in the History of Early American Law* (Chapel Hill, N.C., 1969), pp. 83–120, especially 109–114; Goebel and Naughton, *Law Enforcement in Colonial New York*, pp. 554–58; Frankfurter and Corcoran, "Petty Federal Offenses," 934–65.

predilection was given even greater emphasis for settlers living in a society groping for order and made up largely of males and servants. Lacking the steadying effect of the family, the institutional church, or a well-defined social order, there were few means of calling the people to account for their behavior. In these circumstances, uncertain men were not inclined to tamper with English judicial processes that worked in Virginia without extensive modification.

Virginians, like other Englishmen, linked crime to sin. *The Book of Common Prayer's* invocation of divine intervention to direct and dispose magistrates "to the punishment of wickedness and vice," as well as the line in felony indictments, "not haveing the feare of God before thine eyes but being moved by the instigation of the devill," speak volumes about their assumptions as to why culprits committed their foul deeds.[31] Criminals were sinners who had fallen from grace, and for that fall they must suffer swift punishment, the severity of which increased with the magnitude of the act. The same suppositions were no less valid in the New World. Man's nature did not change when he went over the seas. Hence, there was little need to tinker with the received wisdom of the ages. A man accused was a man guilty of the charges laid to him. His trial was the ritual way of exacting a just penalty for his offense against the laws of God and man, as well as providing a terrifying example to others. Pleading not guilty, calling defense witnesses, presenting exculpatory evidence, defining rules of evidence, all merely prolonged the inevitable.

There is also a practical reason why Virginians did not alter their opinion of criminal due process. Crime was much rarer in

---

31. This is from the prayer for the whole state of Christ's church in the communion service, *The Booke of Common Prayer* (London, 1603), unpaged; indictment of George Caquescough, Northumberland County Order Book, 1652–1665, p. 110. The wording of this indictment closely parallels that of the standard form for English felony indictments.

the colony than the controversies that led to civil actions. Moreover, the content of that civil litigation was, in a sense, more important than the threat posed by the drunkard, the runaway, or the fornicator, for it comprehended the colonists' valuables. Consequently, finding a workable judicial procedure in civil matters carried a somewhat greater urgency than the colonial magistrates' concern for the mechanics of moving criminal trials to a conclusion. For models they turned to their knowledge of common-law practice.

Litigating a civil suit in English courts was a lengthy and expensive undertaking. A suitor needed a lawyer to navigate his case through the proper court by using a complicated battery of maneuvers. The latter ranged from the writs that initiated the suit to the pleadings that laid the facts and the issues before the court. A writ wrongly employed or minor defects in the pleadings voided the case, for such imperfections could be pleaded as a bar to further court action. Much of the business at court itself seemed obscure to litigants who understood neither Latin, the language of the writs, nor law French, the language of the cases the lawyers cited as their precedents. To many laymen, such intricacies seemed as so much mummery that was intended merely to fatten lawyers' purses.

Indeed, such was the hostility to lawyers and courts by the seventeenth century that even as the first settlers sailed for Virginia Englishmen had begun to press for law reform.[32] This agitation for reform had its effect in the colony. Many of the men who sat in the General Assembly and on the colonial bench had left England to exchange a tangle of lawyers and legal restrictions for a freer American environment. That Virginia was a more primitive social organism than the mother country was also an advantage to would-be reformers. English courts

---

32. A brief but useful introduction to the topic of law reform is Barbara Shapiro, "Law Reform in Seventeenth Century England," *American Journal of Legal History*, 19 (1975): 280–312.

and their procedures were too elaborate for a colony made up of dispersed settlements. Modifications were necessary, and that necessity afforded the opportunity to strip common law of some of its complexities. Design and accident therefore combined to simplify procedures in civil matters.

Colonial interest in due process of law in civil lawsuits increased from the moment settlers started acquiring land, labor, and other material possessions. As they had in the criminal sphere, the governor and council experimented with techniques to meet a growing volume of litigation. Of course, a chief reason for the division of judicial authority between county and provincial courts was a desire to expedite civil disputes by reducing some of the council's case load. What emerged from that change was a significant departure from the received English tradition.

At first the division of civil jurisdiction conferred limited authority over small causes to local magistrates. Within a decade that arrangement changed, however, when the General Assembly authorized the county courts to try all cases at common law and in equity. Individual justices tried small causes as assigned to them by statute, and in such matters their determination was final. Cases involving things of greater value were put before the full bench summarily or heard by a jury. Although the use of juries antedates its sanction in statute, litigants seemed to prefer them only when complicated issues were disputed. On its part, the General Court gradually became a high court of appeal. Cases brought on appeal were retried rather than reviewed for errors. The advantage of an appeal lay in the fact that the appellant collected larger damages if it succeeded. As in the local courts, both summary trials and trials by jury were used. However and wherever civil suits were brought the procedure used to hear them was the same. It was a form whose origins can be traced to the late company and early royal period.[33]

As early as the 1620s the governor and the council were experimenting with a procedure for trying civil actions. This was the form known to Englishmen as bill procedure, and it was familiar to anyone who ever brought suit in the High Court of Chancery, the Court of Wards, or the Court of Requests. As bill procedure emerged in Virginia, it worked in the following way: an aggrieved party filed with the court a document, variously called a bill of complaint, a declaration, a petition, or simply a bill, in which he alleged an injury to have been done him by someone else. Receiving the complaint, the court summoned or arrested the defendant for the purpose of making him respond to the plaintiff's allegations. When the defendant answered, the plaintiff could enter a written reply on the record, and the defendant then had an additional chance to present a rejoinder. The purpose of these maneuvers was to settle the issue if possible. If no such resolution was forthcoming, the defendant had to plead to the bill. A guilty plea ended the matter, and judgment passed, but if the defendant pleaded not guilty, the case went to trial. At that point both sides called witnesses who gave their evidence in sworn depositions or in open court. Following the presentation opposing counsel argued their evidence, and the court rendered its verdict.

This method of proceeding possessed several advantages that the Virginians found attractive. First, it reduced the use of writs to commence a lawsuit, and it minimized the importance of

---

33. Hening, ed., *The Statutes at Large*, 1: 224,303–304; 2: 73–74; Lower Norfolk County Order Book, 1637–1645 (transcript), 175; McIlwaine, ed., *Minutes of the Council and General Court*, p. 202; Beverley, *History and Present State of Virginia*, pp. 258–259; Henry Hartwell, James Blair, and Edward Chilton, *The Present State of Virginia, and the College*, ed. by Hunter Dickinson Farish (Williamsburg, Va., 1940), pp. 45, 48–49.

PLEADING, PROCEDURE AND PRACTICE 221

pleadings. To be sure, writs made their way into the colony's civil procedure, but there were fewer of them, they were in English rather than Latin, and they were simple in form. Pleadings were little more than the recitation of presumed fact appearing in the plaintiff's bill or the defendant's answer. Each was set down in plain English without regard to legalisms or technical forms, both of which were usually ignored. Indeed, the General Assembly declared in March 1657/58 that "small mistakes" in form did not bar a case from further action.[34]

Proceeding by bill also fit a peculiarly colonial condition. For most of the century few lawyers settled in Virginia, so most cases were moved by laymen. A litigant frequently acted in his own behalf, although his wife, kinsman, friend, or neighbor might serve as his attorney.[35] Wherever possible, suitors sought representation by experienced people, but since even these lacked formal schooling colonial procedure had to be tailored to the comprehension of settlers who were often barely literate, let alone conversant with the finer points of common-law writs or pleadings. Since anyone could do it, bill procedure eliminated the need for lawyers.

This method could be modified according to the complexities of the case. Unless complicated issues were involved, there was no need for additional maneuvering once the bill and the answer had been filed, so the case could go to trial immediately. The justices were not bound by fast rules; colonial custom and law allowed considerable latitude in rule

---

34. Hening, ed., *The Statutes at Large*, 1: 486–487.
35. Attorney and lawyer were not synonymous terms in seventeenth-century legal usage. An attorney could be anyone who represented another's interest in a court proceeding, while a lawyer was a person with formal legal training at one of the Inns of Court. By definition, all lawyers were attorneys, but not every attorney was a lawyer. See Cowell, *Law Dictionary* under "attorney" and "lawyer."

making.[36] They were therefore likely to admit as evidence whatever seemed to have bearing on the matter, be it the testimony of witnesses, the parties, or even responses to questions they might put to the attorneys. When they heard all that they deemed appropriate, they gave their decision, or if a jury was involved, left the verdict to the jurors.[37] More often than not the process of reaching a resolution of a dispute was achieved by an even more modest effort. In debt litigation, for instance, since most debtors never contested suits lodged against them, settling such matters soon became a routine affair. A creditor commenced his action in the usual way, and the court issued the summons. On court day the debtor came to admit his obligation, judgment passed against him, and the court then ordered an execution to follow. This practice dates from the 1630s; thereafter, it was simplified even further. As of the 1650s it was no longer necessary for the defendant to appear, providing he sent a written avowal of his debt to the court. It was also common by mid-century for both parties to avoid court appearances merely by putting the case in their attorneys' hands.[38]

Bill procedure also contributed to the colonial adaptation of equity as a means of resolving some civil lawsuits. Equity had grown up in medieval England to provide relief to suitors who had none at common law, and from that start had come a body of law consisting of more informal processes for securing justice.

---

36. Hening, ed., *The Statutes at Large*, 2: 171–172; Lancaster County Order Book, 1666–1680, p. 208; Essex County Order Book, 1692–1695, p. 25.

37. For some examples of how bill procedure worked in Virginia courts see Charles City County Order Book, 1677–1679, pp. 371–374; Westmoreland County Order Book, 1675–1689, pp. 374–377; Lower Norfolk County Order Book, 1637–1646 (transcript), 117; Isle of Wight County Deed and Will Book, 1662–1715, pp. 16–17.

38. Northampton County Order Book, 1632–1640, fols. 7–9; Lower Norfolk County Order Book, 1637–1646 (transcript), 6; York County Order Book, 1645–1649, fol. 1; Hening, ed., *The Statutes at Large*, 1: 447, 455.

By the seventeenth century equity's *ad hoc* quality had diminished, but Virginians were attracted to its seeming informality. For that reason the General Assembly invested local courts with equity jurisdiction at an early date. The enabling act provided the method of removing cases from common law to equity. Before a suit was called from the docket the defendant could petition the court for an equity hearing. If the court refused the petition the suit went to trial at law.[39]

Finally, bill procedure possessed the virtue of being rooted in English history. Malleable enough to be bent, it could be fashioned without breaking its links to old ways. That bond with the past made the colonists' variations appear not only suitable but also more comfortable. Comfort slowly turned into acceptance as time dimmed memories of how things ought to be, and what worked eventually became more important than what might have been.

When the seventeenth century gave way to the future, "what worked" was firmly entrenched in Virginia, for colonial lawmakers had created a means of moving all sorts of civil and criminal suits through their courts. They delineated that method in the fashion of John Cowell, not Sir Edward Coke. Still in transition, their version of procedure was receptive to further refinement as were the colony's laws. That very fluidity betokened a changing society whose members were beginning to regard profound change as a condition of life in Virginia. Therein lay the kernel of a later American characteristic—the embracing of change as an affirmation of progress. And, although due process of law is an ancient maxim, it is this attachment to change, not colonial usage, that shapes the modern content of its meaning.

---

39. Hening, ed., *The Statutes at Large*, 1: 303–304; Accomack County Order Book, 1666–1670, fol. 168; Essex County Order Book, 1692–1695, p. 37; Middlesex County Order Book, 1680–1694, pp. 216–17.

ESSAY 10

LOUISIANA LEGAL HISTORY AND ITS SOURCES

Needs, Opportunities, and Approaches

This essay was my first foray into writing about Louisiana law. Edward F. Haas had a hand in its making, first as an oral presentation and then as a book chapter. While Head of the Louisiana Historical Center at the Louisiana State Museum, Haas invited judges, law professors, historians, political scientists, and museum professionals to participate in a symposium he organized around the theme "Louisiana's Legal Heritage." One of the invitees, I demurred out of fear of exposing my ignorance before so eminent a gathering of peers who knew way more than I about the matter at hand. I relented once I knew that Ed wanted a sketch of possibilities that could encourage future research, which was something I felt comfortable doing as a result of my recent involvement with saving the records of the Supreme Court of Louisiana and my growing engagement with those documents.

The talk addressed three broad issues: documentary preservation, coping with mounting quantities of modern court records, and suggesting new ways of regarding Louisiana's distinctive legal order. At the time, Louisiana lawyers, judges, scholars, librarians, archivists, and genealogists were attuned to the need to assure the salvation of court archives. I encouraged those who were at the symposium to join with we who were lobbying the legislature for the funding of a proper state-of-the-art archives facility. Our efforts bore fruit years afterwards, when State Archives finally got the money to raise the building that now sits at Essen Lane in Baton Rouge.

How to cope with an ever-increasing volume of records was the principal reason that led the Supreme Court to deposit its historic archives at UNO. Removing the old documents from the courthouse basement to the campus freed up space, to be sure, but that was a stopgap measure at best, because the growth trend for modern records went only in one direction—upwards. The problem was by no means unique to courts in Louisiana, and neither were potential long-range solutions. Nationally, archivists and records managers touted a procedure they styled "selective destruction" as the way forward, but I was dubious of its application, especially to appellate court records. Instead, I advocated a species of adaptive use that relied upon microfilm and computers.

Drawing notice to these issues pointed toward rethinking ways to do the history of Louisiana law, and articulating some possibilities constituted the main thrust of my remarks. I took a page from my Virginia research to argue that the interpretative scheme that I applied to the Old Dominion might work with equal success if it were adapted to Louisiana, and I sketched what such an application might entail. For me that sketch outlined a framework on which I would hang all of my writing about Louisiana from that day to this. I recommended the published chapter to my students, and others looked to it as well. In that way, that piece became an intellectual mainstay of the New Louisiana Legal History.[*]

---

[*] I first used the phrase "the new Louisiana legal history" in a review of Richard Holcombe Kilbourne, *A History of the Civil Code: The Formative Years* (Baton Rouge, La., 1989) in *Louisiana History: The Journal of the Louisiana Historical Association*, 30 (1989): 324; Mark F. Fernandez, "Louisiana Legal History: Past, Present, and Future," in Warren M. Billings and Mark F. Fernandez, eds., *A Law Unto Itself?: Essays in the New Louisiana Legal* History (Baton Rouge, La., 2001), p. 13. I set forth a more explicit specification of the approach in 1994, when I delivered my presidential address to the Louisiana Historical Association. See "Confessions of a Court Historian," *Louisiana History*, 35 (1994): 261–270.

Originally published as "Louisiana Legal History and Its Sources: Needs Opportunities, and Approaches" in Edward F. Haas, ed., *Louisiana's Legal Heritage* (Pensacola, Fla., 1983), pp. 189–203, the essay is reprinted here with the kind permission of the Louisiana State Museum.

When I was asked to prepare this essay, I hesitated to accept the assignment because my own scholarly interests and work lie mainly in a time and place far removed from Louisiana. Furthermore, my only claim to authority in the subject of Louisiana's legal heritage arises from a familiarity with the state's judicial archives—an acquaintance that developed while I helped rescue the records of our Supreme Court. Not being expert in the study of the state's law, I was somewhat reluctant to attempt to instruct scholars whose knowledge exceeds mine. To do so invited the hazard of unmasking my ignorance; nevertheless, at length it became a risk I was willing to assume. My reason for taking such a chance was this realization: Precisely because I am no specialist, I can play the part of the boy in the tale of the emperor's new clothes and thereby draw attention to some things that need doing in the uncharted regions of Louisiana's legal history. A step towards mapping those regions entails some reconsideration of the sources in relation to a variety of needs, opportunities, and approaches to further research.

One of the more obvious needs is for legal scholars to maintain an abiding concern for the preservation of the sources because until fairly recently, the commitment of Louisianians to saving the records of their legal heritage can only be described as whimsical. The consequences of past failures are now all too readily apparent. For instance, the absence of a state department of archives until 1956—which even now lacks adequate facilities—compelled the state courts to retain their old records in places that were insufficient to insure their security. Under the circumstances, the result of poor care was predictable. Large portions of the earliest records were lost to disasters, carelessness, willful destruction, and pilferage. The colonial documents in the *Cabildo* came near to ruination because of improper storage and the tender ministration of those well-intended amateurs who attempted repairs with scotch tape. Legislative journals have disappeared, along with many of those of city councils across the state. Unhappily, while a limited number of papers belonging to members of the bench and bar have managed to stray into the holdings of our universities, no one ever undertook a systematic accumulation of such collections.[1] It is now therefore quite difficult to document the activities of the judges and lawyers who figured so prominently after 1803 in molding the civilian legal customs with those of the Anglo-American tradition. Equally unfortunate was the neglect of published sources. Often printed on paper highly infected with acid-producing compounds, many reports, compilations, digests, treatises, or how-to-do it manuals have deteriorated to the point of no repair. Such a litany of losses or near losses could go on, but, in the words of a seventeenth-century friend of mine, that recital would "bee too tedious to mention."

More to the point however is a change in attitudes that has come gradually over the past two decades. There now exists among scholars, judges, lawyers, and laymen a keener sensitivity to how fragile are the sources and how great is the

---

1. Connie G. Griffith, "Collections in the Manuscripts Section of Howard-Tilton Memorial Library," *Louisiana History: The Journal of the Louisiana Historical Association*, 1(1960): 320–327; V. L. Bedsole, "Collections in the Department of Archives and Manuscripts, Louisiana State University," ibid., 328–334; Kate Wallach and Elsa B. Meier, "Dear Father-Dear Son, About Southern Law Students, 1800–1860," *Louisiana Law Review*, 23 (1962–1963): 680–708.

need to preserve what remains. The reason for this change is several-fold. During the period of the last twenty years, historians have abandoned the study of great men and great events and turned, in Jesse Lemisch's phrase, to writing "history from the ground up."[2] Accordingly, they now draw attention to the importance of blacks, women, native Americans, Hispanics, and so they have come to prize court records as the window through which to observe this mass of the American people.[3] In the 1960s and 1970s concern for historic preservation played a part, as did the bicentennial celebration, the "roots" phenomenon started by Alex Haley's book, as well as nostalgia for times seemingly less troubled than our own.[4] More specifically, certain individuals and institutions have led the effort to save things that might now be lost. Louisiana's genealogists, through their Friends of the Archives of Louisiana organization, have worked tirelessly to make public officials mindful of the need to secure surviving early records from further loss. The Louisiana Division of the New Orleans Public Library has gathered an impressive array of municipal archives having peculiar significance for studying our legal heritage. Not least among these are the historic records of the Civil District Court for Orleans Parish. The Amistad Research Center now houses an invaluable collection of papers of southern civil rights attorneys while

---

2. Jesse Lemisch, "The American Revolution Seen from the Bottom Up," in Barton J. Bernstein, ed., *Towards a New Past: Dissenting Essays in American History* (New York, 1969), pp. 3–46.

3. For example, see John Demos, *A Little Commonwealth: Family Life in Plymouth* (New York, 1970) and Thad W. Tate and David Ammerman, eds., *The Seventeenth-Century Chesapeake: Essays in Anglo-American History* (Chapel Hill, N.C., 1979).

4. One of the projects that the Louisiana American Revolution Bicentennial Commission subvened was the Louisiana Bicentennial Reprint Series. The series reissued early books about the state's history. It was under the general editorship of the late Joseph G. Tregle, Jr., of the University of New Orleans, and it was published under a Louisiana State University Press imprint.

the Louisiana State Museum has undertaken an ambitious project to repair, arrange, and film the colonial documents. Even the United States Court of Appeals for the Fifth Circuit has an archives-history committee presently at work on ways to preserve federal judicial records. And, my own university, the Supreme Court, and the State Archives are embarked upon a cooperative venture to save the high court records.

These activities are encouraging and they must continue. They should not lull anyone into believing that all is well, however, because there remain categories of sources that are not regularly collected, just as there are those that still face extinction through inadvertence or deliberate choice. For instance, no one routinely gathers the papers of modern law firms, and there is no systematic program of oral history to record the recollections of practitioners on the bench or at the bar. As yet, librarians have not taken many steps towards conserving their old law books, and until book conservation receives greater attention, there is a continuing danger of losing the information which this rich source contains. The singular need in respect to preservation, though, may be deciding how to cope with the mountainous volumes of modern court records.

Since the mid-1950s our federal and state courts have been literally buried under a deluge of paper as the citizenry has come to regard the judiciary as the forum to remedy all manner of social ills. The example of the Supreme Court of Louisiana makes the point. In the past twenty-five years that court has produced more records than it did in its first one hundred-fifty years of existence. Faced with such an onslaught, the inevitable question arose: "To make more space, what can we throw away?" The tempting answer was, those records nobody used anymore, meaning those that were of no value to pending litigation. Yet, giving into temptation was fraught with some peril, for it invited the opprobrium of those who cherished the records for the history they contained as it risked violating both state law and custom. Here, then, was a tension, the existence of which made the concept of selective destruction seem quite seductive. In archival parlance, this conception holds that while some documents have historic merit, others do not, and those that do not may be destroyed. Thus, by having someone earmark certain records insignificant and other significant, it becomes possible to satisfy the urge to retain sources of the past and still solve the problems of space and storage. The weakness in this calculus, though, has been the inability of those to whom the business of choosing has fallen to make their choices. My own experience with selective destruction makes me doubt the concept's value in records preservation, at least as the idea is currently understood. Perhaps it is time to consider an alternative.

In the place of selective destruction I would interpose a variant of what some historic building preservationists call "adaptive use." Restorers who save a building in this way return the structure's exterior form to its original condition while they transform its interior substance to a use other than its original purpose. As it applies to modern court records, adaptive use would reverse this formulation. The substance of the documents, that is their content, would remain unaltered, but their form would be reduced in size through a system of microprocessing.

What makes this variety of adaptive use possible is a fundamental difference between ancient and modern records. Ancient records have both a physical and a functional merit, while those of modern times are merely functional. This distinction arises from how the two types of records were generated. The media of early record keeping exemplify antique techniques of papermaking, printing, and bookbinding, as well as old court hands. Furthermore, a brief in the hand of Edward Livingston is prized not only for what it reveals of nineteenth-century practice, it is also cherished because that Moses of Louisiana law wrote it. In short, ancient records are prized as much for their physical characteristics as for their content. But, technological advances from the late nineteenth century to our day changed the nature of record keeping. The invention of the typewriter eliminated the handwritten record. Newer ways of making paper and books lessened their quality and durability. Dictaphones, tape recorders, word processors, computers, and even television opened new possibilities for information storage. The perfection of copying devices from the typewriter to that ultimate copier, the Xerox machine, made infinite reproduction a reality. Because one piece of Xerox paper is like any other—cheap and short-lived—modern court records are valuable only for what they contain.[5] In their case, then, the medium is not the message; the message lies only in their content. That being so, their content is quite adaptable to some sort of microprocessing.

Microprocessing can be accomplished in one of two ways, employing conventional microfilm or storing the records' texts on computer tapes or discs. The latter technique is still at an experimental stage of development and its possibilities have yet to attract widespread notice or acceptance.[6] Whatever technique of miniaturization is used, though, the result remains the same. The need for paper records diminishes as cases close and they can then be

---

5. On the evolution of the idea, see Warren M. Billings et al., "Towards a Comprehensive Judicial Records Management Program in Louisiana," a report submitted to Chief Justice Joe W. Sanders by the Committee on Records Maintenance and Storage, 15 Mar. 1978, and Billings to Judge Albert Tate, 19 Nov. 1980.

6. The idea for the use of computers for full text storage of court records derives from the example of the Henry Laurens Papers Project. There, the editor, David K. Chestnutt employed the computer to hold transcribed texts of Laurens items. How the Laurens system worked was described in David K. Chestnutt, "Comprehensive Text Processing and the Papers of Henry Laurens," *Documentary Editing*, 2, #2, (1980): 12–14; 2, #3: 3–5.

destroyed after being microprocessed. Microprocessing would do more than merely reduce the amount of space required to house retired records. It would also eliminate the need for someone to distinguish records according to their presumed historical significance because they could all be kept in miniature.

Lest it appear that I have concocted a sovereign remedy, let me hasten to caution adaptive use is still in its infancy. Just as some building preservationists argue the folly of applying the concept to the salvation of old houses, there are archivists and other scholars who balk at the suggestion of destroying paper documents. Others decry microfilm as inconvenient or harmful to the eye, while some undoubtedly object to learning how a computer terminal works. Besides these objections, there are as yet unresolved concerns about the longevity of microfilm or computer tapes, as well as questions about efficient means of retrieval or the costs and staff requirements of a microprocessing system. Admittedly, each of these cares is genuine, but their expression should not be the occasion to ignore this salient fact: If we wish to reduce the tension between the demands of records management and the needs of history, then we cannot continue to blink our eyes to advances in the technology of information storage.

Of course, the object of exploring any means of records preservation is to assure the survival of the greatest array of legal sources. Obviously, the wider scope of the surviving evidence, the broader is the opportunity to understand the impression Louisiana law has made upon the shaping of our state's unique culture and how in turn that culture has helped to fashion our law. It is this bond between law and culture which suggests the need of new formulas to interpret Louisiana legal history.

To date, the scholars of the history of our law are not all that dissimilar from their colleagues who write in the general field of American legal history. That is to say, they fall into two distinct groups, each of which sees the study of things legal as serving particular ends. One of these groups is a band of students who trained primarily as lawyers and only incidentally as historians. Here, as elsewhere, this company consists not only of academicians, but also practicing attorneys and judges as well. Their central interests lie in describing the evolution of judicial doctrines developed by the statutes or the courts, studying the growth of legal institutions, or doing legal biography.[7] But their emphasis upon these seemingly autonomous features of the legal order enhances the idea that only those who speak the special language of Louisiana law are capable of interpreting its history to others. This species, which may be styled "internal legal history," therefore frequently separates the law from its

---

7. Erwin C. Surrency, "Legal History and Rare Books," *Law Library Journal*, 59 (1966): 71; Alice M. Magee, "History of the Courts of Louisiana," ibid., 33 (1940): 253–259; Elizabeth Gaspar Brown, "Legal Systems in Conflict: Orleans Territory, 1804–1812," *American Journal of Legal History*, 1 (1957): 35–76; Henry P. Dart, "Courts and Law in Colonial Louisiana," *Louisiana Historical Quarterly*, 4 (1921): 255–289; Howard Newcomb Morse, "Federal Equity Jurisdiction in Louisiana,' *Loyola Law Review*, 7 (1953): 1–22; Henry G. McMahon, 'The Case Against Fact Pleading in Louisiana," *Louisiana Law Review*, 13 (1952–1953): 369–394; John T. Hood, Jr., "The Louisiana Judiciary," ibid., 14 (1953–54): 811–824; and "The Louisiana Lawyer," ibid., 18 (1957–1958): 661–670; J. Denson Smith, "Law Revision in Louisiana in Retrospect," ibid., 19 (1958–1959): 34–42; Hood, "History of Courts of Appeal in Louisiana," ibid., 21 (1960–61): 531-553; Ginger Roberts, "Edward Livingston and American Penology," ibid., 37(1976–1977): 1037–1067; Mitchell Franklin, "The Foundations and Meaning of the Slaughterhouse Cases," *Tulane Law Review*, 17 (1943–1944): 1–88, 218–62; Walter E. Joyce, "Edward Douglas White: The Louisiana Years, Early Life and on the Bench," ibid., 41 (1966–1967): 752–768; Philip English Mackey, "Edward Livingston on the Punishment of Death," ibid., 68 (1973–1974): 25–42; Max Nathan, Jr., "In Search of a Missing Link: Edward Livingston and the Proposed Code of Commerce," ibid., 43–54; Anne L. Simon, "Inequality under the Law: The Louisiana Story," *Southern Studies*, 16 (1977): 293–308.

cultural links to the past, as it often renders its study mechanical and a trifle tedious. The consequences of these tendencies has been largely to keep professionally-trained historians from entering a field of study that appears beyond their ken.[8] Those who do make the venture comprise the second group, and to judge from their work, two reasons draw them to it. Some see in the legal sources numerous rich episodes that give flesh and color to the Louisiana story, and so they seek to devise diverting narratives about gamblers, highwaymen, or trollops. Others work the sources for evidence of how previous generations used the legal order to settle social imperatives that may now have modern relevance. They are curious, for example, to learn how our ancestors handled women's rights or other personal relationships.[9]

Even though such scholars bring different backgrounds and perspectives to their studies, they are drawn together by common threads. The most obvious of these is a shared assumption about the nature of the legal variety of history. Both groups freight it with didactic or utilitarian ends. They take for granted that the purpose of examining the past is to find the keys to reconciling modern legal problems or maintaining fictions that serve professional purposes.[10]

---

8. The most recent single-volume history of the state all but ignores legal developments, Joe Gray Taylor, *Louisiana, A History* (New York, 1975).
9. Jack D. L. Holmes, ed., "O'Reilly's Regulations on Booze, Boardinghouses, and Billiards," *Louisiana History: The Journal of the Louisiana Historical Association*, 6 (1965): 293–300; Germaine E. Reid, "Race Legislation on Louisiana, 1864–1920," ibid.: 379–393; Robert B. Murray, "Mrs. Alexander's Cotton," ibid.: 393–400; David E. Everett, "Free Persons of Color in Louisiana," ibid., 7 (1966): 21–50; James D. Hardy, Jr., "Probate Racketeering in Colonial Louisiana,' ibid., 9 (1968): 109–121; E. Russ Williams, ed., "Slave Patrol Ordinances of St. Tammany Parish, Louisiana, 1835–1838," ibid., 13 (1972): 399–412.
10. Perhaps the most obvious of these fictions is the one which holds that the law has an existence independent of those who make or enforce it. It

Another of these drawstrings is the fact that existing scholarship was bounded long ago within some fairly narrow limits, and since their drawing they have seldom been crossed.

An outsider like myself therefore discovers that the refrain of the questions asked by Louisiana legal historians is remarkably the same. Among them are these. Is Louisiana a civilian or common law jurisdiction, or is it a mixture of both?[11] If wholly civilian, which tradition, the Spanish or the French, predominated?[12] Parenthetically, those who debate

---

is therefore a neutral, external gauge against which all human conduct may be impartially measured. The necessity for such a fiction is beyond doubt, for it invests the law and its minions with an awesome majesty that compels social obedience. Sometimes the fiction is disbelieved, however. In that case the law is powerless, as in the celebrated confrontation between John Marshall and Andrew Jackson over Marshall's ruling in *Cherokee Nation* v. *Georgia*. Marshall's opinion upholding the validity of treaties guaranteeing the Cherokee the integrity of their lands ran counter to the President's avowed aim to remove all eastern Indians across the Mississippi. Upon learning of the decision, Jackson is reputed to have remarked, "John Marshall has made his decision, now let him enforce it." Apocryphal or not, the fact remains that Marshall had no power to make Jackson obey, and so the Cherokee were removed.

11. John H. Wigmore, "Louisiana: The Story of its Legal System," *Tulane Law Review*, 1 (1916): 1–45; Henry P. Dart, "The Legal Institutions of Louisiana," ibid., 3 (1918): 254–280; Gordon Ireland, "Louisiana's Legal System Reappraised," ibid., 11 (1936–1937): 585–98; Leonard Greenburg, "Must Louisiana Resign to the Common Law?" ibid.: 598–601; John T. Hood, "A Crossroad in Louisiana History," *Louisiana Law Review*, 22 (1961–1962): 709–726; Sidney Pugh Ingram, "Administration of Successions: Anglo-American Influence upon Louisiana Law," ibid.: 24 (1963-1964): 54–105.

12. Dart, "The Influence of the Ancient Laws of Spain on the Jurisprudence of Louisiana," *Tulane Law Review*, 6 (1931–32): 83–93; Mitchell, "The Place of Thomas Jefferson in the Expulsion of Spanish Medieval Law from Louisiana," ibid., 16 (1941–1942): 319–338; and "The Eighteenth Brumarie in Louisiana: Talleyrand and the Spanish Medieval Legal System of 1806," ibid.: 514–561; C. Russell Reynolds, "Alfonso el Sabio's Laws Survive in the Civil Code of Louisiana," *Louisiana History*, 12 (1971): 137–147.

that proposition, really never indicate the importance of that distinction to the growth of law or culture. What were the sources of Louisiana law? When was the law first codified? Was James Brown's and Louis Moreau-Lislet's handiwork of 1808 a code or a digest?[13] After 1803, how were the conflicts between Louisiana and American legal customs resolved?[14] What is the role of our judges?[15] Do they follow something called civilian methodology or do they act like their brethren elsewhere in the Union?[16] Apart from these queries, there is a

---

13. John H. Tucker, Jr., "Source Books of Louisiana Law," *Tulane Law Review*, 8 (1933–1934): 396–405; Ferdinand Stone, "The Civil Code of 1808 for the Territory of Orleans," ibid.: 33 (1958–1959): 3–6; Hood, "The History and Development of the Louisiana Civil Code," ibid.: 7–20; Louis Baudouin, "The Influence of the Code Napoleon," ibid.: 21–28; Radolfo Batiza, "The Influence of Spanish Law in Louisiana," ibid.: 24–39; Franklin, "An Important Document in the History of American Roman and Civil Law: The De la Vergne Manuscript," ibid.: 35–42; Thomas W. Tucker, "Sources of Louisiana's Law of Persons: Blackstone, Domat, and the French Codes," ibid.: 45 (1970–1971): 264–295; Batiza, "The Louisiana Civil Code of 1808: Its Actual Sources and Present Relevance," ibid., 46 (1971–1972): 4–165; Joseph Modeste Sweeney, "Tournament of Scholars over the Sources of the Civil Code of 1808," ibid.: 585–603; Robert A. Pascal, "Sources of the Digest of 1808, A Reply to Professor Batiza," ibid.: 603–628; Batiza, "Sources of the Digest of 1808, Facts and Speculation: A Rejoinder," ibid., 628–653; and "The Actual Sources of the Louisiana Project of 1823: A General Analytical Survey," ibid., 47 (1972–1973), 1–115; Joseph Dainow, "Moreau Lislet's Notes on Sources of Louisiana's Civil Code of 1808," *Louisiana Law Review* 19 (1958–1959): 43–51; Pascal, "A Treatise on the Reprint of Moreau Lislet's Copy of a Digest of the Civil Laws," *Publications of the Louisiana Historical Society*, 2d Ser., 1 (1974): 43–48.
14. George Dargo, Jefferson's Louisiana: Politics and the Clash of Legal Traditions (Cambridge, Mass., 1975).
15. Albert Tate, "The Role of the Judge in Mixed Jurisdictions," *Loyola Law Review*, 20 (1973–1974): 231–244; and "The Role of the Judge in the American Republic," *Louisiana Law Review*, 16 (1955): 386–390.
16. Mack E. Barham, "A Renaissance of the Civilian Tradition in Louisiana," *Louisiana Law Review*, 33 (1972–1973): 357–389.

fascination for demonstrating the uniqueness of Louisiana law that borders on the obsessive, just as there is a frequent preoccupation with comparative analyses.[17]

To be sure, these are vital questions; had they not been asked, there would be no Louisiana legal history, and we would not now be pondering that heritage. Still, constantly asking them yields basically the same results, even as they lead scholars to the same types of sources.

Only a tiny portion of the manuscript sources are now in print, a fact which could open many possibilities for documentary publishing.[18] Unhappily, though, any large-scale documentary project is unlikely to materialize because of the costs in bringing it to publication. At a time when the goal of cutting public spending is being pursued with the dogged conviction of the New England Puritans, it is probably sanguine to expect the state or federal governments to subvene such undertakings. Indeed, if the national administration succeeds in killing the National Historic Records and Publication Commission, documentary publication may cease altogether. In short, unless private philanthropists create endowments similar to the Holmes Devise or the American Historical Association's Littleton-Griswold Fund we are unlikely to see many legal manuscripts rendered into print.

---

17. E. Fabre-Surveyes, "The Civil Law in Quebec and Louisiana," *Loyola Law Review*, 1 (1938): 649–664; Dainow, "The Early Sources of Forced Heirship: Its History in Texas and Louisiana," ibid., 4 (1942–1943): 42–69; Leonard Oppenheim, "The Law of Slaves: A Comparative Study of the Roman and Louisiana Systems," *Tulane Law Review*, 14 (1939–1940): 384–406; Daniel J. Flanigan, "Criminal Procedure in Slave Trials in the Antebellum South," *Journal of Southern History*, 40 (1974): 537–564.

18. What is in print appears variously in the old *Louisiana Historical Quarterly*, *Southern Studies*, and *Louisiana History*, as well as in such collections as the Claiborne papers and the *American State Papers*.

Opportunities for doing legal bibliography also abound. So long as there are no comprehensive guides to the manuscripts, they will be underutilized. Even as simple a compilation as an annual listing of theses, dissertations, articles, and books on Louisiana legal topics, published in a law review or a scholarly journal, would be valuable, as would a union list of Louisiana legal imprints.[19] Apart from the late Kate Wallach, however, Louisiana never produced rivals to the great Virginia bibliographer Earl Gregg Swem or his successor W. Hamilton Bryson. Bryson's bibliographies of the Old Dominion's law and legal history could serve as models here.[20] Despite advances in librarianship that make composing such reference aids easier to accomplish, bibliography remains unfashionable because the investment is great and the return small.

More pointed than these examples are the chances to examine the sources anew for a fresh, broader appreciation of how Louisiana came to possess its distinct legal heritage. The opportunities for imaginative research are manifold, especially in the manuscript court records. These documents are the last great untapped body of evidence about Louisiana's past, and they await exploration and exploitation.

---

19. Back in the 1960s both *Louisiana History* and *Southern Studies* published annual listings of theses and dissertations on Louisiana topics, but the practice was soon discontinued. There does exist a bibliography of doctoral dissertations, Edward F. Haas, *Louisiana: A Dissertation Bibliography* (Ann Arbor, Mich., n.d.).

20. Swem, of course, was the compiler of the monumental *Virginia Historical Index* (Roanoke, Va., 1934), that is keyed a variety of published sources, many of which relate to the commonwealth's legal history. Bryson has compiled three bibliographies, *Census of Law Books in Colonial Virginia* (Charlottesville, Va., 1977), *The Virginia Law Reporters Before 1900* (Charlottesville, Va., 1978), and *A Bibliography of Virginia Legal History Before 1900* (Charlottesville, Va., 1979). While useful, Bryson's work is not flawless; see my review of *A Bibliography of Virginia Legal History*, in the *American Journal of Legal History*, 25 (1981): 80–81.

Among the possibilities for further investigation are detailed studies of the courts from colonial to modern times. Nothing that is written on colonial Louisiana compares to the vast literature on the Virginia country court or the Massachusetts township.[21] Apart from Henry Plauché Dart's essay in the *Louisiana Reports*,[22] there is not a single general history of the Supreme Court, let alone any on the lower courts. Neither the federal district courts nor the Fifth Circuit Court have been subjected to vigorous study, despite their prominent role in refashioning the character of Louisiana's social institutions over the last quarter-century.[23]

It is also possible to achieve a greater appreciation of how legal practices evolved through time. From 1812 onwards, the Supreme Court, by its rule-making power and its control over admissions to the bar always exerted a profound influence on the way in which the legal order routinely worked. Consider the impact of two of the Court's earliest rules not only upon practices but also upon the social habits of early Louisianians. In 1819 the court declared that "candidates for admission to the bar who shall give satisfactory assurances to the Court that they have received a good classical education, altho' they may not have degrees in any college, may be examined on shewing that they have studied two years under an attorney

---

21. Jerry A. Micelle, "From Law Court to Local Government: Metamorphosis of the Superior Council of French Louisiana," *Louisiana History*, 9 (1968): 85–107; Ronald R. Morazan, "The Cabildo of Spanish New Orleans, 1769–1803," *Louisiana Studies* (now *Southern Studies*), 12 (1973): 591–607; Donald Lemieux, "Some Legal and Practical Aspects of the Office of Commissaire Ordonnateur of French Louisiana," ibid., 14 (1975): 378–393.
22. Vol. 133 (1913): xxx–lxxiv.
23. The appeals court has however designated Professor Harvey Couch of the Tulane law school as its official historian. (Subsequent to the appearance of this essay, Couch published *A History of the Fifth Circuit, 1891–1981* [Washington, D.C., 1984]).

duly admitted to practice in this state."²⁴ And in 1821, the Court promulgated this rule:

> The Judges find it necessary to make known that they expect that no application for a licence to plead will be made by any Gentleman not acquainted with the legal language of the State [i.e., English]. It is true we have translations of our laws, and those may suffice to direct the citizen in the ordinary transactions of life. But he who aspires to the high honor of being consulted on, and to explain these laws to his fellow Citizens, and the Court, must be able to read the text. Very few of the acts of Congress, which form a considerable proportion of our written laws, paramount to the acts of our state legislature are translated. The records of suits must be preserved in the same language as the laws, and the judges cannot designate as learned in the laws, and qualified to give legal advice and to carry on a lawsuit, [anyone] who is ignorant of the legal language of the state as not to be able to read the text of the laws or to undergo an examination in it.²⁵

Quite apart from such matters, the records could also be thrown into the debate that swirls around the question of the origins of Louisiana's law. They incorporate hundreds of inventories of personal estates. A systematic analysis of these inventories can furnish clues as to what compilations, digests, treatises, or how-to-do it manuals circulated in Louisiana during the law's formative period.²⁶ Such hints can therefore

---

24. Ms. Minute Book, 1818–1823, 38. This and all other minute books kept between 1812 and 1921 are part of the Court's records that are deposited in the Louisiana & Special Collections Department at the University of New Orleans.
25. Minute Book, 1818–1823, 239.
26. For an example of such a study, see Billings, "English Legal Literature as a Source of Law and Legal Practice for Seventeenth-Century Virginia," Essay 4, above.

inform us how men of law came by their erudition, just as they can lead to a deeper apprehension of legal education and the rise of the professional bar.

Someone interested in explaining the evolution of procedural rights would do well to look to these records too. The examples of a criminal defendant's rights to counsel and appeal suffice as illustrations. At the time of Louisiana's admission to the union, American law did not guarantee a criminal defendant the right of counsel, and his opportunities for appealing a conviction were few or non-existent. By the second third of the nineteenth century, however, attitudes changed and these changes were reflected in the state's courts. At first, appeals went not to the Supreme Court, but to a special tribunal known as the Court of Errors and Appeals. That arrangement proved unworkable, and so the authors of the Constitution of 1845 assigned the jurisdiction to the Supreme Court. From that point forward, the high court began to assume responsibility for developing procedural rights that it has continued to exercise down to the present day.[27]

Then too, the records could be combed for life data on the judiciary. In some instances they are the only evidence of how individual judges discharged their office. The facts accumulated through such a search could be compiled into a biographical dictionary that expands upon the work of Judge

---

27. Upon the demise of the Court of Errors and Appeals, its records were turned over to the Supreme Court. The remnants of that deposit are now housed at UNO. One of my graduate students later wrote her M.A. thesis on the Court of Errors and Appeals, and it was published. See Sheridan H. Young, "Louisiana's Court of Errors and Appeals," *Louisiana History*, 33 (1992): 66–80.

Cleveland Frugé, who has done a directory of the state's modern judges.[28]

Moreover, it is worth pondering anew how conceptions of law transferred to Louisiana and were translated into indigenous legal traditions. In this regard, there are discernible parallels between early Louisiana and Virginia. Both were settled by people who sprang from rule-bound cultures that stressed the importance of law for regulating social conduct. Settlers in both places showed penchants for creating their own laws and legal institutions, for each group believed there could be neither order nor stability without such trappings of civility. For their models, both could draw from richly complex legal inheritances that were somewhat too complicated for the primitive social organisms that first took life on the shores of the James and the Mississippi. Inevitably, there was a good deal of casting about to discover what suited the needs of a frontier existence, and because of the character of the population in both settlements these experiments were initially carried off by laymen. Their concern was always for what met the demands of the moment rather than for professional niceties or what ought to be. By determining what out of the Old World legal baggage could actually be made to work in new settings, these laymen laid the groundwork for indigenous bodies of law that remained receptive to later additions by other hands. Those other hands belonged, of course, to members of the professional bars that arose in the century after 1740. Obviously, the parallels are not exact. They are near enough however to convey the value of comparing Louisiana's legal tradition not only with those of continental Europe but with those of other states in the Union as well.

---

28. J. Cleveland Frugé, ed., *Biographies of Louisiana Judges* (Lake Charles, La. and New Orleans, La., 1971, 1977); Janice K. Shull, *The Chief Justices of Louisiana: Life Sketches* (New Orleans, La., 2007).

A final possibility is to take a closer look at the bond between law and culture. Today, Louisiana law represents an accretion of cultural values that accumulated haphazardly over nearly three centuries. It has come to say how this state's institutions and people ought to be arranged and governed, just as it stands as the measure against which to gauge all manner of conduct. In this way, then, throughout the state's history, the law has always shaped the social order. But that law has also been influenced by the social, political, and economic imperatives that have fashioned Louisiana since its beginnings. Just as its civil law ancestors ultimately defined French and Spanish culture, Louisiana's legal heritage came gradually to describe an identity that set Louisianians off from their antecedents and the rest of the nation as well.

Since the Purchase, some Louisianians have understood this nexus. The rivalry between Louisiana law and American law after 1803 was no mere intellectual exercise for the edification and material benefit of lawyers; it was a conflict of culture in which Franco-Spanish Louisianians sought to preserve their identity. The courts quickly became the forum in which the competing legal systems were harmonized, but the story of that accommodation requires telling.

These examples represent only a tiny sampling of the many opportunities for further study that await the curious researcher. Even so, they testify to the richness of the sources. And, if that evidence is linked to and made part of the larger history of Louisiana, then the importance of the state's singular legal heritage will take on a newer, deeper meaning.

ESSAY 11

A Judicial Legacy

The Last Will and Testament of François-Xavier Martin

François-Xavier Martin, a formidable thinker and a long-time member of the Supreme Court of Louisiana, sits prominently in the pantheon of Louisiana's lawgivers. As such, he was someone I encountered early on as I read printed reports of high court cases. At one point I happened upon a reported case that involved Martin's last will and testament and turned on issues of whether Martin, who was blind, could make a valid holographic will and if there was a state interest in setting aside Martin's wishes. Intrigued, I pulled the manuscript file from the Supreme Court archives to see what more I could learn, though I feared that the docket would be incomplete. The file was largely intact. It contained a wealth of detail about the facts of the case, which the reporter excluded, and clues to the possible whereabouts of the greater corpus of Martin's papers itself. A quick check of the records of the Civil District Court for the Parish of Orleans likewise yielded the original, three-sentence will, and an additional bit of digging in the parish notarial archives turned up a lengthy inventory of Martin's belongings, both of which added to my understanding of the court action.

When I informed Judge Tate of my find, he urged me to write something about it. So did my UNO colleague, Joseph G. Tregle, Jr., who suggested that an article about the case would be an ideal submission to *Louisiana History*. I took their advice, and the result was my second publication on a Louisiana legal topic.

I never found Martin's papers. Either they were lost to neglect or Martin's brother carted them back to France when he returned there, and they may yet rest in some obscure repository. As for the inventory of the judge's property, I regarded it as the basis for a master's thesis, but more than two decades passed before I matched it to Kathy Dugas, who was among the last of my graduate students. Her revised thesis—a close examination of Martin as a real estate magnate and a money lender—appeared in *Louisiana History* in 2009.*

Originally published as "A Judiciary Legacy: The Last Will and Testament of François-Xavier Martin," *Louisiana History: The Journal of the Louisiana Historical Association*, 25 (1984): 277–289, the article is reprinted here with the editor's kind permission.

"Early on yesterday morning [10 December 1846] the honorable Francis Xavier Martin departed this life at his residence in this city. A grand old age, green and vigorous to the last few hours before it yielded to the inevitable destiny of mortals crowned a life spent in devotion to the highest employment of the human—the dispensation of justice among men."[1] So began the *Daily Delta's* notice of old Judge Martin's passing. The obituary's author pronounced Martin one of Louisiana's ablest jurists who for nearly five decades had been a dominating presence in shaping the state's legal system, first as a territorial judge, then as attorney general, and finally as a member of the Supreme Court of Louisiana,

---

*Kathy T. Dugas, "An Immigrant's Journey to Wealth and Power: The Story of François-Xavier Martin," *Louisiana History: The Journal of the Louisiana Historical Association*, 50 (2009): 321–340.

---

1. New Orleans *Daily Delta*, 11 Dec. 1846.

where he served for thirty-one years.² He reminded his readers how Martin's influence extended beyond his contributions from the bench, for he also remarked upon Martin's work as a compiler of an early digest of state statutes³ and the first two series of reports of cases argued before the Supreme Court. All these gifts, concluded the writer, would cause Martin "ever [to] be held in deep veneration by all who study and revere the laws."⁴

---

2. Martin was eighty-two when he died. He has no modern biographer. The basic details of his career may be gleaned from the state's judicial records, and the following biographical sketches. Judith Kelleher Schafer, "Martin, François-Xavier," http://www.anb.org/articles/11/11-00558.html; *American National Biography Online*, accessed 3 Feb. 2010; Michael G. Chiorazzi, "François-Xavier Martin: Printer, Lawyer, Jurist," *Law Library Journal*, 80 (1988): 63–99; R. Don Higginbotham, "Francois-Xavier Martin's History of North Carolina" in Lawrence H. Leder, ed., *The Colonial Legacy* (New York, 1973), 4: 265–282. Henry Adams Bullard, penned the first portrayal shortly after the judge's demise, and it was published by Benjamin F. French in his *Historical Collections of Louisiana* . . . (Philadelphia, Pa., 1846–1853), 2: 17–40. Martin was a member of the Superior Court for the Territory of Orleans between 1810 and 1812, attorney general of Louisiana from 1812 to 1815, and judge of the Supreme Court of Louisiana from 1815 to 1846. Members of the Court in his day were not yet styled "justices," nor was there a "chief justice," though the senior man was called "chief judge." Following the death of Chief Judge George Mathews in 1836, Martin succeeded to the post and held it until it was abolished by the Constitution of 1845, which created the office of chief justice. Martin never became chief justice, however, because he retired from the bench in Mar. 1846, before the new constitution took effect.
3. F. X. Martin, *A General Digest of the Acts of the Legislature of the Late Territory of Orleans and of the State of Louisiana* . . . (New Orleans, La., 1816).
4. Martin published his reports in two series. The first, the so-called "old series," appeared in 1821 under a New Orleans imprint, and it reported cases argued in both the Superior and Supreme Courts. Martin's "new series," covering cases that came to the Supreme Court between 1823 and 1830, were also printed in New Orleans. All are available online via WestLaw or Lexis. Kate Wallach, *Research in Louisiana Law* (Baton Rouge,

Despite the floridity of his pronouncements the newspaperman accurately depicted the significance of Martin's impact upon Louisiana law. But what neither he nor his readers could know, as Louisianians mourned their loss, was that even as Martin grew cold in his grave he would make one last impression upon the state's jurisprudence. That mark came as a result of the controversy that would well up over the disposal of the old judge's estate in accordance with his last will and testament.

François-Xavier Martin died a wealthy man. His passion for riches was no less than his devotion to law; he was as adept at making one as he was at the other. One source of his wealth is explained by his personal frugality. A lifelong bachelor, Martin was economical to the point of being abstemious. He spent little on clothes, household possessions, or food; his house was noted for its slovenliness, just as he was renowned for his own untidiness. Such parsimony, his friend and colleague, Henry Adams Bullard, attributed to early experiences with poverty.[5] As a penniless youth from Marseilles, Martin had landed in North Carolina by way of Martinique during the latter stages of the War for Independence, in which he fought briefly. Mustering out of the service, he took up printing, which, according to Bullard, eventually "became somewhat lucrative," though his prosperity was augmented by a burgeoning law practice.[6] Like others of his generation he saw in a legal career the way to financial advancement: the practice opened doors to lucrative investments in land, besides paving the way to political preferment, which itself could also be turned to profit.

1958), pp. 76–79, provides the most detailed accounting of the various editions of Martin's *Reports*.
5. Henry A. Bullard, "A Discourse on the Life, Character, and Writings of the Hon. François Xavier Martin . . ." in French, ed., *Historical Collections of Louisiana*, 2: 37.
6. Ibid.: 19.

Accepting the appointment as a territorial judge in the Orleans Territory was just such a chance, and no sooner had he settled than he began to acquire considerable holdings in real estate throughout New Orleans. He borrowed against these properties to accumulate more, and he also lent money to friends and associates. Furthermore, he was not above using his influence to enhance his earnings. In 1816 and 1818, he persuaded the state legislature to pass laws requiring the state government to purchase copies of his digest and reports from him.[7] Of course, such conduct by a sitting Supreme Court justice would now be regarded as unethical, but in Martin's day no one was troubled by it. As the years passed his wealth grew; when he died Martin was worth nearly $400,000.[8]

Since Martin had no direct descendants, he intended to leave the entire estate to a brother. He incorporated that intention in an olographic will, that is, one written entirely in his own hand and without assistance, which he wrote in 1844, shortly before sailing to Paris to seek a possible cure for the blindness that had afflicted him for more than a decade. Quite short, the will simply stated, "I institute my brother, Paul Barthélemy Martin, heir to my whole estate, real and personal, and my testamentary executor and detainer of my estate. In case of his death, absence or disability, I name my friend and colleague, Edward Simon,[9] my testamentary

---

7. "An Act to Provide for the Distribution of the Digest of the Laws of this State," *Acts Passed at the Second Session of the Third Legislature of the State of Louisiana* . . . (New Orleans, 1811), pp. 24, 36, 38. "An Act to Authorize the Governor of the State to Purchase, for the Use of the State, Thirty Copies of Martin's Reports of the Decisions of the Supreme Court of the State," *Acts Passed at the First Session of the Third Legislature* . . . *in the Year One Thousand Eight Hundred and Sixteen* (New Orleans, La., 1817), pp. 8, 10.
8. Inventory of the estate of François-Xavier Martin taken by Theodore Guyol, notary, Acts #5, Sept.-Dec. 1846, Notarial Archives, Civil District Court, New Orleans.
9. Simon (b. 1799) was a Belgian who had migrated to Louisiana after first having lived and practiced law in London and Baltimore. He joined the

executor and detainer of my estate. New Orleans, this twenty-first day of May, eighteen hundred and forty-four."[10]

Within days of the judge's demise, Paul Martin began the legal processes of having himself declared his brother's sole heir. The law at that time prescribed an orderly, logical procedure for putting wills out to probate.[11] An executor had to post bond and furnish a district court proof of death. Martin bound himself, and he filed a death certificate with the Second District Court for Orleans Parish on 12 December.[12] Next, he obtained orders from that Court's presiding judge, E.A. Canon, one which permitted him to collect all debts owing to the estate and a second which authorized an inventory of François' properties. Judge Canon also appointed Henry Adams Bullard to represent other heirs who might also claim an interest in the estate. Despite the size of Judge Martin's landholdings and the complexities of his financial transactions, the inventorying and debt-collecting proceeded apace. No additional heirs came forward to

---

Court in 1840, but retired when the Court was reorganized in accordance with the provisions of the Constitution of 1845.

Morphy (1798–1856) came to New Orleans from Charleston. Establishing a law practice, he went on to become attorney general and a state representative before taking his seat on the court in 1839. He, too, left the Court in 1844.

Bullard (1788–1851) was a native of Pepperell, Massachusetts. During a long career in public life he served Louisiana as secretary of state, state legislator, district judge, congressman, and law professor. He sat on the court from 1834 to 1839 and again from 1840 to 1845.

10. The original of the will is in a file of papers that relate to the succession of the estate. That file is part of the archives of the Civil District Court, which are deposited in the Louisiana Division of the New Orleans Public Library.

11. The procedures for probating wills are detailed in Wheelock S. Upton, comp., *Code of Practice in Civil Cases for the State of Louisiana* (New Orleans, 1839), pp. 155–177.

12. The original of Martin's death certificate is located in the file cited in note 10.

demand a share of their relative's bounty, though a niece, Blanche Amalie, who had cared for the judge in his last years, surrendered her putative interest to Paul Martin. All of the legal requirements, save one, were completed by the middle of January; what remained was for Martin to petition for possession of the estate; which he did on the 20th. Judge Canon granted the request, and Paul Martin could now look to living out the remaining years of his life in luxury. His elation over his new-found fortune turned to alarm, as he soon found himself the object of litigation that challenged the legality of his brother's will.

Scarcely two weeks after the will was probated, the attorney general, William A. Elmore, filed a motion with Judge Canon to have it invalidated. Elmore's petition was grounded on three contentions. First, that Paul Martin "[had] caused himself to be recognized as Executor of the Estate of his deceased brother" and "by virtue of a pretended olographic will" took control of the estate. Second, the will was null and void because Judge Martin "was physically incapacitated on account of blindness from making an olographic will." Last, Judge Martin really intended to bequeath his estate to relatives who still lived in France, and since these heirs were not "domiciliated" in Louisiana or some other part of the Union, in accordance with an act of March 1842 governing such instances, the state was entitled to ten percent of the estate's estimated value.[13] In view of

---

13. "An Act explanatory of 924th article of the Code of Practice, for the administration of the succession of strangers dying possessed of property within the State of Louisiana and for other purposes," "An Act to increase the revenue of the State of Louisiana," *Acts Passed at the Second Session of the Fifteenth legislature of the State of Louisiana* . . . (New Orleans, La., 1842), pp. 430–442, esp. 434–436.

these facts, Elmore moved that the will be invalidated and that the state receive $39,608.41.[14]

As was the practice in such suits, Paul Martin, through his attorneys, filed a written rejoinder to Elmore's claims. The state, he answered, had no right to any part of the estate because "it [lacked] direct interest in the succession of François-Xavier Martin." Moreover, even if the will were spurious for the reasons Elmore contended, by law, it was up to the heirs, not the attorney general, to contest it. But, the will was quite valid. Not the least reason for its being so was its having been "duly proved according to the laws of this State and before this Honorable Court and ordered to be executed." Accordingly, Martin was his brother's only heir, and it therefore followed that Judge Canon should dismiss Elmore's suit, a move which he declined to make. Instead, he received supplemental motions from the government, in which Elmore amplified his earlier argument about François's intent to avoid paying the estate tax. That purpose was clearly to be seen in his creation of Paul as "universal legatee and heir" with "the understanding . . . that the property, or some of it, should go to heirs who were not United States citizens." Such a trust arrangement was "under our laws strictly prohibited," and it proved the will's invalidity. Of course, Martin's lawyers denied Elmore's interpretation, and they again asked for a dismissal of the suit.[15] Once more, Canon did not rule in their favor, and so the matter went to trial.

---

14. A copy of Elmore's petition is located in the *State* v. *Martin* case file, Docket #528, June 1847, Supreme Court of Louisiana Archives, Louisiana & Special Collections Department, Earl K. Long Library, University of New Orleans. The file contains transcripts of motions, evidence, and trial proceedings in Judge Canon's court, together with a record of the proceedings on appeal. Subsequent citations to testimony etc. are to this case file.

15. Answer of Paul Barthélemy Martin, ibid.

The attorney general summoned an impressive array of witnesses to prove his allegations. Among them were the late judge's colleagues Bullard, Alonzo Morphy, and Simon, as well as several prominent attorneys and Martin's amanuensis.[16] All of their testimony covered the same basic ground. Everyone agreed that blindness overtook Martin by 1839, and thereafter, they seldom saw him sign more than his name to an opinion or a check. They recalled his speaking of his relations who still lived in France, just as they remembered his consternation at the 1842 estate tax law and his conversations about how it might be avoided, though everyone admitted that his remarks were never made with any specific reference to his own situation. As for the will itself, no one could deny that it was in Martin's handwriting. When queried about it, Bullard replied that "the testator could have written [it] by means of bars to confine the edges or other mechanical means, or by feeling the edges, but . . . he required assistance to take his pen and get the ink; that is the greatest difficulty to know if you have ink in your pen or not." Bullard also testified to being present when the will was first opened. It was, he related, doubled as one might have folded a letter and sealed, but while he believed Martin could have done the folding, he did not think that a blind man could have accomplished the sealing. Morphy, too, did not dispute the will's authenticity, though he also doubted that Martin could do any lengthy writing without some sort of mechanical aid. Indeed, Morphy swore that his colleague admitted using a device when he wrote the will.[17]

Simon offered the most extensive evidence about the existence of Martin's French relations and of his friend's affections towards them. Additionally, he indicated that he and Martin had "many conversations" about the estate. As he

---

16. The witness list is in ibid.
17. Testimony of Henry Adams Bullard and Alonzo Morphy, ibid.

remembered them, Martin had specifically brought his brother to Louisiana in order to entrust his property to him and so avoid the tax. Moreover, Simon offered the opinion that Martin did not wish to deprive his other kin, but he acknowledged that this view of his colleague's intent rested rather more upon impressions than facts. In truth, he testified to never having told Martin of his impressions, as the matter of how the estate was disposed "was none of [my] business."[18]

Once done with these witnesses, Elmore brought Paul Martin to the witness box and interrogated the Frenchman with a series of questions. Suppose, he began, Judge Martin had died intestate; who would his heirs have been? To which the witness replied, "Comme je suis le plus ancien de la famille ce serait d'abord moi. . . . Ensuite les representants de mon frere, Joseph Vincent Martin," and he called all of his nieces and nephews by name. In this circumstance, Elmore then demanded to know what part of the estate would have been his, and Martin allowed "je suppose que cela serait reglé par le Code de la Louisiane," meaning that, according to his understanding of state law, it would have been he. Next, the attorney general wished to know if the old judge ever married and sired children; "no" was the reply. Elmore then shifted the line of questioning towards an inquiry into what understanding the two brothers had about the disposal of the estate. Did the judge and the witness not agree that one part of the estate should pass to the other heirs? Was the witness bound in honor and duty to distribute that portion of the fortune among the relatives? Did the judge instruct the witness as to the disposition of the property? Even if no such instructions existed, did the judge not intend for the witness to apportion property or sums of money to the relatives? Has the witness already transmitted any part of the estate to the judge's other presumed heirs? Martin answered the first query

---

18. Testimony of Edward Simon, ibid.

by saying there was no understanding, adding for emphasis, "il m'a laisse son heriter, et c'est a moi a disposer de son bien comme je l'entenderai." Therefore, he was in no way obliged to give any of it away. As for the question of instructions, Martin commented quite simply there were none. Regarding the judge's intent, Martin related "mon frère m'a dit 'Je te fais mon heriter, de disposer de sa fortune; que c'ètait a moi.'" He concluded his testimony with the comment that he would use his new wealth "selon ma volonte."[19]

Apart from using Elmore's interrogation to justify himself, his brother, and the validity of the will, Paul Martin mounted a brief defense against the state's claims. His attorneys called only three witnesses, whose purpose it was to prove that the judge was quite capable of writing more than his name at the foot of an opinion or on the signature line of a check. Of these, Theodore Guyol,[20] one of the city's notaries, recounted how the old man came almost daily to his office with notes and other documents requiring notarization. These, he averred were without exception in Martin's handwriting. Moreover, Guyol also related that he had known the contents of the will long before Martin's death. He and Martin had discussed them, and in the course of their discussion, Martin said he had left everything to his brother because Paul "was of the same habits and of the same way of thinking as himself."[21] Curiously, other than introducing the probated will, there was no effort taken to refute the state's imputation of fraudulent motives in the drafting of the will. Evidently, the lawyers felt the will, plus Paul Martin's performance sufficiently combatted that charge. Equally, in view of Judge Martin's reputation, they probably believed such an allegation was too preposterous to require a

---

19. Testimony of Paul Barthélemy Martin, ibid.
20. It was Guyol who inventoried the Martin estate.
21. Testimony of Theodore Guyol in *State* v. *Martin*.

rejoinder. They may also have anticipated an unfavorable ruling from Judge Canon, and thus they preferred to try to win their cause on appeal.

When the defense rested, Canon took the case under advisement, and on 15 March, he rendered his judgment. In a nine-page opinion, he came to three fundamental conclusions.[22] He first addressed the question of the state's claim of an interest in Judge Martin's succession, and, basing his conclusion on a section of Article 151 of the Code of Practice, he ruled that Attorney General Elmore had the right to challenge the will.[23] With that, he dismissed the defendant's counterclaim that the State of Louisiana was without standing in the case. Canon next considered whether or not Judge Martin had the capacity to write an olographic will; he held that Martin's blindness incapacitated him. This finding arose from Canon's reading of Article 1581 of the Civil Code, which, as he wrote, enjoined that an olographic will be "entirely written, dated and signed by the hand of the testator." Given, "the acknowledged and notorious helplessness" of Judge Martin, he was manifestly incompetent to comply with either the letter or the spirit of the law, and his inability therefore invalidated his testament. Canon's final judgment was a finding of the old judge's intent to evade the 1842 tax law. For all of these reasons, he nullified the will and ordered Paul Martin to pay the state $39,608.41, plus court costs.

Martin's reactions to the unfavorable rulings are unrecorded, but he clearly did not intend to let things stand as they were. Within a week of Canon's decision, his attorneys

---

22. The opinion is in ibid.
23. The relevant portion reads, "if a plaintiff has several causes of action tending to the same conclusion, not contrary to nor exclusive of each other, though they arise from different contracts, he may cumulate and bring them in the same suit," Upton, comp., *Code of Practice*, p. 26.

filed an appeal with the Supreme Court of Louisiana. The high Court granted a writ of appeal making it returnable "on the fourth Monday of April next [i.e., the 26th]."[24]

The rules governing appeals to the Supreme Court were well established by the time Court agreed to take Martin's case.[25] To insure the appearance of the litigants, they were required to post bonds. A complete transcript of the trial in the lower Court had to be provided to the Court and opposing counsel, as did copies of any supplementary motions. Each side had to furnish the justice with papers known as briefs, in which each party's view of the facts, the appropriate law, and cogent authorities were articulated. All of this documentation had to be filed with the Court's clerk by the return date on the writ of appeal. Then the case was docketed, meaning that it was given a number that determined the order in which the Court would hear it. By the day of the hearing the justices would have presumably familiarized themselves with the issues and would be prepared to question counsel during the oral arguments. (In the 1840s, the Court still allotted up to two hours per case for such argumentation.) Arguments completed, the justices then decided the case and assigned one of their number to write the Court's opinion.

Martin's appeal was called off the docket in June. Neither the case file, the Court's minute book nor the printed report contains a record of the oral arguments or the justices' queries. In truth, the only copies of the contents of the briefs themselves are the texts that the reporter chose to print, but they are hardly complete.[26] Nevertheless, what is there is

---

24. A copy of the writ is in *State* v. *Martin*.
25. For a detailed view of the rules, see Upton, comp., *Code of Practice*, pp. 146–153; Warren M. Billings, ed., *Historic Rules of the Supreme Court of Louisiana, 1813–1879* (Lafayette, La., 1985).
26. These are in 2 *La. Ann.*, 674–715. The likeliest explanation for there not being complete copies of all the briefs is that the reporter borrowed

sufficient to catch the drift of both sides of the argument. Attorney General Elmore and his assistants rehearsed the main points of their case in the district court, but their briefs also included lengthy citations to numerous English, French, and Spanish authorities, which supposedly added weight to their cause. For their part, Martin's lawyers developed their position to a much greater extent than had been their wont during the trial. Their briefs were replete with precedents drawn from the Ten Commandments down to recent case law; they even employed a touch of sarcasm and irony. Étienne Mazureau, for example, opened his brief with the rather acid remark that "he who amasses a great fortune sows the seeds of a great lawsuit which germinate after his death." He then went on to say of his late friend,

> for thirty years his ear was caressed by the most flattering testimonials of a high consideration, both as a savant, and as a judge of integrity and purity. He has descended to the tomb, escorted by a numerous procession composed of all that our city contains of respectability. But in giving up his mortal part to the earth, he has left a will, by which he disposes, in favor of his brother, a fortune of nearly $400,000. And this judge, this president of our Supreme Court, celebrated for his intellectual capacities, and his distinguished judicial mind, who has been able for thirty years, during nine or ten of which he had lost his sight, to write out and to pronounce decisions which many considered as oracles, has not been able to escape the sentence of the Hindu philosopher. His death has given

those that were filed with the Court and set type from them. Such a practice was quite common in the nineteenth century. Indeed, the transcript of the trial bears marginal glosses and editorial directions, all of which evidences the probability of the reporter's having taken the briefs and not having returned them. As for the report itself, a comparison of the testimony it incorporates with the record provides some insight into how much a reporter might compress a record to make it fit his allotted page space.

life to a lawsuit; and this suit is brought in the name of the State, he is represented as incapable of making an olographic testament, and its annulment is demanded! A supplemental petition is presented, in which we recognize manifestly that this alleged incapacity springs only from an imagination burning to obtain at least some scrap of this oppulent succession; and, in which, wishing to arrive more surely at this goal, they accuse him of having made by his will a trust prohibited by our Code.[27]

When the matter was decided, Justice Pierre Rost[28] delivered the Court's opinion. The case, he said, "presented two novel questions." Could the blind Judge Martin make an olographic will? If so, was his naming Paul Martin "his universal legatee, a simulated disposition, made for the purpose of evading the fiscal regulations of the act of 1842?"

Rost made short work of the first query.

Most of the commentators relied upon by [the government], either say or, intimate that a blind man cannot make an olographic will because he cannot write; but as no one doubts that the late presiding judge of the Supreme Court could write, that reason does not create an incapacity in him. . . . we are clearly of the opinion that the alleged incapacity is not established by law. . . . The court of the first instance came to the same conclusion, but considered the physical impossibility established by the

---

27. 2 *La. Ann.*, 690. Mazureau's brief was in French. The quoted passage is William Wirt Howe's translation, which is printed in his edition of Martin's *History of Louisiana*, p. xxv.

28. Rost (1797–1868) was a French immigrant who settled in Natchez before establishing himself in New Orleans. He had served a four-month term on the Court in 1839, and when the Court was reorganized to conform to the Constitution of 1845, he was reappointed to the high bench. At the time of the Martin case, his colleagues were George Eustis, the chief justice, George Rogers King, and Thomas Slidell. Rost left the Court in 1853 to return to private practice.

notorious helplessness of the testator. Public notoriety cannot outweigh, in our minds, the testimony of the three unimpeachable witnesses upon which the will was admitted to probate, and the uncontradicted evidence adduced on behalf of [Paul Martin], that this instrument was in all respects as intended by Judge Martin.[29]

Regarding the judge's alleged intention of defrauding the state of its rightful share of his estate, Rost turned aside Elmore's construction of the reason why Paul Martin was made his brother's sole beneficiary. "There [was]," in his opinion, "another view, far more consistent with his character. . . . His desire that his worldly goods should be kept together after his death, exhibited by the pain he felt at the mere suspicion that his brother would sell them and leave the country far outweighed his attachments for [his other relations]." Accordingly, continued the opinion, "we have no doubt of [Paul Martin's] being really universal legatee;" nor that the late judge's intentions were other than those he had repeatedly expressed, "that his brother should continue to be, in all respects, "*un autre lui-même*."[30]

Towards the end of the opinion, Rost seized the occasion to chide the government for bringing suit in the first place. Public policy, as fixed by law, recognized the authenticity of probated wills until they were overturned by heirs within a prescribed period of time. By that very law, the will, "in the name of the State," had been ordered executed. That done, the state could not, except for "an express warrant of law, interpose to prevent its execution for the purposes of gain." He asserted that the 1842 statute did not apply, because tax laws were in "the nature of penal statutes: they act upon

---

29. Rost's opinion, 2 *La. Ann.*, 718.
30. Ibid., 720.

things as they find them; and their operation should not be extended to cases not contemplated by their framers."[31]

The opinion ended on a salutary note. "Upon us," it concluded, "falls the ... task to determine that ... the name of François-Xavier Martin stands unsullied by fraud;" it reversed Judge Canon and ordered the state to pay all costs. His reputation intact, old Judge Martin could rest peaceably, and Paul Martin could now enjoy his inheritance *selon ma volonte*. Eventually, he returned to France to live out his days. Like his brother, he never married. When he died, the estate passed to one of his nieces and, in the end, it went to the French relations after all.

The entire controversy itself had a transcendent importance. It served to limit somewhat the state's authority to tax inheritances, and in this connection it reflected a typical antebellum desire to keep private property out of government hands. Rost's ruling also limited the state's power to invalidate wills; the impact of the opinion was to say such an authority could only exist if it were granted by legislative action. At a more mundane level, the case imbedded into Louisiana law the principle that the blind could make olographic testaments. Perhaps Judge Martin might have savored the effect of his three-sentence will upon his beloved Louisiana jurisprudence.[32]

---

31. Ibid. 721–722.
32. The case has been cited in subsequent litigation and learned commentary with some regularity, see 2 *Shepherd's Louisiana Citations*, 132.

Essay 12

A Neglected Treatise

Lewis Kerr's Exposition *and the Making of Criminal Law in Louisiana*

I stumbled upon references to Lewis Kerr and *An Exposition of the Criminal Law of the Territory of Orleans* while delving into the origins of the criminal law in Louisiana. Kerr was unknown to me so I poked around and unearthed several salient characteristics about the treatise and its author that eventually led to the next essay.

Commissioned by territorial governor William C.C. Claiborne, Kerr wrote the *Exposition* as an extended commentary upon the Crimes Act of 1805. The book evidently played a part in transplanting Anglo-American conceptions of criminal law to Louisiana. It also ranked among the first-ever printed discussions of criminal law by an American author, and it appeared to be one of the rarest of such books. As for Kerr, he turned out to be quite obscure, and there was no notice of him in any standard biographical directory or reference work. These discoveries piqued my curiosity to the degree that I resolved to look more closely at Kerr and the *Exposition* at a future date.

Years passed before I returned to that project in a concerted fashion. In the interval, though, I acquired a facsimile edition of the *Exposition*, which gradually came to bear an abundance of my marginal annotations. I also developed additional information about Kerr as I pieced together the sequence of events that led to the passage of the Crimes Act of 1805 and to Kerr's employment as commentator on the statute. Close readings of the *Exposition* revealed Kerr as a man with a profound understanding of Anglo-American criminal law and the sources of its intellectual inspiration. How, I wondered, had this little known writer acquired such deep learning. I never arrived at a full answer to that question. A partial explanation seemed to lie in Kerr's prior mastery of an impressive range of authorities that he repeatedly cited throughout the *Exposition*. His recourse to William Waller Hening's *New Virginia Justice* was especially telling because it hinted at a direct connection between legal habits in the Old Dominion and those that emerged in Louisiana after the Purchase. That suggestion tended to confirm a suspicion of mine about which immigrant men of law stamped impressions upon Louisiana's legal order after 1803. Taken as a whole, the *Exposition* was clearly important because of its disclosures about the American origins of Louisiana's criminal justice system. And, like others of its kind, the *Exposition* was noteworthy because it too drew attention to the value of such books as historical evidence. Those considerations led to my writing this essay and preparing an accompanying appendix that listed the sources upon which Kerr relied.

Originally published as "A Neglected Treatise: Lewis Kerr's Exposition and the Making of Criminal Law in Louisiana" in *Louisiana History: The Journal of the Louisiana Historical Association*, 36 (1997): 452-472, the article is reprinted here with the kind permission of the editor.

Treatises are an ancient species of law book. Designed to explicate all manner of subjects, they cover a limitless range of subjects. Some few, notably those of Sir Edward Coke, Sir William Blackstone, Chancellor James Kent, or Justice Joseph

Story, transcended time and became treasures of Anglo-American jurisprudence.[1] Most, however, met a different end. They served a need and fell into disuse, though they often wore out from repeated usage long before obsolescence overtook them. Survivors came to rest in law libraries or private collections, where they sit like so many forgotten antiques. Such relics, individually or collectively, can be for historians fertile veins of inquiry because mining them yields an understanding of early American law and the dissemination of legal information that may be found nowhere else.

Consider the example of Lewis Kerr's *An Exposition of the Criminal Laws of the Territory of Orleans: The Practice of the Court of Criminal Jurisdiction, the Duties of their Officers, with a Collection of Forms for the Use of Magistrates and Others.*[2] Published in 1806, Kerr's volume ranks among the earliest treatises on criminal law produced by an American author.[3] Only six copies are extant, a rarity that accounts for its being virtually unknown to historians of American or Louisiana law.[4]

---

1. Coke, *Institutes of the Laws of England* (London, 1664, 1797); Blackstone, *Commentaries on the Laws of England* (Dublin, 1773); Kent, *Commentaries on American Law* (New York, 1826–1830); Story, *Commentaries on the Constitution* (New York, 1833).
2. Florence M. Jumonville, comp., *Bibliography of New Orleans Imprints, 1764–1864* (New Orleans, La., 1989), p. 38. Extant copies are in The Historic New Orleans Collection, the Library of Congress, and the law libraries of Harvard and Tulane Universities.
3. A comparable example of an early criminal commentary is Henry Toulmin and James Blair, *Review of the Criminal Law of the Commonwealth of Kentucky* (Frankfort, 1804).
4. Jumonville, comp., *Bibliography of New Orleans Imprints*, pp. 38–39. Richard H. Kilbourne, Jr., *A History of the Louisiana Civil Code: The Formative Years, 1803–1839* (Baton Rouge, La., 1987), p. 29, n. 90 and Mark F. Fernandez, *From Chaos to Continuity: The Evolution of Louisiana's Judicial System, 1712–1862* (Baton Rouge, La., 2001), pp. 35–35 are the only

Recently, however, a Florida law book publisher, Wm. Gaunt & Sons, Inc., put the volume in reach of many when it issued a new edition in facsimile. The facsimile affords a convenient, serviceable study text, and armed with a copy, any curious scholar may delve into the inspiration for the *Exposition* or ponder its content. It is also a useful example to those who would discern sources that informed early American treatise writers or to anyone who would assess the marks treatise writers left upon particular branches of law. More generally, exploring the *Exposition* fulfills another purpose. Such an inquiry demonstrates the potential that awaits historians of early American law who parse similar neglected treatises.[5]

The *Exposition* sprang from a climate of thought at once common to the United States and singular to Louisiana. Criminal law across the nation was in transition as the nineteenth century opened, largely because Americans were recasting the intellectual undergirding that had supported it since the beginning of the colonial era. Up through the Revolution, the buttressing premises changed little from those the settlers had brought with them in the 1600s. Foremost among these was an association of criminal conduct with sinful behavior. Miscreants were sinners, whom Satan had seduced from the paths of righteousness. Their misdeeds, went the ancient wisdom, merited the harsh, swift correction of *lex talionis*—an eye for an eye—which mounted

---

modern scholars who recognized the importance of the *Exposition*. George Dargo, an exponent of the clash-of-cultures thesis about the origins of Louisiana law, ignored Kerr's work in his *Jefferson's Louisiana: Politics and the Clash of Legal Tradition* (Cambridge, Mass., 1975).

5. (Holmes Beach, Fla., 1986). As the manager for Gaunt informed me, the facsimile was reproduced from an original that resides in the Tulane University law library (D. Paulette Webb to WMB, 30 Oct. 1995). My copy of the facsimile is the source text for the quotations and citations that appear throughout this essay.

in proportion to the degree of the offense. Trials represented society's ritual way of holding malefactors answerable, but in such accountings there was scant regard for "fairness," at least as that concept is understood in modern criminal proceedings. Finding culpability and apportioning an exemplary sentence was the intent, meaning that the rules of trial weighed heavily against defendants, though there was a proper "Manner of proceeding in every Cause,"[6] and no sentence could be executed unless the right steps followed in due order. Still, accused persons often had no right to an attorney, they could not subpoena witnesses, they lacked the privilege of discovery, they could not adduce exculpatory evidence, and they could not even expect jury trials because such hearings were not routine in every colonial jurisdiction.[7]

---

6. The phrase is that of the seventeenth-century English legal lexicographer John Cowell, who compiled *A Law Dictionary: or the Interpreter of Words and Terms Used Either in The Common or Statute Laws of Great Britain, and In Tenures and Jocular Customs* (London, 1727: originally published at Cambridge in 1607 as *The Interpreter*), under "process."

7. Michael Dalton, *The Countrey Justice: Containing the Practice of Justices of the Peace out of their Session* (London, 1677), pp. 326–394, 411–416, 529–543; Theodore F.T. Plucknett, *A Concise History of the Common Law* (London, 1956), pp. 424–505; Julius Goebel and T. Raymond Naughton, *Law Enforcement in Colonial New York: A Study in Criminal Procedure (1664–1776)* (New York, 1944), Part III, *passim*; Felix Rakow, "The Right of Counsel: English and American Precedents," *William and Mary Quarterly*, 3d Ser., 11 (1954): 3–28; Joseph H. Smith, ed., *Criminal Justice in Western Massachusetts (1639–1702): The Pynchon Court Record* (Cambridge, Mass, 1961), pp. 129–159; Douglas Greenberg, "Crime, Law Enforcement, and Social Control in Colonial America," *American Journal of Legal History*, 26 (1982): 293–325; Kathryn Preyer, "Penal Measures in the American Colonies: An Overview," ibid.: 326–353; Bradley Chapin, *Criminal Justice in Colonial America, 1606–1660* (Athens, Ga., 1983), pp. 25–99; John M. Murrin, "Settlers, Sinners and Precarious Liberty: Trial by Jury in Seventeenth-Century New England," in *Saints and Revolutionaries: Essays on Early American History*, David D. Hall, John M. Murrin, and Thad W. Tate., ed.

Defendants' prospects brightened in the eighteenth century, especially after 1776, when certain basic guarantees found their place in newly-crafted state bills of rights. Typical of this change were the promises of the Virginia Declaration of Rights, which warranted that a defendant had "a right to demand the Cause and Nature of his Accusation, to be confronted with the Accusers or Witness, to call for Evidence in his favour, and to a speedy Tryal by a Jury of his Vicinage; without whose unanimous Consent, he cannot be found guilty; nor can he be compelled to give Evidence against himself."[8]

These and similar pledges inched post-revolutionary criminal practice beyond traditional norms, whereas prohibitions against cruel and unusual punishment,[9] general warrants, or excessive bail bridled state governments in extraordinary ways, though the exact substance of those curbs was left to find meaning in experience. Even so, according

---

(New York, 1984), pp. 152–206; Gail Sussman Marcus, "'Due Execution of the Generall Rules of Righteousness': Criminal Procedure in New Haven Town and Colony, 1638–1658," ibid.: pp. 99–138; Essay 5 above; John M. Murrin and A.G. Roeber, "Trial by Jury: The Virginia Paradox," in Jon Kukla, ed., *The Bill of Rights: A Lively Heritage*, (Richmond, Va., 1987), pp. 109–31; Donna J. Spindel and Stuart W. Thomas, Jr., "Crime and Society in North Carolina, 1663–1740," *Journal of Southern History*, 49 (1983): 232–249.

8. Robert A. Rutland, ed., *The Papers of George Mason, 1725–1792* (Chapel Hill, N.C, 1970), 1: 288; Patrick T. Conley and John P. Kaminski, eds., *The Bill of Rights and the States: The Colonial and Revolutionary Origins of American Liberties* (Madison, Wis., 1992), *passim*.

9. George Mason borrowed the phrase from the English Bill of Rights and incorporated it in the Virginia Declaration of Rights Rutland, ed., *Mason Papers*, 1: 277. What he meant by it is debatable. For certain, he did not intend that it should embrace hanging or maiming, which were common forms of punishment in the Virginia of his day. Likely, he wished to restrain judges from inflicting capital penalties not sanctioned by statute. Warren M. Billings, "'THAT ALL MEN ARE BORN EQUALLY FREE AND INDEPENDENT': Virginians and the Origins of the Bill of Rights," in Conley and Kaminski, eds., *The Bill of Rights and the States*, pp. 349–351.

specific rights to the accused helped launch a reformulation of criminal law. Reform-minded Americans found inspiration not only in the expressions of revolutionary idealism but they drew sustenance from thinkers like Cesare Beccaria, Jeremy Bentham, William Eden, first baron Auckland, or Voltaire.

Therefore, by the time of the Louisiana Purchase, the underlying rationale of criminal law everywhere in the United States was in transition. Visionaries tended to look upon felons less as fallen creatures and rather more as misguided individuals who were capable of being reclaimed through the rational application of humane corrective measures. For that reason, they regarded branding, flogging, maiming, and sometimes death as futile, even barbaric exactions. Thomas Jefferson, for example, abominated the old *lex talionis*, though his success at eliminating it from post–revolutionary Virginia penal statutes was an abject failure.[10] So did that Solon of Louisiana, Edward Livingston, a Benthamite, who disputed nearly every application of capital punishment from an early date in his long career as a reformer.[11] For them, as for others, the ideas of contemporary penologists seemed to contain greater promise for the improvement of criminals than capital punishment. Lawyers, legislators, and laymen in the same way slowly equated the need for fairer trials with the

---

10. A.A. Lipscomb and Albert E. Bergh, eds., *The Writings of Thomas Jefferson* (Washington, D.C., 1903), 1: 64–65; Thomas Jefferson, *Notes on the State of Virginia*, ed. by William Peden (Chapel Hill, N.C., 1954), pp. 143–146; Charles T. Cullen, "Completing the Revisal of the Laws in Post-Revolutionary Virginia, *Virginia Magazine of History and Biography*, 82 (1974): 84-99; Fernandez, *From Chaos to Continuity*, pp. 31–32.

11. William B. Hatcher, *Edward Livingston, Jeffersonian Republican and Jacksonian Democrat* (Baton Rouge, La., 1940), pp. 37, 82–84; Grant Lyons, "Narrow Failure, Wider Triumph: The Response to Edward Livingston's System of Criminal Law in Louisiana" (M.A. thesis, University of New Orleans), Chapters I and II.

rights of citizenship.[12] Likewise, they considered placing restraints on the powers of judicial discretion as a most necessary safeguard, just as they saw in codifying state penal statutes a logical application of reason and a lessening of English influences on American law. Hence the reformers' fascination with civil law methodologies as a means to those ends. Then too, the profession of lawyer was itself in flux. Greater professionalization was the concomitant result of an increasing number of law schools and the rising disposition to look upon "the law" as a science. Those tendencies, by turns, increased an already widening demand for law books of every conceivable sort, especially those like Kerr's *Exposition*, which specifically dealt with American subjects.[13]

Thomas Jefferson purchased more than he bargained for when he bought Louisiana from Napoleon Bonaparte. Having consummated the deal, the president next had to provide for the eventual incorporation of the territory into

---

12. David Brion Davis, "The Movement to Abolish Capital Punishment in America, 1787–1861," *American Historical Review*, 63 (1957): 23ff; William E. Nelson, "Emerging Notions of Modern Criminal Law in the Revolutionary Era: An Historical Perspective," *New York University Law Review*, 52 (1967): 450–482; G.S. Rowe, "Women's Crime and Criminal Administration in Pennsylvania, 1764–1790," *Pennsylvania Magazine of History and Biography*, 109 (1985): 335–368; Kathryn Preyer, "Jurisdiction to Punish: Federal Authority, Federalism and the Common Law of Crimes in the Early Republic," *Law and History Review*, 4 (1986): 223–265; J.R. Pole, "Reflections on American Law and the American Revolution," *WMQ*, 3d Ser., 50 (1993): 123–160.

13. David Hoffman, *A Course of Legal Studies*, 2d ed., (Baltimore, 1836), 1: 19–56, 432–437; 2: 500–558; Maxwell Bloomfield, "William Sampson and the Codifiers: Roots of American Legal Reform, 1820–1830," *American Journal of Legal History*, 11 (1967): 234–252; Charles M. Cook, *The American Codification Movement: A Study in Legal Reform* (Westport, Conn., 1981), pp. 3–96; Kate Wallach, "The Publication of Legal Treatises in America From 1800 to 1830," *Law Library Journal*, 45 (1952): 136–148.

the Union. That task was no small matter. The Purchase's land mass was vast and largely unexplored; its sheer size and its isolation from the east coast rendered it vulnerable to attack and difficult to defend. Its peoples were as exotic as their loyalties to their new rulers were uncertain. Lower Louisiana embraced the city of New Orleans and inhabitants made up of Africans, French, Germans, Spanish, and an escalating collection of brazenly aggressive Americans. Despite an affinity for things Gallic, Jefferson harbored a certain distrust of Louisianians, whom he thought quite unfit for immediate self-government. He expected them to live through an extended period of territorial rule while they learned the habits of American citizenship. For that reason, in 1804, he signed into law the Breckinridge Act, which designated Lower Louisiana as the Territory of Orleans and provided for the establishment of its government. (The statute was also in keeping with provisions in the Northwest Ordinance of 1787 relative to a territory becoming a state.)[14] Shortly thereafter he appointed a fellow Virginian, and kinsman, William C.C. Claiborne as governor.[15]

Claiborne (1775–1817) typified the Americans who poured into Louisiana before and after the Purchase in search of fame, fortune, or escape. Of an old Tidewater Virginia family, he was reared south of the James River in Sussex County and attended the College of William and Mary. At the age of fifteen, he went to work as a deputy to John Beckley,

---

14. "An act Erecting Louisiana into two territories, and providing for the temporary government thereof, " Eight Congress, First Session, 1804, in Francis Newton Thorpe, comp., *The Federal and State Constitutions, Colonial Charters, and Other Organic Laws of the States, Territories, and Colonies Nor or Heretofore Forming the United States of America* (Washington, D.C., 1909), 3: 1364–1371.

15. Walter Prichard, "Selecting a Governor for the Territory of Orleans," *Louisiana Historical Quarterly*, 31 (1948): 269–293.

the Clerk of the United States House of Representatives, which led in turn to an acquaintance with John Sevier and proximity to Thomas Jefferson. Sevier encouraged him to return to Virginia and to read law; he did, but prospects for a young, newly-minted attorney were few in the Old Dominion of the 1790s, so he emigrated to Tennessee. A lucrative career at the Tennessee bar and in Congress followed, and he served as Jefferson's governor in the Mississippi territory before moving on to New Orleans. A mere twenty-eight when he assumed his post in Louisiana, Claiborne was seemingly blessed by credentials that ought to have mitigated the rigors of his assignment.[16]

Things did not go as smoothly as either he or Jefferson initially hoped they might. Neither man fully appreciated the difficulties of attempting to integrate distant people of different ways and hostile attitudes into the bumptious young republic. Nothing about Claiborne in reality adequately prepared him for his extraordinary task. No other American territorial official of his era had ever faced a like responsibility heretofore, whereas the delicacy of the manifold complexities of governing Louisiana eluded the president in far-off Washington. Jefferson's misapprehensions of his governor compounded Claiborne's difficulty because they put an edge on the relationship between the two men that sharpened with the passage of time. Indecisiveness and a readiness to see only malevolence in the actions of others also inhibited Claiborne. So did a lack of fluency in Romance tongues and an unmasked contempt for his new constituents. None of these impediments deterred the governor, who held firm in his

---

16. Joe Gray Taylor, "W.C.C. Claiborne," in Joseph G. Dawson, ed., *Louisiana's Governors: From Iberville to Edwards* (Baton Rouge, La., 1990), pp. 80–86.

determination to school Louisianians in the ways of republicanism, come what may.[17]

Scarcely had French governor Pierre Clément Laussat handed Claiborne the keys to the Hôtel de Ville in New Orleans, than the American realized the magnitude of what lay before him. The ceremonial exchange gave him custody of a place that was immediately without laws or government because Laussat, for reasons known only to him, had suspended both before yielding to Claiborne. Bereft, the young governor groped to re-establish a workable legal order. Among the earliest of his moves in that direction was a reformulation of penal law.[18] When he convened the Legislative Council for its first regular session in December 1804, he charged the members to enact a "system of criminal jurisprudence" for the territory.[19]

Following the progress of Claiborne's proposed "system" in law is difficult owing to the disappearance of the journals of the Legislative Council and all of its working papers, although this much may be inferred with some assurance. Everyone knew that the basis of a crimes bill must rest wholly on American practices because the Breckenridge Act stipulated that the courts "shall have common law jurisdiction;" however the definition of that authority was left to the Louisianians.[20] Accordingly, a committee, chaired by Dr. John Watkins,[21] drew up a preliminary bill, taking advice

---

17. Taylor, "W.C.C Claiborne," 86; Dargo, *Jefferson's Louisiana*, pp. 25–50.
18. Fernandez, *From Chaos to Continuity*, pp. 16–40.
19. Claiborne, Speech to the Legislative Council, ca., 7 Dec. 1804, *Louisiana Gazette*, 7 Dec. 1804.
20. "An act for erecting Louisiana into two territories," Thorpe, ed., *Federal and State Constitutions*, 3: 1366.
21. A native of Chesterfield County, Va., Watkins (1771–1812) emigrated to Kentucky and earned a doctorate in medicine from the University of Edinburgh before settling in New Orleans, where he also served as mayor.

from Claiborne and members of the New Orleans bar, among others. That part of the work stretched into the end of January 1805, when Watkins reported to the full Council.[22] Next, James Workman,[23] one of the clerks, perfected the committee draft into appropriate statutory language for the committee, but the revision sat on the table for several months while the councillors wrote other legislation. Finally, the amended Watkins report was called from the calendar, debated, modified, and adopted. Then, on May 4, 1805, Claiborne signed the final version and immediately promulgated it as the law of the territory.[24]

Styled "An Act For the punishment of crimes and misdemeanors," the statute contained fifty-two sections that fell into three general categories: offenses,[25] prosecutions,[26] and punishments.[27] This arrangement followed a design similar to one in the revised code of Virginia, which was not

---

Jerah Johnson, "Dr. John Watkins, New Orleans' Lost Mayor," *Louisiana History: The Journal of the Louisiana Historical Association*, 36 (1995): 187–196; Thomas Turpin to Watkins, Mar. 2, 1809, Lewis Family Papers, fol. 8, Virginia Historical Society, Richmond.

22. *Louisiana Gazette*, 31 Jan. 1805.
23. Warren M. Billings, "Origins of Criminal Law in Louisiana," *Louisiana History*, 32 (1991): 69. Workman (d. 1832), an Irishman who studied law at the Middle Temple before emigrating to Charleston, dabbled in playwriting and mercantile ventures before settling in New Orleans in 1804. Glen R. Conrad, et al. eds., *Dictionary of Louisiana Biography* (Lafayette, La., 1988), 2: 860–861; Charles S. Watson, "A Denunciation on the Stage of Spanish Rule: James Workman's Liberty in Louisiana (1804)," *Louisiana History*, 11 (1970): 245–259.
24. *Acts Passed at the First Session of the Legislative Council of the Territory of Orleans* . . . (New Orleans, La., 1805), 454. A text of the act appeared in the May 10 and 17 numbers of the New Orleans *Gazette*.
25. *Acts, First Session, 1805*, sections 1–32, 416–440.
26. Ibid., sections 33–37, 440–444.
27. Ibid., sections 38–51, 444–454.

extraordinary, given Claiborne's and Watkins's backgrounds.[28] Rather it was one of numerous examples of how Virginians and their ways would color Louisiana law throughout the first half of the nineteenth century.

The act defined some thirty-two types of offenses. Petty criminals answered in any of the territorial courts, whereas felons stood trial before the superior court. There were pledges for due process and trial by jury, just as there were protections not yet guaranteed everywhere else in the United States. Among the latter was an affirmative right to an attorney as well as "free access" to counsel at "all seasonable hours." An accused was also entitled to a copy of the indictment and the jury list at least two days before trial, and he or she could also subpoena witnesses or "make any proof" of innocence.[29] And, in keeping with the congressional mandate, the statute further stipulated that all criminal misconduct

> shall be taken, intended and construed according to the common law of England; and that the forms of indictment, (divested however of unnecessary prolixity) the method of trial; the rules of evidence, and all other proceedings whatsoever in the prosecution of the said crimes, and misdemeanors, changing what ought to be change, shall be as is by this act otherwise provided for, according to the said common law.[30]

---

28. James Pleasants and Henry Pace, comps., *The Revised Code of the Laws of Virginia: Being a Collection of all Such Acts of the General Assembly, of a Public and Permanent Nature, As Are Now in Force* . . . (Richmond, Va., 1803), table of contents. In turn, the Virginia law was itself patterned on a model advocated by the seventeenth-century English jurist Sir Matthew Hale. Hale, *Pleas of the Crown: or, a Methodical Summary of the Principal Matters relating to that Subject* (London, 1694), "A Table of the Titles and Methods of the Book."
29. *Acts, First Session, 1805*, sections 1–36 417–442.
30. Ibid., section 33, 440.

By and large, then, the Crimes Act matched Claiborne's expectations. It plugged the void created when Laussat abolished colonial law, it classified offenses with some care, it established means for the orderly prosecution of malefactors, and it could withstand congressional scrutiny. Nonetheless, it had its imperfections, some of which were remedied when Claiborne signed corrective legislation at the conclusion of the second session of the Legislative Council in July 1805. Among other things, "An Act Supplementary to the act for the Punishment of Crimes and Misdemeanors" declared that its provisions "shall not extend to any slave."[31]

Given that governor and councillors had created an entirely new basis of penal law and procedure for the territory, there needed to be some means of explaining this novel system to Louisianians, whether attorney or plain citizen, Creole or American. The Legislative Council anticipated just such an eventuality when it called upon Claiborne to draw "up an exposition and explanation of each and every of the crimes and misdemeanors . . ., the rules of evidence, the mode of trial, the forms of writs and indictments, and all other proceedings."[32]

Had Claiborne chosen he might well have penned that explanation himself, for he was a knowledgeable attorney and legal reformer. Too preoccupied with his gubernatorial responsibilities to do it himself, he looked to pass the chore on to someone else. He picked Lewis Kerr.[33] His letter

---

31. *Acts Passed at the Second Session of the Legislative Council of the Territory of Orleans* (New Orleans, 1805), 36–42. After 1806, slave crimes were dealt with under the black code, which constituted a separate body of law in antebellum Louisiana. Judith Kelleher Schafer, *Slavery, the Civil Law, and the Supreme Court of Louisiana* (Baton Rouge, La., 1994), 1–10). Free people of color were tried in the same way as whites.
32. Acts, *First Session, 1805*, section 48, 450.
33. Claiborne to Kerr, Aug. 12, 1805, Kerr, *Exposition*, pp. iv–v.

commissioning Kerr stressed the importance of the assignment. Done properly, wrote Claiborne, the job would "greatly facilitate the operation of the existing Laws of the Territory." For that reason, Claiborne sought "some gentleman learned in the law." Kerr was that person because the governor "repose[ed] great confidence" in him. He charged Kerr "with respect to the work itself" that it would be concise, crafted in a plain "stile," and "ready for the press as speedily as possible." In return, Claiborne offered Kerr no specific compensation, though he promised that Kerr could "rely upon my disposition as a public agent to make a just remuneration for your services."[34]

Unfortunately, details about Kerr are now exceedingly sparse, so the gifts Claiborne found in him are mostly mysterious to the modern eye. This much is incontrovertible. An Irishman, Kerr first turned up in the Mississippi Territory about the year 1802, when he was licensed as an attorney and began a law practice in Natchez. Nearness to Claiborne gained him a place in the gubernatorial household and brought him to the Crescent City when the Virginian took over from Laussat. By turns Kerr then became a major in a battalion of free black militiamen, sheriff of New Orleans, and United States marshal before he received his charge to prepare the *Exposition*. Claiborne afterwards turned against him for his alleged part in the Burr Conspiracy, and he was subsequently indicted, though the government dropped its case for want of compelling proof. Freed of the charges, but not of the suspicions, Kerr left New Orleans and sailed to the British Isles and had no further association with Louisiana.[35]

---

34. Ibid., pp. iv–vi.
35. Claiborne to Seth Lewis, Dunbar Rowland, ed., *Official Letter Books of W.C.C. Claiborne, 1801–1816* (Jackson, Miss., 1917), 1: 204; 2: 289; Thomas P. Abernathy, *The Burr Conspiracy*, repr. ed. (Gloucester, Mass, 1968),

Once commissioned, Kerr fell quickly to his task, finishing it in about five months. Considering the complexity of his assignment, that was a remarkably short time to bring the *Exposition* into print. For his part, though, Kerr regretted his inability to complete it sooner. He was impatient from the start because "magistrates and others at a distance from New-Orleans" clamored for guidance in how to apply the Crimes Act. The "infancy" of the Louisiana press impeded him, leading to "many extraordinary but unavoidable delays." Trouble with his publishers, James M. Bradford and Thomas Anderson, also compelled him to "retrench much of [his] original design," as it forced him to "send every sheet to press almost as soon as it was written," which deprived him of "the common advantages of revision." Whatever the book's stylistic flaws, Kerr expressed his conviction in his letter of transmittal to Claiborne that the *Exposition* would enhance the people's understanding of their new law.[36]

Bradford and Anderson, who were the public printers, executed the official edition of the *Exposition*.[37] Establishing a practice that would remain the rule for legal publications in Louisiana until the 1860s, they printed parallel English and French renditions of Kerr's manuscripts on facing pages of

---

Chapters 3, 14; affidavit of Lewis Kerr, 10 Sept. 1807, United States *v.* Aaron Burr, ms case files, United States Court for the Seventh Judicial Circuit, Ohio District, Library of Virginia, Richmond; indictment of Kerr and James Workman, 21 April 1808, Rowland, ed., *Letter Books of W.C.C. Claiborne*, 4: 170–71; David Williamson to Aaron Burr, 8 Mar. 1809, Mary-Jo Kline and Joanne W. Ryan, eds., *Political Correspondence and Public Papers of Aaron Burr* (Princeton, N.J., 1983), 2: 1080–1081.

36. Kerr to Claiborne, 1 Jan. 1806, Kerr, *Exposition*, pp. 8, 10.

37. On Bradford and Anderson's activities as printers to the Territory of Orleans, see Florence M. Jumonville, "'The People's Friend–The Tyrant's Foe' Law-Related New Orleans Imprints, 1803–1860," in Warren M. Billings and Mark F. Fernandez, eds., *A Law Unto Itself? Essays in the New Louisiana Legal History* (Baton Rouge, La., 2001), pp. 40–58.

text. They engaged Jean Renard to set type in his native tongue, and the Frenchman worked from a translation prepared by a local lawyer, Louis Moreau-Lislet.[38] The end product was a quarto volume measuring approximately 20.5 cm. by 12.5 cm., bound in sheepskin and printed on wove linen paper. It consisted of two hundred and forty-one pages of commentary, plus an additional fifty-eight pages of appendices, plus front matter and an errata sheet. There was no index. The lack of one may well represent one of Kerr's "retrenchments," but its absence was more an irritant than a hindrance to potential readers because of the Table of Contents, which Kerr arranged alphabetically according to subject.[39]

Bradford and Anderson allowed another New Orleans printer, John Mowry, to issue an English only version. As well they may also have licensed Renard to print a separate French edition, though if they did, no copy of it has ever come to light.[40] Neither is there any surviving record to document the initial press runs, the distribution of copies, re-issues, nor later editions.[41]

In keeping with the conventions of treatise writing, Kerr opened his with introductory remarks that served to justify the *Exposition*. He started by giving the reasons for reforming criminal law and practice in Louisiana. The Purchase, he

---

38. Moreau-Lislet (1767–1832), a native of Saint-Domingue, was clerk of the Legislative Council in 1805. He went on to have a long, distinguished career in Louisiana law and politics. Conrad, et al. eds., *Dictionary of Louisiana Biography*, 1: 579–580).
39. Jumonville, comp., *Bibliography of New Orleans Imprints*, p. 38; Kerr, *Exposition*, "Table of Contents, Alphabetically Arranged."
40. Jumonville, comp., *Bibliography of New Orleans Imprints*, p. 39.
41. There was one reprinting at least, and it was published in Plaquamine, La., in 1840. The sole copy of that issue belongs to The Historic New Orleans Collection (telephone conversation between author and Florence M. Jumonville, 8 June 1995).

wrote, rendered the territory a "constituent member" of the United States. Recasting Louisiana's particular "municipal arrangements" thus became necessary in order to unite its people "in sentiment and affection" with Americans as a whole. Moreover, Congress mandated a period when the laws of the territory were to be administered as elsewhere in the nation, wherefore the Legislative Council, "sensible of the advantages of that change," was constrained to adopt a penal statute modelled on common law.[42]

Kerr next posed a rejoinder to French Louisianians who were offended by the imposition of common law, which they saw as quaint, novel, and decidedly foreign. Truth was, he wrote,

> the common law as recognized in the United States is no more the law of England than the civil law can now be deemed the law of Rome. Whatever code be adopted, it must be in some degree foreign . . . The trial by jury, of which the citizens of the United States as a free people are so justly proud and tenacious, is exclusively a creature of the common law, and must therefore be accompanied by many of its forms. Some of these forms may at first sight appear pedantic and obscure, but where is the science whose technicals are less so?

Beyond that Americans enjoyed "the substantial benefits of the English system, without being exposed to many of its asperities or inconveniences." Kerr likewise reminded his Franco-Louisiana readers that the English judiciary, for all of its blemishes, "has stood for ages eminently unrivalled in the European world for its purity and wisdom." And, he dismissed the criticism that French speakers could neither read nor comprehend the "new mode of practice" with the observation that the Crimes Act required simultaneous

---

42. Kerr, *Exposition*, pp. 4, 6.

renderings of both the statute and the *Exposition* into English and French.[43]

His justifications set forth, Kerr then outlined the scheme of his book. First, he would explicate "the several offenses recited by the statute." Those explanations, he noted, would constitute the major portion of the *Exposition*. Next would come "a succinct detail of criminal proceedings, and the principal rules of evidence." Finally, he would conclude with an appendix, which contained the forms of records and other instruments that he had adapted for use in the territorial courts.[44]

Kerr arranged his treatment of offenses to accord with the order of their enumeration in the Crimes Act and its supplement; he therefore began with "Murder" and finished with "Swindling." In each instance, he supplied the statutory definition verbatim, a concise amplification of the particular crime, the standards of proof necessary for conviction, and additional embellishments designed to enlarge upon legislative intent or contemporary practice.[45] The treatment of criminal proceedings was similarly arranged in that Kerr led the reader through all of the steps of a trial, from the arrest of a suspect to the execution of sentence.[46] At every point in all of his commentaries, he took great care to delineate how general American customs or particular territorial usages varied from English standards.

Individually and severally, his discussion reveals much about the differences between Louisiana and English law in 1805. Several examples make the point. One was a statutory distinction between murder in the first degree, which carried the penalty of death, and murder in the second degree, which

---

43. Ibid., pp. 6, 8.
44. Ibid., p. 8.
45. Ibid., pp. 26–137.
46. Ibid., pp. 138–238.

resulted in imprisonment for life, and it fell to juries, not prosecutors or judges, to decide which gradation applied. "This division," observed Kerr "is unknown to the common law." Furthermore, he remarked, the territorial act abolished the common law crime of petty treason[47] and "all other offences of a like nature."[48] What he neglected to note, however, was that the legislators had appropriated these provisions nearly verbatim from a Virginia law.[49]

Kerr showed how the Legislative Council substituted imprisonment at hard labor for the death penalty. In that instance, the Louisianians were several steps ahead of their Virginia brethren, who still executed arsonists and other felons besides first-degree murderers. That change bespoke a general American tendency toward a reduction in the number of capital offenses, just as it represented an evolutionary reconstitution of the meaning of felony.[50]

In similar fashion, Kerr called attention to some of the revolutionizing effects of independence upon American penal law. Quoting Sir Edward Coke, he related how breaking into an English church was said to be burglary. "However," he continued, "as no established religion is recognized in the United States, some new questions may arise whether any, and what religious buildings are entitled to privileges as

---

47. That is, a servant killing his master, a wife her husband, or a clergyman or his superior, Cowell, *Law Dictionary*, under "petit treason." In the colonies and the United States, that definition also extended to slaves.

48. *Acts, Second Session, 1805*, section 1, 36–38; Kerr, *Exposition*, pp. 32, 36.

49. The act passed the General Assembly in 1796, Benjamin Watkins Leigh, comp., *The Revised Code of the Laws of Virginia: Being A Collection of all Such Acts of the General Assembly, of a Public and Permanent Nature; With a General Index* (Richmond, Va., 1819), 1: 616–617. Pennsylvania had a similar law, which was adopted in 1794, Edwin R. Keedy, "History of the Pennsylvania Statute Creating Degrees of Murder," *University of Pennsylvania Law Review*, 97 (1949): 759ff.

50. Leigh, comp., *Revised Code of Virginia*, 1: 587.

such." The Crimes Act was mute on the point, and it remained for later legislation to resolve the matter.[51]

One church-related reform, though, went beyond practice elsewhere in the United States. The Crimes Act implicitly abolished benefit of clergy. A custom rooted in medieval English legal procedure, benefit of clergy was originally devised to protect clerks in religious orders and to shield ecclesiastical jurisdiction from secular interference. In time, it enabled any convict to escape hanging or maiming by reading or reciting the so-called "neck verse" out of Holy Writ (Psalm 51: 1).[52] Benefit of clergy found its way into colonial law and managed to survive for years after the Revolution before reformers outside Louisiana succeeded in eliminating it altogether.[53]

Then there were transgressions that Louisiana law comprehended that its English and American analogues did not yet embrace. Two of the more obvious illustrations of this tendency were the crimes of swindling and levee breaking. The Crimes Act defined a swindler as a person who

---

51. Kerr, *Exposition*, p. 52.
52. Cowell, *Law Dictionary*, under "clergy;" Blackstone, *Commentaries*, 4: 358–369. The verse reads "Have mercy upon me, O God, according to thy loving kindness: according unto the multitude of thy tender mercies blot out my transgressions."
53. A.L. Cross, "Benefit of Clergy in American Criminal Proceedings," *Massachusetts Historical Society Proceedings*, 61 (1927): 154–181; George Dalzell, *Benefit of Clergy in America and Related Matters* (New York, 1955), *passim*; William Waller Hening, ed., *The Statutes at Large, Being a Collection of the Laws of Virginia, from the First Session of the Legislature in 1619* (Richmond, Va., 1809–1823) 13: 30–32; John Bouvier, comp., *A Law Dictionary, Adapted to the Constitution and Laws of the United States of America, and of the Several States in the American Union; With References to the Civil and Other Systems of Foreign Law* (Philadelphia, Pa., 1839), 1: 124. As of 1805, Maryland, Delaware, Georgia and the Carolinas still allowed defendants to plead benefit of clergy.

"knowingly, fraudulently, and designedly" took from another "money or property, with intent to defraud."[54] What is remarkable about this prescription was its novelty; it was among the first definitions of the offense in either the United States or England. Indeed, the very word "swindle" itself—meaning "to cheat" or "to gull"— was a new addition to the English language. It seems to have come into general use as only as recently as 1788, when it appeared in the *Gentleman's Magazine*.[55]

That the Legislative Council should have criminalized swindling was in direct response to the peculiar conditions of the territory. Kerr explained the legislators' rationale this way. "The inhabitants," he declared, "are, for a variety of obvious reasons, . . . exposed to the impositions from which it is the business of the [law] to protect them. The present situation of the country holds out an invitation to nearly all kinds of adventurers; and as the swindler is ever sure to be among the number, it is well that we are provided for his reception." And, in Kerr's estimation, the provision would become "a very useful clause of our criminal code."[56]

Levees were, and remain, vital bulwarks of protection against hurricanes and floods in southern Louisiana, and anyone who "wilfully and maliciously" pulled them down posed a hazard to private property as well as to public safety. Therefore the offense of levee breaking was specified in Section 31 of the Crimes Act, which also dealt with rioting, unlawful assembly, and libel, a juxtaposition of disparate misdeeds that drew from Kerr a single, laconic observation.

---

54. Acts, Second Session, 1805, section 2, 38.
55. *Oxford English Dictionary*, 2d ed., 17: 1448–49. By the third decade of the nineteenth century, the definition had generally worked its way into English and American law. See William Oldnall Russell, *A Treatise on Crimes and Indictable Misdemeanors*, 2d. ed., (London, 1828), 2: 118–119; Bouvier, comp., *A Law Dictionary*, 2: 424; Essay 13, below.
56. Kerr, *Exposition*, p. 132.

"Here again," he declared, "we have several offences which bear no particular relation to each other brought within the compass of one short section."[57]

The commentary on trials is similarly revealing. In truth, that portion of the *Exposition* may be read as a primer on criminal procedure as it was generally understood in America at the opening of the nineteenth century. Such is the fineness of its detail, however, that it merits a separate, extended analysis of its own. Suffice to say, by giving great emphasis to procedural technicalities, Kerr had particular objects in mind. He sought to introduce the Orleanais to the concept of trial by jury, which was a prized benefit of American citizenship. Moreover, the Constitution of the United States guaranteed citizens of the territory a right to a speedy trial, and his guidance would assure the protection of that privilege. Kerr also realized that judges and lawyers throughout the territory were not all learned in the intricacies of American proceedings, so he styled his discussion of them as a detailed set of instructions that took readers step by step from arrest, to arraignment, trail, verdict, and execution of sentence. He concluded on an upbeat note. The "criminal code," he said, contained "what every days experience I am convinced will bring more plainly into view, many valuable principles of energy unpolluted by any sanguinary traits. The best and most celebrated foreign system of criminal jurisprudence has been transplanted among us so pruned and adapted to the nature and circumstance of the soil, that we scarcely know it as an exotic."[58]

Kerr rested the *Exposition* on groundings that he fashioned from a considerable array of written authorities. Aside from the *Acts of the . . . Legislative Council*, some nineteen

---

57. Ibid., p. 110.
58. Ibid., pp. 138–238, 240. I am engaged in just such an analysis, and I expect to publish its results at a future date.

other printed texts served as his sources.[59] This collection represented a fairly sophisticated library on criminal law for its time. Whether Kerr owned all or some of the volumes is conjectural. Given the dearth of information about him, his proclivities for collecting necessarily remain speculative, although the larger question of book ownership by early Louisiana attorneys is a subject that awaits intensive probing.[60]

Significantly, most of the nineteen were composed by Britons. Several things account for this domination. There were the mandates of the Breckinridge and the Crimes Acts that English and American law would be the basis of criminal jurisprudence in the territory. Having been reared in Ireland, Kerr likely trained for the law in the United Kingdom, meaning his studies would have exposed him to some of the titles. More significantly, there were as yet few reliable American treatises from which to seek instruction, but only one of them was evidently available to Kerr. Thus, however much he may have wanted to distance Louisiana from British law, he was of necessity compelled to depend upon the authority of English commentators.

---

59. I identified the nineteen volumes from Kerr's references to them throughout the text of the *Exposition*. Usually, his citations mentioned a particular work only as "Britton," or "Coke," or "Finch," and it sometimes took a bit of detective work to sort out the precise reference. A helpful finding aid in deciphering partial titles was Donald Raistrick, *Index to Legal Citations and Abbreviations* (London, 1981).

60. Such a study is easily undertaken, given the nature of the extant documentation. One need only develop a list of attorneys from the bar admission roles that are recorded in the minute books of the Supreme Court of Louisiana, housed in the Louisiana & Special Collections Department at the University of New Orleans, and then search the succession files in the Notarial Archives of Orleans Parish for estate inventories that enumerated books among dead lawyers' personal belongings.

Several of the volumes merit special attention here, either because of the frequency that Kerr drew upon them, or because they demonstrate the reach of his erudition. Citations to Coke's *Institutes*, Blackstone's *Commentaries*, and Sir Matthew Hale's *Historia Placitorum Coronæ. The History of the Pleas of the Crown* abound throughout the *Exposition*.[61]

Of course, making copious references to Coke or Blackstone was hardly unusual for a lawyer versed in the precepts of Anglo-American jurisprudence. Mastering the *Institutes* was *de rigueur* for any Briton or American who professed law in Kerr's time. Beyond that universal expectation, however, the *Institutes* held singular relevance for treatise writers on criminal law who came after Coke. Sir Edward blazed their trails for them, so Kerr naturally turned to the third and fourth *Institutes*, which provided pertinent general guides to the origins of the American law of crimes and the jurisdiction of courts, respectively.

As for Blackstone, after he brought out the first edition of his tome in 1765, the *Commentaries* quickly rivalled, and in some senses, surpassed the *Institutes*. Blackstone's was the more orderly and elegantly styled of the two masterworks, and Americans soon developed an abiding affection for it. Despite its conservatism and its overtones of monarchy, the *Commentaries* became the American standard because it was more up-to-date than Coke. Especially useful was an edition prepared by the Virginia jurist and law professor St. George Tucker, published in 1803. The judge, who succeeded his mentor George Wythe as professor of law at the College of William and Mary, crafted his lectures into annotations for his edition. That fillet adorned Tucker's *Blackstone* with an American relevance that the *Institutes* could not match. Kerr's

---

61. The complete list of titles follows in the Appendix.

use of Tucker, besides other editions of the *Commentaries*, can be precisely established by specific references to them in the *Exposition*.[62]

Hale's *Historia Placitorum Coronae* was a work of a wholly different order than either Coke or Blackstone. Where the purview of the latter two encompassed the whole of English law, the ambit of the former embraced criminal law exclusively. Indeed, it was the most comprehensive single statement available to Kerr, which made it vital to his undertaking. Plainly put, it had no equal in 1805, despite its having been written more than a century before Kerr took up a pen of his own. The author, Sir Matthew Hale (1609–1676), held various judicial posts throughout the third quarter of the seventeenth century and was a dedicated legal reformer in his own right.[63] Of a studious bent, he wrote voluminously on science, religion, and law.[64] Much of his oeuvre, though, remains in manuscript, while the *Historia* was published posthumously in 1736 in two oversized folio volumes.[65] Just to scan the upwards of fifteen hundred pages is to gain an

---

62. Kerr, *Exposition*, pp. 180, 182. Despite the widespread American affection for the *Commentaries*, that esteem was far from universal. Thomas Jefferson, for one, deprecated the work for its monarchical tendencies, Julius S. Waterman, "Thomas Jefferson and Blackstone's Commentaries," *Illinois Law Review (Northwestern School of Law)*, 27 (1933): 629–659.
63. Hale is the subject of two book-length biographies: Gilbert Burnet, (London, 1682) and Edmund Heward, *Matthew Hale* (London, 1972).
64. A complete bibliography of Hale's writings is in Heward, *Matthew Hale*, pp. 124–156.
65. Sollom Emlyn, a member of Lincoln's Inn, prepared the published version. He discussed his editorial methodology at length in the Preface, which also includes Emlyn's biographical sketch of Hale. Elizabeth Nutt, Richard Nutt, and R. Gosling, whose shop was a significant early eighteenth-century publisher of law books, produced the *Historia*. They artfully combined materials, typography, and design into a singular, exquisitely beautiful example of the English printer's craft.

immediate feel for Hale's gift for reducing masses of information to a manageable, practical account of English criminal law. It is also to appreciate why Kerr cited the *Historia* more than any other of his reference texts.

Two legal dictionaries, John Rastell's *Les Terms de la Ley: or, Certain Difficult and Obscure Words, and Termes of the Common Lawes of this Realm . . .*[66] and Giles Jacob's *The Law-dictionary: explaining the rise, progress, and state of English law*,[67] provided Kerr with definitions of terminology. However, the value of those meanings was limited owing to their irrelevance, in the words of the first American lexicographer John Bouvier, "to our government, our constitutions, or our political or civil institutions." Pertinent or not, Kerr had no choice but to depend upon Rastell and Jacob because he had no dictionary of American legalisms. Such a book did not exist in 1805, and Bouvier's was still decades away from reality.[68]

The sole American authority from whom Kerr borrowed freely was William Waller Hening. Like Claiborne, Hening was Jefferson's protégé, and he enjoyed the esteem of his contemporaries for his sound legal scholarship and numerous published reports, manuals, and editions of Virginia statutes.[69] The sample warrants, bonds, recognizances, indictments, and other forms of process he provided in one of his manuals, the

---

66. London, 1721. Originally published in 1527, *Terms de la Ley* was the first ever type set lexicon in England. It ran through twenty-nine editions before going out of print in 1819.
67. London, 1721. This work is not in the author's library or the Law Library of Louisiana.
68. Bouvier, comp., *A Law Dictionary*, 1: vi.
69. Samuel M. Walker, Jr., "William Waller Hening," in W. Hamilton Bryson, ed., *The Virginia Law Reporters Before 1880*, (Charlottesville, Va., 1977), pp. 19–25.

New Virginia Justice,[70] sufficed as models for the appendix to the *Exposition*. Kerr frequently simplified the phrasing but retained the substance, though in the instance of writs he lifted their texts word for word from Hening's examples.[71]

Resort to Sir Francis Bacon's *Elements of the Common Laws of England*,[72] Sir Heneage Finch's *Law, Or a Discourse Thereof*,[73] Fleta's *Commentariis Juris Anglicani sic Nuncupatus. Sub Edwardo Rege Primo . . .*,[74] and Brown Willis's *Notitia Parliamentaria: Or A History of the Counties, Cities, and Boroughs in England and Wales*,[75] suggests something of the range of Kerr's legal knowledge. Clearly, those citations indicate a person well schooled in the older commentators, like Fleta, and the more obscure, but highly specialized writers, such as Brown Willis. That Kerr had read across such a broad spectrum confirms Claiborne's confidence in his "professional talents and industry."[76]

Lewis Kerr produced a lucid, accessible vade mecum on criminal law that any literate Louisianian might read with profit. In that sense, the *Exposition* helped to content popular concerns about the American take-over. It also smoothed the

---

70. William Waller Hening, comp., *The New Virginia Justice, Comprising the Office and Authority of a Justice of the Peace, in the Commonwealth of Virginia* (Richmond, Va. 1810).
71. See, for example, Kerr, *Exposition*, Appendix, pp. vii, xv, and Hening, *New Virginia Justice*, pp. 526, 300; Fernandez, *From Chaos to Continuity*, 11–117.
72. London, 1639.
73. London, 1651.
74. London, 1647. The identity of the author remains a mystery. "Fleta" was a name derived from the author's incarceration in the Fleet Prison in London, during the reign of Edward I, when the work was supposedly written. John Selden was responsible for printing the first edition, which derived from a manuscript now housed at the British Library. This title is not in the author's library or the Law Library of Louisiana.
75. London, 1716. This title is not in the author's library or the Law Library of Louisiana.
76. Claiborne to Kerr, Aug. 12, 1805, Kerr, *Exposition*, p. iv.

way from Franco-Hispanic conceptions of justice to a variant of American criminal jurisprudence. It matched the expectations of the governor, the legislative councillors, and the author, but it had an impact quite beyond those hopes. It became the textbook that informed judges and lawyers for the remainder of the territorial period and long after statehood.[77] For more than fifty years it remained the standard before giving way to Albert Voorhies's *A Treatise on the Criminal Jurisprudence of Louisiana*, which was published in 1860.[78] By then, Louisiana's law of crime and punishment had attained a degree of refinement and complexity that neither Kerr nor Claiborne could have envisioned.[79]

For historians of Louisiana's legal order, the *Exposition* deserves attention because of its revelations about the origins of criminal justice in the Bayou State. For historians of American law at large, the *Exposition* bears noting as an illustration of the insights to be gained from close study of other neglected treatises.[80]

---

77. Louisiana joined the Union as the eighteenth state in 1812.
78. Voorhies (1829–1913) was an associate justice of the Supreme Court of Louisiana, who had been a criminal lawyer, district attorney, trial judge, state senator, and lieutenant governor before his elevation to the high bench. Conrad et al. eds., ed., *Dictionary of Louisiana Biography*, 2: 815–816).
79. Billings, "Origins of Criminal Law in Louisiana," 72–76; Mark F. Fernandez, ed., "State *v.* McLean et al.: Louisiana's First History of Criminal Law," *Louisiana History: The Journal of the Louisiana Historical Association*, 36 (1995): 313–325.
80. Morton J. Horvitz, "Treatise Literature," *Law Library Journal*, 69 (1976); 459–60 reached a similar conclusion.

APPENDIX

Lewis Kerr's Sources for the *Exposition*

[The following list includes all of the authorities that Kerr cited throughout the *Exposition*. Generally, each work ran through many editions before falling out of print, but it is not always possible to discern the precise edition Kerr used. The ones that can be identified are noted below. Facts of publication refer to first editions, not to those mentioned in the essay itself. Those data derive from John Worrall, comp. *Bibliotheca Legum: Or, A Catalogue of the Common and Statute Law Books of this Realm, And some others relating thereto; From their First Publication to Easter Term, 1777*. London, 1777; Joseph Henry Beale, comp. *A Bibliography of Early English Law Books and Supplement by Robert Bowie Anderson*. Repr. ed. Buffalo, N.Y., 1966; A.F. Pollard and G.B. Redgrave, eds. *Short-Title Catalogue of Books Printed in England, Scotland and Ireland, and of English Books Printed Abroad, 1475–1640*. London, 1926; Donald G. Wing, *Short-Title Catalogue of Books Printed in England, Scotland, Ireland, Wales, and British North America of English Books Printed in Other Countries, 1641–1700*. New York, 1945–1951; Herbert A. Johnson, *Imported Eighteenth-Century Treatises in American Libraries, 1700–1799*. Knoxville, Tenn., 1978; and Florence M. Jumonville, comp., *Bibliography of New Orleans Imprints, 1764–1864*. New Orleans, La., 1989.]

1. *Acts Passed at the First Session of the Legislative Council of the Territory of Orleans* . . . New Orleans, La., 1805.
2. *Acts Passed at the Second Session of the Legislative Council of the Territory of Orleans* . . . *New Orleans, 1805*. {His citations indicate that Kerr took his verbatim quotations of the statutes from these printed texts rather than the engrossed originals.}
3. Sir Francis Bacon. *Elements of the Common Laws of England*. London, 1639.

4. Matthew Bacon. *A New Abridgment of the Law.* London, 1736. {Kerr cited parts of a 3d and 4th editions, which suggests that he worked from broken sets of Bacon's *Abridgment.*}

5. Sir William Blackstone. *Commentaries on the Laws of England.* Oxford, 1765. {Kerr may have worked from one of the later Irish editions, in addition to Tucker's *Blackstone.*}

6. Britton, *Containing the Antient Pleas of the Crown* . . . . London, 1530. {Often attributed to John le Breton, thirteenth-century bishop of Hereford, hence the reference to "Britton."}

7. Edmund Christian. *Notes on Blackstone's Commentaries.* Dublin, 1796.

8. Sir Edward Coke. *Institutes of the Laws of England.* London, 1628–1644.

9. Sir Heneage Finch. *Law, Or A Discourse Thereof.* London, 1613.

10. Fleta. *Fleta, sue Commentarius Juris Anglicani sic Nuncupatus, sub Edwardo Rege Primo* . . ., ed. John Selden, London, 1647.

11. Sir Geoffrey Gilbert, *The Law of Evidence.* London, 1760.

12. Sir Matthew Hale. *Historia Placitorum Coronae. The History of the Pleas of the Crown.* London, 1736. {Kerr's citations are to this rather than the second edition, which was issued in 1778.}

13. Sir Matthew Hale. *Pleas of the Crown: or, a Methodical Summary of the Principal Matters relating to that Subject.* London, 1694.

14. William Hawkins. *A Treatise of the Pleas of the Crown: or A System of the principal matters relating to that subject, digested under proper heads.* London, 1716.

15. William Waller Hening. *New Virginia Justice.* Richmond, 1795. {Kerr used this because the second edition did not come to print until 1810.}

16. Thomas Bayly Howell, comp. *A Collection of State Trials and Proceedings for High Treason and Other Crimes and Misdemeanors from the Earliest Period to the Year 1783.* London, 1789.

17. Giles Jacob. *The Law-dictionary: explaining the rise, progress, and state of English law.* London, 1721.

18. Thomas Leach. *Cases in Crown Law, Determined by the Twelve Judges by the Court of King's Bench, and by Commissioners of Oyer and Terminer and General Gaol Delivery, from the Fourth year of George the Second to the Twenty-ninth Year of George the Third.* Dublin, 1789.

19. John Rastell. *Expositiones terminorum in legum anglorum . . .* London, 1527. {Evidently, as the eighteenth century wore on, Jacob's became the preferred dictionary on both sides of the Atlantic, though as Kerr's citations to Rastell indicates, older lexicons still had their uses. Kerr appears to have drawn his citations from Rastell out of the 1721 edition, entitled *Les Terms de la Ley: or, Certaine Difficult and Obscure Words, and Termes of the Common Lawes of this Realme, now in Use, expounded and Explained.* London, 1721.}

20. St. George Tucker. *Tucker's Blackstone.* Philadelphia, Pa., 1803.

21. Brown Willis. *Notitia Parliamentaria: Or A History of the Counties, Cities, and Boroughs in England and Wales. . .* London, 1716.

22. Kerr probably also used the now lost journals, minutes, and working papers of the Legislative Council.

ESSAY 13

THE SUPREME COURT OF LOUISIANA AND THE ADMINISTRATION OF JUSTICE, 1813 – 1995

I had much to learn after Chief Justice John A. Dixon, Jr., named me Historian of the Supreme Court of Louisiana in 1982. Figuring out how the Court fashioned and was shaped by the legal order that surrounded it daunted me at first. Because state supreme courts seldom caught the eye of legal historians, I was largely bereft of scholarly literature to which I could turn for inspiration or guidance. Answering the most basic of questions demanded endless hours of burrowing through mountains of manuscripts. Of course such rummaging is very much a part of what historians do, so I quickly grew to enjoy rooting around in records that few scholars had ever touched before me. And, whereas the Supreme Court differed markedly from the General Court or the county courts of seventeenth-century Virginia, there were enough parallels between them to enable me to tailor techniques that guided my Virginia investigations to a Louisiana setting.

The first order of business was compiling databases similar to those that I devised for Virginia. One comprised all of the constitutional and statutory definitions of the Court's jurisdiction. Then I made a list of everyone who sat on the Court, which became the foundation for a biographical directory of members. As I assembled both databases, I uncovered clues to reading habits of the judges and members of the bar, which I turned into a compilation of law books that circulated throughout Louisiana between the Louisiana Purchase and Reconstruction. I located rules of procedure that dictated how the Court docketed cases for hearing, how it controlled oral arguments, and who it allowed to appear before it. That spadework led to the publication of the *Historic Rules of the Supreme Court of Louisiana, 1813–1879* (Lafayette, La., 1985), which is now a standard reference tool for Louisiana legal historians.

In time I came to see the Court in an altogether different light. The Court did more than render opinions. Because it sat at the apex of the third branch of state government it had primary responsibility for maintaining the entire judiciary in good working order. That said, it must also be remarked that this administrative aspect of court business since 1813 was less well appreciated than was its role in interpreting the law. That insight opened a line of inquiry that culminated in this essay, a conceptual piece that sketched ways of examining the Court in its administrative capacity, and it suggested how that role evolved over time.

Originally published as "The Supreme Court of Louisiana and the Administration of Justice, 1813-1995" in *Louisiana History: The Journal of the Louisiana Historical Association,* 35 (1996): 389–405, the article is reprinted here with the kind permission of the editor.

"Justice delayed is justice denied." A venerable saying, this ancient maxim bespeaks a fundamental pledge that finds resounding voice in our federal and state constitutions—the warrant of a swift trial in an appropriate judicial forum. Constitutional guarantees, however, are only as good as those who must administer them. Prompt justice therefore depends upon the ability of courts to resolve cases in a timely manner, but for, as long as there have been courts in America, timeliness has proven an elusive ideal to achieve in practice.

How have courts tried to close the gap between the constitutional promise of a speedy trial and reality? Consider the example of the Supreme Court of Louisiana, which has wrestled with the issue for nearly two centuries. On occasion it followed uncommon paths that led to distinctive solutions; at other times its remedies found inspiration in practices elsewhere in the United States. Taken as a whole, these continuities played out against a backdrop of the personal, political, or economic imperatives that defined the state and its legal culture from 1813 to the present. An exploration of these contours not only shows how the Louisiana high bench perfected ways of administering justice but it likewise reveals a side of appellate judging that historians of law have yet to chart to any significant degree. Accordingly, this essay serves to map the outlines.

Any such inquiry could, and probably should, embrace all facets of judicial administration in theory, but for purposes of this discussion, only four command attention: procedural rules, bar regulation, auxiliary staffing, and citation formats. The reason for highlighting these four is a plain one. Rule-making and regulating the bar are the oldest managerial devices at the Court's disposal. The others, by contrast, represent newer techniques that respond to modern legal needs and the digital information age.

Rules are to appellate courts what parliamentary procedures are to legislatures in that each dictates the flow of cases and legislation respectively. Historically speaking, court rules derive from a mixture of custom, constitutional directive, and statutory enhancement. They regulate such procedures as the methods of filing, submission of briefs and other apposite documentation, bonding requirements, hearing dates, or the length of oral arguments. As for the Supreme Court of Louisiana, its rules originated with statehood.

Adoption of the Constitution of 1812 was a condition for the admission of Louisiana to the Union. Consequently, the architects of that document cut the judiciary article to contemporary American patterns, meaning they included in it provision for a supreme court. However, the constitution was mute as to that court's powers of rule-making, so the first state legislature spoke where fundamental law was silent.[1] The Judiciary Act of 1813 stipulated that the Court could "make and issue all mandates necessary for the exercise of [its] jurisdiction over the inferior tribunals," it could control its officers, and it could adopt "all needful rules . . ., which shall not be inconsistent with the provisions of this act or of any other law of this state," just so long as "the said rules once established shall not be altered" without due notice. In essence, then, if the judges did not stray beyond these ample bounds, they might run the Court as they saw fit.[2]

Within days of opening their doors to business on 1 March,1813, Chief Judge Dominck Hall[3] and his colleague

---

1. Article IV created a court of three judges who held appellate jurisdiction over civil actions that exceeded a value of three hundred dollars. They tried cases at New Orleans as well as around the remainder of the state, which comprised a western appellate district. *Constitution or Form of Government of the State of Louisiana* (New Orleans, La., 1812), p. 17; Warren M. Billings, "From This Seed: The Constitution of 1812," in Warren M. Billings and Edward F. Haas, eds., *In Search of Fundamental Law: Louisiana's Constitutions, 1812–1974* (Lafayette, La., 1993), pp. 15–19.

2. "An Act To organize the supreme court of the state of Louisiana, and to establish courts of inferior jurisdiction," sections 17–18, *Acts Passed at the Second Session of the First Legislature of the State of Louisiana* (New Orleans, La., 1813), p. 28.

3. Members of the Court were addressed as "judge" until 1845, when they were styled "justice." Hall became presiding, or chief, judge by virtue of his being commissioned as the first member of the Court, but he resigned his office less than six months after taking his oath. George Mathews replaced him and

George Mathews used these powers for the very first time when they designated five prominent New Orleans attorneys "a Committee to draw up Rules & Regulations for the Government of this Court."[4] Thereby, Hall and Mathews relieved themselves of a lengthy chore that was a necessary prelude to their judging cases expeditiously. Reaching out to senior barristers afforded the wisdom and experience of seasoned practitioners as it instilled in leading advocates a pride of ownership in the court and its work, and it laid down a precedent for the future.

No copy of the first "Rules & Regulations" has come down to us, but the committee seems to have reached for the familiar and borrowed rules from the recently-defunct Superior Court for the Territory of Orleans.[5] Old and new court bore like responsibilities, so with minor tailoring prescriptions that sufficed for the one could now fit for the

---

remained chief judge until 1836, when he was succeeded by François-Xavier Martin. On these matters, see Sybil A. Boudreaux, ed., "The First Minute Book of the Supreme Court of the State of Louisiana, 1813 to May 1818: An Annotated Edition" (M.A. thesis, University of New Orleans, La., 1983), pp. 13–15 and Warren M. Billings, ed., *The Historic Rules of the Supreme Court of Louisiana, 1813–1879* (Lafayette, La., 1985), Appendix II. The third member of the original Court, Pierre Derbigny, was commissioned on 8 Mar. 1813, five days after the others ordered the drafting of the rules, and he took his seat on the 9th, Boudreaux, ed., "The First Minute Book of the Supreme Court," pp. 20–21.

4. Boudreaux, ed., "The First Minute Book of the Supreme Court," p. 16. Abner L. Duncan, Abraham R. Ellery, Edward Livingston, François-Xavier Martin, and Etiènne Mazareau formed the committee.

5. "An Act regulating the practice of the Superior Court, in civil causes," *Acts Passed at the First Session of the Legislative Council of the Territory of Orleans* (New Orleans, La., 1805), pp. 219–260; Mark F. Fernandez, "The Rules of the Courts of the Territory of Orleans," *Louisiana History: The Journal of the Louisiana Historical Association*, 38 (1997): 63–86. Interpretations and additions to the rules were also included in the Code of Practice, but for brevity's sake I have excluded those developments from this discussion. Wheelock S. Upton, comp., *Code of Practice in Civil Cases for the State of Louisiana; With Annotations* (New Orleans, La., 1839), pp. 146–153.

other. Consequently, the committee finished its work in about a week, whereupon Hall and Mathews promulgated its recommendations as the rules of the Supreme Court.[6]

Over the next three decades, Hall, Mathews, and their successors wrote additional rules in a leisurely, ad hoc way.[7] Such a whimsical approach compounded the hindrance brought on by an ever growing jam of appeals and judges who pursued outside interests[8] or who suffered the infirmities of advancing age.[9] Litigation slowed to the proverbial snail's crawl by the mid-1840s.[10] As a result, observers raised the howl that the Court's slothful habits impeded the right to a speedy trial, and they saw in the overhaul of the court rules one remedy for such indolence.[11] Their clamor contributed to a call for the convention that rewrote the state's organic law

---

6. The Court was organized in a matter of days. After the assembly passed the judiciary act on 10 Feb. Gov. William C.C. Claiborne nominated Hall and Mathews, and the state senate confirmed them on the twenty-second. Both swore their oaths of office by the twenty-fifth. They opened the Court six days later for the ceremonial reading of their commissions. On 3 Mar., they named the rules committee and heard their first cases nine days later, Boudreaux, ed., "The First Minute Book of the Supreme Court," 13–22.

7. By 1845, the Court enacted over forty amendments to the original body of rules, Billings, ed., *Historic Rules of the Supreme Court*, pp. 1–6.

8. Martin wrote his history of Louisiana, prepared a digest of Louisiana statutes, and compiled his reports of Louisiana cases while he sat on the Court. To be sure, these activities made valuable contributions to historical knowledge and legal practice and gained an enduring reputation for Martin, but they also kept him from his judicial duties.

9. As Martin aged, he also grew blind. The impediment in no way diminished his mental faculties, though it slowed down his ability to write opinions. See Essay 10 above.

10. Henry Plauché Dart, "The History of the Supreme Court of Louisiana," *Louisiana Reports*, 133 (1913): xlii–xliii.

11. See for example Gustavus A. Schmidt, ed., *Louisiana Law Journal*, 1 (1841): 157.

in 1845.[12] Among other things, the new constitution revamped the jurisdiction of the Court to cover criminal appeals, as it expanded the membership to include a chief and four associate justices, but it left intact the Court's control over the rules.[13]

In 1846, the new justices moved swiftly to recast their governance of the Court. Borrowing a page from Hall and Mathews, they named a committee from the New Orleans bar that drafted a restatement of the rules, which was changed slightly before its adoption.[14] The revised compilation reduced a hodgepodge of repetitive, obsolete, or impractical directives to eleven tersely stated, logically ordered precepts.[15] This collection subsequently assumed a significance that extended far beyond its original purpose because it established a framework for all subsequent revisions, the basic structure of which remains in place to this day.[16]

Regulation of the bar also reached back to the beginnings of the Court. A section in the Judiciary Act of 1813 charged the judges to examine, license, and correct those who wished

---

12. Mark F. Fernandez, *From Chaos to Continuity: The Evolution of Louisiana's Judicial System, 1712–1862* (Baton Rouge, La., 2001), pp. 40–57.
13. Constitution of 1845, title IV, articles 62–64; "An Act To provide for the removal of all cases now pending in the Supreme Court of the State of Louisiana under the Constitution of eighteen hundred and twelve, to the Supreme Court to be established under the new Constitution," *Acts Passed at the First Session of the First Legislature of the State of Louisiana Begun and Held in the City of New Orleans on the 9th Day of February 1846* (New Orleans, 1846), p. 9; Judith K. Schafer, "Reform or Experiment? The Constitution of 1845," in Billings and Haas, eds., *In Search of Fundamental Law*, pp. 21–37, 158–160.
14. Billings, ed., Historic Rules of the Supreme Court, pp. 16–20.
15. Ibid., p. 20, 21–39.
16. Compare the Rules of 1846 with the modern regulations in *Louisiana Revised Statutes*, 8: 293–582. A detailed study of the evolution of the post-1846 rules has yet to be done.

to practice law. The proviso reflected a then-prevailing view that supreme court judges, by virtue of their erudition, were best suited to determine who should be lawyers and to punish those who misbehaved.[17]

Qualifying attorneys quickly became one of the most burdensome of the early Court's administrative chores because of the press of so many applicants. Their rising numbers were attributable to several conditions that prevailed in Louisiana as elsewhere in the nation. For one thing, easy access to the legal profession exemplified a country-wide drift away from its gentlemanly origins in colonial and revolutionary times towards a more modern meritocracy open to all comers. Careers at the bar drew a legion of ambitious individuals who viewed the practice of law as a gateway to political and financial reward. For another, the credentials demanded of a would-be attorney were modest; good character, citizenship, residency, success at passing an oral bar examination were the usual prerequisites. A degree in law helped because a law school education often provided better training than the more common methods of self-study or apprenticeship. Given these conditions, the number of applicants in Louisiana swelled after 1813, so much so that the court grew awash with requests for bar examinations.[18]

The judges finally acted to alleviate their situation in November 1840, when they announced a new regulation that introduced two basic reforms. One raised the level of educational attainment for future lawyers by prescribing a

---

17. "An Act to organize the Supreme Court," *Acts, 1813*, p. 32. The Superior Court enjoyed a similar authority during the territorial period.
18. Warren M. Billings, "The Supreme Court and the Education of Louisiana Lawyers," *Louisiana Bar Journal*, 33 (1985): 74–80; Billings ed., *Historic Rules of the Supreme Court*, p. xviii; Elizabeth Gaspard, "The Rise of the Louisiana Bar: The Early Years," *Louisiana History: The Journal of the Louisiana Historical Association*, 28 (1987): 183–197.

syllabus of books for them to master. This "Course of Studies," which was unique to Louisiana, required learning the statutes of state and nation as well as the contents of a dozen volumes whose subjects ran from the practical to the theoretical aspects of law in general and the law of Louisiana in particular. The other correction addressed the conduct of bar examinations. First, it limited the testing to once a quarter. Then it called for the court to nominate a committee of seven attorneys, who would "strictly and rigidly" screen applicants. The committee certified successful candidates as qualified "in point of legal learning." Certified candidates were then quizzed publicly by the court, and if they jumped that hurdle, then they won their licenses.[19]

These standards met the judges' expectations, and with modifications they remained in effect until the 1920s.[20] Their efficacy nevertheless came into question as the nineteenth century slipped into the twentieth. Challenges to their utility reflected national and local trends that swept aside old verities; the opening decades of the new century were, after all, the era of progressivism. Progressives everywhere preached the gospel of modernization through efficiency and structural reform. This "good news" meshed nicely with reconsiderations within the legal profession regarding practice, education, conduct—even the very nature of law and government itself. For example, Progressives believed that regularity rendered the legal order fathomable,

---

19. Billings, ed., *Historic Rules of the Supreme Court*, pp.10–14; Warren M Billings, "'A Course of Studies': Books That Shaped Louisiana Law," in Warren M. Billings and Mark F. Fernandez, eds., *A Law Unto Itself? Essays in the New Louisiana Legal History* (Baton Rouge, La., 2001), pp. 25–40.
20. *Acts, 1842*, pp. 516–18; Billings, ed., *Historic Rules of the Supreme Court*, pp. 30–31, *Louisiana Annual Reports*, 31 (1879): viii; 51 (1899): xxxvi; *Louisiana Reports*, 134 (1914): xii–xiv. A rule change in 1923 eliminated the syllabus, *Louisiana Reports*, 152 (1923): vii–viii.

symmetrical, sure, so they worked to establish uniform federal, state, and local laws. Others sought to modernize legal education into a more "scientific" discipline taught by professors in a university setting. Reform-minded lawyers transformed state and local bar associations from social clubs into organizations that lobbied legislatures and courts in behalf of their vocational interests, just as they envisioned the American Bar Association as their national voice. More mundanely, attorneys, who specialized in newer fields such as corporation law, elbowed generalists aside as law firms supplanted single practitioners, especially in the cities, where much of the most lucrative work was available.

The Louisiana State Bar Association (LASBA) was the main prophet of this new religion in the state. Not all lawyers heeded its call to salvation, however. Some suspected the motives of a group whose members were overwhelmingly New Orleanians. Others took exception out of philosophical or practical considerations, whereas for older or less-well educated opponents, the issue was change itself. Eventually, the competition for souls got caught up in the politics of the Long Era and nearly cost the Supreme Court its supervision of the bar.[21]

The issue was joined in a roundabout way. Allegations of fraudulent balloting in New Orleans during the election of 1932 led the parish district attorney, Eugene B. Stanley, to launch an inquiry into the charges. Stanley had barely begun his investigation when Attorney General Gaston L. Porterie entered the case, which effectively put it on hold. Opponents of the Long regime immediately smelt a rat, believing that Porterie had intervened because there was something to hide and, more importantly, that Huey Long was calling the shots,

---

21. Ben Robertson Miller, *The Louisiana Judiciary*, 2d ed. (Baton Rouge, La., 1981), pp. 90–92; *Report of the Louisiana State Bar Association*, 20 (1919): 106–107.

and they clamored for Stanley's probe to continue. Acting on Long's orders, Porterie declined to stand aside. His refusal cost him his membership in the Louisiana State Bar Association, which expelled him for what its executive board considered unethical behavior.[22]

Long's minions were quick to exact vengeance. During a special session of the legislature, they enacted the State Bar Act of 1934, which established a new organization of lawyers. The State Bar of Louisiana (SBL), as it was styled, differed from the Louisiana State Bar Association in significant respects. Where the latter had existed as an exclusive, private, voluntary group ever since the 1840s, the SBL was a public corporation with a mandatory membership of *all* licensed attorneys. Governor O. K. Allen was empowered to appoint the first board of directors, representing each of the state's congressional districts; thereafter, the voters elected the members. The board, not the Supreme Court, enjoyed full power to "formulate rules of professional conduct" and to discipline members as well as "exclusive authority to prescribe rules and qualifications for admission to the Bar in Louisiana."[23]

In form, the bar act resembled those of other states, the model being, according to its authors, a California statute. Indeed, Gaston Porterie, SBL's first president, went so far as to assert that it likewise removed any danger of "the profession . . . being controlled by the sentiment of one part

---

22. Harry Williams, *Huey Long: A Biography* (New York, 1969), pp. 654–651; "President's Address," *Reports of the Louisiana State Bar Association for 1935–1941*, 34 (1942): 6–7.

23. "An Act To create a public corporation to be known as 'The State Bar of Louisiana,'" *Acts, 1934, Second Extra Session*, 162 ff. The LSBA traced its roots to 1847, when a group of New Orleans attorneys formed an organization for themselves and their fellow lawyers, "Louisiana State Bar Association: Historical Narrative," *Bar Reports, 1935–1941*, 271–275. The LSBA awaits a close, systematic study but see Essay 14 below.

of our State as against another part of the State." Cloaking the law in such benign pronouncements did not blink the brutal reality of the Longites' attempt to destroy the Louisiana State Bar Association, while diminishing the authority of the anti-Longites Chief Justice Charles A. O'Niell, Wynne G. Rogers, and Fred M. Odom on the Supreme Court.[24]

O'Niell bowed to what he could not overbear, and the Court duly revised the rules to accord with a law of dubious constitutionality. However, the LSBA refused to go away; it loudly commended O'Niell, Rogers, and Odom for standing firm in the face of "repeated public threats of impeachments and removal from office." Its clout was strong enough to keep the American Bar Association from recognizing the legitimacy of its competitor. Even though the LSBA no longer enjoyed its privileges of examining candidates for the bar or assisting the Supreme Court in cases of lawyer misconduct, it continued to promote improved standards of legal education and ethics and other features of its modernization agenda. After 1935, its annual meetings afforded opportunities to attack the rival organization and scheme its destruction. Fairly typical of such ventings was the admonition of New Orleans attorney J. Zach Spearing. "We must not," he said,

> consider the State Bar as a competitor in our advance and our performance of our duties at the Bar. It is not a competitor. Mind you, it has among its members every scalawag and pettifogger, every shyster lawyer, and, more than that, every negro lawyer in the State of Louisiana. Do you know and do you realize that you have been forced into an Association where every negro lawyer in the State

---

24. "An Address Delivered by Hugh M. Wilkinson . . . , Jan. 31st. 1935," *Reports of the State Bar of Louisiana for 1934–1935*, 1 (1935): 163–164, "President's Address," ibid., 18.

of Louisiana is a member on the same footing, and with the same responsibility, rights, benefits and privileges as you? Heavens alive men, are we going to consider such an Association as that a competitor?[25]

In truth, there were some who saw an opportunity in the rivalry between the two associations. Those who did were, in the main, younger lawyers who viewed a single statewide, mandatory bar association as being in the best interests of their calling. Led by the elder Pike Hall of Shreveport, they worked quietly to consolidate the two groups. Long's assassination, Porterie's appointment to a federal judgeship,[26] and Sam Jones's election as governor all set the stage for unification.

Central to the effort was repeal of the 1934 bar act, which the legislature annulled during the regular session in 1940. The repealing statute memorialized the Supreme Court "to exercise its inherent powers" to reorganize the bar as a corporation, which would be called the Louisiana State Bar Association.[27] To that end, the justices picked fifteen lawyers from around the state for an advisory committee, which prepared the corporate charter and other necessary paperwork. The committee elected Pike Hall as chairman. Hall and his colleagues endowed the new association with compulsory membership. They recommended the new association be self-regulating, subject only to the supervision

---

25. *Louisiana Reports*, 180 (1935): ix–xiv; "Senator Long's Louisiana Bar Act," ABA *Journal*, 20 (1934): 744; *Bar Reports, 1935-1941*: 45, 46–48, 14–15. A number of New Orleans attorneys held committee posts and had other connections to the ABA; *Bar Reports, passim*. The relationship between the state and national organizations bears closer study than is appropriate for this essay.
26. Glenn R. Conrad, et al. eds., *Dictionary of Louisiana Biography* (Lafayette, La., 1988), 2: 658.
27. *Acts, 1940*, 365. The wording of repealing statute tracks that of a resolution which the LSBA passed at its meeting in April 1940, *Bar Reports, 1935–1941*, 245–246.

of the Court, though they patterned its governmental structure after that of the much–maligned SBL. The articles of incorporation also contained a canon of ethics and streamlined disciplinary procedures. With respect to bar admissions, the committee brought procedures into greater conformity with national standards, meaning, among other things, that the Court would assume a purely superintending role in the examination of candidates. After some adjustments, the Court promulgated the draft charter on 12 March 1941, and it continues in force.[28]

Regarding auxiliary staffing, if one compares the Court in 1813 to its modern analogue, ponderable contrasts are instantly apparent. The original Court consisted of three judges, a crier, a clerk, and several scriveners. Now there are seven justices, a crier, and a clerk, plus a cadre of budget analysts, computer specialists, deputy clerks, judicial administrators, law clerks, law librarians, staff attorneys, security guards, assorted advisory committees, and even an historian. Lest it be assumed that this latter profile is singularly illustrative of Louisianians' unmatched inventiveness for raiding the public fisc, that thought should be dispelled quickly. The difference merely reflects changes that have happened in every high bench across the country, including the Supreme Court of the United States.

That being so, what accounts for this enlargement? In a word, the Progressives' gospel of efficiency. Efficiency was the watchword as high courts struggled with backlogs of cases that mounted as a concomitant to the expansion of the welfare state over the past eight decades. The question was

---

28. The Court's order for the committee, its enabling orders, the LSBA's charter of incorporation, and by-laws are all conveniently printed in *Report of the Louisiana State Bar Association for 1941*, 1 (1942): 91–135. See also, Pike Hall, Sr.'s presidential address in ibid., 2–19.

how to make the courts more productive and sensitive to society's needs. Adding more justices helped but only marginally in the view of modernizers. Typically, they found surer remedy in redefining court structures. A proficient supreme court embraced more than judges who ruled on cases and clerks who kept records. It had broad responsibilities for the courts below, its chief justice was an administrative traffic cop, and it included staffs of experts and judicial councils. Judicial councils were the key to competent management. Composed of lawyers, judges, legislators and nonpartisan authorities, such bodies provided, in the words of an advocate, "an effective machinery for the advancement . . . of juridical science and the modernizing of justice." Promoters touted judicial councils nationally through the ABA and the American Judicature Society, popularizing them to such an extent that by 1930 twenty states employed them throughout their respective court structures. Louisiana was not in that number.[29]

Some Louisianians warmed to the idea as early as 1910, when the LASBA first suggested it as a means of improving the Court. Walker B. Spencer gave it fuller voice when he tabled a plan for a radical overhaul of the judiciary before the constitutional convention of 1921. His scheme drew a barrage of criticism from lawyers and judges, the most vociferous of whom was Justice O'Niell, and the plan never made it into the new constitution.[30]

Failure did not kill the concept, though thirty years passed before it became a reality in Louisiana. Many hands shared in making it so but those of John B. Fournet left an indelible

---

29. Miller, *The Louisiana Judiciary*, pp. 110–116; Matthew J. Schott, "A Legal Monstrosity? The Constitution of 1921" in Billings and Haas, eds., *In Search of Fundamental Law*, pp. 126–127.
30. *Bar Reports*, 1910, 43.

imprint upon it. That he did seems quite improbable on first glance, considering how he came to the Court.

A St. Martinville native, Fournet practiced law and taught school before turning to politics. Humble circumstances, a populist streak, and vaulting aspirations drew him to Huey Long, whose devoted lieutenant he became. Feisty and crudely partisan, he remained to the end of his days adamant in his conviction that Longism had benefitted Louisianians more than it had harmed them. His fealty to Long got him elected to the Court in 1934 after a canvass that can only be described as rancid.[31]

Fournet obtained his place for the purely political motive of ensuring a Longite majority on the Court, but he turned less partisan after Long's assassination. That change may be laid to his acculturation in the ways of the Court, as well as to his sensitivity to the mood of reform that gripped voters after the scandals of the Leche administration, but it also signalled a deepening interest in making the Court more efficient. His concern arose from a practical necessity. Even though the 1921 constitutional convention increased the number of justices to seven, the extra manpower had not significantly reduced the case load by the time Fournet took his seat, and the backlog mounted thereafter.[32]

Joining forces with the bar association and individual lawyers or judges, Fournet argued long and hard about the need of modernizing the court so as to reduce its workload.

---

31. Conrad, et al. eds., *Dictionary of Louisiana Biography*, 1: 316–117; Williams, *Huey Long*, pp. 288–89, 723–37; Essay 16, below.
32. John T. Hood, "The Court and Its Jurisprudence," *Louisiana Reports*, 245 (1963–64): 24–26; *Louisiana Bar Journal*, 4 (1945): 6; John B. Fournet, "A Judge's Viewpoint on Public Relations," ibid., 8 (1949): 2, 5, 10, 15, 15–16; John B. Fournet, "The Chief Justice Reports on First Ten Years as Administrative Officer of the Louisiana Supreme Court," ibid., 18 (1959): 11, 13; "Chief Justice Fournet Honored by Louisiana Law Institute," ibid., 19 (1950): 2–5, 7–8.

For him, "modernizing" meant, as he put it "[abandoning], temporarily at least, the paths our predecessors trod in solving early problems surrounding their efforts to take the courts to our sparsely settled state—honeycombed, as it was by waterways and marshes—and [setting] our sights upon the problems surrounding innovations that must be devised to care for the people who today find their way to the courts in ever-increasing numbers. And this must be done," he continued "in the expeditious and inexpensive manner that lies at the very heart of the meaning of justice, so that to the people of Louisiana justice will never be so delayed or so costly as to be denied."[33]

Try as he might, Fournet gained little headway as long as O'Niell remained chief and the older associates tarried. The main chance for reform came in 1949, when he succeeded O'Niell. A new office allowed him to put his ideas into practice. He accordingly convinced his colleagues to establish the Judicial Council by rule in 1950, but there were no funds to staff it or to support its work. Within four years, however, Fournet and the others secured a state appropriation, which in turn allowed the appointment of a judicial administrator and councillors who hailed from bench, bar, and legislature. True to its charge, the council gathered information on conditions throughout the entire judicial branch, and those data aided in its preparation of constitutional amendments and statutes that radically rearranged the court structure. Restructuring allowed Fournet and his colleagues to clear their docket for the first time in half a century.[34]

---

33. "Rules. Louisiana Supreme Court. Rule XXI—Judicial Council," *Louisiana Reports*, 219 (1950–51): xciv–xcvi.
34. Ibid., John B. Fournet, "The Problems of the Road Ahead—The Duty of the Courts," 245: 163; "Annual Report of the Judicial Council of the Supreme Court of Louisiana, 1955 (typescript), pp. 1–10, Appendix 1; Hood, "The Court and Its Jurisprudence," 26–28.

Thus, by the time Fournet retired in 1970, he had guided the Court's transition from a bench whose justices judged cases and oversaw the bar into a potent entity that supervised every phase of judicial administration in the entire state of Louisiana. In addition to his preaching the gospel of efficiency he had persuaded lawyers, legislators, and voters alike that the timely exercise of so broad an authority called for sizeable increases in the Court's auxiliary staff, which also happened. Along the way, the Court likewise acquired a marked willingness to experiment with various administrative approaches.

That penchant for experimentation continued as the Court adapted to computer-based technology. Starting in the 1980s, it moved to a sophisticated system of automated records management and a digital format for the immediate transmission of decisions to both print and electronic publishers. Inherent in these advances was the capability of archiving opinions in publicly accessible electronic databases, which was in turn an outcome that could render the law widely available, free or at nominal cost, to more and more people throughout the state. At the same time, publishers of electronic legal information products, such as opinions on CD-ROM, saw profit potential in these developments. Suddenly a competitive market became a real possibility, providing there was a way around a significant roadblock.

Any user of legal information must be able to cite the law, and therein lay the obstacle. Briefly, it was this. For over a century, the West Publishing Company had enjoyed a near monopoly on the publication of court opinions. That made reference to volume and page numbers in its compilation called the *Southern Reporter* the only accepted citation format. Because West claimed copyright to its pagination of the *Southern Reporter*, no other company could employ West page numbers in its product without paying license fees or risking a suit for copyright infringement.[35]

A task force of court staffers confronted the barrier when it studied the implications of information technology. Acting on the group's advice, the justices took a novel step when, in December 1993, they promulgated a vendor-neutral citation format for all of their published actions. The Court was thus the first in the nation to come down on the side of the principle that access to it documents, which are in the public domain, should not be restrained by the intellectual property claims of a private corporation.[36]

At the moment, it is too early to predict the ultimate effect of the new citation system. One result is the presence in Louisiana of publishers besides West who now receive digital copies of opinions, which they competitively produce on CD-ROM for the Court and for sale. Their appearance on the scene has reduced costs significantly.[37] Lawyers around the state have been generally accepting of the change. Federal and state courts across the nation are considering following Louisiana's lead.[38] And, the American Association of Law Libraries adopted recommendations favoring a vendor-

---

35. Byron D. Cooper, "Anglo-American Legal Citation: Historical Development and Library Implications," *Law Library Journal*, 35 (1982): 3–34; L. Ray Patterson and Craig Joyce, "Monopolizing the Law: The Scope of Copyright Protection for Law Reports and Statutory Compilations," *UCLA Law Review*, 36 (1989): 719–815.

36. Rule of Court, 12 Dec. 1993; Carol D. Billings, "Adoption of New Public Domain Citation Format Promotes Access to Legal Information," *Louisiana Bar Journal*, 51 (1994): 557–558.

37. Chief Justice Pascal F. Calogero, Jr., "The Louisiana Public Domain Citation Format: How It Came to Be and What It Has Accomplished," paper delivered at the 88th annual meeting of the American Association of Law Libraries, Pittsburgh, Pa., July 1995.

38. See, for example, Marsha J. Koslov, "What is the Citation Proposal?," *Wisconsin Lawyer* (1995): 10ff.

neutral format similar to Louisiana's in July 1995.[39] Predictably, though, West Publishing welcomed these events with less than open arms, but that is a story for another time.[40]

By way of conclusion, consider the ramifications of this little map. As with any first plotting, this chart merely sketches prominent features that first catch the eye of the explorer. The very crudeness of the depiction calls for refinement. Refinement, in turn, can lead to a more detailed description of how the Supreme Court of Louisiana has administered justice since 1813. Knowing that beckons comparisons with the Court and its companions so that one might isolate the degree of interchange between them, as well as to identify the things that set them apart. An awareness of those distinctions invites deeper inquiry into the way American appellate courts work. And, in the larger sense, probing the twists and turns in techniques of judicial administration through time can be a valuable gauge of not only changing legal technicalities but of the very meaning of fundamental constitutional guarantees such as a the right to speedy trial.

---

39. Lynn Foster, "Report of the Task Force on Citation Formats," pp. 1–26, especially p. 95. Foster presented the report to the Executive Board of the American Association of Law Libraries, 1 Mar. 1995, and it was adopted in July. The report included what was then the most extensive, up-to-date bibliography of the citation format debate among law librarians, publishers, practitioners, and other interested parties.

40. Susan Hansen, "Fending off the Future," *The American Lawyer*, Sept. 1994; Marcia Berss, "West Will Always Be There," *Forbes*, 21 Nov. 1994; Minority Report of Donna M. Bergsgaard and William H. Lindberg, West Publishing Company representatives on the AALL Task Force on Citation Formats, in Foster, "Report," pp. 29–46.

ESSAY 14

A Bar for Louisiana

Origins of the Louisiana State Bar Association

Bar associations originated in antebellum America at about the same time the practice of law passed from a gentleman's calling to a profession. They tended to spring up in courthouse towns, state capitals, and big cities, because those were generally the more fertile areas to find business. Associations with proximity to the supreme courts built on existing bonds between lawyers and high court justices, although the reasons they came into being varied from state to state. Some started as purely social organizations, whereas some mixed pleasure with practical concerns, and some formed to establish law libraries. Private entities all, they were subscription based self-selecting and self-perpetuating societies whose members tended to be judges and prominent attorneys, rather than run-of-the mill practitioners, who were rarely invited to join.

I had only to read a few pages in the Supreme Court's first minute book to see that in Louisiana informal ties between bench and bar dated from 1813. Among its first acts, the Court designated an ad hoc committee of qualified lawyers to assist in easing the transition from territory to statehood by helping to determine whom to admit to practice. Subsequently, the Court turned to similar committees for advice on other administrative matters. The creation of the New Orleans Law Association formalized those links, which drew even tighter with the founding of NOLA's successor society the Louisiana Bar Association. In the twentieth century the bond withstood the Long machine's attempts to shatter it, and it was recast with the founding of the Louisiana State Bar Association in 1941. Accordingly, mapping the contours of those connections became a necessity if I expected to understand this particular aspect of how the court worked.

My interest had less to do at first with plotting the rise of the organized bar than with charting the ways that individual lawyers and the Court cooperated to resolve problems with bar admissions and legal education. It became evident that after the Civil War the collaborations increasingly occurred within the context of the Louisiana Bar Association, which renamed itself the Louisiana State Bar Association in 1929. I noticed something else too. The Louisiana Bar State Association had a rival, the State Bar of Louisiana, and in 1941 both yielded to an entirely recreated society. That discovery set me to wondering. Had there been other rivals as well? What circumstances caused these intermittent reorganizations? For leads I turned to the old association *Proceedings*, the more modern *Louisiana Bar Journal*, and the bar archives. Getting into the latter involved a few phone calls, and much to my delight the staff at the bar association were quite willing to assist. No one there knew all that much about the organization's past, so they were as eager as I to see what I might uncover, and they gave me free access to the documents. Not unexpectedly, there were great gaps in the holdings, but the collection contained nuggets that plugged significant voids in my research. Of particular value were the correspondence and the minutes relating to the 1934 judicial election controversy and the organization's reconstitution in 1941. Once I gained a firmer grasp of the place of an organized bar in the state and its relation to the Supreme Court, I decided to prepare a sketch of how Louisiana attorneys associated formally in the years from the 1840s to the 1940s. That drawing emerged as this essay, and it is also a plan for a forthcoming book that seeks to put the Louisiana bar societies in the context of like associations across the nation.

Originally published as "A Bar for Louisiana: Origins of the Louisiana State Bar Association" in *Louisiana History: The Journal of the Louisiana Historical Association*, 51 (2000): 389–402, the article is reprinted here with the editor's kind permission.

On 9 July 1940, Governor Sam Houston Jones signed into law a bill memorializing "the Supreme Court of Louisiana . . . to create an Association to be known as the Louisiana State Bar Association, which Association shall be self-governing and may be organized as a corporation upon complying with the general corporation laws of this state."[1] Behind those dry, statutory words lies a compelling tale of partisanship, statecraft, and skullduggery that was part and parcel of a decades-long drive to mold a professional society for Louisiana attorneys. By looking at how the state's lawyers associated formally during the century between the 1840s and the 1940s, one can examine some aspects of a neglected yarn from Louisiana's distinctive past that entwines itself with a wider tale of bar organizations throughout the United States. Such an investigation, in turn, invites consideration of its implications for the new Louisiana legal history.

The ancestry of the Louisiana State Bar Association traces through the bill that Governor Jones signed back to the year 1847, when several Crescent City attorneys formed the New Orleans Law Association. Seeking to elevate the status of their group, the founders subsequently incorporated themselves under a state statute encouraging private citizens

---

1. "An Act To Memorialize the Supreme Court of Louisiana to create the Louisiana State Bar Association" . . . , *Louisiana Acts, 1940* (Baton Rouge, La., 1940), 365.

to erect literary, educational, or charitable bodies. The fledgling society closely resembled the design and intent of its counterparts elsewhere, which sprang up all across the country during the first half of the nineteenth century. Similar to a guild, it was a self-selecting, self-governing association that existed for the "purpose of establishing a Law Library, and promoting the interest, integrity, and honor of the Bar of New Orleans."[2]

Details about the New Orleans Law Association (NOLA) are scant, owing to great gaps in the extant documentary record.[3] Certain activities can be sketched broadly nonetheless. Membership dues funded the appointment of a librarian, who soon built the largest, most current collection of statutes, case reports, commentaries, practice manuals, and other appropriate texts anywhere in the city, or the entire state for that matter. Because members enjoyed exclusive use of the library, restricted access gave them a competitive advantage over other attorneys, and that privilege turned into one of the society's chief attractions. Individual members also strove diligently to ingratiate themselves with the Supreme Court of Louisiana, an endeavor that came easily because several justices belonged to the association and had helped in

---

2. "An Act For the organization of Corporations for Literary, Scientific, Religious, and Charitable Purposes," *Louisiana Acts, 1855* (New Orleans, La., 1855), 185–186; *Proceedings of the Louisiana Bar Association, 1898-1899* (New Orleans, La., 1899), 7–9; Anton-Hermann Chroust, *The Rise of the Legal Profession in America* (Norman, Okla., 1965), 2: 129–173.
3. The records of the New Orleans Law Association have all disappeared. Moreover, virtually all of the archives of the later variant organizations that existed before 1941 have been lost too. The remnants consist of the minute books of the executive committee, 1908–1926, and 1934–1941, and the annual *Proceedings*, which date from the end of the nineteenth century. The minute books reside in the offices of the present bar association, located at 601 St. Charles Ave. in New Orleans. Runs of the *Proceedings* are housed at the bar association and the Law Library of Louisiana.

its foundation. Moreover, the Court habitually sought the advice of association members in setting standards for legal education or in devising procedural rules. Then too, some members routinely aided the justices by assuming the task of screening prospects for the bar examination, which the court administered. Other NOLA members sat in the state legislature, whereas the organization as a whole actively touted candidates for judicial office in openly partisan ways.[4]

Luminaries, such as John Randolph Grymes, Christian Roselius, Pierre Soulé, Judah P. Benjamin, Étienne Mazureau, Alfred Hennen, and the Slidell brothers, John and Thomas, were all invited to join the NOLA, and so were lesser lights. However, the membership committee never sought to recruit every attorney in the city, nor did it aggressively solicit prospects from around the rest of Louisiana. The association consequently rarely comprised more than half the state's lawyers, and it in no way presumed to speak for the entire practicing bar on any issue, political or professional. Again, that stance matched a common national and regional practice of the day.[5]

Civil war intervened and threw the NOLA into disarray. After Louisiana seceded from the Union, nearly every able-bodied member volunteered for Confederate military duty. That choice cost dearly. Most of the volunteers squandered their lives on an ignoble cause, so their deaths all but erased the association's membership rolls. Furthermore, once the Crescent City fell to Federal forces in the spring of 1862, the

---

4. Warren M. Billings, "The Supreme Court and the Education of Louisiana Lawyers," *Louisiana Bar Journal*, 33 (1985): 74–80; Essay 13 above; Billings, ed., *The Historic Rules of the Supreme Court of Louisiana, 1813–1879* (Lafayette, La., 1985), pp. 19–20.

5. Henry J. Leovy, "The Ante-Bellum Bench and Bar," *Proceedings of the Louisiana Bar Association, 1900* (New Orleans, La., 1900), 11–27.

organization ceased meeting, and it remained dormant for as long as New Orleans lay under martial law.[6]

Survivors and recruits from among newly qualified attorneys revived the society after the war, and by the midpoint of Reconstruction, the numbers neared prewar levels. The law library, which apparently remained intact, also grew. Encouraging though these signs were, they were not altogether promising. In the best of times, the membership still accounted for less than half the state's attorneys, and it remained tightly confined to the Crescent City, only now social pedigree assumed a higher importance than in former times. Of equal significance, the nature of the association fell increasingly out of tune with a new nationwide trend among bar societies.[7]

Lawyers across the country abandoned groups like the NOLA in favor of ones that openly advocated issues of acute professional and political concern. Beginning in the 1870s, this movement emerged in New York City, then it quickly spread throughout the Northeast and the Midwest,

---

6. Thomas W. Helis, "Of Generals and Jurists: The Judicial System of New Orleans Under Union Occupation, May 1862–April 1866," in Warren M. Billings and Mark F. Fernandez, eds., *A Law Unto Itself? Essays in the New Louisiana Legal History* (Baton Rouge, La., 2001), pp. 117–139; Kathryn Page, "A First-Born Child of Liberty: The Constitution of 1864," in Warren M. Billings and Edward F. Haas, eds., *In Search of Fundamental Law: Louisiana's Constitutions, 1812–1974* (Lafayette, La., 1993), pp. 52–69; Charles Vincent, "Black Constitution Makers: The Constitution of 1868," ibid., pp. 69–81; Ronald M. Labbé, "That the Reign of Robbery Will Never Return to Louisiana," ibid., pp. 81–93; T.C.W. Ellis, "The Louisiana Bar, 1813–1913," *Louisiana Reports*, 133 (1913): lxxix.

7. *Proceedings of the Louisiana Bar Association, 1898–1902*, 18. There are occasional references to the library in Minutes [of the] Association of the Alumni [1869 to 1887], *passim.*, LSBA archives. New Orleans. That volume records activities of graduates of the University of Louisiana, the forerunner of the School of Law at Tulane University.

whereupon it grew until its main engine became the American Bar Association. Brainchild of Connecticut attorney Simeon E. Baldwin, the ABA took life when Baldwin and seventy-four similarly inspired lawyers established it in 1878 at Saratoga, New York. Thereafter, through a series of standing and special committees, the ABA encouraged the translation of state and local bar associations from social clubs and subscription libraries into bodies that lobbied Congress, state legislatures, and courts on behalf of lawyers' vocational interests. It ultimately became the profession's national voice as it attempted to set universal standards for admission to the bar, legal education, the ethics of practice, and law reform.[8]

A blend of pecuniary self-interest, noblesse oblige, and a wish to improve professional standards impelled the bar association movement. Attorneys of Baldwin's stripe expected to ameliorate the social consequences of a nation steaming at flank speed from an agrarian to an industrial economy. The crusade thus drew thinkers and tinkerers who revolted against formalism in the expectation of renovating law into a discipline that boosted the importance of legal realism. These reformers joined with teachers who strove to modernize legal education into a "science" and to make a degree from a university-based law school a prerequisite to practice law. Then there were attorneys who aspired to rearrange the legal order into something intelligible, orderly, and certain, a goal requiring symmetry in local, state, and federal laws. More worldly advocates, who engaged in newer fields of practice, outdid solo lawyers as law firms displaced

---

8. Lawrence M. Friedman, *A History of American Law* (New York, 1973), pp. 561–566; Max Radin, "The Achievements of the American Bar Association: A Sixty Year Record," *ABA Journal*, 25 (1939): 903–910, 1007–1013; 26 (1940): 19–26.135–141, 227–230, 234, 318–321, 358; Edson R. Sunderland, *History of the American Bar Association and Its Work* (n.p., 1953).

generalists, especially in the cities, where much lucrative work was available.[9]

The New Orleans Law Association certainly felt these impulses, given that members Henry Plauché Dart,[10] Thomas Jenkins Semmes,[11] and William Wirt Howe[12] belonged to the ABA and worked diligently to further its aims. Their colleagues, who were slow to respond to prodding, went about business as usual. Membership dwindled, dues fell in arrears, and the library sat in "squalid quarters near the roof in the [New Orleans] court-house." Dart rose to the presidency just when the association "seemed in its last throes." With the aid of Semmes and ABA president Howe, he engineered NOLA's thorough overhaul. The society emerged from its remake in 1899 as the Louisiana Bar Association.[13]

Like its predecessor, the new organization resided legally in the Crescent City. An executive committee—composed of the president, vice president, secretary-treasurer, and five presidential appointees—effectively ran it. Anyone "of the bar of Louisiana in good standing" was eligible for full or library membership, providing he received a favorable vote on his nomination. Federal and state judges were considered

---

9. Oliver Wendell Holmes, *The Common Law* (Boston, Mass., 1880); Morton White, *Social Thought in America: The Revolt Against Formalism* (Boston, Mass., 1949); Robert W. Gordon, "Recent Trends in Legal Historiography," *Law Library Journal*, 69 (1976): 462–463; Friedman, *History of American Law*, pp. 591–592.
10. Marie E. Windell, "Henry Plauché Dart," in Glenn R. Conrad, et al. eds., *Dictionary of Louisiana Biography* (Lafayette, La., 1988), 1: 211–212.
11. Marius M. Carriere, "Thomas Jenkins Semmes," ibid., 2: 732. Semmes was president of the ABA in 1886 and a member of the law faculty at the University of Louisiana.
12. William Kernan Dart, "The Justices of the Supreme Court," *Louisiana Reports*, 133: lxxxviii.
13. Henry Plauché Dart, "President's Address, 1899," *Proceedings of the Louisiana Bar Association, 1898–1899*, 148; *ABA Directory, 1997–1998* (Chicago, 1997), 465.

full members *ex officio*, but they paid no dues or initiation fees, though they could hold office. The corporate charter spoke to local concerns when it committed the association "to exert all due and proper influence to induce the constituted authorities to provide a proper courthouse in the city of New Orleans . . . [And to] maintain a law library." That document also tracked ABA goals because it entailed a code of ethics upon members and called for them collectively to improve legal education, to raise requirements for admission to the bar, and to assist in the trial and punishment of misbehaving lawyers.[14]

Although the charter underwent later amendments, these basic aims served in the office of a compass that fixed the direction of the rejuvenated bar society for upwards of four decades.[15] Eventually that tack nearly caused the organization to founder when it steered into a series of raucous clashes during the Huey Long era. No one in 1899 foresaw that result, of course, though some members lived to experience the nearly fatal consequences of their agenda. Instead, all happily joined Henry Plauché Dart in an aggressive, highly political pursuit of their common objectives.

Adherence to the code of ethics became a condition of membership in the association, but Dart also had something else in mind. He perceived the code as the yardstick to measure the professional conduct of all Louisiana lawyers, and those who were found wanting would be liable to such discipline as the LBA might recommend. Dart failed in his attempt to secure statutory sanction for this scheme, though he boldly persuaded the Supreme Court of Louisiana to

---

14. Charter of the Louisiana Bar Association, *Proceedings of the Louisiana Bar Association, 1898–1899*, 19–28.
15. Later charter revisions appear variously throughout the *Proceedings of the Louisiana Bar Association, 1900–1934, passim*. When the name changed in 1929 to the Louisiana State Bar Association, the members decided to insert the word "state" in an attempt to "emphasize the statewide character of the Association" (ibid., 18 [1929], 120).

enable his plan via the justices' rule-making authority. Empowering the association thus enhanced its reach enormously for it exerted a considerable measure of control over the entire practicing bar, and whether non-members liked it or not, their ability to pursue their livelihood was liable to regulation by an organization in which they had no voice.[16]

The LBA similarly tightened its grip on admission standards to the bar and strengthened its hand in setting criteria of legal education. Its quest for these goals seemed less novel, given that its predecessor had performed likewise in the past. Once again, though, Dart sought the imprimatur of statutory sanction, and once again, the legislature did not accommodate him, so once again, he prevailed upon the state supreme court to grant the authority by rule. The LBA's standing board of examiners enjoyed exclusive power to determine who would become a lawyer. Individually and severally, LBA members gradually also moved the high court and the profession in the direction of accepting a law school diploma as the basic prerequisite to practice.[17]

Dart personally launched a crusade to increase the LBA's library collections. Larger holdings and wider scope made the library an attractive recruiting tool once more, although its

---

16. Dart, "President's Address, 1899," *Proceedings of the Louisiana Bar Association, 1899*, 149. Article 85 of the Constitution of 1898 specifically vested the Supreme Court with jurisdiction over charges of professional misconduct (Michael L. Lanza, "Little More than a Family Matter: The Constitution of 1898," in Billings and Haas, eds., *In Search of Fundamental Law*, p. 10).

17. Dart, "President's Address, 1899," *Proceedings of the Louisiana Bar Association, 1899*, 148–149; "Cases Reported," *Louisiana Reports*, 134 (1914): xii-xiv; "Amendments to Rules, Supreme Court of the State of Louisiana," ibid., 152 (1923): vii–viii. The deans at the Tulane and LSU schools also pushed hard to make the diploma 'a conditio sine qua non to the practice of law," a view that the LBA's committee on legal education generally supported in the 1920s (Executive Committee Minute Book No. 3, June 9, 1920–March 7, 1924, 137).

private nature put non-members at a considerable disadvantage. Lawyers who could not join the association, or who refused to take out library memberships, gained entree only when members extended the privilege surreptitiously. Apparently that practice grew so widespread by the 1920s that President J. Zack Spearing was compelled to enjoin his confreres not to extend "in their names [to non-members] . . . privileges of the Association, particularly of the library." He went on to admonish that "such practice [was] not permissible [because] Membership in the Association [was] individual, personal, and indivisible, and the rights and privileges thereof cannot be delegated even to an associate or employee." The habit nevertheless continued, and while it did, it remained a most unpleasant reminder of distinctions between attorneys who belonged to the association and those who did not.[18]

Improving the library complemented the goal of a new courthouse. Here again, the hands of Henry Plauché Dart were to be found everywhere, pulling this string and that wire in the drive to fund a new abode for the Supreme Court of Louisiana. Construction began once the legislature enacted the first of the enabling laws in 1902, the year after Dart retired as LBA president. The much sought-after pile became a reality once an imposing Beaux Arts courts building rose at 400 Royal Street and opened for business in 1910. Space in the new facility accommodated the bar association and its library, thereby fulfilling the dream of Dart and his associates. A private organization thus secured housing in a publicly funded and maintained building at little cost to itself.[19]

---

18. J. Zack Spearing and W.W. Young to LBA members, June 9, 1920, Executive Committee Minute Book No. 3, June 9, 1920–March 7, 1924, pp. 53–54.
19. "An Act To provide for the construction and maintenance of a court-house building in New Orleans" . . ., *Louisiana Acts, 1902* (Baton Rouge, La., 1902), 106–10; "An Act to provide for the acquisition for,

Apart from lobbying to achieve these particular ends, LBA looked to politics for other purposes. The association routinely backed candidates for judicial office so as to assure the election of judges it favored. It also tried to fashion the outcome of the constitutional conventions of 1913 and 1921. For example, member Edgar Farrar, who was also a president of the ABA, lobbied successfully for an article in the Constitution of 1913 that expanded the New Orleans sewerage and drainage systems. Walker B. Spencer, by contrast, proposed a radical overhaul of the judiciary in 1921. His scheme drew a barrage of criticism from lawyers and judges alike, not least of whom was Supreme Court Justice Charles A. O'Niell, and the plan never made it into the new constitution. O'Niell himself became a lightning rod for political controversy, especially when as chief justice he presided at the impeachment trial of Governor Huey Long. His jurisprudence set him at odds with Long because of his incessant attacks on conflicts of interests among Long's cronies. But the Kingfish also disliked O'Niell exceedingly because of his identification with reform politics and his one-time alliance with former Governor John M. Parker.[20]

---

and or the construction and maintenance of a court house building in the City of New Orleans" . . . , *Louisiana Acts, 1904* (Baton Rouge, La., 1904), 214–221; "An Act to amend Sections 6 and 10 of . . . 'An act to provide for the acquisition of a site for . . . ,' etc.," ibid., 369–370; "An Act to create a Commission which will have custody and control of the new Court House in the City of New Orleans" . . ., *Louisiana Acts, 1910* (Baton Rouge, La., 1910), 408ff; Bernard McCloskey, "The New Orleans Courthouse," *Proceedings of the Louisiana Bar Association, 1909*, 158–160. None of the statutes made any reference to the bar association's occupancy other than to state that "the Louisiana Law Library" would occupy space.

20. Marie E. Windell, "Can a Legislature Control a Constitutional Convention? The Constitution of 1913," in Billings and Haas, eds., *In Search of Fundamental Law*, pp. 114–116; Matthew J. Schott, "A Legal Monstrosity? The Constitution of 1921," ibid., pp. 126–127; Warren M. Billings, "The Supreme Court of Louisiana and Its Chief Justices," *Law*

O'Niell's difficulties with Huey Long and his distaste for reconstituting the judiciary mirrored more than just the personal biases of the chief justice and the governor; they reflected profound differences of opinion among the practicing bar itself. Many Louisiana lawyers mistrusted the LBA. Country attorneys were particularly suspicious of the motives of an overwhelmingly urban professional society, and rural lawyers consistently refused to seek membership. Others objected for philosophical or practical considerations, whereas for some the LBA's boisterous forays into electoral politics set dangerous precedents that might one day harm their livelihood. Older or less well-educated barristers saw the issue as change itself, and they remained hostile to the LBA's push to supplant apprenticeship as the principal means of legal education. Even members had their doubts. Those from rural regions and places like Baton Rouge, Shreveport, or Lake Charles often lacked a voice because Crescent City attorneys dominated the principal offices and held an overwhelming majority of seats on all association committees.

These issues were by no means unique to Louisiana. Neither were they peculiar phenomena of the 1920s and 1930s. They had existed ever since the beginning of the bar association movement, and lawyers across the country had worked toward their elimination. Indeed, a national organization, the American Judicature Society, arose in 1917 for the avowed aim of fostering greater comity among attorneys. Its solution called for the nationwide establishment of what it termed an "integrated bar association," that is, a single, statutorily empowered, statewide entity to which every attorney must belong. Creating such an agency required legislative action, and to that end, the AJS drafted a model bill, which it trumpeted across the length and breadth of the

---

Library Journal, 89 (1997): 458–59; Matthew J. Schott, "Charles Austin O'Niell" in Conrad, et al. eds., *Dictionary of Louisiana Biography*, 2: 619.

United States. In Louisiana, leaders of the LBA were slow to heed the call.[21]

The question of integrating the bar surfaced officially at the LBA's annual meeting in 1929, the year the organization took the name the Louisiana State Bar Association. Walker B. Spencer chaired a committee that reported favorably on the subject and urged its further study. Despite favorable action, the cause of bar integration made slight progress, primarily because of presidential foot-dragging, members' indifference, and Depression-era conditions that "mitigated against any real accomplishment."[22]

The issue was finally forced to a head, when the Longites, with perverse cleverness, seized upon it as a means of humbling the LSBA. Angered at the LSBA's expulsion of Attorney General Gaston L. Porterie from its membership and its interference in the election of Lieutenant Governor John B. Fournet to the Supreme Court, Long loyalists had their revenge in 1934. Governor O. K. Allen called on a special legislative session to pass a law reorganizing the practicing bar. Styled the State Bar of Louisiana, this new society departed from the Louisiana State Bar Association in significant respects. The latter had always been self-selecting

---

21. "Redeeming a Profession: Introducing a Practical and Logical Plan for Bar Organization Which Will Enable the Bar to Realize Its Highest Ideals," *Journal of the American Judicature Society*, 2 (1918): 105–11; "Bar Association Act," ibid., 111–124. According to the statement on the masthead of issue 1 of volume 1 of the *Journal*, and all subsequent numbers, the AJS "exists because of the conviction of its members that earnest and intensive effort with avail to make the administration of justice in the American courts more effective and more economical. Its work is educational. The Society co-operates with all other agencies active in the field. It invites the membership of all persons who are interested in the problem. There are no fees."

22. *Reports of the Louisiana State Bar Association* (1929): 107–110; Charles F. Fletchinger "Presidential Address," ibid. (1930): 135–136, 179; ibid. (1932): 165.

and self-governing. By contrast, the SBL was a public corporation with a mandatory membership of *all* licensed attorneys and an elected board of governors. Members of the latter were drawn from the state's congressional districts and were picked by the voters. Furthermore, the board, not the Supreme Court of Louisiana, enjoyed full power to draft rules of professional conduct, to discipline members, and to set qualifications for entry to the bar. This latter proviso stood in direct contravention of an ancient mandate that reached way back to the Constitution of 1812 and the Judiciary Act of 1813 empowering the Supreme Court to control bar admissions, but Chief Justice O'Niell and the other anti-Long justices were powerless to resist this erosion of their prerogatives.[23]

In form and substance, the state bar act looked like the American Judicature Society's model bill, though in actuality the prototype turned out to be a California law. Gaston Porterie, the SBL's first president, claimed that the act removed any possibility that lawyers from "one part of our State" could control the rest. Honeyed words hardly concealed harsh truth. The intent of the law was as plain as plain could be: to demolish the LSBA and to diminish the influence of Long's opponents on the Supreme Court.[24]

---

23. On Porterie's expulsion, see Essay 13 above. See also complaint of Burt W. Henry, Esmond Phelps, J. Zach Spearing, Charles E. Dunbar, Charles F. Fletchinger, Edwin T. Merrick, J. Blanc Monroe, and Monte M. Lemann against Justices John Land, Harney F. Brunot, and Archibald Higgins, October 19, 1934, Minutes of the Executive Board of the Louisiana State Bar Association, 1934–1937, pp. 377–401, LSBA archives; Essay 16 below; Gov. Allen's call, *Official Journal of the Proceedings of the House of Representatives of the State of Louisiana, Second Extra Session* (Baton Rouge, La., 1934), 4–5; "An Act To create a public corporation to be known as 'The State Bar of Louisiana,'" Acts, 1934, Second Extra Session, 162–167.
24. "An Address Delivered by Hugh M. Wilkinson . . . , Jan. 31st. 1935," *Reports of the State Bar of Louisiana for 1934–1935*, 1 (1935): 163–64; Gaston L. Porterie "President's Address," ibid., 18.

Despite Longite intentions, the SBL largely failed to fulfill its purpose. It had but a single president, it assembled in convention but once, and it published but one volume of proceedings; the organization thus never assumed life as a fully working society that addressed the professional needs of its members. Of course, it controlled who became a lawyer, but, to judge from its one extant minute book, the board of governors met only to vote on admissions to the bar.[25]

The LSBA refused to go away. It publicly supported O'Niell and used its ties to the American Bar Association to prevent the ABA from acknowledging the SBL. After 1935, its annual meetings afforded opportunities to attack the rival organization and to scheme its destruction. Members nevertheless faced continuing dilemmas, for all had to join the SBL to remain practicing lawyers. Loyalty to the LSBA also was expensive for it meant paying dues to two organizations during the Great Depression. Then too, state officials ordered the LSBA to remove its offices and its cherished library from the Royal Street courthouse, an act of spite that drained the treasury and finally forced the library's sale to a book dealer, who eventually scattered the collection.[26]

The American Judicature Society condemned the SBL, while at the same time urging "every decent lawyer" in Louisiana "to strive to make the official state bar serviceable and to plan for improving its form at the earliest opportunity." That line of march appealed to some younger attorneys who discerned opportunity in the contest between the two associations. Led by Pike Hall, Sr., of Shreveport, they worked quietly to consolidate the two groups. Long's assassination, Porterie's appointment as a federal judge, the

---

25. The minute book is now among the LSBA archives.
26. "Senator Long's Louisiana Bar Act," *American Bar Association Journal*, 20 (1934): 20; *LSBA Bar Reports, 1935–1940*, passim.

Louisiana Scandals of 1939–1940, and the election of reform governor Sam Houston Jones, all paved the way for unification.[27]

Indeed, when Governor Jones addressed the legislature in 1940, he urged repeal of "the law which denies the lawyers of Louisiana from selecting the governing authority of their own organization." His audience responded with alacrity and soon crafted the bill that he signed on July 10. It remained only for the Supreme Court to do as the act bid.[28]

Chief Justice O'Niell appointed fifteen lawyers from around the state as an advisory committee, and it was they who drafted the corporate charter and other necessary paperwork. Chairman Pike Hall and his colleagues designed the new association as a compulsory body. They recommended it be self-regulating, subject only to the justices' supervision, and they modelled its governance on the pattern of the much-maligned SBL, though members, not the public, elected the proposed board of governors. The Court made a few adjustments of its own and then promulgated the draft charter by rule on March 12, 1941. A month later, the old LSBA, meeting in Lake Charles, voted to dissolve and to "deliver all of the books and records of this association on condition that the . . . new association preserve the same in its archives." That "new association" continues to this day.[29]

The story of a bar for Louisiana holds local and national significance for the history of law, a fact inviting a closer

---

27. "Statutory Organization for Louisiana Bar: Legislature Adopts Act Intended to Deal with the Profession on a Political Basis—People Will Elect Governing Board," *Journal of the American Judicature Society*, 18 (1934–1935): 110–111.
28. Sam Houston Jones, "Address," 20 May 1940, *Official Journal of the Proceedings of the Senate of the State of Louisiana* . . . (Baton Rouge, La., 1940), 24.
29. *Report of the Louisiana State Bar Association for 1941*, 1 (1942): 91–135. The SBL dissolved on July 30, 1940, SBL Minute Book, Dec. 27, 1934–July 31, 1940, n.p.

exploration, and a far greater accounting, than is possible in a small space such as this. Nevertheless, even this brief essay suggests several leads for future inquiry. Someone should complete collective biographical studies of Louisiana lawyers that extend to the present.[30] Given how the development of bar organizations was a nationwide phenomenon, there is need for sorting out the relationships between various Louisiana and national bar groups over time with a view to discerning the degrees of interchange and. influence between them. In other words, comparative analyses can distinguish between those aspects that were specific to Louisiana and those that were common to all bar organizations. Similarly, the connections between Louisiana bar groups and the American Bar Association, the American Judicature Society, the American Law Institute, the Association of American Law Schools, and the American Association of Law Libraries are ripe for closer scrutiny. A look at changing standards of legal training over the length of the twentieth century provides a way of joining the history of law and the history of higher education in Louisiana. Last, but by no means least, someone with interests in the history of the book ought to examine the beginnings of both the bar library and the Law Library of Louisiana, which now serves the Supreme Court.

These few examples reiterate a point this writer made in his presidential address to the Louisiana Historical Association some years ago. Until these and comparable enquiries are taken up, the new Louisiana legal history will remain incomplete. My hope is that readers of this journal may follow up on my suggestions.[31]

---

30. Elizabeth Gaspard, "The Rise of the Louisiana Bar: The Early Years," *Louisiana History*, 28 (1987): 183–197.
31. Essay 13 above; Mark F. Fernandez, "Louisiana Legal History: Past, Present, and Future" in Warren M. Billings and Mark F. Fernandez, eds., *A Law Unto Itself? Essays in the New Louisiana Legal History* (Baton Rouge, La., 2001), pp. 1–23.

ESSAY 15

MIXED JURISDICTIONS AND CONVERGENCE

The Louisiana Example

My friend Jules Winterton, who directs the library at the Institute for Advanced Legal Studies, University of London, prompted the initial version of this essay. He asked me to address to the International Association of Law Libraries at its annual conference that met in Dublin in 2000. I responded to his invitation with alacrity. The prospect of a week in Dublin in the company of friends and new acquaintances was most appealing. So too was the chance to share my understanding of Louisiana's mixed legal regime with an audience beyond Louisiana. I was one of only two speakers from the United States, and apart from a few other American conferees, the rest were law librarians or academics from the British Isles, Europe, and elsewhere about the globe.

Customarily, an IALL conference program revolves around a single theme, and in the instance of the Dublin meeting the subject was "A Common Law for European legal systems and legal information." A timely topic, it drew notice to an accelerating trend, the convergence of systems of civil and common law throughout the European Union. Evidence for such a convergence could be found in the increasingly greater infusion of supranational law into the domestic law of the EU's member states. It was also apparent in a considerable body of scholarly work that by 2000 identified certain general civil and common law principles that applied to the transnational nature of markets within and beyond the

EU. Convergence between civil and common-law systems was hardly a new phenomenon because the habit of mixing jurisdictions reached centuries deep into the past. To illustrate the historical nature of how divergent legal systems might blend into one over time, Winterton chose to employ the examples of Scotland and Louisiana, which was why he wanted me to talk about the Louisiana example.

To the extent that any of the attendees knew much about Louisiana, they most likely identified with New Orleans jazz, Cajun dancing, or Creole cuisine, which is the way people beyond the borders of the Bayou State stereotypically regard it. Unsurprisingly, therefore, no one would have much of a grasp of its legal order, let alone its progress from the Louisiana Purchase to modern times. I anticipated such a likelihood and prepared my remarks so as to give my listeners a sense of how Anglo-American common law and continental European civil law converged in the first half of the nineteenth century to nurture Louisiana's distinctive jurisdiction, how that system adjusted to major changes, such as the American Civil War, and how it continues to evolve to this day. I used the talk as well to reflect on how cultural assumptions, myths, and practical contingencies contributed not only to giving Louisiana's mixed jurisdiction its distinctiveness but also to imbuing Louisianans with their singular sense of themselves as a breed apart. Subsequently, a revised and extended rendering of those comments became the next article.

Originally published as "Mixed Jurisdictions and Convergence: The Louisiana Example" in *International Journal of Legal Information*, 29 (2001): 272–309, that article is reprinted here with the editor's kind permission.

Once on a plane to New Orleans I chanced to half overhear a conversation between two passengers who shared the same row of seats with me. Somewhere between wakefulness and drowsiness, my ear caught a tell-tale accent that betrayed one of my seat mates as an Orleanian as they chatted animatedly about the Crescent City, Louisiana, and the ways that both diverged from the rest of the country. The native noted reverently the influence of the Roman Catholic Church, he remarked grandly on the extraordinary cuisine, he waxed pridefully about the city as the birthplace of jazz, and he spoke warmly about the manifold ethnic origins of his fellow Louisianians. Then, as if to fortify his contention that he hailed from a truly unusual place, he pointedly observed that Louisiana was the only state in the nation whose legal system rested upon the Napoleonic Code, even as he confessed to an uncertainty about why that difference existed or what it meant precisely.

His tale rang familiar. Indeed, I first encountered a similar version not long after I began teaching at the University of New Orleans in the late 1960s, and since then I have met many others. I mention his particular telling here because it neatly captures sensibilities that imbue Louisianians of all sorts and conditions with peculiar feelings of self and apartness from America at large. And nowhere, I think, does that sense of difference echo more abundantly than in the conversation of the state's judges, attorneys, law professors, and many of its legal scholars. In that account, the story runs this way. Louisiana law is unique. That uniqueness originated in a singular convergence of contingencies which pitted French and Anglo-American legal traditions against one another from the Louisiana Purchase in 1803 to the present. Clashing customs spawned an unusual jurisdiction in which

French ways predominated and distinguished Louisiana from legal regimes elsewhere in the Union.[1]

Assuredly, French precepts informed the substance of law as Louisiana passed from colony to territory to state to modern times. Assuredly too, Louisiana became a jurisdiction apart. However, the special claim for the influence of the one upon the unfolding of the other speaks more to myth than to reality. The reality is a more gripping yarn of cultural dueling, political chicanery, quiet statesmanship, and imaginative adaptations that went hand in glove with a centuries' old quest for a workable legal order—a search that ultimately created the myth. Accordingly, this essay is in the nature of a reflection upon how both came to pass.[2]

After Thomas Jefferson purchased Louisiana, he confronted the daunting task of its incorporation into the Union, and that was no slight chore. The Purchase actually comprised two separate sections. Its vast northern half more nearly resembled the adjoining public domain that lay east of the Mississippi River. Sparsely inhabited, Upper Louisiana could

---

1. See, for example, John H. Wigmore, "Louisiana: The Story of its Legal System," *Tulane Law Review*, 1 (1916): 1–45; Henry Plauché Dart, "The Legal Institutions of Louisiana," ibid., 3 (1918): 254–280; Thomas E. Charbonneau, David A. Combe, and Shael Herman, *The Louisiana Civil Code: A Humanistic Appraisal* (New Orleans, La., 1981); Vernon Valentine Palmer, ed., *Louisiana: Microcosm of a Mixed Jurisdiction* (Durham, N.C., 1999). That view has also suffused more popular writing, such as Carol Flake, *New Orleans: Behind the Masks of America's Most Exotic City* (New York, 1994), pp. 64–67. Recently, though, it has come under scrutiny and revision. See Warren M. Billings and Mark F. Fernandez, eds., *A Law Unto Itself? Essays in the New Louisiana Legal History* (Baton Rouge, La., 2001), pp. 1–23.

2. The origin of the myth is treated in my introduction to Judith Kelleher Schafer and Warren M. Billings, eds., *An Uncommon Experience: Law and Judicial Institutions in Louisiana, 1803–2003* (Lafayette, La., 1997), pp., 11–17 and Mark F. Fernandez, "Louisiana Legal History: Past, Present, and Future," in Billings and Fernandez, eds., *A Law Unto Itself*, pp. 1–23.

develop in the manner set forth in the Northwest Ordinance of 1787, which prescribed the means by which nationally-held lands became states. The smaller portion posed a more vexing problem for the president. Roughly the size of the modern Bayou State, Lower Louisiana contrasted sharply with the upper region. Founded in 1699, Lower Louisiana developed as a French outpost before it passed to Spain in 1765 and France got it back in 1801. At the turn of the eighteenth century, it included the bustling port of New Orleans and boasted an integrity not so different from the English settlements that broke free of British rule after 1776. The town sat at the bottom of the Mississippi River, which gave its merchants control of commerce that floated along the great watery highway and made it the prize Jefferson sought when he first opened negotiations with Napoleon Bonaparte. A disparate gumbo of Acadians, Africans, Britons, Frenchmen, Germans, mixed bloods, Indians, and Spaniards populated city and colony alike. Apart from a small but rising, contingent of United States citizens, these people seemed oddly exotic, possibly threatening, and decidedly unrepublican to Jefferson. Not least of their strange qualities were their legal ways, which descended from the codified law of ancient Rome by way of France and Spain rather than from the English traditions that informed American law. Mr. Jefferson considered these newly-minted Americans quite unfit for immediate statehood, so he envisioned them undergoing a prolonged interval during which they would learn the niceties of republican self-government. To that end, he appointed William C.C. Claiborne governor and secured congressional legislation that organized Lower Louisiana into the Territory of Orleans.[3]

---

3. Treaty ceding Louisiana, 30 April 1803 in Francis Newton Thorpe, comp., *The Federal and State Constitutions, Colonial Charters, and Other Organic Laws of the States, Territories, and Colonies Now or Heretofore*

Still in his twenties, Claiborne (1775-1817) brought formidable legal skill and considerable political seasoning to his new assignment. He also typified many of the Americans who flooded into New Orleans throughout the first half of the nineteenth century in search of fresh beginnings. Of an old Virginia family and a cousin of Jefferson's, Claiborne first drew his kinsman's notice while a teenager, when for a time he held the post of deputy clerk in the United States House of Representatives. Claiborne, acting on the advice of Jefferson and others, subsequently left Washington, D.C. to study for admission to the Virginia bar. The scent of opportunity then drew him to the Tennessee frontier, where he established an enlarging law practice and an equally prospering political career. He was, by turns, a delegate in the constitutional convention that drafted the first Tennessee constitution, a justice of the state supreme court, and a congressman. An advocate of his cousin's politics, he easily cast his state's vote for Jefferson when the House of Representatives decided the disputed presidential election of 1800. That choice earned him an appointment as governor of the Mississippi Territory. His success in dealing with Indian problems there led Jefferson to translate him to Louisiana.[4]

Forming the United States of America (Washington, D.C., 1909) 3: 1359–1362; Convention Between the United States of America and the French Republic, 30 April 1803, ibid., 1362–1363; "An Act to enable the President of the United States to take possession of the territories ceded by France to the United States by treaty concluded in Paris, on the thirtieth of April last, and for the temporary government thereof." Eighth Congress, First Session, 1803, ibid., 1364; "An Act erecting Louisiana into two territories, and providing for the temporary government thereof." Eighth Congress, Second Session, 1804, 3: 1365–1371.

4. Joseph G. Tregle, Jr., " William Charles Cole Claiborne," in Glenn R. Conrad et al., eds., *Dictionary of Louisiana Biography* (Lafayette, La., 1988) 2: 180–181; Joe Gray Taylor, "W.C.C. Claiborne," in Joseph G. Dawson, ed., *Louisiana's Governors: From Iberville to Edwards* (Baton Rouge, La., 1990), pp. 80–86.

Impressive as his credentials were, little in them quite equipped Claiborne to govern Louisiana. Nor could he rely upon the example of other territorial administrators because none of them had ever confronted responsibilities akin to his. An ill-disguised scorn for Orleanians and an inability to converse in Romance tongues hampered his dealings with leading men among his new constituents. So did a propensity toward irresolution and a suddenness to discover only obduracy in anyone who opposed him. Undeterred, Claiborne stuck to his resolve to school his charges in the lessons of republicanism, no matter what.[5]

Immediately Claiborne took formal possession of Louisiana on 20 December 1803, he grasped the enormity of what suddenly had befallen him. He controlled a place in legal chaos, thanks to Pierre Clément Laussat. Dispatched by Napoleon to New Orleans, Laussat carried orders to supervise the official transfer of Louisiana from Spain to France to the United States. But for reasons known only to Laussat, just before yielding to Claiborne, he annulled all remnants of Spanish rule and left nothing in their place.

On first sight, Laussat's gift may have seemed a blessing in that it cleaned the slate for Claiborne. Actually, the Frenchman had thrown a hugely troublesome impediment in Claiborne's way. The absence of courts and laws—even Spanish ones—stifled the commercial vitality of the port and impeded every other activity that daily demanded legal remedy. Claiborne removed the obstacle with a deftness that belied his instinct for caution. In the end, he succeeded in laying ground that eased not only the transition from territory

---

5. Taylor, "W.C.C Claiborne," 86; George Dargo, *Jefferson's Louisiana: Politics and the Clash of Legal Traditions* (Cambridge, Mass., 1975), pp. 25–50; Mark F. Fernandez, "The Appellate Question: A Comparative Analysis of Supreme Courts of Appeal in Virginia and Louisiana, 1776–1840," (Ph. D. diss., College of William and Mary, 1991), pp. 110–115.

to statehood but opened the way for melding separate and sometimes incompatible legal systems into a mixed jurisdiction at once unusual yet akin to those of other southern states and of the nation as a whole.

Temporary courts relieved the backlog of cases and allowed breathing room until the congressionally-mandated Superior Court for the Territory of Orleans opened for business. By law that bench was supposed to seat three members, but difficulties in finding qualified candidates meant that a single judge often comprised the court down to 1812. Presidential appointees, all but one were American born. The first of them, John Prevost, a New Yorker, served until Joshua Lewis, a Kentuckian, replaced him in 1806. An Ohioan, William Sprigg, supplanted Lewis, and Sprigg was followed in turn by, a New Orleans resident, John Thompson, a Virginian by way of Georgia, George Mathews, and a transplanted Frenchman cum North Carolinian, the ubiquitous François-Xavier Martin. To Prevost goes much of the credit for establishing the Superior Court as a working tribunal for it was he who instituted rules and procedures that gave it a decidedly American footing, which his successors built upon.[6]

Additional county benches, erected by the territorial legislature, completed the permanent judicial structure, which was up and running by 1805. In form and procedures, the territorial courts all closely resembled ones that Claiborne had

---

6. Mark F. Fernandez, *From Chaos to Continuity: The Evolution of Louisiana's Judicial System, 1712–1862* (Baton Rouge, La., 2001), Chapter Three; Glenn R. Conrad, "Joshua Lewis," in Conrad et al., eds., *Dictionary of Louisiana Biography*, 1: 510; Elisabeth Kilbourne Dart, "George Mathews," ibid., 1: 557; Warren M. Billings, "The Supreme Court of Louisiana and Its Chief Justices," *Law Library Journal*, 89 (1997): 449–462; Carla Downer Pritchett, "Case Law Reporters in Nineteenth-Century Louisiana," in Billings and Fernandez, eds., *A Law Unto Itself?*, pp. 59–63.

known in Virginia, Tennessee, and Mississippi. That similarity kept faith with Claiborne's instructions and congressional mandates, but it also bespoke the insertion of American law into Louisiana. The suddenness of that intrusion, in addition to the novelty of the courts themselves, provoked sulky reactions from the Orleanians, some of whom grumbled about judicial proceedings in a language they could not comprehend. Others feared the loss of their usual legal customs altogether, and some merely complained; most refused Claiborne's offer of seats on the county courts or other offices. Such disdain compelled the governor to rely more heavily upon American residents than was his wont, and as a result, the judiciary took on ever deeper American hues.[7]

So did the bar. Upwards of sixty percent of the lawyers who practiced before the territorial courts were Americans. The remainder were preponderantly foreign-born Frenchmen or other Europeans and not native Orleanians, who generally lacked the schooling in continental or American law required of a practicing attorney. French emigres such as Pierre Derbigny,[8] Elegius Fromentin,[9] Étienne Mazureau,[10] and Louis Moreau-Lislet[11] identified with the Orleanians culturally, and so they tended to favor retaining the civil law as much as possible. But they recognized that weight of numbers and political reality was against them. Consequently they picked their fights carefully and accepted what they

---

7. Mark F. Fernandez, "Local Justice in the Territory of Orleans: W. C. C. Claiborne's Courts, Judges, and Justices of the Peace," in Billings and Fernandez, eds., *A Law Unto Itself?*, pp. 79–99 and Fernandez, *From Chaos to Continuity*, Chapter Three.
8. Judith Fenner Gentry, "Pierre August Bourguignon Derbigny," in Conrad et al., eds., *Dictionary of Louisiana Biography*, 1: 238–240.
9. Jane B. Chaillot, "Elegius Fromentin," ibid., 327.
10. Jane B. Chaillot, "Étienne Mazureau," ibid., 559–560.
11. Jane B. Chaillot, "Louis Casimir Elisabeth Moreau-Lislet," ibid., 579–580.

could not overbear. In truth, the bar and the bench enjoyed an uncommonly close relationship that enabled generous infusions of Anglo-American law into the territory's legal system.[12]

The locals' consternation over the courts was of a piece with their more general fears of how incursions of American customs upset their legal ways. Always mindful that such concerns carried the potential for political trouble, Claiborne took for granted the likelihood that Louisiana law would become a mixture of American, English, and European precepts that blended civil and common law doctrines in novel ways. And yet he was by no means certain of how to test for such a concoction, but neither was he hostile to the necessity for experimenting. Like other Americans of his day, he saw in the civil law an order and rationality that were lacking in state laws throughout the Union, which made civilian ways a prototype for emulation in appropriate circumstances, but he had no vision for how to apply that model in Louisiana. Furthermore, neither Congress nor the president empowered him to embark on any scheme that involved combining the two legal traditions, and the Americans who lived in the territory were not of one mind on the subject.[13]

Ever cautious, Claiborne moved first to establish a law governing crimes and punishment. He was seemingly constrained on that account by a congressional mandate that the territorial courts should have common law jurisdiction. However Congress left the task of defining that authority to the Orleanians, so Claiborne proposed a bill that the

---

12. Elizabeth Gaspard, "The Rise of the Louisiana Bar: The Early Period, 1813–1839," *Louisiana History: The Journal of the Louisiana Historical Association*, 28 (1987): 183–197.
13. Charles M. Cook, *The American Codification Movement: A Study of Antebellum Legal Reform* (Westport, Conn., 1981), pp. 3–46.

territorial legislature perfected into the Crimes Act of 1805. The statute defined dozens of offenses from murder to slander, as it prescribed which courts tried what crimes and extended to the accused the right of trial by jury, due process, and counsel. It also contained the rather ambiguous provision that "all crimes, offenses, and misdemeanors . . ., shall be taken, intended and construed according to and in conformity with the common law of England."[14] Despite its ambiguities, the Crimes Act on the whole met the governor's hopes. It filled one of the holes Laussat dug when he abrogated colonial law, it codified offenses, it set forth measures for the orderly prosecution of lawbreakers, it could pass congressional muster, and it laid foundations that supported all criminal legislation from that day to this. Nevertheless, the law was not without blemish.[15]

Perceiving the flaws, as well as the novelty of the statute itself, Claiborne commissioned a member of his staff, Lewis Kerr, to prepare a commentary on the law. The result was Kerr's *An Exposition of the Criminal Laws of the Territory of Orleans: The Practice of the Courts of Criminal Jurisdiction, the Duties of Their Officers, With a Collection of Forms for the Use of Magistrates and Others*, which was published in 1806 in parallel English and French versions on facing pages of the text.[16] Kerr's

---

14. Section 33, "An Act For the punishment of crimes and misdemeanors," *Acts Passed at the First Session of the Legislative Council of the Territory of Orleans* (New Orleans, La., 1805), 440.
15. Warren M. Billings, "Origins of Criminal Law in Louisiana," *Louisiana History*, 22 (1991): 63–76.
16. Among the first works of its kind produced by an American treatise writer, the *Exposition* is also among the rarest such texts. Only six witnesses have been identified. Florence M. Jumonville, comp., *Bibliography of New Orleans Imprints, 1765–1864* (New Orleans, La., 1989), p. 38. In 1989, Wm. Gaunt & Sons published a facsimile drawn from the witness that resides in the law library at Tulane University. That reprint is a convenient source text for anyone wishing to examine the *Exposition* at length. The custom of parallel printing in English and French

book was a clear guide to criminal law that any literate Louisianian could easily apprehend. It quieted popular fears about American rules as it eased the transition from Franco-Hispanic to American criminal jurisprudence, and it remained the basic text until Albert Voorhies's *Treatise on the Criminal Jurisprudence of Louisiana* supplanted it half a century later.[17]

On the other hand, determining the nature and substance of the territory's private law offered Claiborne, the legislature, and the courts a more exquisite challenge. No one could say with assurance what laws had been in force before 1803. The only certainty lay in their continental origin, which likely put them at some variance with American ways now being settled upon Louisiana. And, given that private law embraced things that Orleanians held precious, any attempt at defining it threatened controversy precisely because such definition opened the door to further injections of American legal habits. To do nothing continued the confusion Laussat had created, so the search for serviceable private laws began earnestly in 1806, when the legislature authorized James Brown and Louis Moreau-Lislet "to compile and prepare, jointly, a Civil Code for the use of this territory."[18]

Brown and Moreau-Lislet labored for two years before turning their handiwork over to the public printers, who published it under the title *A Digest of the Civil Laws Now in Force in the Territory of Orleans, with Alterations and Amendments Adapted to the Present System of Government*. Like Kerr's *Exposition*, the *Digest* incorporated parallel English and French texts on facing pages, but there the resemblance ended.

---

began with the publication of the territorial acts in 1804 and it remained in use until the 1860s. English was regarded as the official language of the law after 1803.

17. Essay 12 above.

18. Concurrent Resolution of the Legislature of the Territory of Orleans, 17 June 1806, *Acts Passed at the First Session of the First Legislature of the Territory of Orleans* (New Orleans, La., 1807), 214–219.

Where Kerr had relied upon his own knowledge of British criminal law and American practices, Brown and Moreau-Lislet turned for inspiration to civilian authorities such as Justinian, Jean Domat, and Robert Joseph Pothier, as well as the French Civil Code of 1804, the Coutume de Paris, the Siete Partidas, and the Fuero Real, among others. They also took generous snatches out of the commentaries of Sir Edward Coke and Sir William Blackstone, plus bits of territorial legislation. Noticeably, however, they borrowed nothing from the Code Napoleon, which twentieth-century Louisianians would come to revere as a wellspring of state law. The reason Brown and Moreau-Lislet ignored the Code Napoleon is plain enough. It was unavailable to them. Furthermore, the sort of restatement the territorial legislature envisioned, and Brown and Moreau-Lislet delivered, bore scant relation to the European understanding of a code as a primary expression of law that compelled the absolute abrogation of tradition as a source of law and required judicial deference to its prescripts. Instead, the *Digest* compiled existing statutory, customary, or judge-made law into an orderly corpus of first principles that could be bent and shaped, added to and subtracted from as time or circumstances warranted.[19]

---

19. The sources of the *Digest* have long been a bone of contention among Louisiana legal scholars. Some have argued long and vehemently for France as the predominant influence; others have contended with equal force for Spain. A representative sampling of the nature of the disputation is to be found in Henry Plauché Dart, "The Influence of the Ancient Laws of Spain on the Jurisprudence of Louisiana," *Tulane Law Review*, 6 (1931–1932): 83–93; Mitchell F. Franklin, "The Place of Thomas Jefferson in the Expulsion of Spanish Medieval Law From Louisiana," ibid. 16 (1941–1942): 319–338; Franklin, "The Eighteenth Brumaire in Louisiana: Talleyrand and the Spanish Medieval System of 1806," ibid.: 514–561; C. Russell Reynolds, "Alfonso el Sabio's Laws Survive in the Civil Code of Louisiana, *Louisiana History*, 12 (1971): 137–147; John H. Tucker, Jr.,

Although there was agreement that civilian tenets formed the pith of private law in the territory, superior court judges never regarded the *Digest* as controlling. Instead, they treated it just as they might any other source that guided them in resolving litigation. They used it when it fit the case before them; they turned elsewhere when it did not. Then too, their background combined with their rule-making authority to assure routine sprinklings of American procedures and habits into the territory's evolving legal order. And so, by 1811, they sunk the base for Louisiana's mixed jurisdiction.

Mounting clamor for statehood at last moved Congress to act, and on 8 February 1811, President James Madison signed enabling legislation that permitted "the people of Louisiana to form a constitution and a state government."[20] As soon as

---

"Source Books of Louisiana Law," *Tulane Law Review*, 8 (1933–1934): 396–405; Ferdinand Stone, "The Civil Code of 1808 for the Territory of Orleans," ibid. 33 (1958–1959): 3–6; John T. Hood, Jr., "The History and Development of the Louisiana Civil Code," ibid., 7–20; Louis Baudoin, "The Influence of the Code Napoleon," ibid., 21–28; Mitchell Franklin, "An Important Document in the History of American, Roman, and Civil Law: The De la Vergne Manuscript," ibid., 35–42; Thomas W. Tucker, "Sources of Louisiana's Law of Persons: Blackstone, Domat, and the French Codes," ibid., 45 (1970–71): 264–295; Rodolpho Batiza, "The Louisiana Civil Code of 1808: Its Actual Sources and Present Relevance," ibid. 46 (1971–1972): 4–165; Joseph Modeste Sweeney, "Tournament of Scholars over the Sources of the Civil Code of 1808," ibid., 585–603; Robert A. Pascal, "Sources of the Digest of 1808: A Reply to Professor Batiza," ibid., 603–27; Rodolpho Batiza, "Sources of the Digest of 1808, Facts and Speculation: A Rejoinder," ibid., 628–53; Joseph Dainow, "Moreau Lislet's Note on the Sources of Louisiana's Civil Code of 1808," Louisiana Law Review, 19 (1958–1959): 43–51. However the systematic analysis of Richard Holcombe Kilbourne, Jr., *A History of the Louisiana Civil Code: The Formative Years, 1803–1839* (Baton Rouge, La., 1987) settles the argument in favor of the predominance of Spanish influences.

20. "An Act to enable the people of the Territory of Orleans to form a constitution and state government, and for the admission of such state

news of the president's action reached the Crescent City,[21] Governor Claiborne set in motion an election that brought the men who drafted the Constitution of 1812 to New Orleans.[22]

Preparing that document was no easy job, given the clatter of competing interests of the delegates. How to construct a judiciary for the new state became one of the thorniest problems. Gallic members warmed to provisions that preserved existing territorial law and prevented the proposed state legislature from enacting new statutes by general reference. American and Orleanian alike took comfort too in a requirement that judges ground their rulings in writing on explicit points of law and specific legislation. Seemingly that stipulation would slow the further encroachment of common law into Louisiana jurisprudence as it curtailed judicial power. More problematic was the structure of the courts. Everyone understood that a hierarchical judiciary with appellate and trial courts which closely fit American usages was an absolute precondition for admission to the Union. Fashioning a supreme court proved the less troubling task. It emerged from the convention with appellate jurisdiction in civil causes that exceeded a monetary value of $300 and few other duties. As such it seemed no danger to anyone, especially because the drafters, like other Americans of their day, had little sense of what state supreme courts might or might not do. More irksome was how to empower the lower courts. The state could not operate without them, nor would Congress sanction a constitution

---

in the Union, on an equal footing with the original states, and for other purposes," Eleventh Congress, Third Session, 1811, Thorpe, comp., *Federal and State Constitutions*, 3: 1376.

21. The Mississippi River makes nearly a two-hundred seventy degree bend at New Orleans. Hence the synonym "Crescent City."

22. "An Act Providing for the Election of Representatives to form a Convention and for Other Purposes," *Acts of the Second Session of the Third Legislature of the Territory of Orleans* (New Orleans, La., 1811), 126.

that lacked provisions for them, however there was no agreement on the number of lower courts or the authority that should be assigned to them. In the end, the delegates merely vested "the judiciary power . . . in a supreme court and inferior courts" and charged the state legislature "to establish such inferior courts as may be convenient to the administration of justice."[23]

That compromise smoothed the way for final passage of the constitution, which cleared the convention on 26 January 1812. A scribe engrossed copies in English and French, which the delegates all signed. Subsequently, two of their number departed for Washington to seek congressional approval, and on 30 April 1812, Congress voted to admit Louisiana as the eighteenth state in the Union.[24]

Louisiana came into the Union at a pivotal moment in the development of law throughout the United States. Along with proclaiming their independence in 1776, Americans launched an extended conversation about the look, the feel, and the purpose of law that continued well into the nineteenth century. Down the decades until 1860, a booming market economy and dazzling inventions, factories and urbanization, steamboats and trains, banks and politics, immigration and westward expansion, slavery and sectionalism inspired increases of fresh laws and compelled the recalibration of old

---

23. Cecil Morgan, ed., *The First Constitution of the State of Louisiana* (Baton Rouge, La., 1975), pp. 17, 19; Warren M. Billings, "From This Seed: The Constitution of 1812," in Warren M. Billings and Edward F. Haas, eds., *In Search of Fundamental Law: Louisianan's Constitutions, 1812–1974* (Lafayette, La., 1993), pp. 6–20.

24. "An Act for the Admission of Louisiana," Twelfth Congress, First session, 1812, Thorpe, comp., *Federal and State Constitutions*, 3: 1378–1380. The English version of the engrossed constitution has disappeared, but the French text is among the holdings of the Williams Research Center at The Historic New Orleans Collection in New Orleans.

ones. As well some Americans grappled with devices that finally severed ties which bound their law to its English antecedents. Others aimed to make lawyering less a gentleman's occupation and more a professional calling that stood on "scientific" principles. Still others strove to limit the power of judges and to give legislatures opportunity to rationalize common law and procedure into terse, ordered compilations of statutes. Those of that bent saw in civilian methodologies a means to the achievement of their goal, and their push for codification drove an agenda for legal reform that ran vibrant until the outbreak of the Civil War.[25]

This national conversation extended and informed discussions in Louisiana that had gone on since 1803. Much of the debate at first turned on how closely private law should resemble a continental, or more particularly, a French civil code. Foremost among the advocates of a codal restatement

---

25. J. Louis Telkampf, "On Codification, Or The Systematization of the Law," *American Jurist*, 8 (1841-1842): 113–44, 283–329; James Willard Hurst, *Law and the Conditions of Freedom in the Nineteenth-Century United States* (Madison, Wis., 1967); Maxwell J. Bloomfield, "William Sampson and the Codifiers: Roots of American Legal Reform, 1820–1830" *American Journal of Legal History*, 11 (1967): 234–252; Gerard W. Gawalt, "Massachusetts Lawyers: A Historical Analysis of the Process of Professionalization, 1760–1840" (Ph.D. diss., Clark University, 1969); Lawrence M. Friedman, *A History of American Law* (New York, 1973), 202–264; William E. Nelson, *The Americanization of the Common Law: The Impact of Legal Change in Massachusetts, 1776–1830* (Cambridge, Mass., 1975); Maxwell J. Bloomfield, *American Lawyers in a Changing Society* (New York, 1976); Cook, *The American Codification Movement*; Warren M. Billings, "An American Original: John Bouvier's Law Dictionary," *Legal History & Rare Books*, 6 (1996): 8–9; David Dudley Field, et al, comps., *The Code of Civil Procedure of the State of New York. Reported Complete by the Commissioners on Practice and Pleadings*, ed. by Michael Weber, (Union, N.J., 1998), Introduction.

of Louisiana law was not a foreign-born Frenchman or a Creole[26] but an American, Edward Livingston.

To the manor born, Livingston (1764–1836) was of a New York family whose political dominance in the Empire State reached as far back as the seventeenth century. He came of age during the Revolutionary War years, which colored his attitudes towards English law, as did his early fondness for Roman law that in later life blossomed into a passionate belief in the superiority of civil law over common law. The advantages of family and position launched him on a promising start in New York and congressional politics. Suspicions that he had fiddled the accounts in the office of United States Attorney, which he held, led to his abrupt departure from New York City in 1804. Like many others, he set his sights southward and removed to New Orleans, where his formidable legal skills quickly turned him into one of the territory's leading advocates. Marriage into a Creole family and implacable hostility to Governor Claiborne led him to align politically with the Orleanians. In addition to a significant career as a Louisiana lawyer-politician, Livingston also attracted international notice for his work as a penal reformer and drafter of humane criminal codes.[27]

---

26. On the meaning of "creole" in its Louisiana context, see Joseph G. Tregle, Jr., "Early New Orleans Society: A Reappraisal," *Journal of Southern History*, 18 (1952): 21–36 and Joseph G. Tregle, Jr., "Creoles and Americans," in Arnold R. Hirsch and Joseph Logsdon, eds., *Creole New Orleans: Race and Americanization* (Baton Rouge, La., 1992), pp. 131–141.

27. Edward Livingston, "Autobiographical Jottings, " n. d., Edward Livingston Papers, Box 80, Department of Special Collections, Firestone Library, Princeton University; William B. Hatcher, *Edward Livingston: Jeffersonian Republican and Jacksonian Democrat*, (Baton Rouge, La., 1940), pp. 1–10; Fernandez, *From Chaos to Continuity*, pp. 74–89.

Livingston grew vexed in the years just after statehood once it became evident to him that the judges[28] of the Supreme Court showed little inclination to be bound tightly by the *Digest of 1808* as they increasingly leaned towards articulating a Louisiana species of common law. Such tendencies chafed so steadfast an advocate of codification, and he resolved to use his imposing talents to rein them in. Elected to the state legislature in 1820, he banged the drum loudly for a restatement of Louisiana law. His timing was propitious in that his ties to the Creoles, who seethed at a rule of court requiring the use of English in legal proceedings, gave him a ready-built following. Moreover, his friends among the practicing bar whipped up complaints against the Supreme Court's penchant for relying upon domestic and foreign sources in the same fashion as its counterparts in common law jurisdictions. Livingston's tune played well for his colleagues, who in March 1822, authorized the naming of three jurisconsults

> to revise the civil code by amending the same in such a manner as they will deem it advisable, and by adding under each book, title, and chapter of said work, such of the laws as are still in force and not included therein, in order that the whole be submitted to the legislature at its first session, or as soon as the said work have been completed.[29]

---

28. Between 1812 and 1845, members of the court were designated "judges" rather than "justices," and there was no formal recognition of a chief judge as such. However from the first session of court forward, it was the custom for the senior judge in point of commission or length of tenure to preside. The judiciary article in the Constitution of 1845 adopted the style "justice" and "chief justice."

29. Kilbourne, *A History of the Louisiana Civil Code*, pp. 96–130; Fernandez, *From Chaos to Continuity*, Chapter Six; Concurrent Resolution of the General Assembly of Louisiana, 14 March 1822, *Acts Passed at the Second Session of the Fifth Legislature of the State of Louisiana* (New Orleans, La., 1822), 108.

The same legislature also approved the draft of a criminal code, which Livingston had undertaken the year before. His subsequent drafts circulated widely across American and Europe, earning him great praise as one of the country's premier proponents of codification from such contemporaries as Joseph Story and Jeremy Bentham. His proposals influenced the adoption of criminal codes across the nation, particularly in New York, Maine, and Mississippi, but his fellow Louisianians abandoned the project altogether soon after he died in 1836.[30]

Even as Livingston toiled to perfect criminal law he worked with Louis Moreau-Lislet, and former Supreme Court judge, Pierre Derbigny to revise the *Digest of 1808*. In February 1823, the three jurisconsults suggested a batch of alterations to the *Digest*, along with some remedial bills that would correct perceived defects in present law. Those recommendations resounded deafly in the ears of legislators, whose concerns about law revision no longer matched Livingston's. Not to be denied, Livingston persisted, and by the sheer force of his arguments, and the deep respect his erudition conferred upon him, he eventually carried the day. Especially pointed were his attacks on an untidy common law system that offered few restraints on the power of judges to decide cases and to proclaim the law itself. Left unchecked,

---

30. "An Act relative to the Criminal Laws of this State," *Acts Passed at the First Session of the Sixth Legislature of the State of Louisiana* (New Orleans, La., 1821), 30–32; Concurrent Resolution of the General Assembly of Louisiana, Feb. 13, 1821, in Edward Livingston, *The Complete Works of Edward Livingston on Criminal Jurisprudence* . . . (New York, 1873) 1: 4; Billings, "Origins of Criminal Law in Louisiana," 63–77; Grant Lyons, "Narrow Failure, Wider Triumph? The Response to Edward Livingston's System of Criminal Law in Louisiana and Europe" (M.A. thesis, University of New Orleans, 1973); Preliminary Report on the Plan of a Penal Code, *Works of Edward Livingston* 1: 7–79.

judges easily fell prey to their natural propensities for ignorance, error, and corruption. The obvious safeguard against such possibilities was a code more akin to the European understanding than to the meaning that was incorporated in the *Digest*.[31]

Persistence and cogent argument carried the day at length, and in 1824, the legislature accepted the redactors' handiwork. Several observations about the new code, which came off the state printer's press the next year, are in order. Livingston, Moreau-Lislet, and Derbigny clearly used the Code Napoleon for a model, but they just as clearly turned to older French commentators like Jean Domat and Robert Joseph Pothier, as well as to Roman law. However their principle inspiration was neither French nor Roman law; it was Spanish law. American members of the legislature were as receptive to the code as their Gallic colleagues, but their consent did not signify their conversion to Livingston's point of view. Instead, that support spoke to their endorsement of the redaction as part of an ongoing process of bending existing legal practices to contemporary needs that was happening not only in Louisiana but nationally as well. Nevertheless, neither they nor other members of the house and senate could resist the opportunity to tinker with the jurisconsult's work, and so the legislature repealed all laws in force in 1803 as well as every statutory enactment between 1803 and 1823 that the draft code explicitly revised.[32]

Passage of the Civil Code of 1825 seemed a signal victory for Livingston and his adherents. It now appeared as though High Court judges were forever bound to the dictates of legislative will and were forbidden prescriptively from relying

---

31. Edward Livingston, "Draft of a Letter," *ca.* 1823, Livingston Papers, Box 76.
32. Fernandez, *From Chaos to Continuity*, Chapter Six.

upon authorities other than the Code as sources of future rulings. If that were so, then the Livingstonians had transformed Louisiana law into a European style regime which all but abandoned any similarity to an Anglo-American system. But Livingston failed to account for the reaction of the Supreme Court, or more especially, François-Xavier Martin.

Much the opposite of Livingston, Martin (1762–1846) rivalled the great codifier in lawyerly skills, in legal knowledge, and in renown. He left his family in Marseilles as a youth in search of opportunity in the French West Indies, and when that chance failed to prosper him, he set his face westward for the United States, eventually alighting in New Bern, North Carolina after a most inglorious stint as a soldier during the waning days of the War for Independence. In need of work, he turned himself into one of the Tar Heel State's most successful printers. Printing various law books, including the first English rendering of Robert Joseph Pothier's *Traité des obligations selon les règles tant du for de la conscience que du for extèrieur,* kindled his interest in law as a profession, and in due season he gained admission to the North Carolina bar. His politics and his reputation caught the eye of President Madison who first made him a territorial judge in Mississippi before giving him a like post in Louisiana. Martin became the first attorney general for the state before he joined the Supreme Court in 1815, where he remained for over thirty years, the last ten years of which he was chief judge.[33]

Martin, like Livingston, was a close student of Anglo-American law and civilian legal ways, but in contrast to Livingston he was a leading proponent of the view that the

---

33. Robert Joseph Pothier, *A Treatise on Obligations Considered from a Moral and Legal View,* ed. by Warren M. Billings (Union, N.J., 1999), Introduction.

two systems complemented rather than rivalled one another. Accordingly, he devoted much of his inexhaustible energies as a writer and jurist to reconciling the two into a workable jurisprudence that met the legal needs of his fellow Louisianians. Moreover, as a workaday judge, he routinely confronted a constant need to settle cases in a manner that allowed litigants on both sides to leave his court believing the law had dealt with them equitably and justly. In the real world of judging, things that worked usually counted more for Martin than elegant theoretical niceties, and he had the weight of intellect and high office to make his rulings stick.

Then too, Martin prided an independent judiciary, so he was hardly minded to be bound by the new Civil Code in the way Livingston expected. Indeed, no sooner had the Code become law than Martin and his confreres used a series of cases to render it little different from the *Digest of 1808* or other sources. The legislature countered in 1828 with repealing statutes that again invalidated all foreign law in force at the time of the Purchase, the *Digest*, and every territorial or state act that had been revised by the Civil Code. Rather than deterring the judges, the repealing statutes muddied an already cloudy condition, thereby leaving the whip in the Martin's hands. Martin finally clarified matters in 1839. In ruling on the case of Reynolds *v.* Swain, he claimed for the Court the right to say what was law in Louisiana, and who ultimately declared it. Not only that, but Martin's decision strengthened an independent judiciary with an Anglo-American tincture, which yet remains, and it guaranteed that civil and common law precepts would continue to infuse the state's maturing mixed jurisdiction.[34]

---

34. This discussion relies upon Kilbourne, *History of the Louisiana Civil Code*, pp. 131–165 and Fernandez, *From Chaos to Continuity*, Chapter Six. Fernandez's discussion of the issues in Reynolds *v.* Swain is especially

The Court enjoyed two other advantages in the drive to perfect that regime. Clauses in the Judiciary Act of 1813 empowered the judges to "make and issue all mandates necessary for the exercise of [its] jurisdiction over the inferior tribunals," it could supervise its officers, and it could promulgate "all needful rules . . ., which shall not be inconsistent with . . . this act or of any other law of this state," providing that once "the said rules once established shall not be altered" without adequate warning. In other words, the judges had carte blanche, just so long as they stayed within these spacious limits. The Judiciary Act also authorized the court to examine, license, and discipline everyone who intended to practice law in the state. That power was consistent with a custom nationwide which derived from an understanding that High Court judges, by virtue of their merits, were most able to decide who should become practitioners and to correct rogue attorneys.[35]

Shortly after the court sat for the very first time in 1813, it named attorneys Abner L. Duncan, Abraham R. Ellery, Edward Livingston, François-Xavier Martin, and Étienne Mazureau "a Committee to draw up Rules & Regulations for the Government of this Court." No copy of those rules has come to light, but it seems self-evident that the committee merely revised the regulations of the now extinct Superior Court for the Territory of Orleans. Thus from its inception, the Supreme Court not only looked like all the high benches around the country, it proceeded like them as well. Its subsequent rule changes continued that trend too. One in

---

cogent, and it should be consulted for a detailed analysis of the constitutional stakes involved in the case.
35. "An Act to organize the supreme court of the state of Louisiana, and to establish courts of inferior jurisdiction," sections 17–18, *Acts Passed at the Second Session of the First Legislature of the State of Louisiana* (New Orleans, La., 1813), 28, 32.

particular—the rule of 1821 that denied a license to "any gentleman not acquainted with the legal language of the State [English]"—stirred the controversy that launched Livingston's effort at codal revision, but others caused little upset among the bar or the public at large.[36]

Ratification of the Constitution of 1845 set in train changes to the Supreme Court that extended its jurisdiction to take appeals in criminal causes and increased the membership to include a chief justice and four associates, though the Court's rule making authority continued as before. The new justices promptly revised court procedures. As their predecessors had done in the past, they drew a committee from the New Orleans bar which they charged to revamp existing rules. In short order, the committee culled from a jumble of directives eleven succinct rules that the judges promulgated in December 1846. Subsequently, that procedural restatement took on a life of its own because it afforded the basic framework for rules that still guide the modern court.[37]

---

36. Sybil A. Boudreaux, ed., "The First Minute Book of the Supreme Court of the State of Louisiana, 1813 to 1818" (M.A. thesis, University of New Orleans, 1983), pp. 13–15; Mark F. Fernandez, ed., "Rules of the Courts of the Territory of Orleans," *Louisiana History*, 36 (1995): 315–325; Warren M. Billings, ed., *The Historic Rules of the Supreme Court of Louisiana, 1813–1879*, (Lafayette, La., 1985), p. 6. The rules of procedure were also written into Wheelock S. Upton, comp., *Code of Practice of Civil Cases for the State of Louisiana: With Annotations*, (New Orleans, La., 1839), 146–153.

37. Judith Kelleher Schafer, "Reform or Experiment? The Constitution of 1845," in Billings and Haas, eds., *In Search of Fundamental Law*; Mark F. Fernandez, "From Chaos to Continuity: Early Reforms of the Supreme Court of Louisiana, 1845–1852," *Louisiana History* 28 (1987): 19–41; Sheridan E. Young, "Louisiana's Court of Errors and Appeals, 1843–1846," in Billings and Fernandez, eds., *A Law Unto Itself*, pp. 99–117; Billings, ed., *Historic Rules*, pp. 20–21. Compare the Rules of 1846 with the modern regulations in *West's Louisiana Statutes Annotated, Vol. 8, Court Rules* (St. Paul, Minn., 1991), 293–582. A careful treatment of the evolution of the post-1846 rules remains to be undertaken.

Prescribing standards of legal education and testing would-be barristers quickly became one of the Supreme Court's most demanding administrative duties. At first, the requirements were quite modest. An applicant needed only to certify to the judges that he was of good character, that he had apprenticed with "some practising Attorney" for a term of years, and, after 1821, that he had fluency in English, or that he had been licensed elsewhere in the United States. The contentiousness of the English language rule, plus growing numbers of aspirants to the bar at length compelled the Court to refine its admission standards in a novel, if not to say radical fashion, when in 1840 it introduced two fundamental reforms. It required the judges to constitute seven lawyers as a committee that would screen prospects "strictly and rigidly," certifying those whose learning and character qualified them for examination and licensing by the Court itself.[38]

As preparation for both tests, the Court prescribed a syllabus of fifteen books for candidates to master. Cut to the pattern designed by David Hoffman, a law professor at the University of Maryland, the list divided into three broad categories of books that embraced civil law, common law, and the laws of the United States and Louisiana. Thus the range of titles included Jean Domat's *The Civil Law in its Natural Order*, Robert Joseph Pothier's *A Treatise on Obligations Considered from a Moral View*, Sir William Blackstone's *Commentaries on the Laws of England*, Samuel March Philipps's

---

38. Billings, ed., *Historic Rules*, pp. 1, 4–5, 6, 9–11; Warren M. Billings, "The Supreme Court and the Education of Louisiana Lawyers," *Louisiana Bar Journal*, 33 (1985): 74–80; Warren M. Billings, "A Course of Studies: Books That Shaped Louisiana Law," in Billings and Fernandez, eds., *A Law Unto Itself?*, pp. 25–40.

A Treatise on the Law of Evidence, The Civil Code of Louisiana, and James Kent's *Commentaries on American Law.*[39]

The examination and the syllabus raised the level of intellectual preparation of Louisiana attorneys. Indeed, the standards more than matched the judges's hopes because the rule stood, albeit with alterations, until the Court eliminated it in 1923.[40]

However, the Court had something else in mind than elevated educational requirements or mere longevity. The judges intended to impose upon the bar their shared belief that Louisiana's was a jurisprudence that drew equally from civil and common law. They conceived "law" as an age-old aggregation of axioms that regulated human existence. Though law derived from multiple sources, it could be reduced to a logical system that ordered life in Louisiana. Typical of that opinion was Martin's colleague, Henry Adams Bullard.

Bullard (1788–1851), a Massachusetts native and Harvard educated, learned his earliest legal lessons as an apprentice in the office of a Philadelphia attorney. The young lawyer soon concluded that his main chance lay somewhere in Louisiana rather than in the City of Brotherly Love, so in 1813 he settled in Natchitoches. Older than New Orleans, Natchitoches sat along the Red River in the north central part

---

39. David Hoffman, *A Course of Legal Study, Addressed to Students and the Profession Generally* (Baltimore, 1816); Billings, ed., *Historic Rules*, pp. 10–11. The Court owned a copy of the second edition of the *Course of Legal Studies* (Baltimore, Md., 1836), which now sits in the rare book collection of the Law Library of Louisiana in New Orleans.

40. *Acts Passed at the Second Session of the Fifteenth Legislature of the State of Louisiana* (New Orleans, La., 1842), 516–518; Billings, ed., *Historic Rules*, pp. 30-31; "Rules of the Supreme Court Revised and Adopted May 30, 1878, *Louisiana Reports*, 31 (1879): viii; 51 (1899): xxxvi; 134 (1914): xii–xiv; "Amendments to Rules, Supreme Court of the State of Louisiana," 152 (1923): vii–viii.

of the state, a location that rendered the town the major trade center above the Crescent City. It was an ideal location for an aspiring attorney, providing he could master the intricacies of his adopted state's legal order. His law practice and a turn as a district court judge did just that, and they set him on a path to state politics and national office. A vacancy on the Supreme Court opened a seat for him in 1834, by which time he was versed well in American, British, and civil law. Having taught law students, he inclined towards the task of improving the training of lawyers, so he was easily drawn to Martin. He quit the bench in 1846 to become professor of law at the University of Louisiana.[41]

Bullard died bankrupt, and his considerable law library went on the block to satisfy his creditors. The auctioneer's inventory is instructive because it reveals how Bullard's tastes in law books matched the collecting habits of his contemporaries, whose libraries often greatly exceeded his in both scope and size. Nevertheless, his and their libraries shared common attributes: an eclectic array of statutory compilations and cases reports, which embraced the nation as a whole as well as Louisiana; an equally diverse range of digests, dictionaries, treatises, commentaries, and practices manuals, which were the work of British, French, Spanish, and American authorities; and periodicals, a species of legal literature that was just coming into its own across the United States. Moreover, some or all of the titles in the course of studies comprised a significant element in those collections.[42]

---

41. Dora J. Bonquois, "The Career of Henry Adams Bullard," *Louisiana Historical Quarterly*, 22 (1940): 999-1106; Carl A. Brasseaux, " "Henry Adams Bullard," in Conrad et al., *Dictionary of Louisiana Biography*, 1: 127; Robert Feikema Karachuk, "A Workman's Tools: The Law Library of Henry Adams Bullard," (M.A. thesis. University of New Orleans, 1996).

42. Rosemarie Davis Plasse, "Tools of the Profession: New Orleans Attorneys and Their Law Libraries from Statehood to Secession (1813–1861)," (M.A. thesis. University of New Orleans, 2000); Kate Wallach,

Given those characteristics, it becomes evident why Bullard, Martin, and their colleagues chose as they did when they prepared the syllabus for the course of studies. The books were used by practitioners and the Court, their content reinforced the hybrid nature of Louisiana law, and they were accessible.

Availability was further enhanced, at least for some, after a group of attorneys founded the New Orleans Law Association in 1847, the forerunner of the modern Louisiana State Bar Association. The organization differed not at all from similar societies that cropped up before 1860 in cities and towns across the United States in that it existed to maintain a library and to advance the honor and integrity of its members. Membership dues sustained the library, which soon grew to house the largest, most up-to-date collection anywhere in Louisiana. Bullard and other justices helped found the association, and in time the court turned to its members for advice in setting standards for legal education or in devising procedural rules. The association also provided the committee of lawyers who screened applicants for admission to the bar.[43]

By these means, then, the blend of American, British, French, Roman, and Spanish law that started in 1803 became

---

"The Publication of Legal Treatises in America from 1800 to 1830," *Law Library Journal*, 45 (1942): 136–48; Meira G. Pimsleur, ed., *Checklist of Basic American Legal Publications*, (Hackensack, N.J., 1962); Rollo G. Silver, *The American Printer, 1787–1825* (Charlottesville, Va., 1967), pp. 114–145; Friedman, *A History of American Law*, pp. 282–92. A New Orleans attorney, Gustavus Schmidt attempted to found one such periodical. In 1841, he published the first volume the *Louisiana Law Journal*, but it seemingly failed for want of subscribers, which was a common fate for similar publications of the time. See Maxwell Bloomfield, "Law vs. Politics: The Self-Image of the American Bar," in Wythe Holt, Jr., ed., *Essays in Nineteenth Legal History* (Westport, Conn., 1976), p. 309.

43. *Proceedings of the Louisiana Bar Association, 1898–1899* (New Orleans, La., 1899), 7–9; Anton-Hermann Chroust, *The Rise of the Legal Profession in America* (Norman, Okla., 1965), 2: 129–173; Essay 14 above.

by mid-century the mixed jurisdiction that defined Louisiana's legal order to this day. That regime diverged profoundly from the one Edward Livingston envisioned and strove to perfect. Instead, it came nearer to the aim of reformers elsewhere in the South, the frontier West, or the rest of the United States at large. That it did resulted from two contingencies peculiar to antebellum Louisiana. First, no other state began with a dynamic city within its borders. Queen of the South, New Orleans promised peerless possibilities for lawyers and would-be barristers alike. They came in their thousands from every state along the eastern seaboard but Delaware, though the majority were New Yorkers, Pennsylvanians, South Carolinians, and Virginians, and by the 1840s they overwhelmingly outnumbered Creole and foreign-born lawyers alike. Second, in long-established states, codification met resistance because of its novelty. Codification seemed more natural in Louisiana because of the civil law tradition that preceded the Purchase and statehood. And thus the proximity of aspiring attorneys, diverse traditions, and expansive commerce resulted in legal habits at once American and distinctly Louisianian.[44]

Things that made Louisiana an attorney's gold mine also knit its lawyers to the existence of slavery. Quite a considerable part of statute law and judicial opinion sustained the peculiar institution as a matter of course. So did jurisprudence that defined the place of free men and women of color. Attorneys need not have held slaves in order to have benefitted from them. All routinely profited from slavery as advocates for anyone who had a legal interest in the institution, which made their dependence upon it as ordinary as humidity in a Louisiana summer. Besides, for lawyers as for planters elsewhere in the South, slavery marked their region

---

44. Gaspard, "The Rise of the Louisiana Bar," note 15.

off from the rest of the United States and defined a way of life to be protected at all costs. Defenses of that style grew ever more dissonant as it came under attack as Northerners and Southerners contested slavery's place in a democratic republic. John Brown's raid on Harper's Ferry, Virginia and Abraham Lincoln's election to the presidency hurtled the controversy beyond the point of no return, and in April 1861, Confederate general P.G.T. Beauregard ordered the bombardment of Fort Sumter which sparked off four years of horrific conflict.[45]

No sooner did secessionists take Louisiana out of the Union than a majority of able-bodied lawyers answered the Confederacy's call to arms. Those who flew to the rebel standard paid dearly for their flirtation with Southern nationalism. Battlefield casualties thinned their ranks to a shadow, and in the case of the state's largest bar organization—the New Orleans Law Association—the war virtually eliminated the membership. Veteran attorneys and younger ones gradually replenished the losses such that by the midpoint of Reconstruction the number of practitioners

---

45. Judith Kelleher Schafer, *Slavery, the Civil Law, and The Supreme Court of Louisiana* (Baton Rouge, La., 1994); Walter Johnson, *Soul by Soul: Life Inside the Antebellum Slave Market* (Cambridge, Mass., 2000); Judith Kelleher Schafer, "'Forever Free from the Bonds of Slavery': Emancipation in New Orleans, 1855–1857," in Billings and Fernandez, eds., *A Law Unto Itself*, pp. 141–178; Ellen Holmes Pearson, "Imperfect Equality: The Legal Status of Free People of Color in New Orleans, 1803–1860," ibid., pp. 191–211; Jeannine Douglas, "Steamboats and Slaves: Issues of Liability in Louisiana, 1831–1861" (M.A. thesis. University of New Orleans, 1991); Charles G. Rivet, "Commercial Evolution in the Catahoula Basin, With Perspectives on Two Frontier Families" (M.A. thesis. University of New Orleans, 1997); Robert C. Reinders, *End of an Era: New Orleans, 1850–1860* (Baton Rouge, La., 1964); Patricia Brady, "New Orleans in the 1850s," in Samuel Wilson, Jr., et al. eds., *Queen of the South: New Orleans, 1853–1862, The Journal of Thomas K. Wharton* (New Orleans, La., 1999), pp. xx–xxvii.

approached its prewar level. Even so, the devastating economic consequences of slavery's destruction turned Louisiana into a wasteland of little opportunity, which meant that fewer aspiring, immigrant lawyers looked to it or New Orleans for a fresh start as they had before the war.[46]

Constitutional revision in 1864 and 1868 attempted to adjust Louisiana's fundamental law to the realities of defeat and to realize a vision that promised suffrage and civil rights for blacks, desegregated public education, and equal access to public accommodations. Unhappily, that dream fell victim to corrupt politicians, and it suffocated in a cesspit of venality and violence, which the Constitution of 1879 strove to cleanse. Constitutions are no better than the politicians who enforce them; this one was drafted and enforced by corrupt men who reflected white Louisianians' mounting animosity to people of color. Their malice spawned the degradation of black Louisianians and white supremacy that were the most prominent features in the Constitution of 1898.[47]

Louisiana's mixed regime continued as before, although revisions to the statutes and the Civil Code cast out all references to slavery, thereby conforming written law to the change in circumstances. By 1870 too, French was no longer permitted in legal proceedings, just as it was banned from use

---

46. T.C.W. Ellis, "The Louisiana Bar, 1813–1913," *Louisiana Reports*, 133 (1913): lxxix; Thomas W. Helis, "Of Generals and Jurists: The Judicial System of New Orleans Under Union Occupation, May 1862–April 1866," in Billings and Fernandez, eds., *A Law Unto Itself?*, pp. 117–139; *Proceedings of the Louisiana Bar Association, 1898–1902*, 18; Joe Gray Taylor, *Louisiana Reconstructed, 1863–1877* (Baton Rouge, La., 1974).

47. Kathryn Page, "A First-Born Child of Liberty: The Constitution of 1864," in Billings and Haas, eds., *In Search of Fundamental Law*, pp. 52–69; Charles Vincent, "Black Constitution Makers: The Constitution of 1868," ibid., pp. 69–81; Ronald M. Labbé, "That the Reign of Robbery Will Never Return to Louisiana," ibid., pp. 81–93; Michael Lanza, "Little More Than a Family Meeting: The Constitution of 1898," ibid., pp. 99–110.

"in the general exercises in the public schools."[48] Of necessity, the Supreme Court also re-bounded its jurisprudence so as to accord with the end of slavery and federally mandated constitutional guarantees for equal rights. Not every Louisianian greeted that shift kindly. Certainly not white attorneys. Ferociously, they loathed the Court's judgments on "racial and public questions," condemning them as "specious and unsound." Their belief that "the hope of this part of the world ran contrary to the ruling dogmas of that frightful time," tarried long after Congress abandoned Reconstruction.[49]

Such vituperation echoed a strident riff on themes that bespoke the mythology of the Old South. Their cause lost, whites across the battered region conjured a romantically counterfeit past, which for them was an antidote to the toxins of an insufferable present. Lawyers cast particularly saccharine fables of honorable barristers who lived nobly in the idyllic setting of prewar plantation society, only to sacrifice their all in defense of Southern rights. Louisiana versions of such tales appeared right after the war, though the more elaborately polished ones mostly dated to the waning years of the nineteenth century and the early 1900s. Annual meetings of the Louisiana Bar Association, successor to the New Orleans Law Association, afforded a stage from which

---

48. John Ray, comp., *Digest of the Statutes of the State of Louisiana, in Two Volumes* (New Orleans, La., 1870); John Ray, comp., *Revised Civil Code of Louisiana* (New Orleans, La., 1870); Constitution of 1868, articles 109 and 138.

49. Richard Holcombe Kilbourne, Jr., *Debt, Investment, Slaves: Credit Relations in East Feliciana Parish, Louisiana, 1825–1885* (Tuscaloosa, Ala., 1995); Allen Enger, "Valid But Not Enforceable: Decrees Issued by the Supreme Court of Louisiana Involving Contracts for Slaves" (M.A. Thesis, University of New Orleans, 1996); Henry Plauché Dart, "The History of the Supreme Court of Louisiana," *Louisiana Reports* 133 (1913): liii.

to glorify Louisiana's "unique jurisprudence" or to praise antebellum attorneys for their genteel carriage, their forensic prowess, and their inherent grasp of wide-ranging legal principles, all of which made them the envy of the country. Nevertheless, tensions born of cultural differences often resulted in clashes among Creoles and Americans. But, as Charles E.A. Gayarré remarked in 1888, "after a little while everybody became reconciled to what at first had been thought an intolerable inconvenience or annoyance. In the course of time," he continued, "the high-spirited and light limbed Latin genet and the massive, slower tempered Saxon horse, being both harnessed to the car of justice, learned to pull together, and contrived by some means or other to make its wheels work smoothly, notwithstanding the natural difficulties of the road."[50]

Henry Plauché Dart (1858–1934) was the most accomplished of these myth-spinners. Child of a Creole mother and an English father, Dart rose to manhood in New Orleans during its troubled postwar years. Joining the White League, an organization of ex-Confederates, he contested the city's Reconstruction government, and the experience fired his lifelong disdain for blacks, Republicans, and the new

---

50. Paul M. Gaston, *The New South Creed: A Study in Southern Mythmaking* (New York, 1970), pp. 151–187; Tregle, " "Creoles and Americans," pp. 169–85; *Proceedings of the Louisiana Bar Association,* generally; and Charles E.A. Gayarré, "The New Orleans Bench and Bar in 1823," in Judith Kelleher Schafer and Warren M. Billings, eds., *An Uncommon Experience: Law and Judicial Institutions in Louisiana, 1803–2003* (Lafayette, La., 1997), pp. 643–656, esp. 656; William Wirt Howe, "Roman and Civil Law in America," *Harvard Law Review,* 16 (1903): 342–358; Henry J. Leovy, "The Ante-bellum Bench and Bar," *Proceedings of the Louisiana Bar Association, 1899–1900* (New Orleans, La., 1900), 10–27; T.C.W. Ellis, "The Louisiana Bar, 1813–1913," *Louisiana Reports,* 133 (1913): xvi–lxxx; Carleton Hunt, "Address of Mr. Carleton Hunt," in *Ceremonies Attending the Presentation of the Portrait of the Hon. E. John Ellis Deceased to the Supreme Court of Louisiana* (New Orleans, La., 1914), 6–24; Essay 14 above.

order. Law attracted him. Winning his license at twenty-one, he matured into a successful corporate practitioner and an accomplished litigator, who also played an active part in revitalizing the state bar organization and improving legal education. Legal research led him eventually to investigate the history of Louisiana law, and out of that interest came a long stream of work that ran from lectures, to translations of colonial judicial documents, to manifold articles and book reviews.[51]

From first to last, however, Dart's historical oeuvre exhibited tendencies that knit the whole together. Like his elders, he bowed reverently to those of his profession who had fought the good fight during the war, but he heaped bitter words of scorn on Reconstruction supreme court justices "who were contemporaries of the men they now rode with the whip and spur; they had ripened under the same influences, yet they were vindictive, unyielding partisans who abated not one jot or tittle in favor of their ancient fellowship. So far as in them lay they established black supremacy, and drove the last nail into white authority."[52] For the most part, though, Dart's true interests reached far back in time to embrace the transit of European law to Louisiana and to plot its course after statehood. That work, which Dart mainly churned out during the last three decades of his life, called attention to the imprint of Spanish and French rules upon Louisiana jurisprudence. Unparalleled command of the sources combined with polished craftsmanship to impart an unmatched authenticity to his findings. Therein lay his signal contribution. He graced the myth of dueling legal cultures

---

51. Marie E. Windell, "Henry Plauché Dart," in Conrad et al., eds., *Dictionary of Louisiana Biography*, 1: 211–212; Essay 14 above.
52. Dart, "Centennial History of the Supreme Court of Louisiana," liii.

and the supremacy of French ways with the imprimatur of his impeccably sound scholarship.[53]

Dart's collective brief for the myth did not lack doubters. Charles Payne Fenner, for one, challenged the fable when he spoke at exercises commemorating the centenary of the Supreme Court in 1913. The organizers of the observance invited Fenner,[54] a professor of civil law at Tulane, to remark on the court's jurisprudence over the preceding hundred years. He confessed to finding the assignment "a trifle staggering," but his comments undoubtedly seemed equally jolting to many in his audience, which included Henry Plauché Dart among the principal speakers.[55]

Fenner acknowledged the indebtedness of the state's substantive law and jurisprudence to civilian inheritances, but he neither credited the primacy to the French nor attributed any rivalry between Anglo-American and civil law. Conversely, he conceded that "our peculiar system of law . . . differs from that of our sister states." Saying the difference amounted to far less than was "generally supposed," he suggested that Louisiana jurisprudence had long since converged with that of the nation as a whole. Evidence of such a convergence was palpable. The Court used the same process of judging cases "as would be resorted to in . . . any common-law state." Numerous attorneys in New Orleans "engaged in important branches of practice. . . rarely [had] occasion to consult the Code" any longer. Most telling of all,

---

53. Dart, "The Place of the Civil Law in Louisiana," *Tulane Law Review*, 4 (1930): 163–177.
54. Fenner was the son of Associate Justice Charles E. Fenner, who served on the Court from 1880 to 1894 and who was instrumental in organizing Tulane, Glenn R. Conrad, "Charles Erasmus Fenner," in Conrad et al., eds., *Dictionary of Louisiana Biography*, 1: 298.
55. Fenner, "The Jurisprudence of the Supreme Court of Louisiana," *Louisiana Reports* 133 (1913): lxi–lxvi.

perhaps, was the paucity of practitioners who knew the civilian authorities or who mastered Latin or Romance tongues.[56]

Fenner's claim for convergence happened at a key time in the evolution of how certain Louisianians thought about their law. By 1913, the reinvention of legal education across America was well in hand. Courts and state legislatures supplied much of the impetus by tightening licensing requirements and demanding a post-baccalaureate degree as a mandatory credential for lawyering. The changes enhanced the status of numerous university-affiliated law schools that sprang up during the interval between the Civil War and the Great Depression. Law schools concomitantly elevated the quality of their faculties too, which were staffed increasingly with academically-trained professors. Professors in turn claimed the study and teaching of all things legal for their own. Eventually they made good the claim, which allowed them, rather than Dart-like amateurs, to dominate instruction and an ever widening research agenda. Working southward these reforms enlivened a tiny law school at Tulane University, which had struggled ever since its beginning in 1847. They also spurred the founding of the law schools at Louisiana State and Loyola Universities, which opened their doors in 1906 and 1914 respectively.[57]

Once in place, faculty members at all three institutions started exploring the nature and origins of state law. A few followed Fenner's line of march, going so far as to declare most emphatically how "it must be admitted that Louisiana is . . . a common law state."[58] With equal insistence, others

---

56. Ibid.
57. Friedman, *History of American Law*, pp. 293–567; *Louisiana Reports* 245 (1963): 124–52.
58. Gordon Ireland, "Louisiana's Legal System Reappraised," *Tulane Law Review* 11 (1936–1937): 596.

countered, saying that "for considerably more than a hundred years Louisiana has been regarded as a civil law jurisdiction because of its adoption of the doctrines of that great branch of the private law of continental Europe[, and] it remains . . . a civil law jurisdiction."[59] Weight of numbers and quantity of output swept the field for the latter contingent, who launched the so-called "civilian renaissance" in the 1930s. The myth of French civil law as the marrow, the bone, and the spirit of Louisiana jurisprudence greatly sustained advocates of that renewal, who passed on a plain message to generation upon generation of practitioners. All were the collective guarantors of a unique legal system that must be preserved against the onslaughts of the common law.

Born, reborn, and born again, the myth still enjoys a lusty life, which shows no signs of ending any time soon. It is as red beans and rice are to dining, or as king cake is to Mardi Gras. Without it, Louisiana would not be Louisiana.[60]

---

59. Leonard Greenburg, "Must Louisiana Resign to the Common Law?" ibid., 11 (1936–1937): 598–601; Harriet Spiller Daggett, Joseph Dainow, Paul M. Hébert, and Henry George McMahon, "A Reappraisal Appraised: A Brief for the Civil Law of Louisiana, ibid., 12 (1937–1938): 12–41, esp. 41; note 19, above.

60. This version excludes the bibliography that I distributed at the IALL conference in Dublin and which the editor of the *International Journal of Legal Information* appended to the original article.

ESSAY 16

POLITICS MOST FOUL?

*Winston Overton's Ghost and the
Louisiana Judicial Election of 1934*

John B. Fournet (1895–1984), one of the principals in this essay, numbers among the more colorful political figures in twentieth-century Louisiana. An intimate of Huey P. Long, he was by turns, head of the state pardon board, speaker of the state house of representatives, lieutenant governor, a witness to Long's assassination, and Chief Justice of Louisiana. I got to know him, starting in 1977, when Judge Albert Tate arranged for my UNO colleague Raphael Cassimere, Jr. and me to conduct a series of taped interviews with him.

Passing time with Fournet was quite an experience for me because he was the first live historical figure I ever encountered face to face, and he was a compelling storyteller. Cassimere and I interviewed him every month or so for the better part of two years, and while he spoke freely about his career, much of what he had to say sat strangely upon my ears because I was then really quite ignorant of modern Louisiana history. He casually remarked during one of our conversations that his election to the Supreme Court in 1934 had been highly controversial, and it had sent shock waves of animosities throughout the state bar that still reverberated, but it had nonetheless preserved the Longite majority on the Court. The significance of what he said made enough of an impression upon me to make me reach for T. Harry Williams's biography of Huey Long for more information. Williams gave a terse account of Fournet's election that was based mainly on evidence he gathered from interviews with surviving Long-era politicians, though curiously he never talked with Chief Justice Fournet. Nonetheless, his treatment satisfied me, and I gave no further thought to the matter.

Years later, while working on "A Bar for Louisiana" and "The Supreme Court and the Administration of Justice," I discovered that the consequences of Fournet's election in 1934 were vastly more far reaching than Harry Williams had described. The disputed poll nearly destroyed the bar association, it briefly diminished the Supreme Court's control over who practiced law in Louisiana, and it eventually turned Fournet into a nationally-recognized advocate of improved judicial administration. Those findings piqued my interest in the election and why it had inspired so much controversy. Scouring the secondary literature revealed nothing beyond Harry Williams's brief account in his biography of Long, so I looked elsewhere. Eventually, I came across a clue in the archives of the state bar association that looked promising—a citation to an appeal filed in the Supreme Court on behalf of Fournet's opponent, Thomas Porter. I went to the courthouse and requested the file, not knowing quite what I might find. Much to my surprise, and delight, I got a fat folder that contained a wealth of detail about the election, the candidates, and the issues at stake, none of which Harry Williams or any other Louisiana historian had ever seen before.

Reading the documents brought me to the realization that they formed the basis for an account of a poorly understood event in Long-era politics as well as insight into the foibles of judicial institutions and the inherent shortcomings of electing high court judges. My first rendering of such an explanation came in the form of a talk that I delivered at the annual meeting of the Louisiana Historical Association in 2002. Thereafter, I converted the talk into the article that follows.

Originally published as "Politics Most Foul? Winston Overton's Ghost and the Louisiana Judicial Election of 1934" in *Law Library Journal*. 97 (2005): 133–149, that article is reprinted here with the editor's kind permission.

Winston Overton was dead.

Felled by a cerebral hemorrhage on 9 September 1934, he passed away around 7:00 P.M. that evening. The next afternoon family, friends, and dignitaries from across Louisiana crowded into the Episcopal Church of the Good Shepherd in Lake Charles for funeral services. After the Reverend George F. Wharton intoned the closing prayers of the burial rite, pallbearers, including the lieutenant governor and the local sheriff, smartly bore the casket down the long center aisle and to its grave in Graceland Cemetery, where the body of the late associate justice of the Supreme Court of Louisiana moldered to the dust from whence it had come.[1]

In ordinary times, Overton's death would have drawn little public notice beyond the newspaper stories of its occurrence, and it would have been forgotten within a day or two because the judge was not a man many Louisianians thought much about, if at all. Statewide, some who read accounts of his demise recognized him as the younger brother of their junior United States senator. Hometown voters recalled him as their former city attorney, a one-time trial judge, or as their delegate to the state constitutional convention of 1921; but for all of that, he had lived mostly a stranger to those outside Lake Charles and the Third Supreme Court District.[2]

---

1. Petition of E.A. Conway (26 Sept. 1934), Porter v. Conway, 159 So. 725 (La. 1934) (No. 33147), Clerk's Office, Supreme Court of Louisiana, New Orleans.
2. New Orleans *Times-Picayune*, 11 Sept. 1934; James D. Wilson, Jr., "Winston Overton," in Carl A. Brasseaux and James D. Wilson, Jr. eds.,

September 1934 was no ordinary time. It was primary season across Louisiana, and at the hour of his passing, Winston Overton was locked in a strenuous bid to hold his seat and to keep Senator Huey P. Long master of the Supreme Court. His sudden death, which occurred less than two days before the primary election, threatened to snatch victory from Long and exalt his enemies. Not to be denied, the Kingfish and his minions executed a swift, fiendishly clever rearguard action that turned apparent defeat into a stunning success that catapulted Lieutenant Governor John B. Fournet into Overton's empty chair as it demeaned the Supreme Court and nearly destroyed the state bar association.

The manner of that achievement is an engaging, though little appreciated, episode in Long-era politics. It is as well a lesson in the fallibility of legal institutions and the sometimes malign consequences of an elective judiciary.

Seven men—Charles A. O'Niell, Fred M. Odom, Wynne G. Rogers, Harney F. Brunot, John Land, John St. Paul, and Winston Overton—comprised a Supreme Court that reflected political divisions throughout Louisiana during the Long years. Chief Justice O'Niell and Long disdained one another deeply. Their antagonism traced to Long's impeachment while governor in 1929 and to O'Niell's role as presiding judge at the trial itself. The animosity intensified afterward because O'Niell's jurisprudence stressed an independent judiciary and separation of powers as stout bulwarks against overweening executive authority, wherefore that doctrine stood poles distant from Long's way of government. Odom and Rogers typified Louisianians who detested Long for no other reason than his being Huey P. Long. St. Paul wasted no love on the senator either, though he invariably sustained Long's legislative programs on the theory that his court could restrain the legislature only if it

---

A Dictionary of Louisiana Biography: Ten-Year Supplement, 1988–1998 (Lafayette, La., 1999), p. 175.

clearly transgressed constitutional boundaries, and he rarely found that it did. Consequently, he aligned with Brunot, Land, and Overton, thereby guaranteeing Long control of the Court, but only just.³

In the spring of 1934, Long was bent on keeping the Court in his pocket. The likelihood of his doing so seemed secure as the primary season neared. Of the seven justices, only Overton was up for re-election. Overton was sure to draw an opponent, but Long appeared confident of his prospects. The judge was greatly esteemed as a man of honor and a first-class jurist, and his identification with Longism seemed a trifle to Lake Charles voters and others around his district, whom he had served for fourteen years. Besides, he was an incumbent, and that was no small advantage in this or any other election. So probability favored his taking the primary hands down, which was tantamount to retaining the seat and Long's majority.⁴

Justice St. Paul threw an unforeseen crimp into those calculations. Claiming poor health, he announced in April that he would leave the Court when it adjourned for the summer recess. Much as Long might have wished it, he could not induce Governor O.K. Allen to appoint a friendly successor. St. Paul's term of office still had twelve years to go, meaning that under provisions in the Louisiana Constitution

---

3. See Warren M. Billings, "The Supreme Court of Louisiana and Its Chief Justices," *Law Library Journal,* 89 (1997): 449, 458–460; T. Harry Williams, *Huey Long: A Biography* (Baton Rouge, La., 1977), p. 734.
4. Editorial, Lake Charles *American Press,* 10 Sept. 1934; Chief Justice Charles A. O'Neill, Jr., Remarks at Memorial proceedings for Winston Overton, 1 Oct. 1934, in Supreme Court of Louisiana Minute Book, 44, 8 June 1934, 12 Jan 1937, 44–49, Supreme Court Clerk's Office, New Orleans. A daily paper, the Lake Charles *American Press* appeared in two editions. The Home Edition customarily contained fuller, more current, reportage of front-page events than its earlier companion. Unless noted otherwise, the Home Edition is the source of the citations that appear throughout this essay.

of 1921,[5] St. Paul's replacement must stand for election. Long thus faced a race in which the outcome would be very much in doubt. Campaigns for open seats were always uncertain, but this one would be more uncertain still because of where it would occur. St. Paul lived in the First Supreme Court District—a constituency that incorporated Orleans, Jefferson, St. Bernard, St. Charles, St. John, and Plaquemines Parishes (counties)—and it was there that Long's blood rival, Crescent City mayor T. Semmes Walmsley, kept his political stronghold. Walmsley was sure to field a candidate. If his man finished first, then Long would not only forfeit control of the Court, he would suffer the high indignity of a loss to Walmsley.[6]

Looking for a way to shorten the odds in his favor, Long tapped Algiers native Archibald T. Higgins to face off against Walmsley's candidate, Walter Gleason. Higgins, an attractive, well-regarded appellate court judge, came from a fairly typical background for supreme-court candidates of the time. Educated at Tulane University, he initially associated with the law firm of one-time governor Luther E. Hall before branching out on his own. Politics beckoned, and he was by turns city attorney for Gretna, Louisiana, an assistant district attorney in Jefferson Parish, a state representative, and a district court judge before he was appointed and later re-elected to a vacancy on the Fourth Circuit Court of Appeal.

---

5. According to the Constitution of 1921, art. 7, § 7, "if two years or more of an unexpired term remain, the . . . vacancy shall be filled by special election called by the Governor, which shall be held within four months after the vacancy shall have occurred."

6. Williams, *Huey Long*, pp. 669–675. Voters in the first district chose two justices because the bulk of court business originated in New Orleans and because the Court had sat in the Crescent City since its inception in 1813.

He cast his eye on bigger things after St. Paul's resignation, and he willingly accepted the bid of the Kingfish.[7]

Long flung himself unabashedly into the Higgins-Gleason match. That commitment left Winston Overton to fend for himself. Even though Overton enjoyed the advantage of incumbency and Long's verbal support, he found himself locked into a stiff fight with an energetic adversary, Thomas F. Porter, Jr.

Porter's credentials and reputation throughout the district easily rivaled Overton's. A native of Natchitoches Parish, Porter trained at Yale Law School before settling in Lake Charles. There he partnered with E.F. Gayle, married Gayle's sister, and fell into the life of a small town lawyer. He answered the call to arms after Congress declared war on Germany in 1917 and saw action as a gunnery officer in France. Back in Lake Charles, he resumed his partnership with Gayle before an itch for judicial office goaded him to run; and in 1920, he took a seat on the Fourteenth Judicial District Court. An avid campaigner, he earned renown for his oratory on the stump and gained ever greater visibility in subsequent elections, which he always won handily. When the opportunity to challenge Overton came, he jumped at the chance. By his reckoning, his own voter appeal, plus the strength he drew from local attorneys, politicians, and anyone else who despised Long, would carry him to victory, and he aggressively took the fight to Overton.[8]

---

7. Wilson, "Archibald Thomas Higgins," *Dictionary of Louisiana Biography, Ten-Year Supplement, 1988–1998*, p. 111; Louis H. Yarrut, "Justice Archibald T. Higgins," *Louisiana Bar Journal*, 15 (1946): 2, 11–12.

8. Henry E. Chambers, *A History of Louisiana, Wilderness, Colony, Province, State, People*, (New Orleans, 1925), 3: 293; Lake Charles *American Press*, 1 Mar. 1963; Vance Plauché, "Short Sketch of the Fourteenth Judicial District over Fifty Years Ago, 1920–1925," *Louisiana History: The Journal of the Louisiana Historical Association*, 18 (1977): 239, 240–241; E-mails from

Constitutional revision in 1913 made tenure on the Supreme Court of Louisiana subject to popular vote for the first time since before the Civil War.[9] The architects of the Constitution of 1921 retained the practice too, and as a result, judicial elections quickly became an ingrained part of the political culture of twentieth-century Louisiana. Enabling statutes[10] set forth the electoral process in the exquisite detail so beloved of those who believed in the virtues of an expansive administrative state run by great bevies of elected officials. Concern for process, however, did not translate into statutory restraints on the conduct of the elections themselves. Candidates begged money from any open purse, individual lawyers publicly backed their favorites, the state bar association freely touted its choices, and reasoned debate of legal philosophies gave place to less weighty discussion. Indeed, to the chagrin of many, judicial elections became heated, raucous, and ever more costly affairs which by 1934 were scarcely distinguishable from those for the more overtly political offices.[11] So it was with the Overton-Porter encounter.

The campaign formally began after the executive committee for the Democratic Party in the Third Supreme Court District met on 3 July in Crowley. Committee chairman T. Arthur Edwards gavelled the meeting to order and recognized J. Cleveland Frugé. Frugé offered a resolution

---

Kenneth Rudolf, Head of Reference, Yale Law School Library, to Warren M. Billings (14–15 Nov. 2001).
9. Constitution of 1913, arts. 86–87.
10. See, for example, Act of 13 July 1922, No. 97, 1922 *La. Acts* 178 (providing for the "calling, holding, conducting and regulating [of] primary elections"); Act of 15 July 1924, No. 215, 1924 *La. Acts* 394 (amending 1922 act).
11. Wayne M. Everard, "Louisiana's 'Whig' Constitution Revisited: The Constitution of 1852," in Warren M. Billings and Edward F. Haas eds., *In Search of Fundamental Law: Louisiana's Constitutions, 1812–1974* (Lafayette, La., 1993), pp. 47–48; Essay 15, above; Ben Robertson Miller, *The Louisiana Judiciary*, 2ᵈ ed., (Baton Rouge, La., 1970), pp. 120–123.

fixing 11 September as the date of the primary as it invited candidates to file for the seat and stipulated that none but "electors of the white race" could vote.[12] His motion passed without dissent. The committee recessed to await the results. Once the tallies were known, it would reconvene and certify the outcome to Secretary of State E.A. Conway, who by law proclaimed the winner as the party nominee.[13]

Overton and Porter were more opponents than enemies. Both called Lake Charles home. They had long known one another as professional colleagues, they were Episcopalians, and there was no evident animus between them. True to form, however, their match immediately turned personal, though the person in question was neither Winston Overton nor Thomas Porter. It was Huey P. Long. Porter thoroughly loathed the Kingfish. Long abominated Porter in equal measure, once saying of him that "if I owned a whorehouse, I wouldn't let him pimp for me."[14] Given those feelings, Porter adopted a strategy of attacking Long head on while implicating Overton by association. He took the rather unusual step of advertising his candidacy in the newspapers. Typical was an ad that ran in the Lake Charles *American Press* the day before Overton died. It furiously lambasted Long as a power-crazed despot who would stop at nothing to undo the rule of law, and it luridly characterized him as being on the verge of using the national guard to impose dictatorship upon the good people of Louisiana. As for Overton, it said that because he "ha[d] openly announced that he approve[d] and sanction[ed] all of Long's acts, since he fail[ed] to condemn them, and since Judge Overton [was] a part of Long's political

---

12. Resolution of the Executive Committee (3 July 1934), Porter (No. 33147) case.
13. Affidavit of Thomas A. Edwards (19 Sept. 1934), Porter (No. 33147) case file.
14. Quotation attributed to Long by William Cleveland in Williams, *Huey Long,* p. 733.

machine, it must be concluded that the Judge favor[ed] the loss of life . . . if [that were] necessary to maintain Long in power." Porter, by contrast, was "unalterably opposed to Long's dictatorship and his control of the Supreme Court. The sword," the ad blared, "is now in the hands of a madman."[15]

Words in newspapers helped, but the spoken word helped more, and Porter spoke to as many of the voters as he could. Time was of the essence; there being only forty-five days between qualification and election, and the hunt for willing ears throughout the district was a grueling exercise. The Third Supreme Court District sprawled over eleven civil parishes in the mostly rural southwestern section of the state.[16] Traveling by car over rough, often barely passable highways and byways, Porter and Overton crisscrossed the district, talking themselves hoarse at as many as four rallies a day, catching rest, meals, and fresh changes of clothes as best they could. The hectic pace taxed both men, but it put the sixty-four-year-old Overton at the greater disadvantage, because he compounded the wear and tear by refusing to scale back his judicial duties. His forays into the district began and ended with a long, jolting round trip from New Orleans, and as primary day neared, he sickened, though neither he nor anyone else thought the strain might kill him.

Certainly not T. Arthur Edwards. On September 8, Edwards voted absentee before he motored over to Texas for a visit with his brother. Word of Overton's death reached

---

15. Lake Charles *American Press*, 8 Sept. 1934. I am indebted to Linda K. Gill, who photocopied the ad for me. Subsequently, she remarked to me that she had not come across "any ads for Overton while researching [for you]. I sent the one(s) for Porter because I was surprised at finding them (I never noticed political ads like that before!)." E-Mail from Linda K. Gill, Calcasieu Public Library, to Warren M. Billings (2 Jan. 2002).
16. The district embraced the parishes of Acadia, Allen, Avoyelles, Beauregard, Calcasieu, Cameron, Evangeline, Grant, Jefferson Davis, Lafayette, and Rapides.

him around noon on the 10th. He immediately left Beeville for home, knowing that it was too late to cancel the primary and under law he must declare Porter the party nominee. Heavy rains made the roads impassable, and he did not arrive in Lake Charles till midday on September 12.

By then, the votes were in, and Porter had won by a margin of two to one,[17] but because Overton died within thirty-six hours of the balloting, and because the turnout was low, there were mutterings in the Overton camp that Porter was unqualified for the nomination. Edwards harbored no such doubts. When the local press interviewed him just hours after his return from Beeville, he remarked that he had "served . . . as district attorney for four years when [Overton] was district judge, and [Overton had] been [his] close friend for many years," and he noted that "the state ha[d] lost an eminent jurist and a good citizen." As to the Porter situation, Edwards said most emphatically that "Judge Porter will be declared the nominee, being the only legal candidate before the people, whether he got a majority of votes or not since the lamented death of Justice Overton is the same as if he had withdrawn or been disqualified, leaving the field to Judge Porter." And Edwards announced that the executive committee would gather at Crowley on the fifteenth to certify Porter to Secretary of State Conway.[18]

---

17. Lake Charles *American Press*, 11 Sept. 1934; Affidavit of Thomas A. Edwards, in Porter (No. 33147) case file. An accompanying exhibit, labeled "B" in the case file, set forth the official count. It showed that Porter carried all eleven parishes, some by huge margins. The tally, however, revealed no votes were cast in two Evangeline precincts and about a hundred blank ballots were dropped in the boxes in two Lafayette precincts. What to conclude about the Overton vote is problematic because there is no way of ascertaining which voters knew of his death and marked their ballots for him anyway and which learned of his passing only after they voted for him.
18. Lake Charles *American Press*, 12 Sept. 1934.

The law allowed Edwards to set a date of his choosing, but why he put the committee meeting off to the fifteenth is a bit of a mystery. It might be supposed that his friendship with Long and his vote for Overton played into his decision. That supposition would carry weight were it not for his public statement that he deemed Porter the party's nominee. Perhaps he hoped that a little breathing space would allow everyone time to calm down and to accept that his understanding of the controlling statutes was correct. Whatever his reasons, his decision cost Porter dearly.[19]

Long heard of Overton's death almost as soon as it happened. The next day he put out statements to the press that Porter was unacceptable to him, but for the moment he did no more than bluster about "the people always being entitled to an election" and hinting darkly at some sort of legislative intervention.[20] Getting Judge Higgins elected and smashing Mayor Walmsley were uppermost in his mind, and once victory was his, he immediately fixed on keeping Porter off the Supreme Court. He drove to Baton Rouge on the twelfth, and with his principal lieutenants he hatched out a two-pronged battle plan that capitalized on the opening Edwards had unwittingly given him. He instructed his henchmen on the Third District Executive Committee to solicit a legal opinion from Attorney General Gaston L. Porterie as to the validity of Porter's election.[21]

Porterie prepared his opinion within a matter of hours. He rested his ruling on his reading of the primary act of 1922. Overton's death, coming when it did, automatically voided the votes cast on 11 September. Therefore it was imperative

---

19. Lake Charles *American Press*, 15, 17 Sept. 1934. The 1922 primary law merely required that the secretary of state promulgate the results within eight days of an election. Act of 13 July 1922, No. 97, § 27, 1922 La. Acts 178, 196.
20. Lake Charles *American Press*, 10 Sept. 1934.
21. Lake Charles *American Press*, 13 Sept. 1934.

to hold another primary ahead of the general election because the applicable statute plainly forbade picking a nominee by any means other than a popular vote. "Now," Porterie continued, "we look to the law to see if there is anything which says that one may be nominated, except by an election," which brought him squarely to the precise point of the committeemen's query. Had Overton expired seven days or more before the canvass, then Porter would properly be the nominee; but, in the attorney general's words, "the law specifies that such provision shall not apply" because Overton passed away a mere two days before the voters went to the polls on the eleventh. "Therefore," Porterie asserted, "that provision of the law is read entirely out insofar as this case is concerned, and you are left to the other provisions of the law." He concluded:

> [W]here there is ample time as there is in this case the spirit and purpose of our law is always best served by giving the people the right to an election. I rule that you should do so in this case. No candidate can complain over allowing the voters to settle the issue—I doubt that one could be heard to complain if the question is simply submitted to the voters to settle. I would say as a general matter of Committee activity that it would be presumptive to substitute yourself for the people in the selection of the nominee of the Democratic Party which is tantamount to election.[22]

In rendering his opinion, Porterie overlooked a later statute that governed primaries. The pertinent section[23] declared that

---

22. Opinion from Attorney General Gaston L. Porterie to George A. Foster et al. (12 Sept. 1934), in Porter (No. 33147) case file, above, note 1 (citing § 1, para. 2, 1922 *La. Acts*, 178; § 30, para. 3, 1922 *La. Acts*, 201).
23. Act of 15 July 1924, No. 215, § 2, para. 3, 1924 *La. Acts* 394, 397 ("That in the event that after the date has passed on which candidates are

if one of two rivals died, new candidates would have five days to file. However, if the death occurred less than seven days before the primary, the remaining candidate would gain the nomination. Porterie's oversight was deliberate. His opinion armed the Longites for the second, more insidious part of their scheme, seizing control of the executive committee and calling another primary in which they would assure the election of a Kingfish man.

That part of the design was scarcely a secret. As if anyone needed a reminder, a headline in the Lake Charles *American Press* trumpeted "Plan Seen to Depose Edwards, Oust Porter as High Court Nominee." The accompanying story cited rumors of the intention to overthrow Edwards and to prevent Porter's certification. It also noted that Edwards took the reports "calmly" and quoted him as having "anticipated something like that." But, he said, "I am convinced it would not stand up in court. Reorganization of the committee wouldn't be legal; if reorganization had been intended, it should have been done when the committee met to call the primary election." Then he reiterated his earlier conviction that the law entitled Judge Porter to the nomination.[24]

Edwards came in for quite a surprise on the fifteenth. Long collared him, and the two men huddled tête-à-tête outside the Crowley courtroom, with Long trying to persuade him to accept another primary. Edwards would have none of that, and as the two of them parted he was overheard to remark that he would follow "'der furore' [sic] of Louisiana politics" no more.[25]

---

allowed to enter and file their notification in any primary, . . . one or more of the rival candidates . . . shall die, new candidates . . . shall be permitted to enter and file their notification for a period of five days after such death; provided, that this provision shall not be effective when the death occurs within seven days of the date fixed for the primary election.").
24. Lake Charles *American Press*, 14 Sept. 1934.
25. Lake Charles *American Press*, 15 Sept. 1934.

The committee assembled at noon. Porter attended, so did Long, Lieutenant Governor John B. Fournet, and Porterie, who claimed a place at the committee table by virtue of his being a member of the Democratic Party's state central committee. Calling the members to order, Edwards recognized C.F. Hardin, who proposed Porter's certification. Before there was a second, J.W. Bolton, a Longite, demanded that the committee elect a permanent chairman and secretary. Edwards declared the motion inappropriate and refused to put it to a vote, but Bolton appealed to the committee, which overrode Edwards on a division of 11 to 4. Bolton then nominated Cleveland Frugé and L.B. De Bellevue as permanent chairman and secretary respectively, and the nominations carried, again by a margin of 11 to 4. Frugé took the chair and called upon Porterie, who explained that the law compelled the committee to hold another primary. His opinion brought forth the requisite call for an election on 9 October. At that, Porter could keep silent no longer. He vaulted onto a chair, howling heatedly that he was the lawful nominee and bawling that he would make his case in court. Long, who had held his tongue, jumped into the fray. "All we want," he shouted, "is an election. The people are very jealous of an election. I'd hate to think I was claiming a nomination over the graveyard. I'd hate to think we had a graveyard candidate." Then pointing his finger in Porter's face, he bellowed, "You're afraid to face the people." Porter's retort that Long was "a personal coward" ended the verbal sparring. Frugé regained order, whereupon the committee adjourned until "the 12th day of October, 1934, at 12:00 o'clock Meridian for the purpose of canvassing the returns of [the] . . . primary and certifying the results, etc."[26]

---

26. Resolution Certifying Porter; Resolution Calling for a Primary Election; Minute of the Executive Committee Meeting (15 Sept. 1934), in Porter (No. 33147) case file; Lake Charles *American Press*, Sept. 15, 1934;

Now Porter faced two options, look to the law or refile and run again. He grasped enough about odds to appreciate the result of a head-to-head confrontation with the Kingfish and his handpicked candidate, who was supposed to be Lieutenant Governor Fournet. Better, thought Porter, to cast his fate in the courts where, he believed, no reasonable jurist could possibly rule against him. Right and law were manifestly on his side. To make his case, he hurriedly recruited Edward Rightor, P.G. Borron, Charles Vernon Porter, Arséne Pujo, U.A. Bell, C.F. Hardin, Luther E. Hall, Joseph W. Carroll, and T. Arthur Edwards, who were among the sagest attorneys in Louisiana. All of them belonged to the Louisiana State Bar Association as well. Indeed, Bell was its president whereas the others served on various of its important standing committees. They set to work at once, and by 20 September they were ready to go to court.[27]

As Porter's team readied their briefs, the Supreme Court named Archibald Higgins to fill out the remaining three-and-a-half months of Overton's term,[28] and John Fournet entered the October primary.[29] Higgins's appointment responded to a mandate in the Constitution of 1921, which compelled the justices to fill short-term vacancies with a judge from

---

Alexandria *Town Talk*, 17 Sept. 1934; Williams, *Huey Long*, p. 735. Porterie was among those voting to sustain Bolton and to elect Frugé.

27. Lake Charles *American Press*, 17, 19–20 Sept. 1934; New Orleans *Times-Picayune*, 19 Sept. 1934; *Reports of the Louisiana State Bar Organization for 1935-1941* (New Orleans, La., 1942), pp. 2–5.

28. Order Appointing Archibald Higgins to Office (17 Sept. 1934), Supreme Court of Louisiana Minute Book, 44, 8 June 1934–12 Jan. 1937, 29, Clerk's Office, New Orleans).

29. Letter from John Fournet to J. Cleveland Frugé, 21 Sept. 1934; Fournet's Notice of Intent to Run, 21 Sept. 1934, in Porter (No. 33147) case file.

somewhere outside the Third District.[30] Higgins obviously fit that requirement, and he was duly sworn on September 18, 1934.[31]

Nothing in the record hints at why the short mantle fell upon Higgins. The press, seeing nothing sinister in the appointment, reported it as a straightforward news story.[32] Had O'Niell chosen, he might have blocked the nomination because for the moment he and the antis outvoted the Longite justices three to two. That he went along argues his tendering of an olive branch to the Kingfish, which is plausible, although a likelier explanation lies elsewhere. O'Niell and the others saw the interim appointment as a way of giving Higgins high court experience in advance of his taking his own seat. They could certainly use his help in clearing their notoriously clogged docket. Besides, with only months remaining on the Overton term, none of them anticipated the possibility of the Court's confronting anything controversial in the near future.

Fournet's candidacy confirmed what had been rumored for days. Apart from his being a fiercely devoted Long partisan, he seemed an improbable candidate for the Supreme Court, given his relative youth (he had turned thirty-nine on 7 July 1934) and utter lack of judicial experience. Reared in St. Martinville in humble circumstances, Fournet took a law degree from Louisiana State University and fought in World War I before settling in Jennings, where he both practiced and taught school. A fiery, highly ambitious populist, he saw politics as his main chance, which drew him into Long's camp

---

30. Constitution of 1921, art. 7, § 7. ("In case of a vacancy from any cause in the office of any justice, such vacancy shall be filled by selection by the court of a judge of one of the Courts of Appeal from a Supreme Court District other than that in which the vacancy shall occur. . . .").
31. Minute of Higgins's Swearing in, 18 Sept. 1934, in Supreme Court of Louisiana Minute Book, 44, 8 June 1934–12 Jan. 1937, 30, Clerk's Office, New Orleans).
32. For example, Lake Charles *American Press*, 18 Sept. 1934.

when he ran for the legislature in 1928. Thereafter, Long tapped him for speaker of the house and put him in the number two slot on the O. K. Allen gubernatorial ticket in 1932. It was loyalty to his patron and his own abiding belief in the social benefits of Longism that easily persuaded Fournet to go after Overton's empty chair.[33]

On 20 September, Porter's attorneys sued in the district courts at Ville Platte and Baton Rouge. At Ville Platte they entreated Judge Benjamin H. Pavy to stop the October 9 primary because Porter's nomination "was a matter of fact." By virtue of their client's nomination, he "had a vested right in [the] office" and to deprive him violated his constitutional privileges as a citizen of Louisiana and the United States. No doubt Pavy, who was among the bitterest of Long's adversaries, relished the chance to stick a finger in his antagonist's eye, and he wasted no time in setting the case for hearing on the 27th. The Baton Rouge suit made a similar argument, praying for orders to enjoin Secretary of State Conway from "printing or publishing on the official ballots to be used in the general election . . . the name or names of any person or persons other than" that of Porter. The trial judge, W. Carruth Jones, immediately granted the request and gave the state five days to answer why after further trial his temporary restraining order should not become permanent.[34]

Attorney General Porterie appeared for Conway on 25 September. Before addressing the Porter allegations on their

---

33. Mrs. Robert Schoenfeld, "Jean (John) Baptiste Fournet," in Glenn R. Conrad et al. eds, *Dictionary of Louisiana Biography* (Lafayette La, 1988), 1: 316–317; Williams, *Huey Long*, pp. 288–289; Interviews with John Fournet, Warren M. Billings and Raphael Cassimere, Jr. (1977).

34. Petition of Thomas F. Porter, Jr. (29 Sept. 1934); Order for the Appearance of J. Cleveland Frugé et al. (20 Sept. 1934); Order for the Appearance of Gaston L. Porterie (20 Sept. 1934), in ibid.; Petition of Thomas F. Porter, Jr. (20 Sept. 1934); Order for the Appearance of E.A. Conway (20 Sept. 1934), Porter (No. 33147) case file.

merits, he argued three procedural points. The executive committee, not the secretary of state, should have been sued. Judge Jones lacked power to intervene in a purely political matter because "regulation of elections belongs to the political department of the Government." Furthermore, "it is settled in this State that the courts [sic] do not have jurisdiction in election matters unless the statutes particularly confer it [, and] it is a general rule of law that the injunctive process of the Court will not issue against election officials to control them in the discharge of their duties in the conducting . . . an election even though the election or the manner of holding [it] might be null and void." And if the "Courts [were] not clothed with authority to substitute their action for that of the people," then Porter had no grounds for suing Conway.[35]

As to the merits, Porterie insisted at length that the petition lacked foundation in law or public policy. He rejected the claim that the situation of Overton's death automatically conferred the nomination on Porter. If that were the intent of the primary act of 1922, then the legislature would have said so "in plain and explicit terms," but he found no such expression in the statute. Scornfully, he turned aside Porter's claim of having won the vast majority of votes on primary day, saying that by any rational definition of an election, none had happened on 11 September and most voters never wanted Judge Porter anyway. Next, Porterie dismissed the argument that the district executive committee lacked power to call a second primary, asserting that Judge Jones was duty bound "to apply the dominating principle of the law—let the people participate and select their candidate." As an issue of public policy, any finding for Porter threatened "the social and political system of Louisiana" because it would inevitably provoke dissatisfaction among the state's Democratic voters.

---

35. Brief of Thomas F. Porter, Jr., ibid.

"The primary election law," Porterie cautioned Jones, "permits the dominance of the white race in the political affairs of our State." Anything short of an election would lead the voters to "rebel and go to the general election and not only not support the supposed nominee, but fight him openly." Thus, for "strong social, political and philosophical reasons," Jones had no option but to deny the plaintiff's petition.[36]

Judge Jones thought otherwise. Ruling from the bench at once, he turned aside all of the state's arguments and found in Porter's favor. Summing up, he explained his judgment this way: "It is argued that the people have a right to elect their candidates. Is it fair to make the man who made a campaign make it all over again with different candidates and different issues? I believe that the law contemplates that there shall be an end and when death intervenes it is the end of it. The law is clear to me. The election is over and Judge Porter is entitled to the nomination."[37] The attorney general immediately announced he would appeal to the Supreme Court for a writ of certiorari.[38]

Huey Long was not amused. Speaking at a Fournet rally in Oakdale that evening, he hoarsely croaked his refusal to accept Judge Jones's decision. He still believed that there would be a canvass on 9 October but if by hook or by crook "they" stopped it, he urged voters to turn out for the general election, when he promised them "something" to deny Porter. Once again, he reminded his listeners that people like them did not want Porter, and neither did he, because "Porter is against the laws I have had passed and they want to put

---

36. Ibid.
37. Judgment of Judge Jones, in Porter (No. 33147) case file.
38. Notice of Appeal of Gaston L. Porterie, in Porter (No. 33147) case file, above note 1; New Orleans *Times-Picayune*, Sept. 26, 1934; Lake Charles *American Press*, 25 Sept. 1934.

him on the supreme court bench so he can declare those laws unconstitutional."[39]

The lawyers drove down from Baton Rouge to New Orleans in the early morning of the twenty-sixth. They arrived at the courthouse on Royal Street in the French Quarter and handed their hurriedly cobbled briefs to the clerk of the Supreme Court, who in turn marked them as filed and distributed copies to the justices. Within a matter of hours, Porterie obtained his writ of certiorari. The writ required Judge Jones to render up a trial transcript, and it stayed his injunction until the high court decided what to do next. Everyone connected with the case expected those results. After all, it was the business of the Supreme Court to resolve such disputes definitively and speedily. But to the utter shock of the Porter forces, "speedily" signified something vastly different to three justices than to them. The return date on the writ was 26 November and that prevented Porter from making his case to the Supreme Court until three weeks after the general election![40]

Under the prevailing rules of court, any member could grant petitioners hearing, which Justice Brunot did, and that gave Porterie the opening he desired. Land and Higgins then sided with Brunot, which made a number sufficient for the Court to grant the writ.

O'Niell, Rogers, and Odom could only fume because the court rules stipulated that four justices were needed to vacate a writ or to change a hearing date. Of the three, Rogers and Odom joined in a terse, muted dissent that decried their

---

39. New Orleans *Times-Picayune*, 25 Sept. 1934.
40. Petition of Gaston L. Porterie for a Writ of Certiorari, Prohibition, and Mandamus, 26 Sept. 1934; Memorandum of Joseph W. Carroll and Luther E. Hall Opposing Granting of Writs; 26 Sept. 1934; Writ of Certiorari to W. Carruth Jones, 26 Sept. 1934, Porter (No. 33147) case file.

court's substantial damage to Porter's rights.[41] O'Neill, with equal brevity, but with greater fire, heatedly objected, because "on account of the law's delays, which sometimes amount to a denial of justice, the granting of the order staying further proceedings in this case will result in depriving Judge Porter of his nomination, and of the office to which he aspires, no matter how the court may eventually decide the case on its merits."[42]

On the other side, Higgins crafted the reasons why he, Brunot, and Land favored the attorney general. That explanation, which runs to more than thirty pages of double-column print in the *Louisiana Reports*, accepted every one of Porterie's contentions, which Higgins supplemented with copious additional supporting citations from case law. On the critical question of postponing a hearing until 26 November Higgins justified the delay as being in the interests of "broad public policy" and time constraints. All things considered, he concluded, "we have . . . accomplished our purpose of doing substantial justice to all parties concerned. Such is the purpose of equity."[43]

Long's investment in Higgins paid a handsome, speedy dividend. The Kingfish no longer needed to pull a rabbit out of his fedora to have his way. What Brunot, Land, and Higgins did was quite legal. The Court enjoyed sole discretion in deciding whether to grant writs of certiorari, and it was well within its prerogative to set a hearing on the motion for whatever date it chose. What was legal was not necessarily fair, but fairness was not the issue, no matter Higgins's words to the contrary. There would be a primary on 9 October,

---

41. *Porter* v. *Conway*, 159 So. 725, 726 (La. 1934) (Odom, J., and Rogers, J., dissenting).
42. Porter, 159 So. at 726 (O'Niell, C.J., dissenting).
43. Porter, 159 So. at 740.

Fournet would win, and the Supreme Court would still belong to Long.

Despite the setback, Tom Porter showed no inclination to go away. Just as soon as he got the bad news out of New Orleans, he immediately entered the primary, and a day later he withdrew his suit against the executive committee from Judge Pavy's court.[44]

The ensuing contest was really no contest at all. Long trotted out four sound trucks that accompanied him as he travelled the district speaking on Fournet's behalf. Fournet rarely said much, apart from promising to do right by the people. Porter soldiered on. Lawyers and local bar associations all across Louisiana endorsed him. Julius Long came out for him, but that was no surprise, seeing as how he was estranged from his brother. Some judges openly backed Porter too. Benjamin Pavy, the most vocal of them, caught the attention of the media statewide when he accused the Supreme Court of "trickery and corrupt devices," which enabled "those three Long-controlled justices" to steal Porter's nomination. Conversely, Pavy praised the chief justice as a "great and honorable man." The stridency of attacks like Pavy's, plus Porter's own acerbic speeches, did little to impede Fournet, who carried the district by over four thousand votes.[45]

Greatly angered, the Long camp was in no mood for charity. Victory in hand, they inflicted another measure of humiliation upon Porter. Attorney General Porterie petitioned the Supreme Court to dismiss the suit on the

---

44. Notice of Intent to Run of Thomas F. Porter (26 Sept. 1934), in Porter (No. 33147) case file, supra note 1; Motion of L.L. Perrault, 28 Sept. 1934, ibid.

45. New Orleans *Times-Picayune*, 4 Oct. 1934. Between 26 Sept. and 9 Oct. 1934, both the *Times-Picayune* and the Lake Charles *American Press* gave the race extensive coverage, which provided the basis of this summary of the campaign.

grounds that Fournet's election mooted all of Porter's claims.[46] The Porter team offered no rejoinder, and in December the justices halted all further proceedings.[47]

Presumably, the ghost of Winston Overton could rest easy now. That was not to be, however, owing to the intrusion of the Louisiana State Bar Association (LSBA).

The oldest lawyer organization in the state, the LSBA was a private self-selecting, self-regulating society that had close ties with the Supreme Court. Justices were members ex officio, and they nominated members who acted as bar examiners and disciplinarians for Louisiana's entire legal profession. Not only that, the association had taken a leading role in cajoling the state to build the massive Beaux Arts court building at 400 Royal Street, and it was there that it kept offices and maintained the largest law library in Louisiana. (The latter was open only to members.) Although LSBA attracted members statewide, it was very much a creature of New Orleans attorneys, which made it an object of scorn, especially among nonmembers, less prosperous small town practitioners, or poorly educated country barristers. Beyond that, the leaders frequently showed hostility to Long, whom they regarded not only as a loud-mouthed parvenu but a vicious tyrant who also threatened the rule of law and good government. And as recently as 1932, they struck Gaston Porterie from membership because he stopped an investigation of voting irregularities in Orleans Parish. Small wonder then that the organization weighed in on the Porter controversy.[48]

It did so in an extraordinary way. In mid-October, eight of its most prominent members demanded the ouster of

---

46. Petitions of Gaston L. Porterie (Nov. 7 & 26, 1934), Porter (No. 33147) case file.
47. Porter, 159 So. at 741.
48. Essay 15, above; Essay 14, above.

three Supreme Court justices from association membership. Their written complaint, which they directed to LSBA's executive board, charged that by denying Porter a timely hearing, Brunot, Higgins, and Land purposely deprived him of his nomination and left him no recourse at law. That denial so breached their solemn oath of office that it heaped dishonor on themselves, their court, and the LSBA. It was therefore highly appropriate for the executive board to dismiss them. At least one board member objected to receiving the complaint, but only because the Court had yet to determine Porter's suit on its merits. The objection was turned aside, and the charge was accepted. Under the association's charter, the president assigned allegations such as these to a select committee for investigation and recommendation. President Bell immediately recused himself because he was one of Porter's attorneys, so the appointment of the select committee fell to the senior vice president, who named the association secretary and himself, in addition to two others. Their deliberations stretched into the following June before they reached a determination. The operative part of their report minced no words: Regardless of the extent to which the individual members of this Committee deplore the result of the . . . acts of these Justices in the Porter case and the resulting suspicion of, and loss of great prestige, by the Supreme Court, we are of the opinion that the record before us does not require the accentuation of these unfortunate conditions by a formal condemnation of the individual Justices by this Committee . . . This Committee will therefore proceed with caution in any matter involving the motives for judicial action and will find that a judge has been actuated in performing the functions of his office by base motives or influences only when the charge is supported by convincing proof, and not when resting solely on inferences, however strong. Accordingly, the committee recommended dismissing the charges without prejudice, though it lauded the complaining attorneys for their "high sense of duty" and "commendable courage."[49]

That recommendation was too little too late. The original complaint provoked the Long forces to strike the LSBA where it would be hurt the most. Governor Allen called the legislature into special session in December and, among other things, he urged passage of a bill to establish a new bar association. The resulting State Bar Act of 1934[50] contemplated a public corporation of lawyers known as the State Bar of Louisiana (SBL). It also compelled every licensed attorney to become a dues-paying member or forfeit the right to practice. A board of governors, one chosen from each of the state's congressional districts, held executive authority. Its initial members were gubernatorial appointees, but their successors were elected by the voters. Among its powers, the board enjoyed the exclusive prerogative of fixing rules of professional conduct and punishing miscreant barristers. Moreover, it determined standards for legal education, it regulated admissions to the bar, and it quizzed candidates who presented themselves for examination. Those warrants diminished the Supreme Court, whose control of such matters had been ingrained in every state constitution since 1813. Additionally, the act severed the tie between the Court

---

49. Complaint of Burt W. Henry, Esmond Phelps, J. Zach Spearing, Charles F. Dunbar, Jr., Charles F. Fletchinger, Edwin T. Merrick, J. Blanc Monroe, and Monte M. Lemann, 19 Oct. 1934, Executive Committee Minute Book, 2 June 1934–June 1937, 377–79, 380–434, 431–432, Louisiana State Bar Association, New Orleans. Spearing and Fletchinger were past presidents of the association. Merrick was a son and namesake of a former chief justice. Phelps and Dunbar were partners, as were Monroe and Lemann. Lemann also became president of LSBA.

50. State Bar Act, No. 10, 1934 La. Acts 2d Ext. Sess. 162.

and the LSBA, to which the court had delegated effective use of those powers for upwards of a century.[51]

Having no majority, Chief Justice O'Niell trimmed to what he could not overbear, and the Court amended its rules to accord with a statute of questionable legitimacy. The SBL was soon organized, with Porterie as its first president, but it never quite fulfilled its purpose. Even so, bench and bar adjusted to the reality the law imposed on both.[52]

As sparks flew upward and passions cooled, the primary of 1934 receded into memory as the protagonists went their separate ways. Overton's ghost found respite in the shadows of the graveyard. Among the living, the LSBA refused to disappear, and for the remainder of the decade it co-existed uneasily with its rival. Behind the scenes, younger members of both societies worked quietly to effect a merger between them. That goal materialized in 1940, when the legislature bid the Supreme Court to bring the union about, and a year later the present bar organization came into existence.[53] The 1940 legislature also enacted a new primary law. Included in its numerous sections was one that explicitly clarified who would become a supreme court nominee if one of the contestants died at any time before a primary election.[54]

An assassin stilled Long in 1935. Porterie left the presidency of SBL and spent the rest of his apportioned days as a federal district court judge. Edwards passed away in 1962, all but forgotten. O'Niell carried on as chief justice until old age forced him into retirement in 1949. By then, Brunot,

---

51. Essay 14, above.
52. Essay 13, above.
53. Ibid.
54. Act of 8 July 1940, No. 46, § 84, 1940 *La. Acts* 171, 210 ("All vacancies caused by death or resignation or otherwise among the nominees selected by any political party . . . shall be filled by the committee, which has jurisdiction over the calling and ordering of the said primary election . . . ")

Land, and Higgins were years dead. Fournet succeeded O'Niell. Though he came to the bench lacking in judicial experience, and though his pugnaciousness never mellowed, Fournet grew into his black robes. He staunchly championed court modernization and efficiency until he stood down in 1970. Frugé was elected a state judge and abided into his ninety-first year before he died a decade ago. Porter lost his judgeship to the same gerrymandering that put Benjamin Pavy out of office in 1935. He lived till 1963. Fittingly, his funeral was at the Church of the Good Shepherd, and he lies buried in Graceland Cemetery not far from Overton's grave.[55]

With a bit of fancy, one can almost imagine the ghosts of Thomas Porter and Winston Overton sometimes lurking among the tombstones, deep in debate over the ramifications of a controversial, heatedly politicized judicial election. The crux of their argument would be this. Had Huey Long broken the law and stolen a seat on the Supreme Court that Porter believed rightfully belonged to him? Or had the Kingfish, with lots of help from his subalterns, manipulated the law, the courts, and the voters to outwit his enemies?

---

55. E-mail from Linda K. Gill, Calcasieu Public Library, to Warren M. Billings (15 Jan. 2002); Lake Charles *American Press*, 1 Mar. 1963; Alexandria *Town Talk*, 21 Nov. 1991. Porterie died in 1939. Brunot and Land were gone by 1944 and 1941, respectively, and Higgins passed away in 1945. O'Niell lived until 1951, whereas Fournet survived until 1984.

ESSAY 17

SOUTHERN CAUDILLOS
Harry F. Byrd, Sr., and Huey P. Long, Jr.

This essay departs from its companions because of its subject matter. Harry F. Byrd and Huey P. Long were political rather than judicial figures, and Byrd was without formal training in the law. But to ignore them in a legal context would be to overlook how each manipulated their respective legal orders to control Virginia and Louisiana. Being southerners, and yet diametrically opposite one another in all ways save one, their moments on the stage of southern history invites profound questions about the meaning of southern-ness. As I point out, I was drawn to Byrd and Long because I grew up in Virginia and lived most of my adult years in Louisiana. Shadows of both men were well nigh impossible to miss even for someone who did early American history. Intrigued by the impact of two extraordinary politicians, I long wondered what a comparison of the two might teach about southern politics and southern culture, and I wished that a knowledgeable twentieth-century scholar would undertake the task. No one has. Hence, I put this piece together in the hope that it might spur others to look at two southern caudillos in ways that I suggest.

I delivered a spoken version of the essay, which is published here for the first time, at the Fifth Virginia Forum that convened at Christopher Newport University in April 2010. Because my audience consisted of people who knew less about Long than Byrd, I highlighted the Kingfish somewhat more than the man from Winchester.

Arguably Harry F. Byrd, Sr., and Huey P. Long, Jr., were two of the most dominating American political figures of the twentieth century. Byrd was courtly, soft-spoken, and an indifferent orator. Long was crude, loud, and a mesmerizing speaker. Byrd touted limited government. Long advocated an expansive administrative state. Byrd was deeply conservative. Long was unabashedly radical. They shared a ravenous lust to master others. Manipulators of unrivalled skill, they drove political machines that brooked no opposition to their respective views of what was best for "their" people. In short, they rather remind one of the nineteenth-century iron-fisted caudillos who stole democracy in the Latin American republics.

Ronald L. Heineman, J. Harvie Wilkinson, James R. Sweeney, and Brent Tarter have portrayed Byrd elegantly and incisively whereas T. Harry Williams, William Ivy Hair, Glen Jeansonne, and Edward F. Haas have depicted Long with equal trenchancy and shrewdness.[1] The interpreters of both men portray them as uncommon leaders at particular moments in the histories of the Old Dominion and the Pelican State. No one will gainsay that each was a singular politician, but merely regarding Byrd or Long as sui generis

---

1. Ronald J. Heineman, *Harry Byrd of Virginia* (Charlottesville, Va., 1996; J. Harvey Wilkinson, *Harry Byrd and the Changing Face of Virginia Politics, 1945–1966* (Charlottesville, Va., 1968); James R. Sweeney, "Harry Byrd: Vanished Policies and Enduring Legacies," *Virginia Quarterly Review* 52 (1976): 596–612; Brent Tarter, "The Byrdocracy," unpublished ms; T. Harry Williams, *Huey Long* (New York, 1969); William Ivy Hair, *The Kingfish and His Realm: The Life and Times of Huey P. Long* (Baton Rouge, La., 1991); Glen Jeansonne, *Messiah of the Masses: Huey P. Long and the Great Depression* (New York, 1993); Edward F. Haas, "Black Cat, Uncle Earl, Edwin and the Kingfish: The Wit of Modern Louisiana Politics," *Louisiana History: The Journal of the Louisiana Historical Association*, 29 (1988): 213–227; Haas, "Huey Long and the Communists," ibid., 32 (1991): 29–46; Haas, *The Age of the Longs: Louisiana, 1928–1960* (Lafayette, La., 2001).

obscures commonalities that two extraordinary individuals shared, and it is those coincidences that I wish to explore in this essay.

One may wonder why a colonialist and an historian of American law should undertake an expedition such as this. The explanation is plain enough. I cannot be unmindful of the salience of Byrd or Long, given that I was reared in Harry Byrd's Virginia before I moved farther south to take up residence in the Crescent City, where I taught at the University of New Orleans for the better part of forty years. Truth be known, Byrd made no lasting impression upon me until I went off to the College of William and Mary, where for the first time I confronted my upbringing with a hard eye and ultimately rejected all that Byrd represented. Although Long was decades dead when I alighted in New Orleans in the late 1960s, his specter lingered insistently nonetheless. His living adherents and enemies continued their hot debates about his effects upon Louisiana, as did my colleagues and others, all of whose conversations first alerted me to similarities between Long and Byrd.[2] Upon becoming historian of the state Supreme Court, I undertook a crash course in how the Kingfish marked Louisiana, which reinforced that sensibility. More generally my own intellectual engagement with how things work in concert with the interplay of personality upon politics attracted me to Byrd and Long and made me wonder why historians of twentieth-century American politics never compared the two senators at any depth. Regarding them in tandem seemed inviting for another reason. Comparing them

---

2. The arguments turned on whether Long was a dictator, a demagogue, a rogue, a crook, or a great leader who occasionally did bad things in order to advance the public weal, and what was the nature of his legacy. One may follow these disputes in the pages of *Louisiana History* as well as those of the *Journal of Southern History* and the books about Long mentioned in the preceding note. It is not my purpose to revisit those controversies here, though reference to them is plainly unavoidable.

appeared to be a different way of plumbing the meaning of southern-ness and its relation to the history of the nation as a whole.[3]

But I worked in other fields, which made me reluctant to venture into places far from my own; so I filed my curiosity away in a box of idle musings, where it remained until Brent Tarter's talk on Byrd at the 2009 Virginia Forum unexpectedly reinvigorated it. After hearing him out, I remarked that he should compare Long and Byrd some day, but he demurred, whereupon I decided to try my hand.[4] Hence these ruminations. I offer them without any pretense of fashioning new windows into the characters of Byrd or Long or having uncovered startling new information about either one. Instead, my intent is to suggest how a different understanding of both men might proceed if scholars more knowledgeable than I probed these two quite remarkable figures along lines that I am about to suggest.

Because most of you likely have only a superficial acquaintance of Louisiana or Huey Long, let me to introduce you to both. There was more, much more, to Louisiana in Long's day than Mardi Gras, the French Quarter, jazz, or red beans and rice. It was, as it is still, a place of compelling contrasts that set it apart from other southern states and imbued its people with a singular sense of self.

Great rivers and lesser ones punctuate Louisiana, much like Virginia, although they fall south to the Gulf of Mexico. The state's geographical regions also tend to divide north to south rather than east to west, as they do in the commonwealth. Wetlands, prairies, and delta bottomlands

---

3. While reading for this essay, I came across T. Harry Williams's presidential address to the Organization of American Historians, "Huey, Lyndon, and Southern Radicalism," *Journal of American History* 60 (1973): 267–293, which exemplifies the sort of result I had in mind.
4. Tarter, "History and Harry Byrd," paper delivered at the Fourth Virginia Forum, Longwood University, April 2009.

characterize south Louisiana whereas the northern portion of the state contains features that would remind Virginians of terrain west from Richmond to the Piedmont. Fertile soils sustained cotton, sugarcane, rice, and other grains, as well as livestock. Abundant oil, natural gas, salt, sulfur, and timber resources gave rise to lucrative extractive industries, usually controlled by northern capitalists, that loosed changes which moved the labor force away from agriculture in ever increasing numbers after 1900. The people were largely rural, uneducated, and desperately poor. They lived mostly in the southern half of the state, but in their entirety they comprised a population more varied than anywhere else in the South and closer in character to some states in the North or Midwest. A piquant sauce of Indians, Acadians, Spaniards, Africans, English, Irish, Germans, Italians, and Americans, their social habits and religious traditions varied as much as they. South Louisianans were steadfastly Roman Catholic, while north Louisianans were staunchly Protestant. Shreveport and Monroe were the big cities in the north. They were greatly outshone by New Orleans—then the nation's twelfth largest metropolis and its second seaport—which was run by a Democratic Party machine that resembled comparable organizations in Boston, New York, or Chicago.[5]

Coalitions of conservative Democrats not only held the Crescent City in their thrall, they also commanded the entire state, just as they had ever since the end of Reconstruction. For them, politics was a blood sport ruled by chicanery and sharp-edged jockeying for position. Every trick of the politician's craft was theirs, and they had not the slightest qualm in resorting to the basest of them early and often. In

---

5. Glen Jeansonne, "Huey P. Long: A Political Contradiction," *Louisiana History*, 31 (1990): 374–376; Bennett H. Wall, Light Townshend Cummins, Judith Kelleher Schafer, Edward F. Haas, Michael L. Kurtz, *Louisiana: A History*, 5th ed. (Wheeling, Ill., 2008), pp. 298–317.

the rough and tumble scrambles for control of the executive mansion, the state house, New Orleans, and the country parish courthouses, contests played out in the whites-only Democratic Party primaries where victory was tantamount to winning in general elections. Race baiting and appeals to white supremacy on the campaign trail blurred class distinctions and minimized economic disparities. A supercharged racial environment throughout the 1880s and 1890s had contributed mightily to codifications in the Constitution of 1898 and statutory amplifications that stripped black Louisianans from the voter rolls, plus the many whites who were unable to pay newly instituted poll taxes. An alliance between local officeholders, upcountry cotton planters, and the Regular Democratic Organization—as the New Orleans machine was commonly called—gained sway in the early decades of the twentieth century.[6]

No less conservative than their predecessors, alliance members bore reformist tinges nonetheless. They elected governors and legislators who touted "modernization" and "business like" government that was efficient and honest, just as they employed state power to better education, highways, and other services. And they even took halting steps toward corporate regulation and the imposition of severance excises on natural resources as a means of raising state revenues. Those improvements represented a species of uplift not unlike the "very modest progressivism" that Brent Tarter

---

6. William Ivy Hair, *Bourbonism and Agrarian Protest: Louisiana Politics, 1877–1900* (Baton Rouge, La., 1969); Hair, "Henry J. Hearsey and the Politics of Race," *Louisiana History* 17 (1977): 393–400; Michael L. Lanza, "Little More Than a Family Affair: The Constitution of 1898," in Warren M Billings and Edward F. Haas, eds., *In Search of Fundamental Law: Louisiana's Constitutions, 1812–1974* (Lafayette, La., 1993), pp. 93–110; Tarter, "Byrdocracy," 4; Wythe W. Holt, Jr., "The Senator from Virginia and the Democratic Floor Leadership: Thomas S. Martin and Conservatism in the Progressive Era," *Virginia Magazine of History and Biography*, 83 (1975): 3–21.

noted as having arisen in the Old Dominion before and after Byrd consolidated his power. Of equal significance, the reforms lay the ground for Louisiana's transition to an administrative state that afforded ever more benefits to the citizenry at minimal cost to the voters. They also formed the base on which Long would scaffold his vision for Louisiana.[7]

Six years younger than Harry Byrd, Huey Long was born in 1893 in Winnfield, the seat of Winn Parish (county), which sat in north central Louisiana. Winn Parish was a hardscrabble backwater whose inhabitants had earned a deserved reputation for a political perversity that bordered on the radical, opposing as they did secession in 1861, resisting the Confederate cause in the war that followed, and enthusiastically supporting Populism or the odd Socialist throughout the 1890s. The parish was Louisiana's equivalent of Virginia's Fighting Ninth Congressional District. Winnfield itself differed little from other dreary hamlets that abundantly dotted the rural South, although it boasted a more ethnically diverse population than others, Winchester included. The Longs established themselves in Winnfield before the Civil War and were middling sorts of some standing, although they were bereft of the genteel pretensions of Louisiana's great planters and elite New Orleanians who might have regarded them as little better than white trash.[8]

Endowed with a quicksilver mind, Long combined intellect with an innate gift of words, biting wit, and a photographic memory. Coarseness and profanity came easily to him. An affliction of unquenchable energy drove him in a never-ceasing quest for self-aggrandizement, and it is no

---

7. Edward F. Haas, *Political Leadership in a Southern City: New Orleans in the Progressive Era* (Ruston, La., 1988); Wall et al., *Louisiana: A History*, pp. 231–278; Matthew J. Schott, "Huey Long: Progressive Backlash," *Louisiana History*, 27 (1986): 133–145; Samuel C. Shepherd, Jr., "In Search of Louisiana Progressives," ibid., 46 (2005): 389–406.

8. Williams, *Huey Long*, pp. 3–25; Hair, *The Kingfish and His Realm*, pp. 1–39.

reach of the imagination to say that his ambition to dominate others was his pole star. He received little by way of a formal education. Never finishing high school, he read broadly and honed his oratorical skills in discussions around the dinner table and in debates with friends. Exposure to the populist leanings of his neighbors likely reinforced his avowed sympathies for plain folk and braced his visceral animosity toward concentrations of great wealth and corporate power. Long started fending for himself while still a teenager. He hit the road and became an accomplished traveling salesman who crisscrossed north Louisiana hawking cooking oil and other household items. An interlude at the University of Oklahoma proved fleeting, and he took up sales once more. Selling profited him little financially but acquainted him with hundreds of plain, struggling folk, whose names and faces he never forgot. His experience of such a wide clientele sowed the seeds of a future constituency and whetted his talent for marketing his most beloved merchandise—himself. Next, he turned to lawyering. He enrolled in law courses at Tulane University and read every law book within his grasp but did not earn a diploma. Undeterred, he inveigled the state Supreme Court into quizzing him for the bar examination, which he passed, dazzling the judges with a mastery of the law that surpassed theirs. License in hand, and barely twenty-one years old, the newly minted lawyer set up practice in Winnfield with his brother Julius. Their partnership soured quickly, whereupon he decamped to Shreveport and gradually gained a comfortable, if unspectacular, living representing ordinary people against large corporate interests. In his mind, however, arguing cases was merely a step toward his true aspiration, politics.[9]

Thus it was in 1918 that Long tested the political waters by running for a vacant seat on the state railroad commission.

---

9. Ibid., pp. 71–106; 73–86.

The railroad commission—renamed the Louisiana Public Service Commission in the Constitution of 1921—was a good government reform that looked mighty on paper but was utterly toothless in reality. Its three members regulated intrastate rail traffic and also enjoyed jurisdiction over public utilities, steamboats, and oil and natural gas pipelines. If elected, he could exploit the commission's inherent powers and earn the statewide recognition he needed to reach the higher offices that in his mind were undoubtedly his to pluck. What the twenty-five year old Long lacked in political experience he more than offset with his aggressive, sometimes novel, methods of canvassing the electorate. Traversing the wretched north Louisiana roadways in a used automobile, a first for political aspirants across the state, he relentlessly scoured the twenty-eight-parish district in search of votes. Gathering crowds anywhere he could assemble them, he effortlessly entranced them with his spellbinding depiction of himself as *the* friend of the people and their *true* paladin against the corporate moguls who kept them down. Often, he bedded down at night with former customers who thrilled when he drove up, remembered them by name, and identified with them. Campaign fliers filled voters' mailboxes and hung from all available light poles and trees, which made the name "Long" a household word too. As a result of his prodigious effort, Long came second in the primary and narrowly captured the runoff.

Over the ensuing six years, Commissioner Long whetted his political skills and honed his pitch to voters. His uncanny ability to bend the rules within the limits of the law resulted in piping inexpensive natural gas into New Orleans, lower utility rates, and cheaper rail fares for consumers across the state. Those successes combined with his singular aptitude for bulldozing his opponents, heightened his growing reputation as the common people's champion, and emboldened him all the more. He tried to extend the commission's regulation of the Louisiana branches of the Standard Oil of New Jersey colossus and supported the election of reformer John M. Parker. Long quickly broke with Parker after he decided that the governor's coziness with Standard Oil resulted in a severance tax law far too modest to generate adequate revenue for governmental programs. That conclusion led him to his first run at the governor's mansion in 1923. He lacked money, a statewide organization, and the benediction of established politicos and businessmen. Long turned those obstacles to his advantage, arousing voters by resorting to the same boisterous campaign style that had served him in the past. This time, he added a wrinkle—the novel medium of radio and a sound truck—that hugely extended his voice in his bid for popular support. Aroused voters flocked to him and brought him within eight thousand votes of a spot in the second primary.

Defeated, but hardly chastised, Long immediately set his sights on the next election. To that end, he allied with a dissident faction of New Orleans politicians whose backing was sufficient to bring in a substantial number of city votes, which when combined with his northern strength and the support he expected to glean in rural south Louisiana would assure victory. Gaining the latter region was easier said than done, given that its voters were largely French speaking, heavily Catholic, and suspicious of a north Louisiana Protestant. Long succeeded however by convincing wary Acadians that poverty was no respecter of the downtrodden anywhere in the state and by stumping for Catholic southerners who ran for the Senate of the United States in 1924 and 1926. His strategies effectively assured him the top spot when voters streamed to the polls in January 1928, though his margin was too thin for an outright win in the first primary. Victory was his after the second place finisher dropped out.

Governor Long established an iron-fist control of nearly every level of state government, and despite an attempt to impeach him he reeled off stunning achievements in the period between his inauguration as governor and his assassination. Among other things, Baton Rouge gained a new gubernatorial mansion and a new capitol building, which symbolized visions that he imposed on Louisiana. He bettered public schools and higher education. The state also boasted the best highways in the nation. Its government provided free textbooks for school children, free adult education, pensions for the aged, and free charity hospitals for the needy—programs that in their day surpassed anything elsewhere and anticipated programs later partially replicated by the federal government. Expanded boards, commissions, and state construction projects turned government into a major employer, and that lessened the dire effects of the Great Depression upon many Louisianans. Exactions from business and industry covered a significant chunk of massive increases in public spending, as did the expansion of the state's bonded indebtedness. Voters bore some of the expense through increased fees and nuisance taxes, though they also received reductions in their real estate levies through expanded homestead exemptions. To be sure, these and like changes improved Louisiana, but they were incomplete, and the costs far outran the returns.

Even as he forcibly reshaped Louisiana, Long aimed at bigger targets. He took a seat in the Senate of the United States, but kept his enemies at bay by remaining governor until shortly before that term expired in 1932. Secure in his powerbase back home, he began playing for national audiences. He backed Franklin Roosevelt for the presidency, but the two fell out once Long concluded that Roosevelt was Wall Street's tool and not a true reformer. More to the point, the Kingfish lusted after the White House. To improve his odds of shoving FDR aside, he launched his "Share Our

Wealth" platform. Trumpeting its virtues in person and over the airwaves, he drew huge followings across the country, scared the hell out of New Dealers, and likely pushed Roosevelt farther leftward than was his wont to lean. No one will ever know if Share Our Wealth would have worked as the basis of a countrywide coalition that could have catapulted Long into the presidency because he died before mounting a concerted challenge to Roosevelt.

The Kingfish captivated the eastern press and opinion makers who never quite decided what to make of him or his remedies for the nation's economic woes. National pundits tended to brand him as a corrupt redneck, a southern clown, a communist, a fascist, a lunatic, a demagogue, a dictator, or worse. Their opinions echoed the inflammatory rhetoric of his enemies at home, some of whom also openly counseled killing him as the only way finally to be rid of so vile a fellow. Whether such talk actually sealed Long's fate can never be resolved conclusively, though it may well have added inspiration to a young Baton Rouge physician who fatally shot Long in September 1935. Dead at forty-two, Long's like would never be seen again.[10]

Harry Flood Byrd flowered in an altogether different environment. Like Long, he grew up in a small town, although Winchester was no hothouse for radicalism. Scion of an extended First Family of Virginia, Byrd inherited impeccable political credentials. His father was Speaker of the House of Delegates and a leading organization Democrat. Hal Flood, his namesake and uncle, was a prominent organization fixture too. Another uncle served in the United

---

10. The foregoing analysis rests upon Williams, *Huey Long*, passim.; Hair, *The Kingfish and His Realm*, passim., and Wall et. al., *Louisiana: A History*, passim.; Huey P. Long, *Every Man and King: The Autobiography of Huey P. Long* (New Orleans, La., 1933); Long, *My First Days in the White House* (Harrisburg, Pa., 1935); and Alan Brinkley, *Huey Long, Father Coughlin, and the Great Depression* (New York, 1982).

States House of Representative, and both his grandfathers held seats in the General Assembly. Again like Long, Byrd received little formal education. Bored with learning he quit school and started making his way while still in his teens. Energetic and relentless, he salvaged a decrepit newspaper and bought two more. He managed a telephone exchange while he presided over the Valley Turnpike Company. The profits from those ventures enabled him to take up apple growing, which brought him immense wealth and national renown as an orchardist. Politics beckoned, especially after his father schooled him in the arts one needed as a successful Virginia politician.[11]

The Old Dominion way of politics was staid, if not downright insipid. A plaything of white gentlemen, it had neither the overt brutality nor the ethnic and cultural cleavages that divided Louisianans. It did have a mean, undemocratic side to it, however. Constitutional revision in 1902 and subsequent enabling statutory provisions disfranchised black Virginians along with great numbers of white voters, who could not pay poll taxes. The result was a small electorate that skillful manipulators easily managed to the benefit of the commonwealth's conservative, business-oriented elite. Actually, one might say that politics in the Old Dominion was of the elite, for the elite, and by the elite. So as it had been all the way back to the days of Governor Sir William Berkeley who struck the bargains with the great planters—Byrd's ancestors among them—that consolidated the elite's sway for generation unto generation.[12]

Byrd's insider credentials handily inserted him into an already well-oiled political mechanism. Following an appointed term on the Winchester city council, he lost his bid

---

11. Heineman, *Harry Byrd*, pp. 1–32.
12. Tarter, "The Byrdocracy," 3; Warren M. Billings, *Sir William Berkeley and the Forging of Colonial Virginia* (Baton Rouge, La., 2004), pp. 79–113.

for re-election, but he won a seat on the state senate. He served on committees dealing with finance and highways that typified his subsequent career. Working behind the scenes, he exhibited a tirelessness and organizational genius that steadily boosted him up the ranks. In 1922, he succeeded his late uncle Hal Flood as party chairman, and he soon fastened his grip on the party machinery with an adroit cleverness that avoided rantings, bloodlettings, or much in the way of public scrutiny. From that date until his death forty years later, Harry Byrd was master of Virginia. A one-term governor, he displayed an imaginative leadership not seen in generations. By the time he left office in 1930 he streamlined state government into an entity that looked like a corporation with the governor resembling a powerful business-like executive. He also imposed his belief in pay-as-you go philosophy on state finance, which combined with love of minimal taxation and his hostility to any but the most basic public expenditures. That attitude kept Virginia in the ranks of the most backward states in the nation and caused considerable suffering throughout the Great Depression.

Byrd retired from active public life when he left the executive mansion, though he held the levers of power tightly in his grasp. There he might have stayed but for Franklin D. Roosevelt's naming Senator Claude A. Swanson his secretary of the navy, and he succeeded Swanson. Six times re-elected to the Senate of the United States, Byrd became vehemently hostile to the New Deal and an expansive federal government, and he vigorously opposed the national Democratic Party's support for civil rights. The latter stance led to the fatal embrace of Massive Resistance and the undoing of Byrd's organization.[13]

Byrd had no personal acquaintance with Long until the national Democratic Party convention of 1932. Long backed

---

13. Heineman, *Harry Byrd*.

Roosevelt, whereas Byrd opposed the New Yorker, which was reason enough for Long to turn on him. Byrd thought Long dangerously deranged, all the more so after the Kingfish reputedly threatened to kill him over a dispute about seating the Louisiana delegation. Later on, when they sat next to one another in the Senate, Long so vexed Byrd that the Virginian was heard to observe in 1934 that at the next Congress he would seek another chair even if that meant sitting with the Republicans. Personal dislikes aside they differed in other ways. Byrd lacked media savvy, which he may not have needed because news outlets across the Old Dominion usually endorsed everything he represented. Long developed a mastery of mass communication that rivalled the great Roosevelt. Democrats in name only, they hewed to viscerally antithetical constituencies and visions of governance. For Byrd, personal probity and tight-fistedness led naturally to scrupulously honest, minimalist government that had no duty to ameliorate the lot of the less fortunate or to mitigate the shocks of modernization. In the world of the Kingfish, every man had a price, and one's integrity was a changeable virtue, or none at all. Government, especially large centralized ones, was a means of easing the condition of the people, or those who controlled it. Such characterizations, or emphasizing the buffoonery of one and the courtliness of the other, obscure the commonalities shared by two quite notable politicians.[14]

Intuitive, not philosophical, they had little use for the science of politics, elaborate economic theories, or grandly articulated public policies. Supremely adept at navigating their respective milieus to their advantage, they crafted parallel courses that brought them to similar heights of officeholding. Avowed segregationists, they posed as racial agnostics, which both could do at small cost because black citizens were

---

14. Heinemann, *Harry Byrd*, p. 150; Hair, *The Kingfish and His Realm*, pp. 268–269.

political nullities. Therefore neither needed to resort to race baiting in their bids for white votes. These likenesses are self-evident, as are others that require no comment here. The resemblance that interests me most for the purposes of this piece is their common understanding of the play of politics.[15]

In contrast to Thomas P. "Tip" O'Neil, who said famously that all politics was local, to Byrd and Long all politics was personal. Politics, in their estimation, could be retailed to the voters as the mechanism for advancing their respective versions of the public weal, which chiefly meant cherishing friends, confounding enemies, and aggrandizing themselves. To accomplish those ends, both sought to acquire and to maintain personal power. That is why power captivated Byrd and Long as nothing else. That is also why the more they got, the more they wanted, and the more they grabbed until they wielded absolute authority and supreme jurisdiction over people they presumed to lead. Thus, by seizing untrammeled power they became strongmen—caudillos, if you like. Once in power they modified the engines that made caudillos into machines that maintained their absolutism.

Those machines were versions of the same model. Leaving nothing to chance Byrd and Long prided themselves on their attention to detail. Each understood that the more he knew about friends or foes, the more he could dominate them. They relied upon small circles of confidants but ultimately trusted only themselves. Beneath the inner rings were loosely strung networks of local officials, sheriffs, and legislative leaders who turned out the vote or moved favored bills into law. The money needed to keep both machines lubricated properly was raised by similar methods. Long had his "deduct system," into which state employees above certain pay grades contributed ten-percent of their salaries,

---

15. Jeansonne, "Huey P. Long," 377–380; Tarter, "The Byrdocracy," 3–5.

whereas Byrd's people were dunned varying sums of money to buy votes by paying the poll taxes of potential voters. A steely lock on the electoral apparatus and the levers of state patronage emasculated their enemies and reduced them to a puny, sputtering opposition. Moreover, their control of patronage also kept FDR at bay and the New Dealers largely out of their states. (That the president turned the Internal Revenue Service loose on the Kingfish, instead of merely tempting Byrd's opponents with federal largess, says which caudillo Roosevelt feared most.) Byrd and Long believed in rewarding their friends, and they also recognized the value of fear and swift retribution for disloyalty.

For all of that, there were glitches. For Long it was his near impeachment in 1929, and for Byrd it was the election of James H. Price as governor in 1937. In the end, both recovered and strengthened their control.[16]

Long's machine, never finely tuned even with him at the wheel, crashed after his death with all the force of a piston rod thrown through an engine block. None of his mechanics could fix it, especially in the wake of the scandals that sent LSU president James Monroe Smith and Governor Richard Leche to prison and led to the suicides of other underlings. The wreck resurrected Long's enemies into an effective opposition that touted the same social programs as had Long. Thereafter these so-called "anti-Longites" contested the remaining Longites, and the two factions vied to "reform" the state, which usually meant little more than replacing one set of rapscallions with another. There were improvements, starting with the election of Governor Sam Huston Jones in

---

16. Williams, *Huey Long*, pp. 355–389, 384–409; Alvin L. Hall "Politics and Patronage: Virginia's Senators and the Roosevelt Purges of 1938, *VMHB*, 82, (1974): 331–350; Heinemann, *Harry Byrd*, pp. 184–200; John Syrett, "The Politics of Preservation: The Organization Destroys Governor James H. Price's Administration," *VMHB*, 97 (1989), 437–462.

1940, which continued into the 1960s, but to this day Louisiana remains at the bottom of every measure of progress and retains its notoriety as a sinkhole of corruption and a bastion of backwardness.[17]

The Byrd machine lasted much longer before it rusted into oblivion after World War II. Its manner of corroding rather reminds me of the wear upon an earlier Virginia caudillo, Sir William Berkeley. Berkeley lost touch as he tarried beyond his prime. Newer politicians depended upon his patronage but feared him and wished him gone. None dared raise a hand to unseat him until Nathaniel Bacon rebelled and broke him. Similarly, Byrd fell out of step with voters and younger members of the organization who increasingly regarded him as a dinosaur. Massive Resistance was his Bacon's Rebellion. Its failure accelerated the machine's corrosion and led to better days for *all* Virginians.[18]

Not at all unlike political bosses elsewhere in the United States, Harry F. Byrd and Huey P. Long shared much in common. They acquired massive power, they massaged a corrupted electorate at will, and they ultimately stole democracy. That said, Long exemplified a radical streak of southern behavior whereas Byrd represented just the opposite impulse. They came from states, though of the South, that differed profoundly, which raises equally deep questions about definitions of southern-ness. Those differences also inspire questions about why Virginia and Louisiana cast up two such intriguing political figures. Perhaps answers lie in more extensive probing of two southern caudillos along the lines I have suggested in this little essay.

---

17. Mark T. Carleton, "Four Anti-Longites: A Tentative History," *Louisiana History* (30 (1989): 249–262.
18. Billings, *Sir William Berkeley*, pp. 210–267; Heinemann, *Harry Byrd*, 247–407; Numan V. Bartley, *The Rise of Massive Resistance: Race and Politics in the South During the 1950s* (Baton Rouge, La., 1969).

ESSAY 18

Needs and Opportunities in Virginia's Legal History and Culture

In March 2006, the editors of the *Journal of Southern History* invited me to contribute to a special issue that they intended to devote wholly to redefining and reconsidering the colonial South. I grabbed the opportunity because capitalizing on it represented another step towards my getting back to something scholarly in the wake of Hurricane Katrina. The essay—"Law in the Colonial South"—emerged as a reflection on the rise of legal studies as a field of southern history and a guide to topics that I thought might spur research in long-neglected subjects.

That article bears a kinship with the essay that follows. In it I contended that the fashioning of legal architectures was crucial to the South's beginnings, and I argued that the making of legal cultures across the region is a facet of southern history much overlooked by scholars and general audiences alike. That neglect seemed a curiosity, given the existence of a literature that consisted of an enormous bounty of books, diaries, memoirs, specialized monographs, scholarly articles, popular works, documentary editions, finding aids, dissertations, theses, government publications, fiction, television, and movies, not to mention an equally plentiful harvest of manuscript resources, much of which is readily accessible to anyone. The explanation for that curiosity was not a lack of trying. Instead, the answer lay with those who wrote about the subject and their approach to it. They were a small, disparate lot. Working largely independent of one another, they never constituted a "school" that trained their successors or postulated master narratives and overarching interpretations. There was little agreement among them about what constituted "southern legal history," topics in need of exploration and which means of analysis were most appropriate to exploit available resources. What held true for the colonial southern legal history generally was no less true for all of Virginia legal history. That realization led me to map out the dimensions of existing scholarship in this essay and to suggest areas of research that others might choose to undertake.[1]

Virginians boast legal traditions that are now more than four centuries old. Those habits were unquestionably decisive in Virginia's becoming a colony, a member of the Union, and even a state of mind. I venture to warrant, however, that the proverbial "average Virginian" standing on a Richmond street corner or the ubiquitous general reader knows little of the commonwealth's legal past. And why should they? Acquaintance with legal history is not a requirement in the current secondary school standards of learning or in university curricula, and no graduate history department in the Old Dominion emphasizes the subject.[2]

---

1. Warren M. Billings, "Law in the Colonial South," *Journal of Southern History*, 78 (2007): 602–616. A decade earlier I drew notice to some of these characteristics as they related to colonial Virginia. See Warren M. Billings, "Seventeenth-Century Virginia Law and Its Historians, With an Accompanying Guide to Sources," *Law Library Journal*, 87 (1995): 556–576.
2. Commonwealth of Virginia Board of Education, *History and Social Standards of Learning for Virginia Public Schools* (Richmond, Va., 2008);

Although law scarcely figures in the most recent book-length histories of the state, the record of its iteration and reiteration from 1607 to modern times is huge nevertheless.³ Virginians have been writing about their law ever since the seventeenth century, but the commonwealth's legal history, as we know it, is a creature of the nineteenth century.⁴ Its

---

Virginius Dabney, *Virginia: The New Dominion* (Garden City, N.Y., 1971); Ronald L. Heineman, John G. Kolp; Anthony S. Parent, Jr., and William G. Shade, *Old Dominion, New Dominion: A History of Virginia, 1607–2007* (Charlottesville, Va., 2007); Peter Wallenstein, *Cradle of America: Four Centuries of Virginia History* (Lawrence, Kan., 2007). See also "Judicial Independence in the New World: The Evolution of Virginia's Early Court System and it Effect on the Nation," a documentary production of WCVE-TV, Feb. 2009.

3. Locating that literature presents a challenge because there is no comprehensive bibliography of all that is. W. Hamilton Bryson's *A Bibliography of Virginia Legal History Before 1900* (Charlottesville, Va., 1979) is useful for identifying ante-1900 materials. Earl Gregg Swem's outdated *Virginia Historical Index* (Roanoke, Va., 1936) is helpful as well, as is Richard R. Duncan *Theses and Dissertations on Virginia: A Bibliography* (Richmond, Va., 1986). To get a *very* rough feel for what is available in scholarly magazines, using the term "Virginia legal history," I browsed five journals on JSTOR: the *William and Mary Quarterly*, the *Virginia Magazine of History and Biography*, the *Journal of Southern History*, the *American Journal of Legal History*, *Law and History Review*, and the *Virginia Law Review*. I picked those five for several obvious reasons. Both the *WMQ* and the *VMHB* began publication in the 1890s and metamorphosed from outlets for antiquarians to venues for early Americanists and Virginia historians. The *Journal of Southern History*, which commenced publication in 1934, is the leading magazine devoted to southern regional subjects of all sorts. The *American Journal of Legal History* and *Law and History Review* started in 1957 and 1983, respectively, and they primarily attract historians based in law schools. Begun in 1913, the *Virginia Law Review* is a publication of the University of Virginia School of Law. My search yielded an aggregation of over 6400 items that ranged from articles to biographical sketches, documentary collections, genealogical data, and book reviews.

4. Billings, "Seventeenth-Century Virginia Law and Its Historians," 555–556.

pioneers first undertook historical enquiries as detours from their vocations as lawyers, politicians, physicians, or clergymen. Of two sorts collectively, one group consisted of gentlemen-dabblers who rummaged Virginia's past for subjects for their speeches at special or patriotic observances or for occasional essays some of them published in newspapers and popular magazines. Their works were mostly ephemeral because, as Philip Alexander Bruce once noted, "the new historical information gathered up in these more or less casual investigations was preserved in so loose and perishable form that it was virtually lost to serious students."[5]

Himself a "serious student," Bruce stood in a second cadre—that band of gentlemen-scholars who bounded the field in the decades before and after the Civil War. Antebellum gentlemen-scholars shared a number of attributes in common. All nurtured a characteristically Virginian pride of place and family. Some were antiquarians who mounted salvage efforts that shielded early records from destruction. They frequently joined hands in founding such institutions as the Library of Virginia and the Virginia Historical Society as places of safe haven for old legal records and ancient law books. Still others published documentary collections or initiated magazines that became outlets for essays on legal topics and printed runs of legal manuscripts. Then there were those like Thomas Jefferson, who amassed his own law library and archive of seventeenth-century legislative journals and statutes, much of which he later sold to the Library of Congress. (He even helped himself to a pair of bound

---

5. See, for example, Henry Augustine Washington, *The Virginia Constitution of 1776: A Discourse Delivered Before the Virginia Historical Society* (Richmond, Va., 1852); Bruce Scrapbook, 1888–1926, n.p., Philip Alexander Bruce Papers, Mss 2889, Manuscripts Department, Alderman Library, University of Virginia, Charlottesville, Va.

volumes of early provincial archives that he removed from the General Court office in Williamsburg.)[6]

To the extent that antebellum gentlemen-scholars looked for point or purpose in the history of Virginia law and culture, they found inspiration in the colonial and revolutionary eras. That they did should surprise no one. Their ancestors started the colony whereas their fathers and grandfathers brought off the Revolution and launched the republic. For them the seventeenth century was chiefly about the transit of English ways, especially the common law, to America, and in no other state was that passage or its effects more palpable than in the Old Dominion. The Revolution had been about severing Virginians' legal bonds with Great Britain and about the beginnings of a legal order *de novo*. Although new, that order did not snap all ties to the mother country, the source of so much they held dear. These gentlemen-scholars also regarded all history as sum of the human experience of rational choices that led inevitably to betterment and liberty. "The lamp of experience," in Patrick Henry's phrase, history thus illumined the inevitable march of

---

6. Jefferson amassed the huge collection of seventeenth-century Virginia legal records that now rests among his papers at the Library of Congress. Those records, part of Series 8: Virginia Records, 1607–1737, have been digitized, and they are available at http://memory.loc.gov/ammem/collections/jefferson_papers/mtjser8.htm. The two record volumes that he appropriated are "Virginia Miscellaneous Papers, 1606–1692" and "Virginia Foreign Business and Inquisitions, 1665–1676. They originally belonged in a provincial record group that Conway Robinson styled "Inquisitions etc." in the inventory he took in 1829, which is discussed at length below. See also, Harry Clemons, ed., "Some Jefferson Manuscript Memoranda of Colonial Records," *VMHB*, 65 (1957): 154–168.

progress from former times to the present and to the ages yet to come.[7]

Like-mindedness did not dispose gentlemen-scholars to explore their legal history systematically, either in choice of topics or modes of analysis. Theirs was a scattergun engagement that yielded an omnium-gatherum of books, articles, and editions that investigated doctrine, jurisprudence, courts, the bar, legal education, biography, remembrances, and especially the rise of representative government. Although their take on such matters seems quaintly naïve now, and most of their publications go largely unread, the achievements of two antebellum gentlemen-scholars, William Waller Hening and Conway Robinson stand out.[8]

Hening (1768–1828), by turns a member of the General Assembly and a chancery court clerk, prepared assorted legal texts.[9] His *The New Virginia Justice: Comprising the Office and*

---

[7]. Quoted in H. Trevor Colbourn, *The Lamp of Experience: Whig History and the Intellectual Origins of the American Revolution*, (Chapel Hill, N.C., 1965), p. x.

[8]. Some representative examples are "Brief Sketch of the Courts in this Commonwealth," in William Brockenbrough, comp., *A Collection of Cases Decided by the General Court of Virginia, Chiefly Relating to the Penal Laws of the Commonwealth, Commencing in the Year 1789, and Ending in 1814* (Richmond, Va., 1826), 2: v–xv; Nathaniel Beverly Tucker, Lecture to Law Students at William and Mary, Nov. 1834, *Southern Literary Messenger* 1 (1834): 145–154 Henry St. George Tucker, *Commentaries on the Laws of Virginia* (Winchester, Va., 1846); Robert Reid Howison, *A History of Virginia, From Its Discovery and Settlement by Europeans to the Present Time* (Philadelphia, Pa., 1846–1848); Peter V. Daniels, Jr., *Preface to A Vindication of Edmund Randolph, Written by Himself and Published in 1795* (Richmond, Va., 1855); Hugh Blair Grigsby, *The Virginia Convention of 1776* (Richmond, Va., 1855).

[9]. For biographical treatments of Hening, see William J. Van Schreeven, "William Waller Hening," *WMQ*, 2d Ser. 22 (1942): 161–164 and Waverly K. Winfree, "Acts Not in Hening's *Statutes*, With a Biographical Sketch of W.W. Hening" (M.A. thesis, College of William and Mary, 1959).

Authority of a Justice of the Peace, in the Commonwealth of Virginia . . . (Richmond, Va., 1795 and later) turned out to be the standard manual for local magistrates in both the Old Dominion and several other states, and it likewise remains a fruitful introduction to the formalities of county courts in Hening's day.[10] He collaborated with William Munford to compile a series of higher court case reports before he joined with Munford and Benjamin Watkins Leigh to draft the Revised Code of 1819.[11] His *chef d'oeuvre*, though, was *The Statutes at Large; Being a Collection of all the Laws of Virginia, From the First Session of the Legislature in the Year 1619*, a project that Thomas Jefferson inspired him to undertake. Published between 1809 and 1823, the thirteen-volume set includes acts of assembly adopted between 1619 and 1792. *The Statutes at Large* never rose to the height of a best seller, but it turned into an indispensable tool for his contemporaries who studied early Virginia legal history, and so it remains.[12]

That *The Statutes at Large* endures as a basic source speaks to Hening's considerable abilities as a legal historian and documentary editor. Meticulous to a fault, Hening took great care in tracking down manuscripts and reconciling variations among them. A stickler for textual fidelity, nothing was more improper in his mind than varying "the spelling of the words, to suit the fluctuations of a living language." Such a method of transcription, he asserted, would be as wrong as a painter who copied the picture of an ancient Turk with his mustachoes, [and gave] him the beardless face of a modern

---

10. *The New Virginia Justice* went through three later editions before it fell out of print in 1825 (Morris L. Cohen, comp., *Bibliography of Early American Law*, [Buffalo, N.Y., 1998], 3: 176–178). On its influence outside of Virginia, see Essay 12, above.
11. Published at Richmond in 1819.
12. The University of Virginia Press reissued *The Statutes at Large* as a facsimile edition in 1969.

American Indian."[13] He also included appendices of pertinent ancillary documents, a significant number of which are no longer available anywhere else, and he provided helpful annotations without falling into the cardinal sin of editorial excess. Despite some noticeable gaps in his coverage, Hening was a remarkably thorough scholar, whose research and editorial methods match favorably with those in use nowadays.[14]

Hening bequeathed two additional legacies. *The Statutes at Large* was the first in a long line of scholarly editions that in the course of two centuries intermittently put printed volumes of vital primary resources at the disposal of historians and other legal scholars.[15] His second gift proceeded from his view of history. In the preface to *The Statutes at Large*, Hening contended that learning the laws of the commonwealth enabled one to understand its polity and the march of republican government. The statutes, in particular, afforded models of sound conversation because they were the handiwork of men of superior abilities. He went further. Virginia's earliest acts, he held, "will be found to contain a rich treasure of information relative to the *state of society among its first settlers; their religious intolerance; the rise, progress and establishment of our civil institutions; and generally such political events as afford a lesson to posterity of something worthy to be imitated and something to be shunned.*" In other words, if one had no understanding of the law, its mechanisms, and its makers,

---

13. Hening, ed., *The Statutes at Large*, 1: xi.
14. His most notable omissions were statutes from the early 1650s and 1660s. See Warren M. Billings, ed., "Some Acts Not in Hening's *Statutes*: Acts of Assembly April 1652, July 1653, and November 1653," *VMHB*, 73 (1975): 22–72 and Jon Kukla, ed., "Some Acts Not in Hening's *Statutes*: The Acts of Assembly, October 1660, ibid., 77–98.
15. Brent Tarter, "Long Before the NHPRC: Documentary Editing in Nineteenth-Century Virginia," *Documentary Editing* 30 (2008–2009): 36–47.

then one had no understanding of Virginia. So expansive an outlook on the utility of legal history foreshadowed views that inform the thinking of present-day historians.[16]

A Richmonder by birth, Conway Robinson (1805–1884) practiced law, saved a railroad from bankruptcy, sat on the Richmond city council, served in the General Assembly, redacted the state's civil and criminal codes, and wrote prodigiously.[17] His version of *A Collection of Forms Used by the Clerks of Courts of Law and Equity in Virginia*,[18] published in 1826, was at one end of a lengthy string of legal texts and histories that stretched all the way to his incomplete *History of the High Court of Chancery and Other Institutions of England*, the sole volume of which appeared two years before his death. The *Practice of Courts of Justice in England and the United States*, perhaps his masterpiece, was an early foray into the realm of comparative law that might also be thought of as a primitive forerunner of Atlantic history.[19]

---

16. Hening, ed., *The Statutes at Large*, 1: iii. Hening's remarks paraphrase a passage from Joseph Priestly, *Lectures on History and General Policy* (Philadelphia, Pa., 1804), pp. 148–149. I am grateful to my colleague Maria Kimberly at the Library of Virginia who tracked down the Priestly passage for me.
17. John Selden, "Conway Robinson," *Virginia Law Register*, 1 (1896): 631–646; E. Lee Shepherd, "Robinson, Conway," http://www.anb.org/articles/11/110723.html; *ANB Online*; accessed 15 Dec. 2009; Richard A. Claybrook, Jr., "Conway Robinson," in W. Hamilton Bryson, ed., *The Virginia Law Reporters Before 1880* (Charlottesville, Va., 1977), pp. 57–65; Christopher M. Curtis, "Codification in Virginia: Conway Robinson, John Mercer Patton, and the Politics of Law Reform," *VMHB* 117 (2009): 140–181, esp. 175–176.
18. His father, clerk of the City of Richmond Hustings Court, compiled the original edition, which he published in 1809.
19. Among his other books are *The Practice in the Courts of Law and Equity in Virginia* (Richmond, Va., 1832–1839); *An Essay upon the Constitutional Rights as to Slave Property* (Richmond, Va., 1840); *An*

Robinson was both a charter member of the Virginia Historical Society and its first treasurer. As one of its principal executive officers for more than half a century, he strove to augment its holdings, and when he died, he willed the Society a portion of his library together with a large accumulation of his papers, both of which are yet worthy of mining.[20] An inveterate gatherer, he used personal connections and his extensive knowledge of English and American law to track down all sorts of fugitive documents. Perhaps the most prominent of these finds is the only known contemporaneous text of the journal of the General Assembly of 1619, kept by its secretary John Pory, which Robinson located while on a visit to London.[21] (His discovery resulted in the journal's publication on four separate occasions, first by the historian George Bancroft in 1857 and then in three later printings.[22]) He prepared a detailed inventory of colonial archives that were stuffed in cubbyholes and crammed into barrels at the General Court offices in the Capitol, apparently as a preliminary step to preserving those records in a more friendly environment, but the scheme came

---

Account of Discoveries in the West Until 1519 . . . (Richmond, Va., 1848); *Views of the Constitution of Virginia* . . . (Richmond, Va., 1850).

20. Virginius Cornick Hall, Jr., "The Virginia Historical Society: An Anniversary Narrative of Its First Century and a Half," *VMHB*, 90 (1982), 8.

21. The Pory document is in Colonial Office Papers, Class 1, vol. 1, fols. 139–154, the National Archives, Kew, United Kingdom.

22. George Bancroft, ed., "Introductory Note to Proceedings of the First Assembly, 1619," *Collections of the New-York Historical Society*, 2d Ser., 3 (1857): 331–334. The second and third printings occurred in 1874 and 1907, respectively, whereas the fourth, and best, rendition is William J. Van Schreeven and George H. Reese, eds., *Proceedings of the General Assembly of Virginia, July 30–August 4, 1619: Written & Sent from Virginia to England by Mr. John Pory, Speaker of the First Representative Assembly in the New World* (Jamestown, Va., 1969), which presents facsimiles of the original manuscripts and Reese's transcriptions on facing pages.

to naught.[23] His "Notes and Excerpts from the Records of Colonial Virginia, 1624–1689" was either a spin-off from the inventory project or an aid to his other legal research. Whatever reasons lay behind their creation, the "Notes" and the inventory attained considerable importance after 1865. They comprise the surviving record of the bulk of the seventeenth-century archives that fire destroyed in the waning days of the Civil War, and their existence is well nigh indispensable for research on the origins of the General Assembly and the General Court.[24]

Until Robinson retired from his active participation in Virginia Historical Society activities, he collaborated with younger gentlemen-scholars who picked up the pieces and slowly resuscitated Virginia legal history after the Civil War. Much as before, this generation focused on colonial times, although theirs was a collectively darker view of human progress than their elders once espoused. In their opinion, law and its supporting institutions linked politics, social arrangements, and economic conditions, and the people of the Old Dominion into a distinctive polity. They expressly regarded law as the crucial element of a culture that delineated and was delineated by Virginia norms. Nostalgia figured in their thinking too. Some of them had soldiered in the war or lost loved ones whereas others were youngsters or came into the world amidst the fighting, or they were born after the conflict ceased. Whatever their individual circumstances, none of them regarded postwar Virginia as the

---

23. Robinson, "Memorandum of the Records in the General Court Office with a statement of the condition of the same," 3 June 1829, Accession Number 21779, Library of Virginia, Richmond.

24. Robertson's "Notes" are among his papers at the Virginia Historical Society, and large portions of them appeared in early volumes of the *VMHB*. See also Lawrence J. Friedman and Arthur H. Schaffer, "The Conway Robinson Notes and Seventeenth-Century Virginia," *VMHB*, 78 (1970): 259–267.

most congenial of places, and their researches into the founding era took them back to a more glorious time and fed an Old South mythology that intoxicated southern whites even to this day. Last, but by no means least, they invested their scholarship with more system and rigor than had their predecessors, although their approaches were no less scattershot than before.

This group of gentlemen-scholars was a remarkably fruitful lot, who by the opening of the twentieth century added greatly to the increase in the ever-growing body of Virginia legal historiography. That abundance was quite remarkable, especially if one recalls that theirs was a sparse working environment that lacked funding, xerography, computers, and every other research nicety that historians now take for granted. Their names and theirs works are unrecognizable in the main to all but the most erudite of modern scholars. Who knows anything of, say, William P. Palmer, Edward Ingle, or Frederick Johnston? The group cast up some exceptional members, nonetheless, and of these, Philip Alexander Bruce commands notice here, and so does his contemporary, Thomas Jefferson Wertenbaker.[25]

---

25. See, for example, Tarter, "Long Before the NHPRC;" William P. Palmer, et al., eds., Calendar of Virginia State Papers and Other State Papers and Other Manuscripts . . . Preserved at Richmond, 1652–1869 (Richmond, 1875–1893); Edward Ingle, *Local Institutions of Virginia* (Baltimore, 1886); Edward D. Neill, *Virginia Carolorum: The Colony Under the Rule of Charles First and Second, A.D. 1625–A.D. 1685* (Albany, N.Y., 1886); Neill, *The Earliest Contest in America on Charter Rights, Begun A.D. 1619, In Virginia Legislature: With Documents Now First Printed* (St. Paul, Minn., 1890); Frederick Johnston, *Memorials of Old Virginia Clerks, Arranged Alphabetically by Counties, with a Complete List of Place Names* (Lynchburg, Va., 1888); Alexander Brown, *The First Republic in American* (New York, 1898); Lyon G. Tyler, *The Cradle of the Republic: Jamestown and the James River* (New York, 1900); Herbert Levi Osgood, *The American Colonies in the Seventeenth Century* (New York, 1904–1907); Oliver P. Chitwood, *Justice in Colonial Virginia* (Baltimore, Md., 1905);

Bruce (1856–1933), a grandson of a Virginia Historical Society founder, read history at the University of Virginia before he gained an L.L.B. from Harvard University. Veering off from law and politics, he plotted a career in journalism, a course that eventually steered him toward scholarly pursuits. He landed positions as recording secretary and librarian at the Virginia Historical Society in 1892 and started the *Virginia Magazine of History and Biography* shortly thereafter. Generous samplings of the Old Dominion's legal records became that journal's staple fare, and so it remained long after he quit the society in 1896. Noteworthy in and of itself, that boon to scholarship pales in comparison to the one Bruce made with *The Institutional History of Virginia in the Seventeenth Century: An Inquiry into the Religious, Moral, Educational, Legal, Military, and Political Condition of the People Based on Original and Contemporary Records*, which appeared in 1910.[26]

The *Institutional History* was a massive work. As its title implies, the two-volume set presented an exquisitely detailed exposition of the structures that bounded seventeenth-century Virginians into society with one another. It immediately commanded an authority that few others could rival, grounded as it was on Bruce's exhaustive pioneering

---

Elmer I. Miller, *The Legislature of the Province of Virginia: Its Internal Development* (New York, 1907); Robert T. Barton, ed., *Virginia Colonial Decisions: The Reports by Sir John Randolph, and by Edward Barradall, of Decisions of the General Court of Virginia, 1714–1728* (Boston, Mass., 1909); Philip Alexander Bruce, *Institutional History of Virginia in the Seventeenth Century: An Inquiry into the Religious, Moral, Educational, Legal, Military, and Political Condition of the People Based on Original and Contemporary Records* (New York, 1910); Thomas Jefferson Wertenbaker, *Virginia Under the Stuarts, 1607–1688* (Princeton, N.J., 1914).
26. Darrett B. Rutman, "Philip Alexander Bruce: A Divided Mind of the South," *VMHB*, 68 (1960): 387–407; Hall, "The Virginia Historical Society," 67–68,72; L. Moody Simms, Jr., "Bruce, Philip Alexander," in Sara B. Bearss, John T. Kneebone, J. Jefferson Looney, Brent Tarter, and Sandra Gioia Treadway, eds., *Dictionary of Virginia Biography* (Richmond, Va., 2001), 2: 338–341.

research in local court records, which he employed as the stuff of his interpretations. Despite its length and comprehensive coverage, *The Institutional History* seemed quite accessible to readers in Bruce's day, and it proved to have great staying power deep into the twentieth century. No longer the must-read volume for Virginia legal scholars that it once was, it yet remains occasionally useful nonetheless.

As for Wertenbaker (1879–1966), he is noteworthy because he represented something that Bruce and his fellow gentlemen-scholars did not. A Charlottesvillian, he too worked in journalism until he answered a scholar's call, albeit in contrast to Bruce, he found his ultimate place in the academy. He gained a Ph.D. in history at the University of Virginia, where he was a student of Richard Heath Dabney. Thereafter he taught at Texas A&M and UVa before Woodrow Wilson lured him to Princeton, where he spent much of his career. Professionally trained, his appreciation of legal matters was of a different order than that of gentlemen-scholars. Not only that, he was also a harbinger of changes that altered the direction of Virginia legal historiography in ways that have yet to run their course.[27]

Wertenbaker concentrated on the Old Dominion in the seventeenth century, and he too carried out careful, orderly siftings of original manuscript collections. His first book, *Patrician and Plebian, Or the Origin and Development of the Social Classes of the Old Dominion* (Charlottesville, Va., 1910), while not specifically devoted to law, held signal implications for the future crafting of Virginia history, legal or otherwise. Its reliance upon class and conflicts between classes as analytical concepts marked a turn toward an interpretative mode that was soon engrafted into later writers' thinking. In a second

---

27. William H. Brackney, "Wertenbaker, Thomas Jefferson," http://www.anb.org/articles/14/14-00686.html, accessed 15 Dec. 2009; John C. Willis, "Dabney, Richard Heath," *DVB*, 3: 649-650.

book, *Virginia Under the Stuarts, 1607–1685* (Princeton, N.J., 1914), Wertenbaker covered much the same territory as Bruce had in *The Institutional History*, but his treatment differed from Bruce's in three pertinent respects. *Virginia Under the Stuarts* was shorter, and Wertenbaker based the research for it principally upon manuscript sources that he scoured in London at the Public Record Office (now the National Archives of the United Kingdom). This book extended his class analysis to early Virginia politics, and he argued that leaders like Governor-General Sir William Berkeley, together with their "venal" henchmen, designed an emerging legal order in ways that stifled opportunity for ordinary planters and oppressed them sorely. Such oppressions loosed struggles for democracy that led to rebellion in 1676 and foreshadowed revolution in 1776.[28]

Interest in Virginia legal history waned even as Bruce and Wertenbaker published their books. A reason for the decline was generational. Age and obsolescence had overtaken the gentlemen-scholars. One by one they passed away, and fewer of their kind stepped into their places because there were fewer of them. Their successors, not all Virginians, were academic scholars who were educated at graduate departments of history or university-affiliated law schools that were permanent fixtures on university campuses across the nation by the opening of the twentieth century.

The guild of academic historians owed its existence to teachers such as Richard Heath Dabney and Dabney's more celebrated contemporary, Herbert Baxter Adams. Adams taught at Johns Hopkins University, the first American

---

28. The preface to the 1957 edition of *Virginia Under the Stuarts* contains a charming tale about how Wertenbaker arranged his research trips to London in 1910, 1912, and 1914, and he retells his excitement at sifting through what were then seldom used documents and the joy of discovery.

institution of higher learning founded expressly to encourage advanced graduate education. Commencing in the 1880s, Adams hosted a seminar that quickly garnered renown as a hothouse for new modes of historical inquiry. He, like Dabney, stressed the utility of ordered historical knowledge. In the estimation of both men such wisdom could come only through the application of scientific methods to American historical questions, and in particular to an overarching type of institutional approach that they learned from their own doctoral training at the University of Heidelberg. Although they never saw themselves as professionals, their students—Wertenbaker, Richard Lee Morton, Charles M. Andrews, Charles H. Haskins, J. Franklin Jameson, Frederick Jackson Turner, and Woodrow Wilson, among the more noted—developed a keen sense of professionalism and a penchant for dismissing gentlemen-scholars who to their way of thinking merely played at the historian's craft. They would also distance themselves from academic legal scholars.[29]

Acute feelings of self-interest, noblesse oblige, and political activism impelled lawyers across the nation to start associations that pursued professional endeavors in the years that followed the Civil War. These statewide organizations joined forces with the American Bar Association, founded in

---

29. In addition to his teaching, Adams started the *Johns Hopkins Studies in History and Political Science* as an outlet that publicized his students' work, and he was a founder of the American Historical Association. See John Martin Vincent, "Herbert Baxter Adams," in Howard W. Odum, *American Masters of the Social Sciences* (New York, 1927); John Higham et al., *History: Humanistic Scholarship in America* (Englewood Cliffs, N.J., 1965), pp. 8–16; Laurence Veysey, "The Plural Organized Worlds of the Humanities," Alexandra Oleson and John Voss, eds., *The Organization of Knowledge in Modern America, 1860–1920* (Baltimore, 1979), p. 99; Raymond J. Cunningham, "The German Historical World of Herbert Baxter Adams: 1874–1876," *Journal of American History*, 68 (1981): 261–275; John Higham, "Herbert Baxter Adams and the Study of Local History, *American Historical Review*, 89 (1984): 1225–1239.

1878, openly to lobby legislatures, courts, and universities to realize a set of complementary goals. One prodded members to engage with the larger community so as to ameliorate the grosser features of national life and to better the public weal. Another encouraged a thorough rearrangement of the legal order into something intelligible, systematic, and certain, an end that demanded symmetry in local, state, and federal law, as well as political activism. Yet a third took aim at reforming the training of lawyers, and it was this latter goal that resulted in the improvements in legal education and the attachment of schools of law to universities. Faculty members in those schools were mostly attorneys. They came to regard legal history as the study of law's self-governing attributes, and they sought to elucidate its autonomous characteristics via a distinctive interpretation, now called "internal legal history." In a like mood, they insisted that their training uniquely qualified them to construe legal history to others, especially those they educated for careers at the bar, on the bench, or in the statehouse.[30]

So narrow a view of the past had less and less appeal to non-specialists as legal history grew into the highly technical field of research that it already was at the end of the 1800s. Thus academic historians increasingly went looking elsewhere well before *Virginia Under the Stuarts* came out. The effect of that shift insofar as its implications for doing Virginia legal history was consequential. Apart from documentary publication, additions to the literature fell to levels of

---

30. Alfred F. Konefsky, "The Legal Profession: From the Revolution to the Civil War," in Michael Grossberg and Christopher L. Tomlins, *The Cambridge History of Law in America* (Cambridge, 2008), 2: 68–106, 708–715; Robert W. Gordon, "The American Legal Profession, 1870–2000," ibid., 3: 73–127, 771–780; Gail J. Hupper, "The Rise of An Academic Doctorate in Law: Origins Through World War II,"*AJLH* 49 (2007): 1–61.

disinterest not seen before.³¹ New work, such as it was, came largely from the handicraft of university-based writers outside Virginia. Much of that production took form in masters' theses and doctoral dissertations, but little of it actually saw print because the authors abandoned their topics soon after they earned their degrees. And so the field languished until after World War II.³²

---

31. Lyon Gardiner Tyler initiated *Tyler's Historical Magazine and Genealogical Quarterly* in 1919, which churned out reams of legal records until it ceased publication in 1952. Henry Read McIlwaine, the Virginia state librarian from 1907 to 1934, continued publication of the colonial higher court records and legislative journals. See Oscar Handlin, et al., eds., *The Harvard Guide to American History*, 1ˢᵗ ed., (Cambridge, Mass., 1954), pp. 138–139 and Jon Kukla, "Preface to the Second Edition," in H.R. McIlwaine, ed., *The Executive Journals of the Council of Colonial Virginia* (Richmond, Va., 1979), pp. vii–xi. Susan Myra Kingsbury completed her edition of the Virginia Company records, Kingsbury, ed., *Records of the Virginia Company of London* (Washington, D.C., 1906–1935). Amidst the Second World War, Julian P. Boyd launched the Thomas Jefferson Papers project, an undertaking that turned documentary editing into a professional subspecies of history. Boyd pioneered techniques that are the foundations of modern documentary editing, which he set forth in the first volume of Julian P. Boyd et al., eds., *The Papers of Thomas Jefferson* (Princeton, N.J., 1950–).

32. Clarence W. Alvord, *Governor Edward Coles* (Springfield, Ill., 1920); Fairfax Harrison, *Virginia Land Grants: A Study in Colonial Conveyancing* (Richmond, Va., 1925); Cyrus H. Karraker, *The Seventeenth-Century Sheriff: A Comparative Study of the Sheriff in England and the Chesapeake Colonies, 1607–1689* (Chapel Hill, N.C., 1930); Leonidas Dodson, *Alexander Spotswood: Governor of Colonial Virginia, 1710–1722* (Chapel Hill, N.C., 1932); Henry H. Simms, *Life of John Taylor: The Story of a Brilliant Leader in the Early Virginia States Rights School* (Richmond, Va., 1932); Arthur P. Scott, *Criminal Justice in Colonial Virginia* (Chicago, Ill., 1930); June Purcell Guild, *Black Laws of Virginia: A Summary of Legislative Acts Concerning Negroes From the Earliest Times* (Richmond, Va., 1936); George Lewis Chumbley, *Justice in Virginia; The Development of a Judicial System, Typical Laws and Cases of the Period* (Richmond, Va., 1938). Other books devoted space to legal matters. See Susie M.

As the renaissance picked up in the postwar era, it drew inspiration from at least three sources. Spawned by the G.I. Bill of Rights and the federal investment in colleges and universities, a fleet but golden moment of higher learning opened hitherto unavailable opportunities to women and men who flocked to campuses across the nation, new and old, where faculties scurried to accommodate seemingly endless numbers of graduate degree candidates. Historians of all stripes set their discipline on new interpretative gimbals. No longer was history merely about American exceptionalism, politics, diplomacy, rational decision making, or about the comings and goings of great white men. Now it embraced oft-ignored subjects—material culture, women, Indians, African-Americans, ordinary citizens, race, class, gender—just to list the more recognizable ones. Tapping into those topics also led to sifting overlooked sources, which were best exploited by the employment of a host of social science methodologies.[33] These advances also enchanted certain law school professors who contended that legal history as they knew it stood in dire need of refreshing.[34] Richard B. Morris,

---

Ames, *Studies of the Virginia Eastern Shore in the Seventeenth Century* (Richmond, Va., 1940); Louis B. Wright, *The First Gentlemen of Virginia: Intellectual Qualities of the Early Colonial Ruling Class* (San Marino, Calif., 1940); Wesley Frank Craven, *The Southern Colonies in the Seventeenth Century, 1607–1689* (Baton Rouge, La., 1949); Duncan, comp., *Theses and Dissertations on Virginia History*, (Richmond, Va., 1986), 125–131.

33. Although its focus is on early American studies, Joyce Appleby, "A Different Kind of Independence: The Postwar Restructuring of the Historical Study of Early America," *WMQ*, 3d Ser., 50 (1993): 245-267 nicely captures at length the changes I outline here.

34. Daniel J. Boorstin, "Tradition and Method in Legal History," *Harvard Law Review*, 54 (1941): 424–436; George Lee Haskins, "Colonial Records and History," *WMQ*, 5 (1948): 547–52; Haskins, "Law and Colonial Society," *American Quarterly*, 9 (1957): 354–364; J.A.C. Grant, "What Areas of Exploration in Legal History Are Appropriate?" *American Journal of Legal History*, 3 (1959): 370–378; Paul L. Murphy, "Time to Reclaim: The Current Challenge of American

George Lee Haskins, Leonard Levy, Lawrence M. Friedman, and Harry N. Schieber were among the more prominent of these scholars, but as Schieber himself once observed, it was James Willard Hurst who "virtually [rewrote] the conceptual foundations of American legal history."[35]

Drawn to history while a student at Harvard Law School, Hurst (1910–1997) taught at the University of Wisconsin Law School for most of his career. He came to scorn internal legal history as remote, barren, much too formal, and so divorced from reality that it obscured the importance of what Hurst styled "the social functions of law." Unraveling those purposes required learning how lawmaking entities actually worked, and so he mined the widest possible array of legal

---

Constitutional History," *American Historical Review*, 69 (1963): 64–79; George Athan Billias, ed., *Law and Authority in Colonial America* (Barre, Mass., 1965); Stanley N. Katz, "Looking Backward: The Early History of American Law," *The University of Chicago Law Review*, 33 (Summer 1966): 867–884; Lawrence M. Friedman, "Heart Against Head: Perry Miller and the American Mind," *Yale Law Journal*, 77 (1968): 1244–1259; David H. Flaherty, ed., *Essays in the History of Early American Law* (Chapel Hill, N.C., 1969); Alden T. Vaughan and George Athan Billias, eds., *Perspectives on Early American History: Essays in Honor of Richard B. Morris* (New York, 1973); David J. Rothman, "The Promise of American Legal History," *Reviews in American History*, 2 (March 1974): 16–22; Warren M. Billings, "The Law in Colonial America: The Re-examination of Early American Legal History," *Michigan Law Review*, 51 (1983): 953–962.

35. Harry N. Schieber, "American Constitutional History and the New Legal History: Complementary Themes in Two Modes," *Journal of American History*, 68 (1981): 340; James Willard Hurst, *The Growth of American Law: The Law Makers* (Boston, Mass., 1950); Hurst, *Law and Economic Growth: The Legal History of the Lumber Industry in Wisconsin, 1836–1915* (Cambridge, Mass, 1964); Hurst, "Legal Elements in United States History," in Donald Fleming and Bernard Bailyn, eds., *Law in American History* (Cambridge, Mass, 1971), 3–95; Hurst, "Old and New Dimensions of Research in United States Legal History," *AJLH*, 23 (1979): 1–20. A complete bibliography of Hurst's writing can be found at http://law.wisc.edu/ils/works_by_hurst.htm.

sources. He drew freely from the methods of different fields of inquiry as he reached for analyses that revealed the cultural dimensions of law and how it shaped and was shaped in the real world. (Although Hurst never recurred to William Waller Hening, one can find faint intimations of the Virginian in Hurst's way of doing legal history nonetheless because his version bore similarity to Hening's.)[36] Without question Hurst had his greatest effect on law faculties but his ideas drifted into history graduate departments, which influenced some faculty and their students to look upon the law as an appropriate area of research once again, myself included.[37]

Documentary projects restarted or began from scratch.[38] The Library of Virginia, the University of Virginia Library, the Virginia Historical Society, and the Colonial Williamsburg Foundation founded the Virginia Colonial Records Projects, a microfilm archive that captured duplicates of lost documents

---

36. Hurst offered a succinct statement of his views in "The Law in United States History," *Proceedings of the American Philosophical Society*, 104 (1960): 521ff.

37. David H. Flaherty, "An Approach to American History: Willard Hurst as Legal Historian," ibid., 14 (1970): 222–234; Robert W. Gordon, "J. Willard Hurst and the Common Law Tradition in American Legal History," *Law and Society Review*, 10 (1975): 9–55; "Engaging Willard Hurst: A Symposium," *Law and History Review* 18 (2000); Shirley S. Abrahamson, et al., "Tributes to James Willard Hurst," *Wisconsin Law Review*, no 6. (Nov–Dec 1997): 1123–1210.

38. Here I have in mind such projects as William T. Hutchinson, William M. Rachal, et al., eds., *The Papers of James Madison* (Chicago, Ill., 1962–1977); Charlottesville, Va., 1977–); Herbert A. Johnson, Charles F. Hobson, et al., eds., *The Papers of John Marshall* (Chapel Hill, N.C., 1974–2006); William J. Van Schreeven, Robert L. Scribner, and Brent Tarter, eds., *Revolutionary Virginia, The Road to Independence: A Documentary History* (Charlottesville, Va., 1976–1983), as well as the Virginia Historical Society's now defunct *Documents Series*.

that rested in British and continental European repositories.[39] Changes in editorial policies at the *Virginia Magazine of History and Biography* and the *William and Mary Quarterly* transformed the two magazines into professional publications, and those alterations opened outlets for new, shorter scholarly works, as did the emergence of such serials as the *American Journal of Legal History* or *Law and History Review*. In the 1960s the pace of book publication also quickened, and the output has remained constant to this day.

Contemporary Virginia legal historians reflect characteristics similar to those of their colleagues across the South and the nation at large. Most have doctorates in history rather than law, but some sport both degrees. More reside in history departments or state agencies than in law schools, and they are likely neither Virginians nor residents of the commonwealth. Some belong to a gang of "usual suspects" who have long immersed themselves in Virginia's legal history. Others are ascending stars or newcomers. A number are not legal historians in any strict meaning of the term but they are attracted to legal subjects as a means of illuminating aspects of Virginia society that captivate them. Collectively, all validate an observation by Michael Grossberg and Christopher L. Tomlins, who edited the recent stylish *Cambridge History of Law in America*, that the broader field is now blessed with an exuberant vitality and an "astonishing variety." Grossberg and Tomlins attribute such liveliness to present-day practitioners who they say are deeply engaged "across the range of historical investigation in demonstrating the inextricable salience of law in human affairs."[40] The

---

39. For a brief description of the VCRP see John T. Kneebone, "The Virginia Colonial Records Project," American Historical Association *Perspectives* 30 (Dec. 1992): 15–20.
40. Michael Greenberg and Christopher L. Tomlins, ed., *The Cambridge History of Law in America* (Cambridge, 2008), 1: xiii.

authors of the books about seventeenth-century legal developments, which appeared during the run-up to the quadricentennial anniversary observances of the founding of Jamestown commemoration, or soon thereafter, exemplify those characteristics abundantly.[41]

Even so those volumes stand as reminders of just how much the writings of the past six decades have not strayed far beyond long-established investigatory boundaries. The period from the 1600s to the 1820s is still the most studied.[42]

---

41. The Federal Jamestown 400th Commemoration Commission sponsored a number of law-related conferences in 2007. (A list of those conferences is in Frank B. Atkinson and Warren M. Billings, eds., *Final Report of the Jamestown 400th Commemoration Commission* [Washington, D.C., 2009], Appendix 14.) Selected presentations from the conferences will appear in Frank B. Atkinson and Warren M. Billings, eds., *The Jamestown Commentaries*, which will be published in the near future by the University of Virginia Press. Among the more significant books published between 1990 and 2008 were James R. Perry, *The Formation of a Society on Virginia's Eastern Shore, 1615–1655* (Chapel Hill, N.C., 1991); James Horn, *Adapting to a New World: English Society in the Seventeenth-Century Chesapeake* (Chapel Hill, N.C., 1995); John Ruston Pagan, *Anne Orthwood's Bastard: Sex and Law in Early Virginia* (Oxford, 2002); Terri L. Snyder, *Brabbling Women: Disorderly Speech and the Law in Early Virginia* (Ithaca, N.Y., 2003); Warren M. Billings, *A Little Parliament: The Virginia General Assembly in the Seventeenth Century* (Richmond, Va., 2004); and William E. Nelson, *The Common Law in Colonial America, Volume 1: The Chesapeake and New England, 1607–1660* (Oxford, 2008).

42. See, for example, Robert Kenneth Faulkner, *The Jurisprudence of John Marshall* (Princeton, N.J., 1969); Richard E. Ellis, *The Jeffersonian Crisis: Courts and Politics in the Young Republic* (New York, 1971); W. Hamilton Bryson, *The Virginia Law Reporters Before 1880* (Charlottesville, Va., 1977); Herbert A. Johnson, *Imported Eighteenth-Century Law Treatises in American Libraries* (Knoxville, Tenn., 1978); Edward Dumbauld, *Thomas Jefferson and the Law* (Norman, Okla., 1978); Raymond C. Bailey, *Popular Influence upon Public Policy: Petitioning in Eighteenth-Century Virginia* (Westport, Conn., 1979); W. Hamilton Bryson, *A Census of Virginia Law Books in Colonial Virginia* (Charlottesville, Va., 1979); Bryson, *A Bibliography of Virginia Legal History Before 1900* (Charlottesville, Va.,

Treatments of time between the 1820s and the 1950s are few and far between, which confines developments in those years to largely unknown regions.[43] Conversely, the civil rights era seems to be a most promising area of growth.[44]

1979); A.G. Roeber, *Faithful Magistrates and Republican Lawyers: Creators of Virginia Legal Culture, 1680–1810* (Chapel Hill, N.C., 1981); Frank Dewey, *Thomas Jefferson: Lawyer* (Charlottesville, Va., 1986); Philip J. Schwarz, *Twice Condemned: Slaves and the Criminal Laws of Virginia, 1705–1865* (Ithaca, N.Y., 1988); Thornton J. Miller, *Juries and Judges Versus the Law: Virginia's Provincial Legal Practice, 1783–1828* (Charlottesville, Va., 1994); Thomas D. Morris, *Southern Slavery and the Law, 1619–1865* (Chapel Hill, N.C., 1996); Charles F. Hobson, *The Great Chief Justice John Marshall and the Rule of Law* (Lawrence, Kans., 1996); Philip J. Schwarz, *Slave Laws in Virginia* (Athens, Ga., 1996); Herbert A. Johnson, *The Chief Justiceship of John Marshall, 1804–1835* (Columbia, S.C., 1997); David Robarge, *A Chief Justice's Progress: John Marshall from Revolutionary Virginia to the Supreme Court* (Westport, Conn., 2000); R. Kent Newmyer, *John Marshall and the Heroic Age of the Supreme Court* (Baton Rouge, La., 2001); Linda L. Sturtz, *Within Her Power: Propertied Women in Colonial Virginia* (New York, 2002); Cliff Sloan and David McKean, *The Great Decisions: Jefferson, Adams, Marshall and the Battle for the Supreme Court* (New York, 2009).

43. See, for example, John Ritchie, *The First Hundred Years: A Short History of the School of Law of the University of Virginia for the Period 1826–1926* (Charlottesville, Va., 1978); W. Hamilton Bryson, *Legal Education in Virginia, 1779–1979: A Biographical Approach* (Charlottesville, 1982); Robert J. Brugger, *Beverley Tucker: Heart over Head in the Old South* (Baltimore, Md., 1979); Dickson D. Bruce, Jr., *The Rhetoric of Conservatism: The Virginia Convention of 1829–30* (San Marino, Calif., 1982); Anne Hobson Freeman, *The Style of a Law Firm: Eight Gentlemen from Virginia* (Chapel Hill, N.C., 1989); Robert P. Sutton, *Revolution to Secession: Constitution Making in the Old Dominion* (Charlottesville, Va., 1989).Thomas E. Buckley, S.J., *The Great Catastrophe of My Life: Divorce in the Old Dominion* (Chapel Hill, N.C., 2002).

44. See, for example, Donald G. Neiman, *To Set the Law in Motion: The Freedman's Bureau and the Legal Rights of Blacks* (Millwood, N.Y., 1979); Ronald J. Bacicagal, *May It Please the Court: A Biography of Judge Robert Merhige* (Lanham, Md., 1992); John C. Jeffries, *Justice Lewis F. Powell, Jr.* (New York, 1994); Phyl Newbeck, *Virginia Hasn't Always Been for Lovers: Interracial Bans and the Case of Richard and Mildred Loving*

Here then is the present state and condition of the writings about Virginia law and culture. If nothing else, this survey points to two plain, palpable conclusions. Anyone so minded can now learn more about the Old Dominion's legal order than at any time in the last two hundred years. Yet, despite all that is known, much remains to be known. So, what are the needs and opportunities for further research? Ways of answering the question are manifold, but rather than frame a laundry list that runs to the last jot and tittle of needs, let me suggest the following possibilities by way of example.

Someone ought to propose ways of dividing Virginia's long legal history into manageable temporal units. The gentlemen-scholars casually marked an imaginary line between what they took to be Virginia's formative era and their own times. Their border sufficed because they diligently attended to the one and completely ignored the other. That boundary was useless once their successors looked beyond the seventeenth and eighteenth centuries. Hence, the reason to recalibrate the dividing lines more precisely. The art lies in breaking the whole period from 1606 to the present into time sequences that are consistent with the play of legal events over the course of four hundred years. One possibility is a tripartite division. The first would start in 1606 and run to the early 1800s, the second would extend from that nineteenth-century terminal point to the 1950s, whereas the third would embrace the 1950s to the present. Another scheme might be a permutation of one Brent Tarter devised for "The New Virginia Bookshelf." Yet a third could blend the topical with

---

(Carbondale, Ill., 2004); Peter Wallenstein, *Blue Laws and Black Codes: Conflicts, Courts, and Change in Twentieth-Century Virginia* (Charlottesville, Va., 2004); Paul A. Lombardo, *Three Generations, No Imbeciles: Eugenics, the Supreme Court and Buck v. Bell* (Baltimore, Md., 2008); James R. Sweeney, ed., *Race, Reason, and Massive Resistance: The Diary of David J. Mays, 1954–1959* (Athens, Ga., 2008); Pippa Holloway, *Sexuality, Politics and Social Control in Virginia, 1920–1945* (Chapel Hill, N.C., 2006).

the temporal. No matter the option, any serviceable method of periodization should be consistent with the reality that legal changes moved in their own way and at their own pace. (Marking a line at, say, the Revolution would not be especially helpful. The political breech with England preceded legal independence by as much as two generations, meaning that the appropriate demarcation ought to be struck at a spot at least fifty years later than 1776.)[45]

The need for better timelines is a reminder of another need. The greatest opportunities for engaging, fruitful original research lie in scouring the records of the nineteenth-, twentieth-, and twenty-first centuries. For starters, one might begin with a series of questions about public men and women. Who were they? Were they exemplars of what William Waller Hening called "the best talents" that the Old Dominion could offer? What were their backgrounds? What was the extent of their legal sophistication? How did that knowledge inform their actions in constitutional conventions, the General Assembly, the courts, and other entities? What about Virginians who played parts as voters, suitors, offenders, witnesses, petty officials, or jurors? And what of ordinary folk who, despite being put upon by their powerful "betters," went to law to again and again to claim the free exercise of their rights which that very law so often denied them?[46]

Whenever possible, full-dress biographies of these Virginians await their authors. There is ample room too for more compact treatments, as in biographical dictionaries or in instances where the evidence is far too limited to sustain full-scale portrayals.[47] No matter the scope of the undertaking a

---

45. Tarter, "The New Virginia Bookshelf," *passim.*
46. Hening, ed., *The Statutes at Large,* 1: xii.
47. For example, Cynthia Miller Leonard, comp., *The General Assembly of Virginia, July 30, 1619–January 11, 1978: A Bicentennial Register of*

caveat bears mentioning. As a rule legal biographers typically find inspiration in a venerable proposition: lessons of history and law arise from the contemplation of exceptional legal lives. For that reason their choice of subjects tends mainly towards jurists. So tight a focus has not wanted detractors, however, and their criticisms are a caution of the need for broader approaches to future assessments of Virginia legal lives.[48]

Attention to the character of legal education and the transition of legal practice from a genteel calling to a professional vocation can fill in some blank spaces. The scholarship of W. Hamilton Bryson, E. Lee Shepherd, and others is a convenient starting place. It identifies opportunities for lengthier investigations into such variables as law faculties, curricula, and student bodies and whether

---

Members (Richmond, Va., 1978) and Elizabeth R. Herberner and Jon Kukla, comps., *The General Assembly of Virginia, 11 January 1978–27 April 1989: A Register of Members* (Richmond, Va., 1990). The latter also contains short biographies of members who sat between 1978 and 1989. An accurate roll of colonial governors-general and state governors to the year 1994 is in Emily J. Salmon and Edward D.C. Campbell, eds., *A Hornbook of Virginia History*, 4th ed. (Richmond, 1994), pp. 101–113. *The Dictionary of Virginia Biography* is an undertaking of the Library of Virginia that was conceived in the mid-1980s and now runs to three printed volumes. The in-house staff prepared many of the entries, although the editors frequently invited outside, singularly knowledgeable scholars to contribute. A classified index to the published volumes is available at http://www.lva.virginia.org/public/dvb/classified-index.asp. Then there is the *Encyclopedia Virginia*, which is a project of the Virginia Foundation for the Humanities and Public Policy. An on line publication, it has broader scope than the *DVB*, but its newness limits its coverage at present. Its contributors are all outsiders who are recruited by the various section editors. It can be visited at http://www.encyclopediavirginia.org.

48. Warren M. Billings, "Judges' Lives: Judicial Biography in America, 1607-1995," in Coggins, ed., *The National Conference on Legal Information Issues*, pp. 192–205.

alterations to them over time reflected prevailing conditions nationally, or not. A pertinent question in this regard is the effect of the influx of women and African Americans into faculties and student populations that in turn raises a broader interplay between the legal order and issues of the holy trinity of race, class, and gender.[49]

Something else to consider is the pattern of how the state's law schools grew. As everyone knows, the first law school anywhere in the United States opened in 1779 at the College of William and Mary, followed in order by the University of Virginia (1825), Washington and Lee University (1849), and the University of Richmond (1870). A few proprietary law schools flowered before the Civil War and again in the early 1900s, only to wither away almost as swiftly as they blossomed. The Great Depression killed an attempt at Virginia Union University to found a place for African Virginians to become lawyers without having to leave the state. Those failures meant that four universities were the chief providers of formal legal education until deep into the

---

49. W. Hamilton Bryson, *Legal Education in Virginia, 1779–1979*, pp. 1–67. (Bryson recruited a variety of scholars to profile the law professors he included in the volume. He and Shepherd also wrote many of sketches too.) See also Shepherd, "Lawyers Look at Themselves: Professional Consciousness and the Virginia Bar, 1790–1850," *AJLH*, 25 (1981): 1–23; Shepherd, "Breaking into the Profession: Establishing a Law Practice in Antebellum Virginia," *JSH*, 48 (1982): 393–410; Bryson, *Essays on Legal Education in Nineteenth-Century Virginia* (Buffalo, N.Y., 1998); Bryson, "Legal Education" in Bryson, ed., *Virginia Law Books: Essays and Bibliographies* (Philadelphia, Pa., 2000), pp. 316–397; Craig Evan Klafter, "The Influence of Vocational Law Schools on the Origins of American Legal Thought," *AJLH*, 37 (1993): 307–331; Davison M. Douglas, "The Jefferson Vision of Legal Education," *Journal of Legal Education*, 51 (2001): 185–212.

last century.[50] Then in the span of just sixteen years the number doubled, dramatically some might say. A new law school opened its doors at George Mason University in 1979. Next came one at Regent University (1986), another at the Appalachian School of Law (1994), and the most recent one started at Liberty University in 2004. Did the founding of these schools track demand, or were other reasons in play? What significance attaches to the fact that Regent and Liberty have tight bonds with the Christian Right? Does their location in Virginia mean anything culturally or legally? If so, what? As for Appalachian what circumstances were afoot that led to its establishment as private, freestanding non-profit academic institution?[51]

Regarding the practice of law itself, perhaps someone might look at how workaday attorneys responded to changing demands on lawyering. The law's increase in scale inevitably compelled alterations in the very nature of practice, as did its ever-rising complexity. Complexity begot specialization, and specialization spawned corporate-sized law firms. Did locating the big outfits in the cities siphon away talented practitioners from rural areas, or did large firms recruit out of state? How did urban and/or suburban growth upset the lawyer-client-county courthouse nexus that long characterized practice? And to what extent did barristers involve themselves in professional development and improving legal education? These types of questions inevitably lead to enquiries about the role of local and state bar associations.[52]

---

50. Bryson, "Legal Education," pp. 342–354, 355–357, 357–359, 365–366; Bryson and Shepherd, "The Winchester Law School, 1824–1831," *Law and History Review*, 21 (2003): 393–409.
51. Mark F. Grady, "Two Visionary Law Deans of George Mason University," *University of Toledo Law Review*, 33 (2001–2002): 59–67.
52. E. Lee Shepherd, "'The Ease and the Convenience of the People': Court House Locations in Spotsylvania County, 1720–1840," *VMHB*, 87 (1979): 279–299.

A greater awareness of the law books that practitioners, jurists, teachers, and pupils read in the 1800 and 1900s would be worthwhile. Figuring out those habits could proceed outward from existing studies of seventeenth- and eighteenth-century tastes in legal literature. The insights of book historians, who unraveled the culture of reading and book ownership, would be helpful to any demonstration of which law books actually shaped Virginia's legal architecture. Necessarily, a grasp of tastes and influences requires identifying the books in circulation and their owners, which opens additional lines of exploration.[53] Records of book ownership, for example, document the contents of private collections. Knowing who owned what allows for estimations of such things as the variety of books in circulation and the proportion of English authors to foreign, American, or Virginia writers. There are clues to printeries, to sales figures, and the law book trades. In the context of antebellum times, that information would helpful for pinpointing when Virginia law passed from a derivative of its British antecedents to a law unto itself. Especially telling too would be detailing the effect of the digital revolution on modern law libraries.[54]

Moving in another direction, new renderings about the working of the courts and the General Assembly are needed. They ought mainly to focus on changes that have happened since the early 1800s. Local and municipal governments are there for probing too. So too the state boards and commissions, which exercise considerable executive, legislative, and judicial power. Two in particular, the Board of Public Works and the State Corporation Commission, warrant special notice. Created by statute in 1816, the Board of Public

---

53. David D. Hall, "The Chesapeake in the Seventeenth Century," Hugh Amory and David D. Hall, eds., *A History of the Book in America*, (Cambridge, 1999), cha. 2; Essay 4 above.
54. Bryson, ed., *Virginia Law Books*, pp. 220–316, 387–479, 500–519.

Works was the first of its kind in the nation. An arm of state government, the board administered a private-public development fund that it doled out to local citizens who built roads, canals, and railways before the Civil War. This so-called Virginia system of mixed enterprise was but a refined variation on a relationship that existed between the state and entrepreneurs as far back as the seventeenth century. Although justified as a bulwark against radical reform and socialism, the State Corporation Commission was a harbinger of the administrative state. It took life in the Constitution of 1902, and its primary purpose was rationalizing non-partisan regulation of utilities, common carriers and limited liability companies. Success bred its reputation as an inventive way around the complications of corporate expansion, and to this day the commission stands as a potent independent mechanism of governance. The richness of their archives is the thing that makes these boards especially compelling objects to investigate enduring linkages between law and private enterprise.[55]

As a phenomenon of legal history, examining state constitutions anywhere in the Union has lured few takers, and

---

55. Billings, *Sir William Berkeley and the Forging of Colonial Virginia*, pp. 174–210; Brent Tarter, "Constitutions Construed: Outline for a Constitutional History of Virginia," (unpublished paper, Dec. 2009) pp. 65–67; Carter Goodrich, "The Virginia System of Mixed Enterprise," *Political Science Quarterly*, 64 (1949): 355–387; Allen Caperton Braxton, "The Virginia State Corporation Commission," *Virginia Law Register*, 10 (1904): 1–18; Thomas Edwin Gray Jr., "Creating the Virginia State Corporation Commission," *VMHB*, 78 (1970): 464–480; George Harrison Gilliam, "Making Virginia Progressive: Courts and Parties, Railroads and Regulators, 1890–1910," *VMHB*, 107 (1999): 189–222. The archives of both commissions rest at the Library of Virginia. A description of the library's holdings for the Board of Public Works is Marianne M. McKee, comp., "The Internal Improvement Movement in Virginia: Early Canals, River Navigations, Roads, Turnpikes, Bridges, and Railroads, Records and Resources at the Library of Virginia," http//www.lva.virginia.gov/public/guides/inter_improvements.pdf.

it would also be educational to learn more about how they were made in Virginia.[56] Virginians drew up their first written constitution in 1776, they enacted their most recent one in 1971, and they adopted six more in between. Taken together, the eight charters offer an important guide to how the weight of experience and years led to periodic restatements of fundamental law in settings both unique to Virginia and common to other states, so each characterized the Old Dominion at an exact moment. Who wrote them? What did they say? Why were seven cast aside? Why was each longer than its predecessor? Did increased length reflect a nation-wide trend toward a kind of anti-law that curbed state legislatures? Who favored constitutional revision? Who opposed it? Is greater weight to be ascribed to one constitution above another? If so, which one, and why? Were they models for fundamental charters in other parts of the country?[57]

As yet unpublished papers by Sara B. Bearss, John E. Stealey, III, and Brent Tarter offer some preliminary answers. Bearss looked at the Constitution of 1864. In her estimation, its unionist authors achieved reforms the conventions of 1829–1830 and 1850–1851 could not, they abolished slavery, and they closed sectional rifts by recognizing the state of West Virginia. The document lived a short life and dropped from memory after Reconstruction, all but disappearing

---

56. Warren M. Billings, "Introduction," in Warren M. Billings and Edward F. Haas, eds., *In Search of Fundamental Law: Louisiana's Constitutions, 1812–1974* (Lafayette, La., 1993), pp. 1–2.
57. A.E. Dick Howard, "'For the Common Benefit': Constitutional History in Virginia as a Casebook for the Modern Constitution-Maker," *Virginia Law Review* 54 (1968): 816–902; Howard, *Commentaries on the Constitution of Virginia* (Charlottesville, Va., 1974); John Dinan, *The Virginia State Constitution, A Reference Guide* (Westport, Conn., 2006), pp. 1–32; Judith Kelleher Schafer, "Reform or Experiment? The Louisiana Constitution of 1845," in Billings and Haas, eds., *In Search of Fundamental Law*, pp. 21–22.

before Bearss resurrected it.[58] Stealey argued that the failure to cut constitutionalism to suit western Virginians in 1830 and 1851 contributed greatly to the creation of West Virginia, a thing that he maintains might never have occurred but for the intransigence of eastern delegates at both constitutional conventions.[59] Tarter viewed all eight charters with the intent of outlining the entire constitutional history of the state.[60] Both methods of analysis have their uses. Bearss and Stealey demonstrated the results from closely scrutinizing a single constitution. Tarter's search for predominate themes is indicative of what a fully featured, overarching constitutional history might resemble.

The Declaration of Rights also merits greater attention in its own right. A ringing, soaring brief for the ideals of equality and liberty, the Declaration was the first of its kind in America, and the model for the Bill of Rights. Nevertheless, its authors chose not to combine it with the Constitution of 1776, which they wrote too. The convention of 1829–1830

---

58. Sara B. Bearss, "Restored and Vindicated: The Virginia Constitutional Convention of 1864" (delivered at the Fourth Virginia Forum, Longwood University, April 2009). The document resembled the Louisiana constitution of 1864, which unionists crafted in rather remarkably comparable circumstances and was also quickly forgotten when it was replaced. See Kathryn Page, "'A First-Born child of Liberty: The Constitution of 1864," in Billings and Haas, eds., *In Search of Fundamental Law*, pp. 52–69.
59. John E. Stealey, III, "Western Virginia's Constitutional Critique in 1861; Reflections of Antebellum Virginia's Undemocratic Reality" (delivered at the Fourth Virginia Forum, Longwood University, April 2009).
60. Brent Tarter, "Constitutions Construed: Outline for a Constitutional History of Virginia" (unpublished paper, Dec. 2009); Tarter also presented a portion of that paper as "Constitutions Construed: Or Politics and Law in Early Virginia" to the Fifth Virginia Forum, which met at Christopher Newport University in April 2010. I am indebted to all three authors for sharing their papers with me. Because those papers represent work in progress I deliberately refrained from more than the briefest summary of each.

enshrined it as article 1 of the second constitution, and it has retained that place ever since. Curiously, however, later conventions, the state courts, and the General Assembly rarely saw fit to translate stirring words on paper into actual practice. If anything, all three merely honored the Declaration in the breach. Was that because, as Tarter argues, the precepts of the Declaration ran contrary to anti-democratic tendencies that he regards as having defined politics from colonial times to the present? Or are there alternative interpretations? Either way, the possibilities for further inquiry are apparent, and an anthology similar to Jon Kukla's *The Bill of Rights: A Lively Heritage* (Richmond, Va., 1987) might be a practical medium for hashing out differing explanations.[61]

Acts of the General Assembly deserve greater notice too. They contain a nearly unbroken record of Virginia's passage from a colony bounded by few rules to a modern state bordered by all-encompassing laws. Their words bespeak the good, the bad, and the ugly applications of legislative power to regulate the common weal. Their corpus is massive. (By itself Hening's compilation of the laws from 1619 to 1792 barely occupies a library shelf, whereas the assemblage of printed statutes passed between 1792 and the latest assembly session fills an entire section of library stacks.) Tackling them in one fell swoop is obviously too unruly and too unlikely to yield meaningful results, which makes topical approaches to any number of specific areas of regulation the more realistic alternative. Finally, for those who fancy renderings on a

---

61. Tarter, "Constitutions Construed," pp. 10–13, 24. See also Warren M. Billings, "'THAT ALL MEN ARE BORN EQUALLY FREE AND INDEPENDENT' Virginians and the Origins of the Bill of Rights," in John P. Kaminski and Patrick T. Conley, eds., *The States and the Bill of Rights, 1607–1791* (Madison, Wis., 1991), pp. 335–370; Brent Tarter, "The Virginia Declaration of Rights," in Josephine F. Pacheco, ed., *To Secure the Blessings of Liberty: Rights in American History* (Fairfax, Va., 1993), pp. 37–54.

grander scale, opportunities to craft master narratives or overarching analyses from scratch are there for the taking. Virginia's legal order has always differed from those of other southern states, and its disparities raise profound questions about definitions of southern-ness. How distinctive a part of the South was/is the Old Dominion? How Virginian was/is the South? How much was/is Virginia kin to other American regions? To what degree did/do Virginians regard themselves as Southerners? Is there value in looking beyond the region and seeing the centrality of law to Virginia history as a means of comprehending American history generally?

Admittedly, all of the foregoing suggestions mirror my own interests, which make them merely illustrative. Nevertheless, they are reminders of the need for basic research in primary documents of many sorts, and this is where the impact of Cyberspace upon the ways of doing the commonwealth's legal history comes into play. Until fairly recently, exploring any topic presupposed reliance upon the physical materials themselves. Now there is an alternate universe of virtual reality. An area in that world embraces huge, but always growing, digitized chunks of the corporal record which live at addresses such as JSTOR, Westlaw, Lexis, HeinOnline, Early English Books on Line, Google Books, the American Memory Project, and elsewhere. Then there is a class of virtual documents that are born, reared, and sometimes allowed to die digitally. Until someone calls them up on a computer screen, digital documents exist only as bits and bytes on institutional servers, which are maintained at considerable public or private expense. Their range is as ubiquitous as it is vast, running as it does from court records to tweets. And they bid fair to replace all other species of future legal records.

Presumably, anyone can tap this limitless, ever-expanding storehouse of virtual information without leaving one's study. Ostensibly, the price of entry requires no more than a personal computer, a broadband Internet connection, and a password, but to quote A.S. Gilbert and Arthur Sullivan's *HMS Pinafore* character Little Buttercup:

> Things are seldom what they seem,
> Skim milk masquerades as cream;
> Highlows pass as patent leathers;
> Jackdaws strut in peacock's feathers.[62]

In other words, access is rather more complicated than searching a library's directory of databases before going on line, typing in a desired URL and hitting the return key. Usually, there are subscriptions that involve the payment of site license fees to the database owners. Site licenses are not cheap, though they cost qualified users nothing because repositories pick them up. Generally, someone without a formal connection to a licensee is excluded, however, since private subscriptions are frequently unavailable or prohibitively expensive. Here is a digital cleft between the haves and the have-nots that will surely widen. In times of severe fiscal constraints, few institutions can afford to sign up for every new database that comes along. They struggle to keep pace with rising costs, whether the expenditures go to maintaining subscriptions or to digitizing their own collections. Primary documents born digitally create problems of sustainable preservation even as they raise exquisitely vexing issues about access, authentication, citation, privacy, and security.

The spread of electronic publications as alternatives to printed books and articles engendered another class of digital documents whose existence causes comparable concerns, but

---

62. Little Buttercup sings this in her duet with the Captain in Act II of W.S. Gilbert and Arthur Sullivan, *HMS Pinafore*. The quotation comes from the text of the libretto that is available at http://math.boisestate.edu/gas/pinafore/.html/index.html. Accessed 1 June 2010.

this is not the venue for airing them, except to say that the last word on the impact of new media upon the traditional outlets for publication is far from being written. Meanwhile, Virginia will continue to tempt its share of legal historians.[63]

---

63. These issues are discussed at length in the following places Patrick E. Kehoe, Lovisa Lyman, and Gary Lee McCann, eds., *Law Librarianship: A Handbook for the Electronic Age* (Littleton, Col., 1995); Timothy L. Coggins, ed., *The National Conference on Legal Information Issues: Selected Essays* (Littleton, Col., 1996); *The State of American Libraries: A Report of the American Library Association* (annual report, April 2010), available as a PDF file at http://www.ala.org; *Sustainable Economics for a Digital Planet: Ensuring Long-Term Access to Digital Information* (Final Report of the Blue Ribbon Task Force on Sustainable Digital Preservation and Access, Feb. 2010), available as a PDF file at http://brtf.sdsc.edu; and the Legal Information Preservation Alliance web site http://www.aallnet.org/lipa/.

Index

Adams, Herbert Baxter, 431–432
Allen, O.K., 305, 328, 375, 388, 396
Anderson, Thomas, 278, 279
Andrews, Charles M., 432
Andros, Sir Edmund, 196
Argall, Samuel, 101
Armiger, William, 114

Bacon, Sir Francis, 78–79, 289, 292
Bacon, Matthew, 292
Bacon, Nathaniel, 113, 147–148, 161, 168
Bailyn, Bernard, 21
Baldwin, Simeon E., 321
Bancroft, George, 426
Beale, Joseph Henry, 291
Bearss, Sara B., 448–449
Beauregard, P.G.T., 363
Beccaria, Cesare, 269
Beckley, John, 271
Bell, U.A., 386, 395
Benjamin, Judah P., 319
Bennett, Richard, 109, 135, 136, 137, 138–139, 162
Bentham, Jeremy, 269, 352
Berkeley, Charles, 1st viscount Fitzhardinge of Berehaven, 121, 125, 145
Berkeley, Dame Elizabeth Killigrew, 120
Berkeley, Dame Frances Culpeper Stephens, 118, 146, 150
Berkeley, Henry, 121
Berkeley, Jane, 121
Berkeley, John, 1st baron Berkeley of Stratton, 121, 122, 125, 145
Berkeley, Margaret, 121
Berkeley, Maurice (d.1627), 121, 124
Berkeley, Sir Maurice, 121
Berkeley, Sir William, 43, 59, 66–67, 106–113, 117–152, 155–156, 159, 161, 162, 168, 170, 171–172, 411, 416, 431
Berry, Sir John, 149–150
Beverley, Robert, 144
Blackstone, Sir William, 189, 264, 286–287, 292, 345, 358
Blaney, Edward, 103
Bolton, J.W., 385
Bonaparte, Napoleon, 270, 337
Borron, P.G., 386
Bouvier, John, 16, 288
Bradford, James M., 278, 279
Britton, 292
Brooke, Sir Robert, 80
Brown, James, 237, 344, 345
Brown, John, 363
Bruce, Philip Alexander, 428, 429, 430, 431
Brunot, Harney F., 374, 375, 391, 392, 395, 397
Bryson, W. Hamilton, 239, 443
Bullard, Henry Adams, 248, 250, 253, 359–360, 361
Bulstrode, Edward, 83
Byrd, Harry F., 399, 400–401, 402, 405, 410–413, 414, 415, 416

455

Calvert, Cecilius, 2d baron Baltimore, 143
Canon, E.A., 250, 252
Carroll, Joseph W., 386
Cary, Lucius, 2d viscount Falkland, 123
Cary, Tom, slave, 196–197
Cassimere, Raphael, Jr., 371
Charles I, King, 65, 103, 107, 109, 123, 124, 125, 126, 129–130, 134, 159, 204
Charles II, King, 134, 135, 136, 138, 140, 141, 142, 145, 150, 155, 168
Chew, John, 102
Christian, Edmund, 292
Claiborne, William, 102, 130, 132, 135, 136, 137, 139
Claiborne, William C.C., 263, 271–277, 289, 290, 338–344, 347
Coke, Sir Edward, 55, 78, 83, 84, 179, 204–205, 264, 282, 286, 292, 344
Conway, E.A., 379, 381, 388, 389
Coopy, Robert, 180
Coventry, Henry, 150
Cowell, John, 81, 82, 205, 206, 207
Craven, Wesley Frank, 29
Croke, Sir George, 83
Cromwell, Oliver, 134, 138
Cromwell, Richard, 138
Culpeper, Thomas, 2d baron Culpeper of Thoresway, 114, 155, 162, 195
Curtis, Edmund, 135, 136

Dabney, Richard Heath, 430, 431–432

Dale, Sir Thomas, 64, 99, 100
Dalton, Michael, 12, 15, 87, 88, 89, 192, 205, 207
Dart, Henry Plauché, 240, 322, 323, 324–325, 366–369
De Bellevue, L.B., 385
Dennis, Robert, 135
Derbigny, Pierre, 341, 353
Devereaux, Robert, 2[d] earl of Essex, 121
Digges, Edward, 32, 109, 137, 139, 162
Dixon, John A., Jr., 295
Domat, Jean, 345, 353, 358
Downing, Mary Clark Roane, 11
Dugas, Kathy, 246
Duncan, Abner L., 356
Dunn, Richard S., 190
Dyer, James, 83

Eden, William, 1st baron Auckland, 269
Edward, Prince, 85
Edwards, T. Arthur, 380–382, 384, 385
Elay, Lancelott, 108
Ellery, Abraham L., 356
Elmore, William A., 251–255, 258
Elsynge, Henry, 165
Elyot, Sir Thomas, 163
Emmanuel, slave, 194
Evans, Emory G., 3, 4

Farrar, Edgar, 326
Fenner, Charles Payne, 368–369
Fernandez, Mark F., 153
Fernando, slave, 173, 193
Finch, Henry (Sir Heneage), 84, 289, 292
Fitzherbert, Sir Anthony, 80

INDEX 457

Fitzhugh, William, 83–84
Flaherty, David H., 72
Fleta, 289, 292
Flood, Hal, 410, 412
Fortescue, Sir John, 55, 84, 85
Fournet, John B., 309–312, 328, 371, 374, 385, 386, 387–388, 398
Frankfurter, Felix, 202, 203
Friedman, Lawrence M., 436
Fromentin, Elegius, 341
Frugé, J. Cleveland, 243, 378, 385, 398
Fulbeck, William, 84

Gates, Sir Thomas, 99, 100
Gawler, Henry, 114
Gayarré, Charles E.A., 366
Gayle, E.F., 377
Gilbert, A.S., 452
Gilbert, Sir Geoffrey, 292
Gleason, Walter, 376
Gregory, George C., 98
Grossberg, Michael, 438
Grymes, John Randolph, 319
Gutierrez, Joseph A., 153, 154
Guyol, Theodore, 255

Haas, Edward F., 225, 400
Hair, William Ivy, 400
Hale, Sir Matthew, 286, 287–288, 292
Haley, Alex, 229
Hall, Dominick, 298, 300, 301
Hall, Luther E., 376, 386
Hall, Pike, Sr., 307, 330
Hamor, Ralph, 99–100, 102
Hardin, C.F., 385, 386
Hartley, Leslie P., 16
Hartlib, Samuel, 137
Hartwell, Henry, 114

Harvey, Sir John, 31, 65, 102, 103–105, 127, 130, 162
Haskins, Charles H., 432
Haskins, George Lee, 436
Hawkins, William, 293
Hayes, Robert, 211
Heineman, Ronald L., 400
Hening, William Waller, 58, 289, 293, 422–425, 437, 442, 450
Hennen, Alfred, 319
Henrietta Maria, Queen, 123
Henry VIII, King, 197
Henry, Patrick, 421
Higgins, Archibald T., 376–377, 382, 386, 387, 391, 392, 395, 398
Higginson, Humphrey, 190–191
Hoffman, David, 358
Howard, Francis, 5th baron Howard of Effingham, 114, 155, 162, 170
Howe, William Wirt, 322
Howell, Thomas Bayly, 293
Hunt, Thomas, 110
Hurst, James Willard, 436–437
Hutson, James H., 5
Hyde, Edward, 1st earl of Clarendon, 121, 124, 145

Ingle, Edward, 428

Jacob, Giles, 288, 293
Jameson, J. Franklin, 432
Jeansonne, Glen, 400
Jefferson, Thomas, 269, 270, 271, 289, 336, 337, 338, 420
Jeffreys, Herbert, 114, 149–150, 162
Jermyn, Henry, 126
John le Breton, bishop of Hereford, 292

Johnson, Herbert A., 291
Johnston, Frederick, 428
Jones, Inigo, 123
Jones, Sam Huston, 317, 331
Jones, Spotswood Hunnicut, 2, 93
Jones, W. Carruth, 388, 389, 390
Jumonville, Florence M., 291
Justinian, Roman Emperor, 345

Kelso, William M., 94, 98
Kemp, Richard, 104, 105, 132
Kendall, William, 197
Kent, James, 264, 359
Kerr, Lewis, 263–293, 343–345
Key, Elizabeth, 173, 190–191
Key, Thomas, 190
Kitchin, John, 79
Knight, Peter, 108
Kukla, John, 450

Lambarde, William, 86, 205, 207
Land, John, 374, 375, 392, 395, 398
Laud, Archbishop William, 133
Laussat, Pierre Clément, 272–273, 275, 339
Lawrence, Richard, 148
Leach, Thomas, 293
Leche, Richard, 415
Lee, Richard II, 83
Leigh, Benjamin Watkins, 423
Lemisch, Jesse, 229
Levy, Leonard, 436
Lewis, Joshua, 340
Lincoln, Abraham, 363
Little Buttercup, 451
Littleton, Sir Thomas, 55, 84, 85
Livingston, Edward, 231, 269, 350–352, 353, 354, 355, 356, 362

Long, Huey P., 303, 304, 305, 310, 326, 27, 328, 330, 371, 372, 374, 375, 276–377, 379–380, 382, 384, 385, 386, 387, 388, 390, 392, 393–394, 396, 397, 398, 399, 400, 401, 402, 405–410, 412, 413, 414, 315, 416
Long, Julius, 393
Lovelace, Francis, 136
Ludwell, Philip, 114, 118
Ludwell, Thomas, 112, 146

Macon, Ann, 114
Madison, James, 346, 354
Martin, Blanche Amalie, 251
Martin, François-Xavier, 245–261, 340, 354–355, 356, 361
Martin, Joseph Vincent, 254
Martin, Paul Barthélemy, 249–252, 253–261
Mason, Lemuel, 169
Mathews, George, 299, 300, 340
Mathews, Samuel, Jr., 109, 137, 138, 139
Mazureau, Étienne, 258–259, 319, 341, 356
Mendelson, Wallace, 202, 203
Menifie, George, 102
Moreau-Lislet, Louis, 237, 278, 341, 344, 345, 353
Morphy, Alonzo, 253
Morris, Richard B., 435–436
Morton, Richard Lee, 432
Moryson, Francis, 149–150
Mottrom, John, 190–191
Mowry, John, 279
Munford, William, 423

Necotowance, 133
Nicholas, Sir Edward, 140

INDEX 459

Nicholson, Francis, 115, 155, 162
Noye, Sir William, 79

O'Neill, Thomas P. "Tip," 414
O'Niell, Charles A., 306, 309, 311, 326, 327, 329, 330, 331, 374, 387, 391, 392, 397, 398
Odom, Fred M., 306, 374, 391
Opechancanough, 131–132
Overton, Winston, 373, 374, 375, 377, 379, 398

Palmer, William P, 428
Parker, John M., 326, 410
Pavy, Benjamin H., 388, 393, 398
Payne, Marion, 3
Percy, George, 97
Phillips, Samuel March, 358
Pierce, William, 103
Plowden, Edmund, 83
Pollard, A.F., 291
Porter, Charles Vernon, 386
Porter, Thomas E., Jr. , 372, 377, 379, 380, 381, 382, 383, 384, 385, 386, 388, 389, 390, 391, 393, 395, 398
Porterie, Gaston L., 304, 305, 328, 329, 330–331, 382–384, 388–389, 390, 393–394, 397
Pory, John, 170, 426
Pothier, Robert Joseph, 345, 353, 358
Pott, John, 102
Prevost, John, 340
Price, James H., 415
Price, John M., 47
Pujo, Arséne, 386
Pulton, Fernando, 13

Rastell, John, 80, 81, 288, 293
Rastell, William, 80
Redgrave, G.B., 291
Renard, Jean, 278
Richards, Thomas, 196
Rightor, Edward, 386
Robinson, Conway, 422, 425–427
Robinson, Sam, 2
Roe, Sir Thomas, 124, 126
Rogers, Wynne G., 306, 374, 391
Rolfe, John, 100, 177, 187
Roosevelt, Franklin D., 409–410, 412, 415
Roselius, Christian, 319
Rost, Pierre, 259–260

Sandys, George, 123
Sandys, Sir Edwin, 102
Scarburgh, Edmund, 34
Schieber Harry N., 436
Semmes, Thomas Jenkins, 322
Sevier, John, 271
Shepherd, E. Lee, 443
Simon, Edward, 249, 253–254
Slidell, John, 319
Slidell, Thomas, 319
Smith, James Monroe, 415
Smith, John, 95, 96
Smith, Roger, 103
Soulé, Pierre, 319
Spearing, J. Zack, 306–307, 325
Spencer, Nicholas, 194–195
Spencer, Walker B., 309, 326, 328
Spicer, Arthur, 83
Sprigg, William, 340
St. Paul, John, 374–376
Stanley, Eugene B., 304
Stealey, John E., III, 448–449

Stegge, Thomas, 135
Stephens, Richard, 102
Story, Joseph, 264, 352
Suckling, Sir John, 123
Sullivan, Arthur, 452
Swan, John, 196
Swanson, Claude A., 412
Sweeney, James R., 400
Swem, Earl Gregg, 239
Swinburne, Henry, 12, 87, 88, 89, 91, 192–193

Tarter, Brent, 400, 402, 404, 441, 448, 449, 450
Tate, Albert, 7, 245, 371
Tate, Thad W., 3
Thompson, John, 340
Thorpe, Otho, 114
Tomlins, Christopher L., 438
Tradescant, John, 123
Tregle, Joseph G., Jr., 245
Tucker, St. George, 287, 293
Turner, Frederick Jackson, 432
Tyler, Lyon G., 97–98

Voltaire, 269
Voorhies, Albert, 290, 344

Wallach, Kate, 239
Walmsley, T. Semmes, 376, 382
Watkins, John, 273–274
Wentworth, Thomas, 1st earl of Strafford, 126
Wertenbaker, Thomas Jefferson, 428, 430–431, 432
West, Thomas 3d baron De La Warre, 99
West, William, 88, 89
Wharton, George F., the Rev'd, 373
Wilkinson, J. Harvey, 400

Williams, T. Harry, 371–372, 400
Willis, Brown, 289, 290, 293
Wilson, Edith Bolling, 146
Wilson, Woodrow, 146, 430, 432
Windebanke, Sir Francis, 125
Wing, Donald G., 291
Wingate, Edmund, 80
Wingfield, Edward Maria, 97
Winterton, Jules, 333
Woodhouse, Thomas, 110
Workman, James, 273
Wormeley, Ralph II, 83
Worrall, John, 291
Worsley, Benjamin, 135
Wyatt, Sir Francis, 102, 103, 105–106, 123, 126–127, 158–159, 162
Wythe, George, 287

Yeardley, Sir George, 162, 168
Yonge, Samuel H., 98

www.ingramcontent.com/pod-product-compliance
Lightning Source LLC
Chambersburg PA
CBHW022006300426
44117CB00005B/55